# VISIONS OF THE SOCIOLOGICAL TRADITION

D0827094

# DONALD N. LEVINE

# VISIONS *of the* SOCIOLOGICAL TRADITION

THE UNIVERSITY OF CHICAGO PRESS
*Chicago and London*

DONALD N. LEVINE is the Peter B. Ritzma Professor in the
Department of Sociology and the College, University of
Chicago. His previous books include *Wax and Gold: Tradition
and Innovation in Ethiopian Culture* (1965), *Greater Ethiopia*
(1974), and *The Flight from Ambiguity: Essays in Social and
Cultural Theory* (1985), all published by the University of
Chicago Press.

The University of Chicago Press, Chicago 60637
The University of Chicago Press, Ltd., London
©1995 by The University of Chicago
All rights reserved. Published 1995
Printed in the United States of America
04 03 02 01 00 99 98 97 96 95    1 2 3 4 5
ISBN: 0-226-47546-8 (cloth)
          0-226-47547-6 (paper)

Library of Congress Cataloging-in-Publication Data

Levine, Donald Nathan, 1931–
      Visions of the sociological tradition / Donald N. Levine.
          p.      cm.
      Includes bibliographical references and index.
      1. Sociology—History.   2. Sociology—Philosophy.
      I. Title.
      HM19.L48   1995
      301'.01—dc20                                    95-3389

*My book is both a key to the past, and a plea for the future, of the social sciences.*
  —WERNER STARK

# CONTENTS

PART THREE / VISIONS OF THE PRESENT
SOCIAL SCIENCE IN CRISIS OR TRANSFORMATION?

# LIST OF FIGURES

# ACKNOWLEDGMENTS

A number of colleagues with special knowledge of the various traditions reviewed pertinent chapters in Part Two. For examining the chapter on the Hellenic tradition, I am grateful to Arthur Adkins and Alan Gewirth; on the British tradition, to Kevin Brown and Charles Camic; on the French tradition, to Lewis Coser and Loic Wacquant; on the German tradition, to Uta Gerhardt, Robert Pippin, and Jeffrey Rubenstein; on the Marxian tradition, to Kevin Anderson, Dan Brudney, and Moishe Postone; on the Italian tradition, to Federico d'Agostino, Irving Louis Horowitz, and Raffaele Rauty; on the American tradition, to Susan Henking, Hans Joas, and Norbert Wiley.

Several other colleagues examined chapters from Parts One and Three. Particularly helpful comments came from James S. Coleman, Shmuel Eisenstadt, Ivan Ermakoff, Arthur Frank, Robert K. Merton, Roland Robertson, Barry Schwartz, Chris Shilling, and Tom Smith.

For help in typing the manuscript and carrying out library work, I am indebted to David Ciepley, Emanuel Gaziano, Jay Feist, Eric Wiland, and Lisa Parsons Wiland. Lisa Wiland also artfully produced a number of the figures. David Ciepley and Emanuel Gaziano gave the complete text a close reading and made invaluable suggestions.

Jeffrey Klein provided moral support and editorial wisdom at critical junctures. My longtime editor and multispangled colleague, Doug Mitchell, performed an array of essential functions—challenging, restraining, facilitating, supporting.

My debt to generations of administrators, teachers, colleagues, and students at the University of Chicago is so patent it needs no mention.

# PROLOGUE

The social sciences play a double role. They study human behavior and they exhibit it. Changes in culture and human conduct show up in the ways social scientists act as well as in what they investigate. When observers comment on a new crisis in sociology, one wonders whether that could reflect something of the broader cultural situation.

In writing this book I have held that question in mind. What is one to make of the crescendo of plaints about the state of sociology?[1] I see at least one problem that finds its parallel in our general culture. This has to do with a shortage of ideas and ideals suitable for lending us purpose and moral direction under radically changed social and technological conditions. You may call it a problem of the depletion of our symbolic resources. This problem may not seem so critical as the spread of nuclear weapons, urban violence, accelerated destruction of habitats and species, expanding world hunger, or continued oppression of women in many countries. Even so, addressing the cultural problem may facilitate effective action on those other fronts.

In broaching so bold a theme I seek to return social science to one of it roots—to concern about the moral dilemmas of industrial civilization voiced early in the nineteenth century. Just as secular elites bred for waging war were giving way to captains of industry, Saint-Simon and Comte argued, so traditional clergy were to be replaced by new spiritual elites equipped to pursue a scientific approach to social health. Leaving all control to the temporal powers would weaken the sentiments and moral codes essential to the functioning of society. Unconstrained by the moral force of a new spiritual elite, the secular management of industrial society would lead to social disintegration. Not a few observers of contemporary societies find such prognoses confirmed.

---

1. Warnings were sounded in Gouldner's forecast of a coming crisis in sociology (1970). Before long, Eisenstadt would document and diagnose the malaise (1976). In recent years, the plaints have become more shrill, with diagnoses of sociology as an "impossible science"; in need of "unthinking," not just rethinking; professionally "fragile"; and in a state of utter "decomposition" (Turner and Turner 1990; Wallerstein 1991; Halliday 1992; Horowitz 1993). I examine the question of sociology's imputed crisis directly in chapter 14.

Alas, the intellectuals whom Saint-Simon and Comte wanted to counterbalance the fragmentation of modern society have themselves become part of the problem. When they have not lost themselves in pursuing minute specialities, they have tended to become apologists for partisan outlooks. They have reduced the standards for truth and the vision of our common humanity to matters of gender, race, ethnicity, class, or narrow ideology—or else to a nihilistic worldview justifying nothing save combat. In so doing, as Julien Benda once put it, intellectual elites have betrayed their calling.

Their betrayal is abetted by a poverty of symbolic resources for coping with the problem. The resources needed should not be mistaken for the universally compelling doctrines that Saint-Simon and Comte strove to create. For too long it has seemed as though consensus could be built only from a great fund of common beliefs, whereas theory and experience alike indicate that uniformity of belief produces stagnation if not repression. The remedy for fragmentation is communication, not uniformity.

This means communication not in the everyday sense—what we do when we ask for directions or exchange recipes—but communication in the sense of grasping truly alternative points of view in a calm and understanding way. What we see in sociology, and in other social and humanistic disciplines, is so often an assertion of narrowly partisan rectitude that borders on arrogance and grandiosity, conveying the notion that what others are up to is worthless. I don't know whether ignorance or insecurity is more to blame when we behave this way.

The cultural challenge, in any case, is to figure out how to construct new kinds of consensus while retaining different modes of believing. By discovering new ways to combine independence with being connected, diversity with mutuality, a new generation of intellectuals can provide a more capacious conscience and a sharper consciousness for directing human affairs.

Such insights are easy to hear but hard to listen to. I wish there were an easier way to grasp and internalize them, but some disciplined effort seems essential. I hope the experience involved in following the argument of this book will facilitate such growth and may inspire today's intellectual leaders to take some steps toward recovering their calling.

The book is organized about three arguments. The first focuses on the role of narratives in the life of disciplines. After discussing the ways in which narratives provide coherence and meaning generally, Part One exhibits one such narrative by representing the story of modern sociology in the form of a sequence of narratives about the sociological tradition told by a succession of its leading figures.

That examination leads to the centerpiece of my exposition, a new kind of narrative appropriate to the current state of sociology—the "dialogical" narrative presented in the seven chapters of Part Two. Readers new to the literature of sociology may prefer to begin with this part. My account documents the salience both of national traditions and of ethical concerns in the early history of sociology. It takes its departure from one massive fact: when it came time to set forth the theoretical underpinnings of the new science of sociology at the turn of the last century, the preeminent British, French, German, Italian, American, and Marxian scholars did so in radically different ways. Why was this so? What has come of it? These are the questions that prompted me to undertake this project in the first place, and that led me to appreciate the extent to which those different sociological approaches were embedded in contrasting traditions of moral philosophy.[2] Caveats about the limitations of such an approach appear at the end of chapter 5.

In Part Three I face the current condition of sociology and the social sciences with a focus on problems of fragmentation. I suggest that the dialogical narrative presented in Part Two offers the possibility of a constructive foundation for coping with those problems, both by linking currently disconnected parties into common universes of discourse and by providing grounds for a communal ethic based on the prerequisites of dialogue. I direct your attention to parallels between features of the sociological tradition and features of the current human condition.

The term 'visions' in the title thus carries multiple meanings. It refers, first of all, to the variety of ways in which sociologists have envisioned their own past. In the second part, it refers to varying projections for the future created by a long line of Western social thinkers. In the final part of the book, it refers to diagnoses of the present situation in the social sciences. I leave it to readers to speculate on how these animating visions may relate to one another.

2. I also began fully mindful that a famous earlier work on the sociological tradition had largely discounted those national differences and argued instead that the exciting thing about the turn-of-the-century period was the convergence of different traditions behind a single theoretical framework (Parsons 1937). The more I thought about it, the more I realized that sociologists have created an array of contrasting representations of their past, that these different stories carried profound implications for how they should practice sociology in the present, and that the very practice of telling such stories is a quintessentially human activity (the argument of Part One).

# Visions of the Past

## SIX HISTORIES IN SEARCH OF A TRADITION

We preserve certain memories of each epoch of our lives. Incessantly reproduced, these memories perpetuate—through an unbroken filiation, as it were—the sense of our identity.
MAURICE HALBWACHS

# CHAPTER ONE

# Disciplines and Their Stories

## FRAGMENTS AND COHERENCES

**M**ore and more, experience comes in bits. Videos roll images; TV watchers flip channels. Symphonies become packaged themes. Art becomes collages of ingredients. Tourists buy copies of segments of monuments. Aesthetic theories dissolve texts into congeries of sentences and words. Computers reckon in bytes, politicians in sound bites. Nourishment comes from food court stations, through drive-up windows, in microwaved nuggets. Specialists treat bits of illness, located in whole body-minds. "MTV-generation" students reportedly show decreased ability to follow or formulate sustained arguments and evince a blindness to history that is not just ignorance of the past but the loss of a sense of historical connectedness altogether.

It has been called the fragmentation of experience.[1] This means that the coherence of life is lost as it is reduced to bits of sensation, torn from the rounded flow of experience, from contexts of encompassing meaning that unfold in frames of long memory. Such fragmentation stems from three sources. The supply side reflects the growth of analytic technologies—cognitive, visual, auditory, medical, gustatory. The demand side (not unmanipulated) reflects the consumerist hunger for immediate gratification. The cultural side reflects both an exalted valuation of novelty and an assault on history.

All three trends represent a late manifestation of that world-historical process often described as rationalization.[2] A secular impulse toward instrumental rationalization in a context of competitive indus-

---

1. In a seminal analysis of this phenomenon, Fredric Jameson (1984) characterized it as a breakdown of chains of significance producing an aesthetic and a cultural style marked by "schizophrenic fragmentation." "In the postmodern force field," writes Jameson, "the subject has lost its capacity . . . to organize its past and its future into coherent experience [so] it becomes difficult . . . to see how the cultural productions of such a subject could result in anything but 'heaps of fragments'" (71). On the burgeoning contemporary commerce in fragments, see, for example, Nedelmann 1989, Bauman 1992, and Ritzer 1993.

2. Max Weber offered the classic formulation of this process, although many others, including Tönnies and Simmel, made important earlier contributions. See Levine 1985a, ch. 7.

tries drives the unceasing effort to make technologies increasingly efficient. It also sharpens a calculating consumerist mentality that feeds the demand for such efficiencies. Moreover, the rationalization process in the modern era was advanced through appeals to overthrow the "benighting" effects of tradition, said to have kept humanity from enjoying the full range of goods essential to a good life and creative persons from giving full expression to their individuality.

Since the 1960s, all these trends have accelerated. As parental and communal authorities have waned, hedonic calculation has waxed. Therapies emphasizing the here and now—through behavioral reinforcement, dramatic abreactions, or medications—have replaced those oriented to slow historic reconstructions. Mystical philosophies emphasizing the authenticity of the present moment have challenged ethics grounded on universal claims or historic developments. The modern sensibility seems finally to have awakened from what James Joyce's hero Stephen Dedalus described as the burdensome nightmare of history.

However valid these comments on the fragmentation of experience may be, they must be balanced against contrasting accounts that regard our experiences as tied to frames of meaning more extended than ever before. The same technologies that chop our experiences into bits bring us close to the entire world. The rationalism that erodes particular traditions opens the ethical imagination to extensions of compassion never before experienced by so many toward so many. The sales pitch for the immediate moment accompanies media presentations on civilizational frames of extraordinary scope. One historian even describes a recent rash of books and journals devoted to retrieving the past and ruminating on the act of recollection as a new culture industry that expresses an "addiction to memory."[3] Although it is hard to say whether the pull toward greater coherence may be as strong as the push toward fragmentation, it cannot be overlooked as an integral part of the human condition in our time.

Not surprisingly, a similar opposition between fragmentation and coherence has appeared in the ways that social scientists construct accounts of behavior. Many students of human behavior—psychologists and economists, in particular—explain conduct in terms of measurable responses to discrete positive or negative stimuli. When cars swerve,

3. This description, however, occurs in the context of critique of that culture industry for focusing recollection predominantly on particularistic grievances instead of representing more inclusive civic arenas (Maier 1993).

joggers jump. When prices soar, sales drop. Such actions can be observed and measured easily, a boon for efforts to secure reliable knowledge about behavior.

Even so, many social scientists understand that more is at stake. Some economists have argued that humans are moved not just by immediate pressures but also by distant goals that are contemplated in the imagination and that, while these goals can shift in response to changes in current information, they exhibit a good deal of stability. Some psychologists maintain that consistent organization of conduct around firm identifications is a hallmark of stable personality. Against the view that choices reflect momentary responses stands the view that choices reflect *who persons think they are.* This contrasting view notes how hard it is to rally behind decisions for long—difficult decisions, certainly—without a firm sense of what one stands for. The link to history lies not only in the effects of past events; it inheres in the fact that enduring commitments depend as much on regard for the past as on thoughts for the future.[4]

If stability of character depends on a coherent notion of one's past—on a narrative that relates the formative episodes which gave rise to one's identity—then perhaps the threats to coherence unleashed by the fragmenting forces of modern life can be offset through attention to the stories people tell about their lives and about the communities in which their lives find meaning.

## THE ROLE OF NARRATIVES IN SYSTEMS OF ACTION

Human beings attempt to make sense of their experience by interpreting their actions as part of a coherent life story. When unexpected or novel life events occur, they weave them into their narrative so that their story continues to make sense over time. Such work helps persons preserve a sense of self-consistency.

Much research in psychology supports the proposition that life changes that disrupt one's ability to maintain a plausible autobiography tend to increase inner tension, ultimately leading to feelings of emptiness or fragmentation. In a seminal synthesis of this and related work,

---

4. In the language of what Wiley (1995) calls the semiotic self, the 'I' requires a (Meadian) 'Me' based on past experience as well as a (Peircean) 'You' oriented to one's prospective projects. In asserting that "memory extends the sentiment of identity to all the moments of [a person's] existence," Rousseau offers an early formulation on the significance of remembered experience for the unified functioning of selves ([1762] 1979, 72).

Bertram Cohler (1982) has described some salient features of these self-narratives. Like all stories, they present a beginning, a middle, and an end. Their key feature is a consistency of perspective embodied in a plot line that makes sense to others in terms of socially shared under-standings. As time goes on, the authors of these stories transform ear-lier material so that it figures in different ways in the overall plot line. In other words, as humans grow older they tend to revise earlier memories continually as a function of subsequent experience. Points of major transition in the life cycle—notably, the shift from early childhood in the five- to seven-year-old period, the shift from adolescence into young adulthood, and the transition to middle age—are times when the mind is particularly active in creating new constructions of the past. Consequently, an illuminating way to represent the course of a person's life is to chart the successive reconstructions of the personal narratives he or she has produced over time.

In this perspective history is not a luxury, but an essential condition of an optimally functioning personality. By extension, the same can be said of human collectivities. In his pioneering work on the social fram-ing of memory, Maurice Halbwachs investigated the linkage between personal and collective dimensions of recollection. Accepting intro-spective accounts of memory utilized by psychologists, Halbwachs showed that in most instances these individual recollections showed the stamp of collective representations. He argued that society obligates people to mentally reproduce previous events in their lives and peri-odically to touch them up, shorten them, or complete them.

What is more, he demonstrated the indispensability of collective memories for the functioning of social groups of all kinds—families, social classes, religious communities, and the like. With this notion, Halbwachs filled in the missing piece of Durkheim's argument about the mechanisms that maintain social solidarity and commitment to a group's values and purposes. Collective memories recall great events of the past, which form a focus for group solidarity. They also keep alive the sense of affiliation with the group and its purposes during periods of routine activity between times when the group assembles to reaffirm its collective existence (Halbwachs 1992, 25). In recent years, another function of collective memories—their defensive purposes—has be-come conspicuous in international discourse, as publics in Germany and Japan have debated the record of atrocities during World War II, former apologists for communist regimes in Eastern Europe have has-tened to forget, Arabs and Israelis have nursed wounds of resentment based on divergent recollections of the past century, and secessionist groups in Ethiopia have rewritten histories to justify their claims.[5]

Like all human communities, those organized to cultivate intellectual disciplines depend on some view of their past. Such views give their disciplines identity and direction, important for functioning effectively in the present. These accounts differ from those provided by professional historians. The latter proceed from an outside perspective, chronicling events in the framework of some externally supplied interpretive scheme. The former take the form of collective autobiographies. The selective process at work in these stories is geared more to commemorating and to forgetting than to mere chronicling. Such tales, like the tales any group tells of itself, often assist the process of educating and inducting new members into those disciplines.

Examination of disciplinary histories produced by practitioners of those disciplines reveals a variety of narrative forms. Looking at a selection of such accounts—of disciplines ranging from geology and medicine to philology and psychology—a team of historians of science has identified a wide range of purposes served by internal histories (Graham, Lepenies, and Weingart 1983). In some cases they simply emphasize the value of scientific work in their field, as when they laud the achievements of great scientists or glorify science as the preeminently progressive human activity. In other cases they valorize certain directions in scientific work, as when they strengthen a particular approach to science or herald a conceptual transformation in the field. Still others serve to demarcate the boundaries of an intellectual domain, as when they celebrate the emergence of a distinctive new discipline or trace its connections with antecedent philosophical systems. Generally speaking, internal histories of scientific disciplines serve to legitimate either previously existing patterns or newly emerging patterns.

Over a period of time disciplines inevitably alter the prevailing accounts of their histories. Discovery of new facts, creation of new ideas or methods, ascendance of new research groups, and new relationships with external systems provide occasions to reinterpret the significance of prior developments. If one looks at the context in which these varying accounts appear, one is likely to discern a distinctive set of circumstances that occasioned their construction. Accordingly, just as the life cycles of individuals can be illuminated by representing the succession

5. Of the voluminous literature on these matters, I might mention Harms et al. 1990, Marcus 1992, and Gordon 1993.

of their autobiographical accounts, so the history of a discipline can be traced by recalling the succession of disciplinary histories produced by their practitioners.

## RECONSTRUCTING NARRATIVES AND LIVES

One outcome of every successful psychotherapy is a different view of one's biography. This may come about by recovering buried memories, reinterpreting past experiences, or revising stories about one's capabilities. Indeed, professional counselors have come to appreciate the therapeutic potential of encouraging clients to rewrite their life scripts and to create new stories that lead to more positive feelings and accomplishments. They advise that this be done not by assaulting the old stories but first by helping clients to appreciate what their old stories have done for them, then by offering them the alternative of constructing a more productive story. First they "get into gear with the client's story," then encourage the client to "shift it to a more healthy story" (Lee et al. 1993; Gilligan 1987).

That is the larger purpose I hope this book will serve. My goal is to review the earlier stories sociologists have told themselves in an empathic way in order to reveal the value that those stories contained for earlier moments of adaptation. After doing that, I hope to suggest the kind of story that may reduce unproductive tensions and impaired functioning within the community of social scientists.

In the first part of this book I apply Cohler's paradigm for the study of personal lives to the discipline of sociology. That is, I tell a history of sociology over the past century by presenting the sequence of stories sociologists have told themselves about their tradition. In so doing I find it instructive to subsume them under a set of ideal types. I designate these narrative types as positivist, pluralist, synthetic, humanistic, contextual, and dialogical.

Two things are true of these narrative types. One is that they emerge in a chronologically significant sequence in the course of the twentieth century. The other is that at the time they first appear they respond to identifiable problems that confront the discipline. The latter consideration gives us the key to determining what kind of narrative structure might be most suitable for the sociological tradition at the dawn of the twenty-first century. I offer these analyses in the belief that it is time for social scientists (and perhaps other communities as well) to begin telling themselves another story about the history of their enterprise.

# CHAPTER TWO

# Positivist and Pluralist Narratives

S ociology was born with a ready-made history. The father of the discipline, Auguste Comte, was at the same time the father of the history of the discipline (as indeed of the history of science more generally).[1] In the very lecture in which Comte introduced the term 'sociology,' he recounted a number of efforts that prefigured the new science.[2] This account reflected the theme of Comte's grand story about the way human knowledge evolves: its transformation from speculative notions about occult causes to empirically grounded laws about relationships of co-occurrence and succession. Although the evolutionary schema Comte used had been suggested nearly a century before by the young Baron de Turgot—who spoke of a progression in human thought, from imputing the causes of things to gods, to accounting for phenomena by abstract expressions, to basing hypotheses on the observed movements of bodies—Comte actually sought to document this progression as a fundamental law of historic development and to adduce it in expounding the fundamental sciences of astronomy, physics, chemistry, and biology.

## THE COMTEAN MYTHOS

The time had arrived, Comte held, for ideas about human society to become rigorously grounded, or "positive," as they had in the established natural sciences.[3] That is why he initially referred to what he

1. So George Sarton, in *The Study of the History of Science*, describes Comte as "the first scholar to conceive [the history of science] as an independent discipline and to realize its importance" (1936, 3). See also Sarton 1952.

2. This was lecture 47 of his *Course of Positive Philosophy*, entitled "Brief Appreciation of the Principal Philosophic Attempts Undertaken So Far to Found Social Science," written in the spring of 1839 and presented at his apartment at 159, rue Saint Jacques. See note 4 below.

3. Comte used the word 'positive,' the central notion of his philosophic system, to carry three distinct meanings: (1) knowledge based on observation as opposed to knowledge based on speculation, which he termed 'metaphysical'; (2) ideas that were certain as opposed to notions whose validity was questionable; (3) ideas useful for reconstructing social order as opposed to ideas used in a negative way, to combat the social order.

later called sociology as social physics.[4] The pure sciences stood in a hierarchy reflecting the increasing complexity of the phenomena they studied. It was essential for the "simpler departments of science" to become positive before those examining highly complex phenomena could be so transformed. Although it thus had not been plausible for positive social science to emerge until biology became positive—and until humanity had developed sufficiently to disclose the natural laws of human progress—Comte could identify some earlier attempts to establish a social science. These precursors included Aristotle, Montesquieu, Condorcet, political economists, and descriptive historians.

To Comte, Aristotle's *Politics* seemed remarkable for approximating a positive approach at a time when political observation was restricted

---

4. Comte introduced the term 'social physics' in 1822 in a landmark essay, heavily influenced by Saint-Simon, where he first set forth the positivist agenda. Soon after, he offered a definition of social physics as "that science which occupies itself with the study of social phenomena considered in the same light as astronomical, physical, chemical and physiological phenomena, that is to say as being subject to natural and invariable laws, the discovery of which is the special object of its researches" ([1825] 1974, 192). Seventeen years later, in lecture 46 of the *Course of Positive Philosophy*, he complained that this term had recently been spoiled (*gâté*) by a Belgian scholar, who adopted it as the title of a work dealing with nothing more than "simple statistics." He was alluding to the distinguished statistician Adolphe Quetelet, whose work *Sur l'homme et le développement de ses facultés, ou Essai de physique sociale* (later retitled *Physique sociale*) had appeared in 1835. When introducing the new name 'sociology' in the following lecture, however, Comte remarked simply that he wished to venture the new term as an equivalent to social physics "in order to be able to provide a unique name for the part of natural philosophy concerned with the fundamental laws of social phenomena." It was this alleged need for such a distinctive appellation, Comte averred, that induced him to overcome his "deep repugnance for neologisms of any sort." Unfortunately, neither of these revealing comments by Comte regarding the origin of the term 'sociology' appears in the English translation ([1830–42] 1877, 4:15, 185), but they have recently been published in a volume of social science quotations (Sills and Merton 1991, 42).

In what may be his only other published comment on the term 'sociology,' Comte provides a note in his *System of Positive Polity* to the passage where he argues that as theocracy and theolatry once depended upon theology, so sociology is required as the systematic basis of sociocracy and sociolatry. His note anticipates the howls that the term would soon elicit: reporting others' reactions to "the horrible hybrid that has ever since designated the science of society," Merton observes that "scholars then and today have protested the now domesticated barbarism" (1968, 2 n. 2). In the note Comte expresses his own regrets about the hybrid character of the term, but quickly provides a clutch of consoling defenses: the inadequacy of any purely Greek root for 'socio'; the fact that its hybrid character "recalls the two historical sources—one intellectual, the other social—from which modern civilization has sprung"; the existence of other equally hybrid scientific terms, such as mineralogy; and the fact that "the word Sociology has already been adopted by all Western thinkers from my Positive Philosophy" ([1848–51] 1875, 1:326). Comte goes on to express the hope that the words 'sociolatry' and 'sociocracy' will also be accepted. We may be grateful this devout wish was never consummated.

and the nascent positive spirit lived feebly in geometry alone. Even so, Aristotle's treatise could not possible disclose anything regarding the natural progress of humanity, since civilization had not progressed very much when he wrote, and his work remained overly occupied with metaphysical discussions about the principles of government

Closer to Comte's time, Montesquieu advanced toward an acceptable social science by using observational methods to examine political facts and by conceptualizing them in the form of general laws. Montesquieu's effort, however, was premature, both for trying to apply the positive approach to social phenomena before it had been successfully introduced into biology and for violating a fundamental sociological law by proposing to reorganize society during a period destined for revolution. Comte hailed Condorcet for making the next great addition to sociology after Montesquieu. Condorcet's breakthrough consisted of grasping the general conception that the various social states of mankind exhibit a lawful sequence of progressive improvement. Since Condorcet's mind was rationally prepared by mathematical study and informed by the contemporary expansion of the physical sciences, he went a long way toward creating positive sociology; but Condorcet's project remained premature owing to the primitive condition of biological knowledge, which led him to wander off after chimerical notions about the perfectibility of cerebral faculties.

Although Comte credited only Montesquieu and Condorcet for taking notable steps on the right road to social science, he mentioned two other signs that his time was ripe for subjecting social researches to positive methods. One was the upsurge of interest in political economy. In that field he commended the work of Adam Smith while criticizing other political economists for metaphysical speculation and for pursuing their investigations in isolation from other societal phenomena. Another sign was the growing inclination for historical studies, in which he especially commended the work of Bossuet; yet he criticized historical productions for remaining literary and descriptive, thus failing to produce propositions that correlate social occurrences so as to yield systematic predictions.[5]

5. In his 1822 essay, Comte had already sketched a version of this prehistory of what he then called social physics. Besides differing in some details from his 1839 interpretations of Montesquieu and Condorcet, the earlier version makes no mention of political economy and descriptive history; it focuses instead on what Comte considered misguided ambitions—to apply mathematics to the study of social phenomena or to derive their laws from biology (in the manner of present-day sociobiology).

For Comte, then, the prehistory of sociology consisted of a succession of stages through which human cognition became increasingly liberated from the limitations of commonsense knowledge. In its mature, positive condition human cognition could be trained on social phenomena. The process involved a lengthy sociocultural evolution that depended in the first instance on the emergence of a stratum of cultural specialists: magicians and priests, then theologians and philosophers, culminating with practitioners of positive science. The work of those specialists enhanced the human capacity to solve societal problems by producing intellectual disciplines that could be used, finally, to produce reliable social knowledge.

Comte's prehistory offers a prototype for a way to characterize the sociological tradition that may be labeled positivistic.[6] We can represent his narrative in the shape of an upward-sloping curve, moving from uncertain knowledge toward increasingly robust science, but a curve that is jagged, owing to the resistances of tradition and emotionality. Its generic features include:

*a plea to consider human social organization as a natural phenomenon investigable through methods of the natural sciences;*

*a campaign against subjectivist thinking, waged through a two-pronged strategy of empirical rigor and theoretic coherence;*

*a conception of scientific activity as both cumulative and progressive; and*

*a quest for empirically grounded general laws that permit predictions that can empower humans to solve practical problems.*

These features reappear in a number of twentieth-century narratives about the development of sociology. We shall consider three of them: Park and Burgess ([1921] 1924), Madge (1962), and Catton (1966).

### THE PARK AND BURGESS STORY

*Introduction to the Science of Sociology* has often been described as the single most influential textbook in the history of the field. In this remarkable compendium of source materials, Robert Park and his junior colleague Ernest Burgess sought to define the status of the field and make the case for regarding this upstart as a serious discipline. In so

---

6. It is important to keep in mind that using the term 'positivist' to designate a type of narrative does not imply that the author in question supports a particular methodology that may be labeled positivist and even less a particular view of human action. On Parsons's confounding of the two latter meanings of positivism, see chapter 3, note 4.

doing, they not only raised by several notches the intellectual level at which the discipline presented itself to the anglophone public, they also revealed the linements of a historical framework that underlay their "systematic treatise."

Park and Burgess begin their story by citing Comte, not for creating the science, but for giving it "a name, a program, and a place among the sciences" ([1921] 1924, 1). They recall his conception of the social organism and contrast it with that of Spencer, whom they identify as "after Comte the first great name in the history of sociology" (24). They divide followers of Comte and Spencer into schools, which they classify as realists, nominalists, and students of collective behavior. These scions gradually transformed sociology from a speculative philosophy of history into a true science of society. The steps in this transition, they note, mark the periods in the history of the science, that is:

> 1. The period of Comte and Spencer; sociology, conceived in the grand style, is a philosophy of history, a 'science' of progress (evolution).
> 2. The period of the 'schools'; sociological thought, dispersed among the various schools, is absorbed in an effort to define its point of view and to describe the kinds of facts that sociology must look for. . . .
> 3. The period of investigation and research, the period into which sociology is just now entering. (44)

Sociological research is at present, they wrote in 1921, about where medicine was before Pasteur and the germ theory of disease, with plentiful information about cases, but few systematic investigations to check out hypotheses. Accordingly, their preface exhorts: "The first thing students in sociology need to learn is to observe and record their observations. . . . Until students learn to deal with opinions as the biologists deal with organisms, that is, to dissect them—reduce them to their component elements, describe them, and define the situation (environment) to which they are a response—we must not expect very great progress in sociological science" (v, vi).

In keeping with their stress on empirical rigor, Park and Burgess's short bibliography includes only fifteen references to authors listed as representatives of schools (e.g., Durkheim, Simmel, Cooley, Tarde, Le Bon), but twenty-five references to writings on methods of sociological investigation. Park advised his students to become super-journalists, like the writers for *Fortune*, only reporting more accurately and with greater detachment. Burgess went on to perfect the genre of the scientific paper in sociology as a report of research findings; at the close of his career, his grandfatherly advice to beginning graduate students was to learn shorthand in order to make their field notes more reliable.

Like Comte, Park and Burgess conclude a sketch of the prehistory of scientific sociology by heralding their own time as the occasion for authentically empirical social research. The difference is that they do to Comte what he does to Montesquieu and Condorcet: they make him a precursor, not a truly positive sociologist, because the skills needed to conduct empirical social research were not yet available to him. Four decades later, John Madge would update the story.

## POSITIVIST ACCOUNTS FROM THE 1960S

Madge's *Origins of Scientific Sociology* (1962) stands not as prolegomenon but as history proper. He credits Comte for the vision of a science of society that would rival the established sciences in rigor, but he considers the realization of that vision to have taken place only in the United States in the preceding few decades, a view the more credible for coming from a European scholar.

Following Comte, Madge sets up positive criteria to select works for his history of the field. They must all make significant contributions in three respects: investigative technique, theoretic coherence, and understanding of social problems. These criteria permit him to justify the exclusion of such figures as Spencer, Sumner, Tönnies, Simmel, and Weber. Madge's account of the tradition starts with Durkheim's *Suicide* and proceeds through a series of landmarks in the history of American social research: Thomas and Znaniecki's *Polish Peasant* (1918–20), the urban ethnographies of the "Chicago School" students of Robert Park (ca. 1930), Robert and Helen Lynd's *Middletown* studies (1929, 1937), the Hawthorne Experiment studies (1933–39), William Whyte's *Street Corner Society* (1943), Gunnar Myrdal's *American Dilemma* (1944), the American soldier studies of Stouffer et al. (1949–50), the Kinsey studies on human sexual behavior (1948, 1953), the authoritarian personality studies by Adorno et al. (1950), R. F. Bales's studies of interaction in small groups (1950), and Festinger and Kelley's *Changing Attitudes through Social Context* (1953).

In treating this series of pathbreaking works, Madge highlights the ways in which each advances the positivist agenda of securing rigorous methods of social research and of linking the findings they produce to coherent theories and practical dilemmas. Thus, he flags the Lynds' work in Middletown for having combined such a wide array of data sources, including census data, court files, school records, local newspaper, statistics on wages, casual interviews, personal diaries, and systematic sample surveys. He notes the methodological innovations of the Hawthorne Experiment studies in formalizing rules for nondirective interviewing, pioneering the use of content analysis, and introducing such theoretical tools as systems analysis and the interplay of formal and informal organization. He stresses the improvements in scaling methods achieved by Samuel Stouffer and his colleagues as well as the theoretical consolidations represented by their use of the concept of relative deprivation (which Merton and Kitt would subsequently extrapolate into the theory of reference group behavior).

After reviewing a half-century of sociology's growth as a positive science, Madge signals his appreciation of the heightened quality of its work and its attendant rise in status. He notes with approval the sophistication of sociological methods of quantitative and qualitative analysis; the diffusion of standard concepts such as norms, values and interaction; and the establishment of wider contexts for understanding human miseries previously thought to need merely local remedies. He concludes with words that might well have been penned by Comte, or by Park and Burgess, had they lived through the chapters of the story Madge relates:

> Without the advances in systematic inquiry described in this book we should still be operating at the level of vague generality. Without the emergence of a specifically sociological frame of reference we should be unable to discipline the data that modern techniques enable us to collect. And yet these advances, indispensable as they may be, are only the means to an end for those who believe that the value of knowledge is control over nature, and that the world still has an overwhelming need for the large instrumental truths of sociology. (1962, 567)

William Catton, Jr. tells an essentially similar story about the sociological tradition, albeit in a less triumphant tone. Catton's tale is about a great transformation, which he calls *From Animistic to Naturalistic Sociology*. Naturalism is Catton's term for those nineteenth-century movements of thought that advocated extending the methods of natural science into areas from which they previously had been barred. These movements sought to remove the gulf that formerly had been supposed to separate humans from the rest of the natural universe. Catton refuses to regard 'nature' as a term distinguishing one thing from another since, he argues, "all being is included in nature" (1966,

50). Naturalists refuse to attribute benign or hostile qualities to the environment; they simply look for regularities in the phenomenal world. When natural scientists ask the question "why?" they never mean by it "for what purpose?" but only "as an instance of what more inclusive generalization does this pattern prevail?" (55).

Catton specifies four markers of a naturalistic outlook:

1. It asks only those questions whose answers depend upon sensory observation—a precondition of "objectivity" in the sense that findings are subject to independent corroboration by other investigators. Scientific advance thus often depends on technical improvements that bring additional variables within the purview of observation.

2. It seeks to explain phenomena by referring only to occurrences prior to the phenomenon being explained, thereby excluding all teleological explanations.

3. It considers change intrinsic to social systems, and the process of change, not continuity, as the problem requiring explanation.

4. It refuses to imagine "unmoved movers," that is, it never explains a change in terms of something that does not itself change (5, 21).

Adapting these features of the naturalistic outlook to sociology, Catton rejects commonsense views that consider human phenomena in terms of notions like will, purpose, and morality. Commonsense notions of that sort yield what Catton calls animistic sociology. Animistic thought expresses the irrepressible urge to ask "why" questions, which tends to make human desires the causes of impersonal phenomena.

Before genuine social science could emerge, Catton maintains, two conditions had to be met: it had to become possible (and respectable) both to view social phenomena naturalistically and to suspend ethical judgment when examining them. Most sociologists have been "marginal men" in transition between previously prevalent animistic thoughtways and emerging naturalistic conceptions. Catton credits Comte for having identified this transition as a critical problem, but not for having understood the naturalistic approach well enough to produce a truly naturalistic sociology. Later sociologists who advanced the naturalistic orientation include Spencer, Ward, Giddings, Small, and Sumner. In spite of these pioneers and their successors, the animistic orientation remains tenacious; sociologists still have not outgrown the temptation to view the universe teleologically, to ask questions regarding the human purposes served by diverse social phenomena. It was to counter these persisting roadblocks to scientific progress in sociology that Catton wrote his tract.

Each of the positivist narratives about the sociological tradition just reviewed casts it in the form of a jagged upward-sloping curve in which a base cognitive condition of misleading, undisciplined notions about social facts progressively gets replaced, more or less haltingly, by views grounded on controlled observation and technical analysis. The differing circumstances that elicited the four versions of the narrative confronted the positivist enterprise with slightly different challenges. For Comte, the challenge was simply to legitimate the transfer of a naturalistic approach to the study of humanity. For Park and Burgess, it was to enhance the utilization of direct observational techniques in testing sociological hypotheses. For Madge, it was to consolidate appreciation for the achievements of positive sociology to date and to defend them against would-be detractors: "We must be very circumspect in criticizing such developments," Madge advises when concluding his tale (1962, 567). For Catton, the challenge is to uphold the purity of the positive persuasion in the face of backsliders.

For all these variants, however, the situation that elicits their narrative is defined as one in which the methods of natural science are eminently applicable to the study of social phenomena and to the solution of social problems. The moral of their stories is the wisdom of promoting a vision of scientific sociology as a cumulative and progressive discipline, animated by empirical rigor and theoretic coherence, oriented to the discovery of general laws.

The positivist vision of the sociological tradition still possesses some plausibility. To be sure, its pristine Comtean form harbors flaws that must be corrected. On three points there is broad consensus today. First, rather than holding that theology and rational philosophy were displaced by positive science, we are likely to see them as constrained to share intellectual territory with positive science, such that their proper sphere of jurisdiction becomes more limited and specialized—as Lévy-Bruhl and Scheler already remarked. Second, rather than downgrading the empirical validity of prepositive cognition, we are likely, since Malinowski and Dewey, to affirm the validity of the pragmatic lore of prepositive cultures. Third, although Comte and others are surely correct in noting the important preparatory role played by disciplines lower in complexity on the positivist hierarchy, we know that cross-disciplinary fertilization can go in either direction. Around the time Comte wrote, for example, biologists were borrowing from social scientists, as when biologists like von Baer and Milne-Edwards adapted Smith's concept of the division of labor to analyze individual organisms, or when

Darwin was led to the notion of natural selection by reading Malthus's analysis of the pressure of population on human economies, not to mention the cross-fertilization in all directions among natural sciences of the present century.

If one corrects the positivist narrative in these respects, its central mythos remains intact. Its chief remaining vulnerability concerns the status of general theory. For each of the positivist historians of sociology, theoretic coherence is not inherently problematic. They share a sense that as sociological propositions becomes increasingly sharp and robust, they will coalesce into more general, consensually supported theories. The division of sociological opinion into divergent schools was a transitional phenomenon, destined to be overcome. Meanwhile, as Catton exclaimed, "We do ourselves an injustice when we thrust ourselves into reified pigeonholes, labeling ourselves as adherents of supposedly discrete isms or schools of thought" (1966, 56). The positivistic historians of sociology assume it is just a matter of time and continued progress before sociologists share a coherent body of rigorously grounded theoretical conceptions. Precisely this assumption gets reversed in those accounts of the tradition we now turn to consider.

## PLURALIST NARRATIVES: THE PROTOTYPE

Seven years after the first edition of Park and Burgess's treatise, Pitirim Sorokin published a strikingly different account of the sociological tradition. Not that Sorokin rejected the positivist touchstone of empirical accountability; far from it. "The primary task of a scholar is to deal with facts rather than theories," he insisted (1928, xvii). However, rather than taking progress in naturalistic fact-gathering as the organizing principle of his account, Sorokin used empirical rigor as a critical constant; and instead of regarding the existence of divergent schools as a residual matter—a mere transitional phenomenon—Sorokin translated it into the very heart and substance of his view of the field.

As its title indicates, Sorokin presents his account as a survey of *Contemporary Sociological Theories*. Even so, we can justifiably regard it as implying a kind of narrative about the growth of sociology. For one thing, the contemporary theories in question, Sorokin announces, are those of the previous *six to seven decades*. Indeed, when it suits his purpose, Sorokin does not hesitate to refer to authors writing well before 1860. Moreover, when describing the several schools into which he divides sociology, Sorokin frequently begins by describing the "prede-cessors" of the school. Finally, Sorokin repeatedly offers an image with which to symbolize the development of sociology: not an upward-sloping curve but the growth of a field of flora.

During the "contemporary" period of sociology, Sorokin writes, "various theories . . . have been produced in a great abundance, and have been appearing like mushrooms after rain. At the present moment the field of sociology is overcrowded by a multitude of various and con-tradictory systems" (1928, xix). Sorokin accordingly saw his task as trying to provide the novitiate to this confusing field with a guide and, shifting the metaphor slightly, to separate out its "sterile flowers" and its "weeds" from its worthwhile species (758–60). Thus, while Park and Burgess saw sociology in the 1920s as emerging from a period of warring schools into a no-nonsense time of investigation and research, Sorokin plotted a trajectory of continuing theoretical profusion. When, four decades later, he updated his account—much as Madge updated the Park and Burgess story—Sorokin retained the floral metaphor, claiming that *Sociological Theories of Today* was needed "to orient our-selves in what looks like a jungle of diverse and often discordant theo-ries" (1966, 12).

Sorokin's guide to the teeming forest of sociological theories pro-ceeds by segregating them into several genera or schools, then analyz-ing the fundamental principles of the diverse schools and their major subdivisions. Here is the taxonomy he employs (1928, xxi):

   I. Mechanistic School
       Social mechanics
       Social physics
       Social energetics
       Mathematical sociology of Pareto
  II. Synthetic and Geographical School of LePlay
 III. Geographical School
 IV. Biological School
       Bio-organismic branch
       Racialist, Hereditarist and Selectionist branch
   V. Bio-Social School
 VI. Bio-Psychological School
       Instinctivists' sociology
VII. Sociologistic School
       Neo-positivist branch

Durkheim's branch
Gumplowicz's branch
Formal sociology
Economic interpretation of history
VIII.  Psychological School
Behaviorists
Instinctivists
Introspectivists of various types
IX.  Psycho-Sociologistic School
Various interpretations of social phenomena in terms of culture, religion, law, public opinion, folkways, and other "psycho-social factors"
Experimental studies of a correlation between various psycho-social phenomena

Updating this survey in 1966, Sorokin began by reflecting on what had transpired in sociology during the four-decade interval. During the 1925–65 period, sociology as a profession had expanded considerably. Its intellectual energy had concentrated on techniques of research and narrowly demarcated problems. As for theoretical orientations, the bulk of recent sociological research was marked by continued application of most of the sociological approaches set forth in the 1928 volume. Even so, not all schools of the preceding period developed equally well, and many of them underwent changes in their claims. As a result, the map of sociology in this period had to look somewhat different from that of the preceding period, a circumstance that prodded a number of other sociologists to try their hand at classifying its diverse approaches. Sorokin listed eight such classifications, and offered several reasons to account for this pluralism of classificatory schemes. Since his evaluation of the various currents of sociology differed from those of the scholars who created the other classificatory schemes, Sorokin needed to lay out a revised taxonomy of his own. This taxonomy, he claimed, allows for most of the significant theories of the recent period as well as for all the schools discussed in the earlier volume (1966, 10).

1.  Singularistic-Atomistic theories, divided into two main classes:
Physicalistic-Mechanistic
Quantitative-Atomistic
2.  Systemic Theories, subdivided into four Macrosociologies of *Cultural* Systems and Supersystems or Civilizations:
Totalitarian

Nontotalitarian
Dichotomic
Typological
3. Systematic Theories of *Social* Systems, subdivided into six main classes:
Social-Action and Analytic theories
Functional-Structural and Nomenclature theories
Dialectic theories
Pseudo-Behavioral (Mixed) theories
Mixed Taxonomies of Social Systems (Groups)
Mixed Theories of Social Change
4. Integral system of structural and dynamic sociology

The 1966 taxonomy differs from the 1928 version not only by including new kinds of work but also in its simplified, more logical schematization. A division into nine major schools has been reduced to four, and this division has been undergirded by a coherent theoretic schema—the two dichotomies of units versus systems, and culture versus social systems. The new schema reflects the inclusion of Sorokin's own mature theoretical orientation, which he called the integral system of structural and dynamic sociology, listed as a fourth major approach. The "integral system" was so called because it integrates the analysis of individual motivation, cultural patterns, and social systems—dimensions that constitute bases for special attention in the first three groups of approaches.

Together the two Sorokin volumes offer an overview of the sociological tradition from its earliest time through the mid-1960s. This overview comprises an account of the sociological tradition we may call pluralistic. The generic features of this way of constructing the tradition include the following assumptions:

*the development of sociology has taken the form of an evolution of divergent theoretical approaches and research agendas;*

*these differences are bound to perdure, although their distribution patterns vary;*

*these differences are valuable, not harmful;*

*periods of fecund growth are intermittent, alternating with periods of stagnation, regression, or crisis.* [7]

Kindred assumptions inform a number of portrayals of the world of

---

7. Not all pluralist authors affirm Sorokin's additional assumption that those diverse theoretical approaches can legitimately be represented in a plurality of ways, though to be consistent they should. But see note 8 below.

contemporary sociology, including such works as Walter Wallace's *Sociological Theory: An Introduction* (1969), Jonathan Turner's *The Structure of Sociological Theory* (1974), and George Ritzer's *Sociology: A Multiple Paradigm Science* (1975). Our concern here, however, rests with efforts that weave these pluralistic assumptions into the warp and woof of a historical tapestry. Extensively developed narratives appear in two other accounts that explicitly follow Sorokin, those of Don Martindale and Shmuel Eisenstadt.

## LATER PLURALIST NARRATIVES

Half a dozen years before Sorokin issued the second volume of his inventory, Don Martindale published *The Nature and Types of Sociological Theory*. Although Martindale glossed Sorokin's first volume as "perhaps the finest single systematic study of sociological theory that American has produced" (1960, 115), his own account followed only the spirit of Sorokin's narrative, not the way its materials were divided.

Martindale's account manifests a more explicitly historical cast. He starts, not unlike Comte, by locating sociology in the history of human thought, preceded by folk wisdom, theology, philosophy, history, and natural science. "With all historical time to develop in, sociology is only about a hundred years old," his story begins (3). When it finally emerged, sociology absorbed its points of view from philosophy, its materials from history, and its cognitive model from natural science. Its emergence took place in a context marked by the sprouting of a number of related disciplines, including political science, economics, social geography, historical jurisprudence, psychology, and anthropology. The story of sociology proper is the story of the working out of ways to conceive and pursue sociology as a distinctive social science in its own right.

As is true in the early stages of all scientific disciplines, alternative ways of construing its basic ideas divide the field into diverse schools of thought. When a science matures, its schools tend to disappear. We do not hear of "schools" of physical theory, Martindale avers, but we do hear of schools of psychology and sociology. Rather than grieve over sociology's continued division into schools, or to ignore that fact, it is important to discover what the schools are and how they differ. Martindale's circumspect and illuminating overview presents the key ideas of what he identifies as the five major schools of sociological thought, and

their respective subdivisions, in the order of their historical emergence.
These are as follows:

1. Positivistic Organicism
    Idealistic
    Bio-organismic
    Voluntaristic
2. Conflict Theory
    Marxism
    Social Darwinism
3. Formal School
    Neo-Kantian branch
    Phenomenological branch
4. Social Behaviorism
    Pluralistic Behavioral branch
    Symbolic Interactionism
    Social-Action branch
5. Sociological functionalism
    Macro-functionalism
    Micro-functionalism

Like Sorokin, Martindale issued a revised version of this schema, but soon enough after the first—in 1981—as to require only a second edition, not a whole new book. Like Sorokin, too, Martindale undertook to make his revised schemata simpler and more coherent. He replaced the inductively based division into five schools with a deductively based typology consisting of four schools. The humanistic and scientific poles of Western intellectuality form one axis of this typology, the distinction between individualism and holism the other, yielding the schema in Figure 1.

By adding a distinction between orientational emphases (rationalism/nonrationalism) under elementarism, and an ideological distinction (left-wing/right-wing) under holism, Martindale refined his typology to accommodate the full inventory of theoretical types he identified in his history. This more differentiated schema is reproduced as Figure 2.

Although Martindale does not explicitly tell his story in the language of biological evolution, many features of his narrative suggest associations to that model. He consistently depicts disciplines and schools as particularly sensitive to environmental influences in their earliest

BASIC NOTION OF SOCIAL REALITY

| METHODOLOGICAL ORIENTATION | ELEMENTARISM | HOLISM |
|---|---|---|
| SCIENCE | SCIENTIFIC ELEMENTARISM | SCIENTIFIC HOLISM |
| HUMANISM | HUMANISTIC ELEMENTARISM | HUMANISTIC HOLISM |

Figure 1. Martindale's Typological Schema

stages; he analyses the emergence of new schools as though they were responding to openings like intellectual niches; and he views the historical outcome not as the triumph of a positivist outlook but as an enrichment of culture by a diversity of intellectual formations.

In all other respects, Martindale forcefully elaborates the key features of the pluralist prototype forged by Sorokin. Sorokin began by referring to the antagonistic relationship among schools as "contradictory systems" (1928, xix); later on he suggested that the schools were mutually exclusive on their wrong points but mutually complementary on a number of other points (1966, 646). Martindale straightforwardly articulates the pluralist premise:

> That the schools are true alternative formations of theory has been established beyond any doubt. They form independent systems of concepts that cannot be arbitrarily intermixed. This fact appears over and again whenever one type of theory attempts to account for evidence of another branch. (1960, 538)

In his second edition, Martindale suggests that the irreducible differences which persist among sociological theorists reflect the responses of persons of varying temperaments to deep intellectual problems that cannot be settled once and for all (1981, 620).

To Sorokin's argument that sociology requires a plurality of approaches owing to the enormous complexity of social phenomena

BASIC NOTION OF SOCIAL REALITY

|  | *Elementarism* | | *Holism* | |
|---|---|---|---|---|
| METHODO-<br>LOGICAL<br>ORIENTATION | Rationalism | Nonrationalism | Left-Wing | Right-Wing |
| Humanism | Social-Action<br>Theory<br>Symbolic<br>Interactionism | Phenomenolo-<br>gical Sociology | Critical<br>Theory | Traditional<br>Christian Social<br>Theory<br>Absolute Idealism,<br>Hegelianism<br>Structure-<br>Functionalism,<br>Macrofunctionalism |
| Science | Neo-Kantian<br>Sociology<br>(Formalism) | Pluralistic<br>Behaviorism<br>Behavioristic<br>Sociology | Marxian<br>Sociology | Positivistic<br>Organicism<br>Conflict Theory<br>Structure-<br>Functionalism:<br>Microfunctionalism |

Figure 2. Martindale's Typology of the Sociological Theories

(1928, 757; 1966, 646), Martindale adds the point that theorists derive much benefit from the stimulation afforded by contrasting ideas (1960, 52). Martindale also confirms Sorokin's skepticism about the inexorably progressive character of scientific development: to Sorokin's point that the much-vaunted developments of the 1925–65 period were "improvements of details only, and sometimes even no improvements at all" (1966, 5), Martindale joins in with the plaint that later developments in some of the schools have tended to result in a retreat to a more primitive stage of activity (1960, 537).[8]

S. N. Eisenstadt's account of the sociological tradition (1976) is even more assiduously historical than Martindale's. His chronicle divides into two broad phases, the generations prior to World War II (chs. 1–5) and the postwar developments (chs. 6–13). In the earlier phase, sociological thought crystallized when its proponents abandoned philosophical questions about the "natural" conditions of social order or the "best" type of in favor of analyzing the mechanisms of continuity and chage in different types of orders. Efforts to address these

8. For Martindale's argument that the diverse schools of sociology can legitimately be represented in a plurality of ways, see 1960, 537–40.

questions led to a number of empirical generalizations, research programs, middle-range theories focused on concrete areas of social life, and "broad explicative paradigms" of social order. These various explicative paradigms have formed the crux of sociological analysis. Following Sorokin, Eisenstadt classifies them into four major types: individualistic approaches (Tarde, Thomas, Homans, game theory), sociologistic (Simmel, Tönnies, Durkheim, MacIver), culturalistic (Dilthey, Spengler, Alfred Weber), and environmental (Buckle, Gumplowicz, Duncan).

Alongside this classification of sociological paradigms in terms of the "basic units" of social life, Eisenstadt also classifies the approaches according to what he calls their analytic properties, namely, their level of analytic sophistication and openness. On this dimension he distinguishes three types: (1) the "discrete" mode explains social phenomena in terms of nonsocial forces, such as biological traits or geographical features (McDougall, Ratzenhofer); (2) the "closed-systems" approach views the components of social order in ways that represent their relationship as relatively fixed and that emphasize one element as predominant (Marx, early Durkheim); (3) the "open-systems" approaches give up the assumption of some type of fixed relationship among the components of social order and examine their internal systemic dynamics (late Durkheim, Weber).

In the postwar period, the structural-functional school became the central focus of theoretical discussion in sociology. Although it exhibited many characteristics of open-system models, structural-functionalism was perceived as a closed-system paradigm in many sectors of the sociological community. Their criticisms of the structural-functional model led to a number of "countermodels," along the following lines: (1) the "conflict model" (e.g., Dahrendorf, Mills) argues that control of resources and power, not presumed consensus on common values, constitutes the core institutional structure of any society and the primary basis of its continuity; (2) the "individual-rational" model (e.g., Harsanyi, Homans, Blau) explains the development and variability of individual behavior in terms of the rational choices of individuals and exchange among them, instead of appealing to societal needs; (3) the "symbolic interactionist" model (e.g., Schutz, Mead, Blumer) claims that the individual's social essence lies in a continual process of personal definition of and interpersonal negotiations about the social situation; (4) the "symbolic-structuralist" model (e.g., Lévi-Strauss) stresses the autonomy of the cultural symbolic dimension of human life and looks for the hidden structures of social reality; (5) the "group interest" model (e.g., Bendix and Collins) see society as a field of groups, each struggling to further its political, ideal, or economic interests; and (6) the "historic-systemic" model (e.g., Frankfurt School, French Marxists, Touraine) emphasizes the specific systemic characteristics of different historical situations.

The resulting plethora of debates led to two contradictory outcomes. On the one hand, the debates produced a number of "openings" with constructive theoretical implications. For example, proponents of individual-rational approaches admitted openings to the symbolic dimension, as in John Harsanyi's shift to accept prestige and culturally defined status as goals of individual behavior. The emphasis on distributive justice in Homan's exchange model was modified by Peter Blau's arguments for conceptions of justice that transcend immediate exchange situations. Proponents of the "ecological-group approach" showed openings toward the systemic dimension of analysis, as in arguments that competition among groups for limited resources involves institutionalized patterns of division of labor and organized structures to mediate those struggles. What distinguished these analytic developments is that they resulted from combining theoretical analysis with empirical research (ch. 10).

On the other hand, the intense theoretic debates of the 1970s led to an "abdicative" mode of response to the perceived disunification of sociology, shifting the center of sociological discourse either into marginal fields like methodology and social philosophy or into partisan, ideologically charged camps. The heightened sectarianism among the compartments of this pluralistic community moved sociology to a state "consisting of completely closed, 'totalistic' paradigms which differed not only in their analytic premises but also in their philosophical, ideological, and political assumptions, minimizing the possibility of scholarly discourse on problems of common interest" (311).

Eisenstadt's history thus concerns more than the emergence of diverse sociological paradigms. In contrast to Sorokin and Martindale, he presents not just an unfolding panorama of schools of sociological thought but a full-blown history of the discipline. As its title indicates, *The Form of Sociology—Paradigms and Crises* concerns the periodic crises that have threatened the field as well as its pluralistic contents. Eisenstadt's interpretive focus in fact centers on the health and well-being of the sociological enterprise. Interwoven in his account of major trends in the historical development of its intellectual content is an analysis of the problems of institutionalizing sociology as a profession and an academic specialty.

In representing the process by which sociology came to be institutionalized as an academic tradition, Eisenstadt follows Shils and others in portraying a sequence of four stages: the forerunners, the founding fathers, the growing institutionalization between the two World Wars, and the full institutionalization of the postwar era. He adds further depth to such portrayals by relating fluctuations in its level of institutionalization to two distinguishing features of the history of sociology. One is the considerable extent of discontinuity it exhibits, evident in the disjunctive development of various research programs and sizable gaps between such developments in different periods and places. The other is the chronic difficulty sociology has faced in maintaining its autonomy, given its continuing involvement with external intellectual traditions and social roles.[9] These conditions have made sociology particularly susceptible to perceiving itself in a state of crisis.

Eisenstadt takes the outcries about crisis in sociology in the 1970s as a call for searching diagnostic analysis. Sociology's perennial vulnerability to being absorbed into other intellectual traditions or social roles was exacerbated by an upsurge of opposition to the discipline from outside quarters. His diagnosis thus pointed to two manifestations of sociology's pluralism in this latter period, a pathological one in which sectarian divisions undermined scholarly discourse within the community and a constructive one in which divergent paradigms nourished openings to other approaches. Eisenstadt concludes by celebrating the healthy pluralism that transforms these approaches "from mutually exclusive models into different, yet mutually relevant, research paradigms . . . capable of enriching each other and the more general framework of sociological analysis" (373).

One could assess the pluralist narratives by asking how inclusive they are, how trenchantly their typologies reveal intellectual issues, how fairly they represent the authors surveyed—questions beyond the scope of this study. On the differences of their typologies, we might simply note here that those differences lead them to divergent interpretations of what their authors signify. Marx, for example, was categorized by Sorokin as a *sociologistic* theorist akin to Durkheim, by

9. Eisenstadt offers the interesting suggestion that sociology fares best when institutionalized in settings that permit the coexistence of a variety of sociological approaches and that involve a mixture of roles: technical investigator, undergraduate and graduate teacher, social philosopher, publicist, ideologue, and reformer.

Martindale as a *conflict* theorist akin to proponents of Social Darwinism, and by Eisenstadt as a *closed-system* theorist akin to Simmel; while Weber was categorized by Sorokin as a *psychosociologistic* theorist akin to Le Bon and Fustel de Coulange, by Martindale as a *social action* theorist akin to Veblen, and by Eisenstadt as an *open-system* theorist akin to Parsons.[10]

The narratives by Sorokin, Martindale, and Eisenstadt exhibit different thematic emphases as well as different classificatory schemes. Their various themes reflect the differing circumstances that elicited them. For Sorokin the challenge, in 1966 as in 1928, was both to counter sociology's growing narrowness of focus by connecting its practitioners to its rich theoretical heritage and to provide a guide to this heritage, one that would help practitioners sort out fruitful approaches from sterile ones. For Martindale in 1960 the challenge was to correct a simplistic picture of sociology divided between global philosophizing and visionless empiricism by presenting the field as in fact constituted by five major active theoretical divisions with their associated research traditions. For Eisenstadt in 1976 the challenge was to promote a view of the constructive potentials of the pluralistic structure of sociology in a way that would contribute to rebuilding the sociological community during a highly divisive period (which led him to adumbrate the dialogical type of narrative I shall discuss in chapter 5). For Martindale in 1981 the challenge was not only to remap the field of sociological theory in light of its tumultuous developments in the previous two decades but also to enlighten those

> inclined to throw up their hands in dismay at the theoretical fragmentation and institutional counterformations of contemporary professional sociology. [They are applying] social and political criteria to a sphere where they are inappropriate. . . . In the world of the mind variety is the essence and not simply the spice of life. (627)

For all of these variants, the situations that elicited their narratives were similarly defined as ones of intellectual confusion. A clarifying representation of the multifarious schools of sociological thought was badly needed. The moral of their stories is the wisdom of acknowledging both the importance of the theoretical dimension of sociological analysis and the fact that the complexity of social phenomena requires a diversification of theoretical approaches. All of the narratives empha-

---

10. Sorokin, in fact, repudiates Martindale's characterization of him as a "positivistic organicist" (1966, 613ff.).

size the poverty of mindless empiricism. And despite their acknowledgment of moments of convergence at later points within the sociological
tradition, the pluralistic narratives feature the inexorable and largely
beneficial diversity of its schools. The aspiration to counteract such diversity and its attendant centrifugality animates the narratives to be
considered in the chapter that follows.

# CHAPTER THREE

# Synthetic Narratives

Of the many efforts to tell the story of the sociological tradition, *The Structure of Social Action* by Talcott Parsons ([1937] 1968) stands as the most influential and enduringly controversial. Little heeded by the sociological community for a decade or so after it appeared, during the postwar period it came to be viewed as a compellingly authoritative text and subsequently appeared to many as a turning point in the history of the field.[1] If ever one needed evidence to support the claim that disciplinary narratives function to provide collective identity and practical orientation, *Structure* may serve as a case in point.

In a way this is ironic, because when Parsons first published *Structure*, he pointedly described it as a study in social theory, not as a narrative. In prefacing the 1949 edition he reaffirmed this point, insisting that *Structure* "was intended to be primarily a contribution to systematic social science and not to history, that is the history of social thought" (1968, xv-xvi). Two decades later, however, in the preface to the paperback edition of this work, Parsons acknowledged that although *Structure* was not meant in the first instance to be a study in intellectual history, he considered its selective organization of materials to be "in fact appropriate to the *core* line of development in sociological theory" (xiv).

Indeed, like his senior colleague Sorokin at Harvard, the account Parsons gives of social theory relevant to contemporary sociology goes back to the seventeenth-century Hobbes. Yet his vision of that past diverges radically from Sorokin's. The heart of Parsons's account concerns four authors—Marshall, Pareto, Durkheim and Weber—who in his judgment "represented an altogether new phase in the development of European [social] thought" (viii). In the 1968 preface, Parsons revealed for the first time that his project

---

1. Camic (1989) lists several of these descriptions. He also observes: "The historical argument of *Structure* is the most famous interpretation ever offered of the development of the sociological tradition and has long been accepted, in varying degrees, by scholars in and out of the discipline. . . . Few theoretical developments in the discipline over the past half century have been launched without an engagement with Talcott Parson's towering first book" (56, 39).

began with my conviction of the unacceptability of the common view of the time, especially as expressed in Sorokin's *Contemporary Sociological Theories* (note the plural). He stated that the three sociologists in my study—Pareto, Durkheim, and Weber—belonged in radically different schools, and that Marshall, as an economist, belonged in a still different intellectual universe. I regarded their works not simply as four discrete and different alternative theories, but as belonging to a coherent body of theoretical thinking, understandable in terms of the major movements in the period's intellectual history. (x).

In composing *The Structure of Social Action,* Parsons was pursuing a number of other ambitions as well. Like the authors of the positivist narratives we have considered, he was seeking to bolster the cause of empirically grounded science—at a time when virulent currents of irrationalism, in Europe especially, were eroding the Western commitment to reason. He was also seeking, like the authors of the pluralist narratives, to define and legitimate the role of theoretic work in the enterprise of science in general and sociology in particular. Within that enterprise he was working to promote a certain epistemic notion—of the constitution of discrete disciplines, and of sociology in particular, as abstract analytic sciences rather than disciplines concerned with concrete subject matters. In addition, we shall see, he was striving to counter certain conceptions of human action he regarded as inadequate if not noxious—conceptions that denied the role of ultimate values and free agency in human conduct. Yet above all loomed his commitment to replacing the Sorokin-type view of sociology as a field consisting of "as many systems of sociological theory as there are sociologists" ([1937] 1968, 774) with a grand synthesis that would eliminate the warring schools which had divided sociology—and therewith provide an intellectually respectable theoretical charter for its investigative activities.[2] In order to accomplish this, Parsons needed to produce a vision of the past that started with plurality and culminated in unity.

## CONVERGING POSITIVISMS

Because its plot features the transcendence of vexing antagonisms through seemingly heroic intellectual attainments, *Structure* perhaps

---

2. For arguments that support and supplement this formulation, see Alexander 1987 and Camic 1989.

possesses the most dramatic interest of any of the many versions of sociology's history. Parsons refers to its two main antagonists as the positivistic and the idealistic traditions. The dramatic interest in these two is not equal, however. The former not only commands the bulk of Parsons's attention in the book—ten chapters on the positivists to five on the idealistic tradition—but was clearly the primary object of his personal investment in constructing the story. Parsons even opens his saga with a fantasy about the murder of the latter-day defender of the utilitarian branch of the positivist creed, Herbert Spencer. "Spencer is dead," he exclaims. "Not . . . that nothing in his thought will last. It is his social theory as a total structure that is dead.[3] . . . Who killed him and how? This is the problem" (3).

Parsons suggests that the attack on Spencer was directed primarily against three of his notions, which had come under fire from many quarters: his views on evolution, individualism, and religion. In the early decades of the twentieth century, Parsons maintains, lineal evolutionism had been giving way to cyclical theories; individualisms had been giving way to collectivistic and organic theories; and views of religion as a product of prescientific ignorance and error were being challenged by anti-intellectualistic theories of human nature and behavior. In the course of *Structure,* Parsons makes some mention of the critique of evolutionary thinking but directs virtually all of his argument to the problems associated with the assumptions of individualism and rationalism in modern European social theory. These two assumptions are embedded in the branch of the positivistic tradition Parsons calls utilitarianism, and the nub of Parsons's theoretic argument is that Pareto, Durkheim, and Weber concur in undermining those assumptions through empirically substantiated theoretic argument.

Parsons couches his discussion of these matters in a frame of reference he calls the theory of action. By so doing, and by identifying the concurrence of Pareto, Durkheim, and Weber in the assault on utilitarian premises as *the* preeminent episode in the sociological tradition, Parsons construes "the *core* line of development in sociological theory" as a series of efforts to interpret the nature of human action. Although the concept of action had long been a subject of philosophical investigation, Parsons does not present a considered philosophic anal-

---

3. One of the ironies of Parson's career was his eventual reversal of this famous judgment. Two dozen years later Parsons would write that "very much of the framework of a satisfactory sociological scheme was already present in Spencer's thinking" (1961, x).

ysis of the term; he simply identifies "action theory" as a plausible frame of reference for representing reality—with a status comparable to that of the space-time framework of classical mechanics—and represents it as referring to "unit acts," which include four components: (1) an agent, (2) an end, (3) a situation, comprised of (a) conditions and (b) means, and (4) at least one selective standard regulating the choice of means.

Parsons's story begins with Thomas Hobbes, whom he treats as progenitor of the utilitarian tradition of positivistic action theory. For Parsons, the generic feature of a positivistic theory of action is that it "treats scientifically valid empirical knowledge as the actor's sole theoretically significant mode of subjective orientation to his situation" (79).[4] To this generic assumption of "rationality" the utilitarian branch of positivistic action theory adds the assumption of atomism—that social organization consists solely of the aggregation of the unit acts of individuals—together with an assumption that the ends of action are statistically random.

For Parsons, Hobbes initiated the central dynamic of the story by defining the basic units of a utilitarian conception of action and by posing one of the most fundamental empirical difficulties of utilitarian thought, the "problem of order." This dynamic led the positivistic tradition to become ensnared in "the utilitarian dilemma." This imputed dilemma consists of adopting premises that require one either to assume that the actor's choice of ends is independent of the situation, in which case ends must be random and one cannot account for order, or to deny the randomness of ends, assimilating them to conditions of the situation. In that case, the factor of subjective agency disappears and utilitarian theory typically yields to theories that interpret human action solely in terms of heredity or environment—other branches of positivism like Darwinian biology, psychological instinct theory, or behaviorism. In the end, one could save the assumption of voluntaristic agency in conjunction with the need to account for order only by incorporating the normative dimension into the core conceptualization of action. At the conclusion of *Structure*, Parsons will define action as "the

4. It should be noted that Parsons here employs the term 'positivistic' in a sense quite different from the more commonly accepted sense, which refers not to a substantive theory but to an epistemology descended from Comte. Confounding his readers, Parsons slips into this other meaning of the term at times (181, 293, 305). It takes on a third meaning in the present text when I use it to designate a kind of narrative akin to that of Comte.

process of alteration of the conditional elements in the direction of conformity with norms" (732).

In revealing how the positivistic tradition of action theory worked its way out of the utilitarian dilemma, Parsons calls first on an economist, Alfred Marshall. Since utilitarian assumptions were embedded in classical economics, what made Marshall especially significant to Parsons was his apparent dissatisfaction with those assumptions. For Marshall was concerned not only with the ways in which individuals satisfy their everyday wants—through "the study of wealth," or utility theory, with its postulate of rationality in adapting means to individual ends—but also with the ways in which human character gets formed under the conditions of work. Marshall endorsed the free enterprise system not just because of its efficiency as an adaptive mechanism but mainly because it offered a superior venue for cultivating those traits of character he valued on ethical grounds. Although Marshall wanted economics to consider these value elements of action as well as its instrumental dimension, Parsons found such an agenda unacceptable. For that would entail inflating economics into a comprehensive science of social man, thereby abandoning its historic attainment in becoming an abstract analytic science as well as leaving no place for the distinctive discipline of sociology.

Parsons turns next to Pareto, who, like Marshall, found it important to consider aspects of action other than those that could be subsumed under calculations of utility. For two reasons, however, Pareto does not follow the Marshallian move to include such elements under the purview of economics. For one thing, Pareto casts his gaze over the entire panorama of historical action and does not restrict it to the domain of want satisfaction under the free enterprise system. He finds it necessary to appeal to such "nonlogical" aspects of action as values and sentiments because the vicissitudes of history cannot be comprehended without appealing to them.

In addition, epistemological considerations keep Pareto from pursuing the kind of economistic imperialism that Parsons ascribed to Marshall. Pareto has abandoned the "empiricist" position that scientific propositions reproduce concrete reality in favor of an appreciation of the role of abstraction in the constitution of scientific facts. For Pareto, economics provides a good example of a science of human behavior that proceeds by abstracting certain elements of its subject, namely, those dealing with logical actions. It would therefore take another abstract analytic discipline to account for the structure of nonlogical actions. This was the mission Pareto assigned to sociology, and which he attempted to fulfill by producing a complex classification of social sentiments. Pareto's work decisively broke through the limitations of the positivistic theory of action in ways that later sociology could fully embrace.

Quite independent of Pareto, and working in a totally different intellectual world and social milieu, Durkheim experienced what Parsons interpreted as a similar break from positivism, albeit from a different starting point and via a much more complicated route. What made the experience of Durkheim so interesting to Parsons was that Durkheim's theoretical and methodological views developed in the course of struggling to solve the empirical problems with which he was faced in his major monographic studies. Parsons also considered it integral to his representation of Durkheim to treat his theorizing as a process in which Durkheim underwent "a fundamental change, from one set of sharply formulated ideas to another" (304). Indeed, this depiction of the vicissitudes of Durkheim's thinking heightens the dramatic appeal of the narrative Parsons unfolds.

Instead of an initial acceptance of classical economics, as he found in Marshall and Pareto, Parsons finds Durkheim beginning with a rejection of economic theories, since the individualistic assumptions of classical economics could not account for social order, yet neither could the rationalistic assumptions of socialist economics. With *On the Division of Labor in Society* Durkheim launched a polemic against utilitarian rationalistic individualism, centering his critique on the inability of the principle of mutual advantage between negotiating parties to account for the body of rules that provides the binding force behind contractual agreements.

Parsons identifies Durkheim's critique of this inability of utilitarian theories to represent the "non-contractual elements of contract" as the central empirical insight that initiated his theoretical journey. It led him to search for a factor that transcends the decisions of individual parties. When Durkheim came to articulate the properties of that factor in *Division,* however, Parsons finds him ignoring the normative dimension of action and dealing instead with population pressures. Parsons glosses this as a biological factor and not what Durkheim would later consider to be a social factor (323, 350).[5] Dissatisfied with that posi-

---

5. It is hard to imagine a more vulnerable interpretation. For one thing, Durkheim not only introduced his key normative social factor, the *conscience collective,* in this book,

tion, Durkheim went on to explore alternatives ways to represent the social factor.

He proceeded by appealing to the distinctiveness of emergent higher-order realities, drawing analogies with the domains of chemistry and biology. In this phase of his development, Durkheim remained tied to his "positivistic" (here used, confoundingly, in the methodological sense) requirement to regard social facts as observable external things which, in the book on method, he defined by the criteria of "exteriority" and "constraint." Since that definition would include such non-societal elements as heredity and environment, however, he went on in *Suicide* to argue against a group of theories that employed hereditary and environmental factors in favor of theories that appealed to social integration and normative regulation as independent variables. The concept of anomie, in particular, helped him to clarify his notion of the collective conscience as a pervasive factor that not only imposes normative constraints from outside the individual but also penetrates the individual personality. This value element helps to organize purposive action in ways that the mere pursuit of interest cannot encompass.

Durkheim then achieved a further significant breakthrough, Parsons holds, when in *Moral Education* he came to redefine the nature of constraint as "the moral obligation to obey a rule—the voluntary adherence to it as a duty" (383). This insight enabled him to accommodate the reality of binding norms to the principle of subjective agency. Durkheim's final achievement appeared in the monograph on religion, where he analyzed religious beliefs as collective representations of "ultimate-value attitudes" and examined ritual symbolism as a distinc-

---

as Parsons acknowledges, but he never repudiated its causal efficacy, as Parsons claims. Durkheim treated the *conscience collective* both as a significant secondary factor in explaining the rise of social specialization and, largely differentiated in the form of civil laws and related normative codes, as the source of cohesion in specialized societies. Indeed, since Parsons here ignores the normative structures Durkheim analyzed in differentiated societies—the state, the legal codes, and the moral obligations incurred through cooperative relationships—it seems hard to avoid the conclusion that he has failed to grasp what Durkheim considered the principal basis of organic solidarity after all. How else could Parsons claim that "Durkheim has conspicuously failed to account for the specific element of organic solidarity beyond the very general formula that it must lie in features of the social milieu" (323)?

What is more, Durkheim never repudiated the relevance of demographic and ecological variables as social forces. He even came to erect a division between two branches of sociology, one of which, "social morphology," had precisely the mission of analyzing such variables. For some reason, Parsons never represents Durkheim's later consistent employment of the category of social morphology.

tive expression of those sacred values. The existence of ritual conclusively testified to an order of phenomena that unmistakably transcend the pursuit of individual profane interests. Rituals amount to socially constituted expressions of ultimate-value attitudes that are essential for social order and that stand in periodic need of revivification.

With this triple achievement in combatting the tenets of utilitarian positivism—by viewing social norms as empirical facts, acknowledging their status as voluntarily accepted duties, and identifying their symbolic expression in ritual—Durkheim's pivotal role in the evolution of modern sociology was assured. He succeeded in retaining the utilitarians' emphasis on subjective agency in action in a way that solves their putative dilemma: by providing the piece of the action system they left out—the role of socially constituted norms as an independent variable. In so doing he arrived, thanks to his persistent questioning of the nature of social facts, at essentially the same position Pareto reached from the quite different path of analyzing individual action. The sheer weight of the evidence they considered, Parsons tells us, led both men strongly predisposed in favor of the positivistic theory of action to consummate its breakdown (470).[6] They did so by converging on a common conception, which Parsons calls the voluntaristic theory of action—defined as a theory encompassing both normative and situational-adaptive dimensions of action.

Durkheim's commitment to this position was not stable, however, In his later work, Parsons holds, Durkheim veered toward the tradition that excludes situational-adaptive factors from systematic consideration, that of idealism. Parsons proceeds then to examine the tradition of idealism in Germany and its greatest exponent, Max Weber.

### PARSONS ON WEBER

Although Parsons's own social theory resembles Durkheim's more closely that its does that of any other predecessor, Parsons spent con-

---

6. If the defining feature of a positivistic theory of action is, as Parsons states it, the exclusive reliance on instrumental rationality in accounting for human action, then it is incorrect to say that Durkheim was initially disposed toward a positivistic theory of action. At no point did Durkheim exclude normative constraints as an essential determinant of action. Of course he was, and considered himself to be, a positivist in the Comtean, methodological sense—another instance of the mischief Parsons commits by confounding two such discrepant meanings of the term.

siderably more effort in trying to promote the appropriation of Weber's work.[7] Parsons's activity on behalf of Weber began with his dissertation essay on Sombart and Weber ([1928–29] 1991), followed shortly by translation of *The Protestant Ethic and the Spirit of Capitalism* in 1930. Although the translation was seriously flawed (and to this date, regrettably, has not been overhauled), that translation arguably did more to bring Weber to the attention of the modern sociological community than any other single act. In 1947, Parsons cotranslated and wrote an extended critical introduction to the first substantial segment of Weber's *Wirtschaft und Gesellschaft* to be translated into English. He also provided an important critical exegesis of Weber's sociology of religion as an introduction to the first English translation of that chapter from *Wirtschaft und Gesellschaft* (1963). Yet it is for expounding Weber's work in *The Structure of Social Action* that Parsons is perhaps best known as a champion of Weberian sociology.

The section of Weber in *Structure* is shorter and more subdued than the chapter on Durkheim. Even though Weber's intellectual trajectory was arguable more turbulent than that of Durkheim, Parsons presents Weber's views as of a piece, not the outcome of a long siege of strenuous inner conflicts. The dramatic component of Weber's story gets reserved for the final comparison with Durkheim.

In contrast with Parsons's treatment of the positivistic tradition, which centers on issues regarding the structure and content of human action, his treatment of the idealistic tradition deals almost exclusively with methodological matters. After a perfunctory genuflection to Kant he moves very quickly to the central thema: that a putative ban on analysis led German scholars to advocate recording human acts and their effects in their concrete wholeness, and to philosophize about those actions in terms of their significance for the totality of human develop-

---

7. Moreover, when Parsons had occasion to compare the types of mind possessed by his two major protagonists—Weber's as the encyclopedic mind in which theoretical notions rarely stand out above the enormous mass of detail, Durkheim's as the rigorously theoretical mind that spells out the implications of carefully advanced postulates ([1937] 1968, 501)—Parsons must surely have been conscious that his own mind exhibited the Durkheimian type.

Parsons observed more than once that he had staked a good part of his career on advancing the cause of Weberian theory. In a personal communication to the author he once remarked that the source of Sorokin's negative attitude toward him was probably the fact that he had translated and dealt so much with Weber, which Sorokin, given his Russian Orthodox roots, presumably found objectionable.

ment.[8] This led to a legitimation of two major modes of historical interest: an interest in the concrete detail of historical processes for its own sake, and an interest in the organization of historical data around the notion of a particular spirit (*Geist*) of a period or system ([1937] 1968, 475–78). These emphases produced a chronic conflict between "idealism" and "positivism" pitched in terms of three epistemic oppositions: organicism as opposed to atomism, irreducible qualitative individuality as opposed to general laws, and interpretation of meanings as opposed to uncovering causal relationships.[9]

As the principal proponents of the idealistic tradition prior to Weber, Parsons focuses on Marx and Sombart. Earlier Parsons had considered Marx briefly within the positivistic tradition, treating him as a variant utilitarian by virtue of his rationalistic assumptions, but he devotes more space to Marx in the idealistic context because of his historicizing of the capitalistic system. Although Marx took over the main framwork of the classical economic theory, Parsons observes, "he turned it from an analytical theory of the economic aspects of social phenomena in general into a historical theory of the functioning and development of a particular economic system. . . . Marx's difference from the classical economists is merely this: . . . he threw his attention from the rational process itself back to the situation which dictated its course," and he saw "that the fundamental character of these situations was subject to historical change" (489, 493).

8. In outlining that transition Parsons commits a certain sleight, which ought to be noted: he makes the strange claim that for Kant an intellectual apprehension of human life and action "could be attained only by the speculative methods of philosophy, especially by a process of the intuition of total wholes (*Gestalten*) which it was illegitimate to break down by 'atomistic' analysis" ([1937] 1968, 475). Nothing in Kant's writings familiar to me or to any Kantian scholar I have consulted would justify such an interpretation. Another idiosyncratic interpretation of Kant appears a few pages later, where Parsons, struggling to find some way of grounding the German quest for historical specificity, attributes to the followers of Kant a predisposition toward "a certain 'particularistic' mode of treatment of human action," despite the fact that Kant is the archetypical figure of modern universalism. For more extended consideration of Kant's role in the German tradition, see chapter 9.

9. Parsons's use of the term 'idealism' is nearly as idiosyncratic and misleading as the way he uses the term 'positivism.' What he has in mind is more commonly referred to as "romanticism," with its linkage with what is often called "historicism," a movement that arose in opposition to Enlightenment rationalistic universalism including Kantian idealism (see ch. 10). Indeed, in a 1935 publication Parsons never refers to that tradition as idealism but, more appropriately, either as "the German Historical School" or as "romantic empiricism" or "the 'romantic' school of thought" ([1935] 1991, 188, 206, 204, 227).

Like Marx, Sombart emphasized the qualitatively unique and historically specific character of the capitalist system. But where Marx saw capitalism developing out of comparable forms of class-based socioeconomic structures, Sombart viewed it as the creation of a historically novel *Geist*. For Sombart, the *Geist* of capitalism comprises the principles of acquisitiveness, competition, and rationality, and manifests two aspects, the spirit of enterprise and the bourgeois spirit. Sombart's theory of capitalism, while derivative of Marx, departs from the Marxian theory in eliminating everything from the capitalist system but its historical character and in couching its interpretation in terms of the epistemic notions of German idealism.

For Marx, capitalism developed through the progressive emergence of contradictions inherent in its socioeconomic basis; for Sombart, it emerged through the progressive objectification of its spirit, which Parsons glosses as "unquestionably a common value element" (499). The delineation of the Marx-Sombart conflict sets the stage for Weber to transcend this dilemma in ways consonant with what Parsons depicts as the emerging voluntaristic theory of action.

In contrast with his relatively broad selection of materials by Durkheim, Parsons restricted his treatment of Weberian materials to a narrow band: the essays on Protestantism and the religions of China and India; the methodological essays of 1903–6; and a few passages from the introduction to Part One of *Wirtschaft und Gesellschaft*. Parsons used these materials to document three major claims. The first was that Weber had effectively countered the position of Marxian historical materialism by demonstrating the role of value elements in the genesis of capitalism. The other two arguments were directed against the idealistic tradition. Here he argued that Weber rejected the emanationist model of scholars like Sombart by arguing that value elements "exert their influence in complex processes of interaction with the other elements of a system of action, not by simply 'becoming real'" (715). In his methodological essays, moreover, Weber countered the idealist refusal to apply general concepts to the field of human action, by arguing the need for general concepts in order to demonstrate any objective empirical proposition.

The climax of the treatment of Weber in *Structure* comes when Parsons relates Weber's demonstration of the role of value elements in historical action to Durkheim's demonstration of the role of social norms. In particular, he likens Weber's concept of charisma to Durkheim's concept of the sacred. Conceding that Weber's explicit systematic theorizing ran in a different direction from his own—toward a system of ideal types rather than a system of generalized analytic categories— Parsons was content to "elicit by analysis a definite scheme of the structure of a generalized system of action which appears at the most strategic points of Weber's work" (716).

In concluding, Parsons advances the claim that Marshall, Pareto, Durkheim, and Weber converged on "the outline of what in *all essentials* is the *same* system of generalized social theory" (719–20). This theory specifies the elements of a generalized system of action, which fall into three relatively well-defined groups: (1) the factors of heredity and environment, seen subjectively as the ultimate means and conditions of action; (2) the intermediate intrinsic means-end sector, representing the technological, economic, and political elements of instrumentally rational action; (3) the elements clustering about the ultimate-value system as a complex of meaning not reducible to the random ends of utilitarianism. With this convergence, the major lines of controversy in the early history of sociology have been erased, and the sociological community could unite behind a consensually established paradigm, granting economics jurisdiction over the aspects of action concerned with rationality in terms of the supply-and-demand schema, and granting sociology jurisdiction over the aspects of action concerned with ultimate value attitudes. Reviewing the field some thirty-five years later, Parsons reaffirmed his sense that the "war of schools" had diminished drastically during the period from the turn of the century to the mid-1930s, that subsequent work had furthered the crystallization of sociological thought around a consensually supported theoretical scheme, and that further statements supporting pluralism or "formless eclecticism" would "positively impede progress" in the discipline (1961, 138–39).

### THE PARSONIAN MYTHOS

For all its grandeur and sweep, *The Structure of Social Action* must be judged a deeply flawed work of scholarship. As a self-avowed effort to take stock of the theoretical resources of the sociological tradition, it has been indicted for ignoring the French tradition before Durkheim, the entire American tradition, and the work of Georg Simmel, as well as for its strikingly partial appropriation of the utilitarian tradition, the tradition of German idealism, and the work of Marx, Durkheim, and Weber. As an effort to systematize those theoretical resources that pertain to the analysis of human action, it has been faulted for focusing so exclusively on situational facts and normative dispositions that it neglects affects (an omission Parsons arguably corrected in later work) and cognitive orientations (an omission he arguably never corrected), and for construing what theories it does represent in the terms of an artificially constructed theoretical dilemma.[10] As an effort to clarify presuppositional issues in sociological theory, it has been criticized for using virtually all of its key terms—action, empiricism, order, positivism, rationality, and voluntarism—in aggravatingly vague and/or inconsistent ways. And as an effort to argue the case for mainstream convergence in modern sociology, it has suffered repeated contradiction by pluralistic accounts that challenge the convergence hypothesis.[11]

Even so, these flaws do not ruin its value as a plausible and appealing sort of narrative. After all, every history must be selective. Parsons's version was surely no more so than Madge's and those of many others.[12] The annoying ambiguity of his central concepts is more harmful to his

10. "If motivation is as essential a feature of the action process as means and ends, then, were randomness of ends to characterize an action model, it could be overcome not only (as Parsons asserts) at the level of means and ends, but at the level of motivation as well. When, for example, one abandons the assumption that actors are motivated by diffuse egoism and endows them with more specific motives, the problem of statistical randomness disappears—and, with it, the utilitarian dilemma, for any dilemma from which one can escape without ending up on either horn is no dilemma at all" (Camic 1979, 522). This issue remains open.

11. So great have been the expectations aroused by *Structure* that it has even been chided retrospectively for failing to address historic societal crises during the time of the Depression, the Spanish Civil War, and approaching conflict with the Fascist states (Bottomore 1969). This line of critique shades into extreme and counterfactual allegations about Parson's alleged reactionary and even pro-Nazi sympathies. The facts are clear: Parsons was one of the first American sociologists to voice alarm about Nazism in the 1930s and wrote a number of articles about the problem. See Uta Gerhardt's important edition of Parsons papers on Nazism and her introductory essay (Parsons 1993). See also below, chapter 4, note 9.

For a masterly overview of the properly academic criticisms of *Structure,* see Camic 1989. For Parsons's distorting selectivity, see Camic 1979 and Levine 1980. For a careful representation of Durkheim that provides a corrective to readings by Parsons and others, see Gane 1988. For not giving cognitive belief systems their due, see Warner 1978. For Parsons's conflations regarding positivism and other methodological matters, see Alexander 1982–83. For criticisms of vagueness and inconsistency in his day concepts, see Von Dohlen 1973 and Camic 1989. For pluralistic rejoinders to his convergence hypothesis, see Levine 1980 and 1985a, ch. 6, in addition to the authors cited in the previous chapter. For critiques focused on the posited relationship between Durkheim and Weber, see Bendix 1971; Pope, Cohen, and Hazelrigg 1975; and Yang 1986.

12. For a spirited justification of Parsons's selectivity in *Structure* in spite of its historical flaws, see Alexander 1989.

work as a theoretic treatise than as a narrative discourse. Further, although others have argued the greater salience of theoretical divergence, it should be noted that each of our pluralist raconteurs has referred to significant moments of convergence in postwar sociological theory. Sorokin, for example, concludes his second survey of the disparate currents of sociological thought in the twentieth century by mentioning "a considerable agreement of diverse sociological theories in the past and by a growing concordance of these theories at the present." Among the points of convergence, he includes such Parsonian themes as the value-laden and superorganic character of sociocultural phenomena, which differentiates them from inorganic and organic phenomena, and the fact that they possess distinguishable cultural, social, and personal aspects (1966, 635ff.).[13]

Whatever its flaws, *Structure* remains the preeminent construction of the sociological tradition of the genre I am labeling synthetic. Its essential defining features consist of the following assumptions:

*theoretic formulations are quite as important as empirical techniques and findings for the advancement of sociology;*

*sociological theory was organized among contending schools in its early phases;*

*our present perspective enables us to view each of these earlier schools as at best partially correct, and to advance a new way of thinking that deserves to dominate the field.*

The synthetic narrative might thus be represented in the form of two or more streams that flow along for a while and then converge in one mighty river. Such an image was likely to appeal to a discipline tired of longstanding internal cleavages. That appeal was manifest not only in the resonance evoked by Parsons's own narrative in the 1950s but also in a number of subsequent efforts to compose narratives of this genre.

## LATER SYNTHETIC NARRATIVES

Two fresh examples of a synthetic narrative appeared in the 1960s. Both of them configured the sociological tradition in terms of a perduring opposition between two root metaphors, the mechanical system and the organism, and conveyed a message that the time is ripe for that opposition to yield to some superseding synthesis.

13. For comparable passages referring to theoretical convergence, see Eisenstadt 1976 (245–47, 270–73) and Martindale 1981 (603).

Werner Stark's treatise of 1962 covers not just the past century of sociological theory but, as his title indicates, *The Fundamental Forms of [Western] Social Thought* starting with classical antiquity. His grand view of that panorama discloses a kind of cyclical movement in which certain powerful doctrines about social life constantly tend to reappear. The first doctrine thinks of society as a unity; he calls it organicism, or holism, or sociological realism. Its normative form appeared in Aristotle's conception that societies exist by nature and have a natural telos in the good life for humans, and in Aquinas's view that the body social comes to resemble the body physical the more that its members cease to be selfish and become social; its positive form appeared in Spencer's view of society as an organism; its "extreme" forms appeared in the detailed applications of the "body social" metaphor by thinkers like Schäffle and Lilienfeld. This doctrine finds its disciplinary home in "classical anthropology." The second doctrine, mechanicism (or atomism, or sociological nominalism), thinks of society as a multiplicity. Its normative form propounds that model of society as a balance of forces in equilibrium (Rousseau)[14] and the model of peace secured through an automatically operative balance between actions and reactions (Kant); its positive form may be found in Pareto's notion of systemic equilibria; its extreme forms in thinkers who depict social forces in terms of molecular gravitation or rational mechanics. This second doctrine finds its disciplinary home in classical economics.

Stark demonstrates that the doctrines of organicism and mechanicism have long coexisted; he traces the debate between them as far back as Plato's *Crito*. Although supporters of both positions see these doctrines as competitive, Stark argues that since each model misrepresents social reality by exaggerating one or the other of its basic features, the two are not competitive. Instead they are

> right only when taken in conjunction, but decidedly wrong when taken in isolation. . . . Organicism shows us what society would be like if the tendencies toward integration gained the upper hand . . . over the tendencies toward individual independence. . . . Mechanicism on the other hand shows us what society would be like if the tendencies toward individual independence gained the upper hand . . . over the tendencies toward integration. (vii, 264)

Although Stark forwards the suggestion that holistic and atomistic doctrines tend to be associated, respectively, with historical milieus fa-

14. For an alternative reading of Rousseau, see chapter 8.

voring social integration and individual freedom, the main conclusion of his study of the development of social thought is that the partiality of both contending doctrines evinces above all a need for synthesis. He accordingly identifies the outlines of a third theory, which proves to be "a synthesis, a reconciliation of opposites, truer than they because it bears in itself both their fundamental truths" (vii). The third theory views society as a "process" and features the expression of human agency. Stark finds it prefigured in the work of Fouillée, Tönnies, Simmel, Sumner, and Cooley, each of whom strove to overcome the traditional dichotomy between social realism and social nominalism and so to conjoin self and society. Stark designates this approach "cultural sociology" to signify that it has overcome the materialistic limitations of both organicism and mechanicism. Revealing the deeper agenda of every disciplinary narrative, he adds, "My book is both a key to the past, and a plea for the future, of the social sciences" (vii).

Five years after Stark, yet with no apparent awareness of Stark's book, Walter Buckley (1967) set forth an argument that the time had come to replace mechanical and organismic models in sociology with a "general systems perspective" akin to the "process" model advanced by a few prophetic sociologists. The temporal horizon of these two scholars differed: Stark looked at the past two millennia, Buckley at the preceding two decades. Stark's synthesis came from inspecting the vicissitudes of Western social thought, Buckley's from the postwar efflorescence of modern systems theory. But their visions of the sociological tradition proved similar, for Buckley maintained that

> sociological theory has been living for some time off the intellectual capital of previous centuries. . . . Current dominant theory is built on mechanical and . . . organismic systems models laid down during previous centuries which are quite inappropriate in dealing with the type of system represented by the sociocultural realm. (1967, 1)

Buckley, like Stark, tells us that he uses the term "sociocultural" to make explicit the difference between the human and subhuman levels of organization. And, like Stark, Buckley includes Simmel and Cooley (along with Mead) as exponents of a process model that anticipates the basic principles of the cybernetic model he advocates.

The main features of this new systems model include information processing and exchanges, tension production as constitutive, organizational openness, and indeterminacy. These features converge in the notion of *morphogenesis,* a process in which systems transform themselves through internal and external interactions. Exemplars of this newer approach include Karl Deutsch, Leo Srole, Theodore Newcomb, and Peter Blau.

While Stark found Parsons's synthesis congenial and cited the work of Parsons to illustrate his "third sociology" (249), Buckley considered Parsons a key part of the problem that needed to be overcome. For Buckley, the chief contemporary instantiations of outmoded theories are the Paretan equilibrium model of Homans and the "equilibrium-function" model of Parsons. Parsons erred doubly, claimed Buckley, referring now to the work of Parsons's middle period, for having embraced both the mechanical and organismic equilibrium principles, and thereby having failed to incorporate the cultural level of analysis into his systemic model. There is immense irony in Buckley's characterization of Parsons, given that Parsons conspicuously bore a lifelong commitment to featuring the cultural dimension of action and served as a major conduit into sociology of precisely the ideas from cybernetics theory Buckley adduces to ground his putative countermodel. Even so, one must appreciate the way in which Buckley's book reproduces the key features of the kind of narrative for which Parsons's *Structure* provided the archetype: both sides of an age-old antinomy are inadequate, but a new overarching conception offers great hope for the future of sociological theory.

The 1970s were so filled with the clamor of opposing schools in sociology that no one dared propose a synthetic narrative. By the 1980s, however, the mood began to shift—not least owing to the death of Parsons in 1979—and the scene came to resemble in certain respects the condition of the 1930s.

Recall that the situation that elicited Parsons's grand synthetic narrative was one he considered acutely demoralizing for sociology. A thousand disparate theories had created "a strong current of pessimism [among] students of the social sciences, especially those who call themselves sociologists. We are told . . . that there is no common basis, that all is arbitrary and subjective." This had produced lapses into mindless empiricism or else aesthetic intuitionism. In concluding *Structure*, Parsons expressed the hope that his study would counteract those dangerous tendencies and that the convergence of thought it demonstrated might reverse the prevailing pessimistic judgment of the social sciences. "We have," he affirmed, "sound theoretical foundations on which to build" ([1937] 1968, 774–75).

Nearly half a century later, a young sociologist deeply identified with

Parsons would introduce a similar synthetic effort with a similar definition of the situation. "If sociology could speak it would say, 'I am
tired,'" he began. Its pervasive fatigue and pessimism stemmed from
the trivializing effects of technocratic fetishism and the disabling effects
of theoretical confusion and ideological poverty. If sociology is to be
revived, it must recapture a strong and vigorous body of theory. With
that bold diagnosis Jeffrey Alexander embarked on the most ambitious
effort to reconstruct the tradition in a generation—the four volumes of
*Theoretical Logic in Sociology* (1982–83; hereafter TLS) followed by
*Twenty Lectures: Sociological Theory since World War II* (1987).

Like Parsons, Alexander presents his narrative not as a history but as
an exercise in systematic theory. Under the banner "Against Histori-
cism/For Theory" (1989) he explicitly rejects historiographic criteria
for assessing works like *Structure*. Yet even when analysis of Alexander's
work as systematic theory reveals flaws, it still offers an inviting way to
reconstruct the history of social thought.

Indeed, much of the appeal of Alexander's work comes from its energetic revivification of the original Parsonian mythos.[15] It is difficult to
think of Alexander's 1980s corpus as anything other than a massive updating of *Structure*, quite as we regarded Madge's *Origins of Scientific
Sociology* as an update of Park and Burgess, or the later volumes by
Sorokin and Martindale as updates of their previous ones. Like these
later publications, Alexander's work tells about the literature produced
in the interval since his predecessor's work appeared—in this case, the
entire oeuvre of Parsons himself and a substantial number of sociological theorists of the postwar decades. He also devotes half a volume to
Karl Marx (albeit ignoring the early utilitarians and idealists whom
Parsons considered briefly).

As with those other later publications, the benefit of time enabled
Alexander's TLS to rework the earlier interpretive schemes in a more
deductively systematic fashion. Thus, Alexander formalizes the Parsonian framework by locating the category of "presuppositions" at the
pole of maximum generality on a continuum of different types of scientific statement,[16] by identifying the problems of "action" and "order"

15. This is why the "older generation" of sociologists attached to that mythos were
generally so much more sympathetic to TLS than were the author's peers (Turner
1985a).

16. His discussion here benefits from the intervening work on the history and philosophy of science, though he shows no awareness of the "anti-positivistic" epistemologists
prior to Kuhn—men like Whewell, Peirce, Poincaré, Husserl, Jaspers, Whitehead, with
most of whom Parsons was familiar.

as *the* two presuppositional issues in sociological theory, and by specifying the criterion of "multidimensionality" as the universal criterion by which methodological and substantive theoretical statements are to be evaluated. In practice, he uses multidimensionality to signify a disposition to incorporate both poles of two substantive oppositions—rational versus nonrational grounds of action and individualistic versus collectivistic grounds of social order—and both poles of an epistemological opposition between idealistic and positivistic views of theory.[17]

Volume 1 of TLS sets forth Alexander's claims about presuppositional logic in sociology, along with critiques of authors who debase discourse about presuppositional issues by conflating them with questions about ideology, methodology, models, and empirical propositions. The remaining volumes consider the contributions to presuppositional discourse found in the works of Marx and Durkheim, Weber, and Parsons. Although Alexander introduces his tetralogy by implicitly disclaiming any narrative aspiration, referring to TLS as a single book with four separated parts pursuing "one consistent theoretical ambition" (1982–83, 1:xv), it is hard not to get a sense that he is projecting what he regards as "the *core* line of development in sociological theory," especially when one considers the subtitles: "*The* Antinomies of Classical Thought: Marx and Durkheim," "*The* Classical Attempt at Theoretical Synthesis: Max Weber," and "*The* Modern Reconstruction of Classical Thought: Talcott Parsons" (emphases mine).

In telling his story, moreover, Alexander imitates the most dramatically effective device in Parsons's *Structure*: the interpretation of Durkheim's work in the form of a saga about persisting internal conflicts heroically grappled with. Alexander applies this stratagem with gusto to the early writings of Durkheim, then to the oeuvres of Marx and Weber, and finally to the writings of Parsons himself.[18] In Alexander's scenario, as in that of Parsons, the overarching struggle takes place between the presuppositional commitments to materialism and idealism. Marx played out this struggle by proceeding from idealism to materialism, Durkheim did so by proceeding from the latter to

17. In all of this, again, Alexander follows Parsons by presenting these terms with little awareness of their philosophic antecedents and complexity, and without expending the effort needed to define them sharply or justify the usages being made of them. For critiques of Alexander's cavalier treatment of his own basic concepts, see Wallace 1984, Turner 1985a, Levine 1986b, and Warner 1988.

18. In the words of one reviewer, "the narrative structure of Alexander's analyses depends on his showing that the thinkers he discusses are in the grip of deep internal presuppositional conflicts which drive them hither and yon" (Turner 1985b, 211–12).

the former. Weber wavered between emphases at the idealist and the materialist poles but, in his treatments of religious evolution, social class, and medieval European cities, succeeded in integrating both perspectives. Even so, Weber relapsed into a more monotonic materialist perspective in his later treatments of classical Chinese society and of modern political structures.

The story of Parsons, so Alexander tells it, resembles that of Weber for shifting back and forth between multi- and unidimensionality. To begin with, Alexander chronicles the development of Parsons as a "multidimensional" theorist. In his early period, culminating with *Structure,* Parsons set forth his arguments for the irreducible role of theory in empirical science, the articulation of the problems of action and order, and the solution to both through a multidimensional focus on the significance of both normative and conditional elements in action. Alexander assigns the essays after *Structure,* culminating in the two books of 1951—*Toward a General Theory of Action* and *The Social System*—to Parsons's middle period. In these years Parsons was "specifying" his multidimensional assumptions by engaging them with empirical analyses, as in his well-known discussions of pattern variables; his discrimination of culture, social and personality systems as distinct levels; his theories of consensus and deviance; and his interpretations of modern societies. In the later period Parsons drove his multidimensional commitments into the theoretical elaborations of the four-function AGIL scheme and the analysis of interchange and its media. This period also witnessed the culmination of Parsons's sweeping analyses of the evolution of freedom in modern societies.

Alongside Parsons's continuing commitment to multidimensional analysis, however, Alexander finds a chronic tendency toward more simplistic thinking. The second half of TLS criticizes Parsons for veering toward idealistic reductionism—for example, in treating the occupational system in terms of socialization issues at the expense of attending to clashes of interest. Alexander also faults Parsons for conflating presuppositional statements *proprement dites* with statements about ideology, methodology, models, and empirical matters.

In other words, Alexander's narrative about the tradition is more like Catton's than like Madge's. Multidimensionality for him, like naturalism for Catton, represents not a triumphantly secured outlook but an intellectually warranted position, one that preeminent figures in the tradition move toward but often defect from. This perception sets up the exceptionally revealing part of the tale that Alexander relates in his 1987 sequel.

In *Twenty Lectures* Alexander talks about sociological theory after World War II. He begins by asserting "the empirical fact of Parsons's theoretical hegemony" in the postwar period (1987, 111). By the late 1960s, however, assaults on Parsons had produced an anarchic situation in which warring schools once again flourished. Alexander analyzes key figures from these schools: conflict theory, exchange theory, symbolic interactionism, ethnomethodology, cultural sociology, and Marxism. Each school is said to elaborate one theoretic element from the multidimensional theory Parsons had tried ambivalently to promote. The larger drama, then, is that while Parsons preached an ecumenical synthesis to end warfare among sociological schools, in practice he undercut this aspiration through one-sided positions that provoked a series of counterresponses.

Alexander's account of postwar sociology resembles Eisenstadt's a decade earlier. However, where Eisenstadt saw the diverse "counter-models" to Parsons's paradigm as valid alternatives under the umbrella of a pluralistic/dialogic view of the tradition, Alexander sees them all— like the one-sided digressions of Weber and Parsons—as regressions from a multidimensional synthesis, which those two authors at their best so brilliantly embodied. In keeping alive the dream of synthesis despite the polemics of his first volume, Alexander offers a narrative to promote solidarity in the wake of sociology's civil wars of the 1960s and 1970s.

A different sort of synthetic narrative emerged from the work of Jürgen Habermas in the early 1980s, his two-volume *Theory of Communicative Action* (hereafter TCA), published in German in 1981 and in English a few years later (1984/1987a), followed by his *Philosophical Discourse of Modernity* (hereafter *Discourse*; 1987b), which offers a philosophical grounding for the TCA project.[19] In contrast to the narratives of Parsons and Alexander, TCA appeared not at the outset of a career but as a culminating statement. It climaxed a quarter-century of work in which Habermas sought to synthesize materials from a variety of philosophical and empirical traditions, work that began from the viewpoint of Western Marxism and aimed to develop a theory of history with practical import.

As Parsons intended in *Structure,* Habermas wrote TCA as an essay in systematic theory rather than history, yet (coupled with the *Discourse*) it in fact offered a narrative account of what he considered the

---

19. Whether the promise of the *Discourse* is redeemed in TCA remains an open question; in any case the *Discourse* can be viewed as a text that governs TCA's trajectory as a "regulatory ideal" (Frank 1992).

core line of development in Western social theory. Whereas the convergence of Pareto, Durkheim, and Weber formed the focus of Parsons's synthesis, Habermas included Marx, Durkheim, Mead, Weber, Parsons himself,[20] Goffman, and work from adjacent fields including hermeneutics (Gadamer), linguistics (Chomsky), psychology (Freud, Piaget), phenomenological philosophy (Husserl, Schutz), and philosophy of language (Austin, Wittgenstein).

The purpose of Habermas's narrative was not to define legitimate boundaries for sociology but to transcend such boundaries in the service of a more encompassing synthesis. Habermas proceeds through a succession of critiques geared not so much to securing an adequate analytic scheme as to reaching a proper theoretic and practical understanding of modernity. His narrative begins with the German philosophical tradition.[21] In the wake of Kant, Fichte, and Schelling, Hegel posits the distinctive quality of modernity as the determination not to follow the models of other epochs but "to create its normativity out of itself" (1987b, 7). Hegel was right to locate that self-generated normativity in the reason of acting subjects, but he took a problematic turn in deriving the subjects' source of reason. Although in his earlier work Hegel glimpsed what Habermas regards as the proper derivation of human reason—"*the higher-level intersubjectivity of an uncoerced formation of will* within a communication community existing under constraints toward cooperation" (1987b, 40)—he made a highly consequential error by developing the derivation of subjective reason in another direction. This direction was through the philosophy of consciousness, which led to the conception of monological self-knowledge and, beyond that, to an externalization of subjective rationality in an institutional order. What Hegel's conception of rationalized law did permit was a synthesis of two distinct mechanisms of social control: "mechanisms of social integration, which attach to action orientations, and mechanisms of system integration, which reach right through action orientations" (1987a, 202). After Marx, however, this synthesis of ac-

20. Habermas found Parsons's synthesis an indispensable point of departure for progressive work in social theory: "The body of work [Parsons] left us is without equal in its level of abstraction and differentiation, its social-theoretical scope and systematic quality, while at the same time it draws upon the literatures of specialized research. . . . No theory of society can be taken seriously today if it does not at least situate itself with respect to Parsons" (1987a, 199). Indeed, after 1937 Parsons went on to become a polymath like Habermas, incorporating ideas from anthropology, cybernetics, economics, linguistics, political science, and psychology into his ongoing work.

21. See chapter 9 below.

tion theory and systems theory broke down and the two theoretical interests were pursued along divergent lines.

For Habermas, then, social theory after Hegel flowed in three separate channels. (1) In the dominant line that culminates with Parsons, the monological view of rationality gets picked up by Dilthey, Husserl, and Weber and comes to constitute a general theory of action. (2) Economic theory develops the idea of an instrumental order into the conception of a system steered by the medium of money. This led to wide-ranging analyses of objectified manifestations of rationality in the modern world, such as the reifications of functional rationality so criticized by Lukács and the Frankfurt School. Parsons strove to combine the traditions of action theory and systems theory through a synthesis that gives a privileged place to rational action as resource mobilization in the service of upgrading adaptation to the environment.

(3) The other line picks up the train of thought adumbrated by the early Hegel. The pivotal figure here is George Herbert Mead, who strove to capture the structural features of symbolically mediated interaction.[22] Habermas sees Mead as the prime thinker who challenges the monological view of rationality, for Mead developed foundations for a modern theory of communicative action in which rationality becomes the offspring of intersubjective discourse. What Mead's theory lacked was a conception of a prelinguistic root of communicative action that has a symbolic character, a gap Habermas fills using Durkheim's theory of collective consciousness.

In the synthetic work of Habermas, the three lines are brought together: the first two with a theory of institutionalized rationality that pertains to the domain of economic, political, and bureaucratic systems; the third with a theory of communicative rationality that pertains to spheres of everyday experience, which Habermas refers to as the "lifeworld."[23] This is the domain of the transmission of culture and of consensual social integration. Although the mature Parsons attempted to synthesize the domains of action and of systems, he failed because of his alignment with the monological view of rational action. For

22. Oddly, Habermas fails to mention the young Mead's preoccupation with Hegel; see chapter 12 below.

23. This theoretical synthesis bears an extraordinary resemblance to that produced a century earlier by Tönnies in *Gemeinschaft und Gesellschaft*. Tönnies brought together the conception of instrumental rationality and contractually established institutions theorized by Hobbes with the conception of personalized communal forms oriented to values and sentiment theorized by the German Romantics.

Habermas the theory of communicative action also provides criteria for the rational evaluation of society. His story thus serves to legitimate a role for social theory as a means to evaluate the state of the modern project for normative autonomy.

Habermas's own report on that state is mixed. On the one hand, modernity is willy-nilly increasing the number of cases in which interaction must be coordinated through a consensus reached by participants themselves. On the other hand, the capacity to participate in norm-setting communicative action is diminishing. This capacity depends on nurturing experiences in lifeworld structures like the family. However, lifeworld territory is being encroached on by integrative processes that stem from the "system" world and its impersonal media, money and power. In effect, Habermas ends up conjoining the form of Marx's critique of the contradictions of capitalism with the substance of Durkheim's analysis of anomie in modern society, and does so using the terms of Mead's theory of communication.

Habermas's interpretation of the "colonization" of the lifeworld by macrosocial systemic structures and his vague notion of the lifeworld have provoked much controversy.[24] However vulnerable his substantive assertions, his synthesis remains notable for three features that have not been thematized in previous narratives of the sociological tradition. Habermas offers the first narrative in which ethical concerns appear prominently interwoven with assessments of the progress of sociology as a scientific discipline. He emphasizes the constitutive role of dialogue in all structures of human action.[25] And he provides an account of the sociological tradition in which the boundaries of sociology are made permeable if not dissolved. As will be clear by the end of my story, I consider these features valuable—indispensable, even—for the kind of narrative I believe appropriate for the coming generation.

24. For insightful critiques of Habermas's lifeworld concept and the thesis of colonization, see Alexander 1985; also Olafson 1990 and Postone 1990. For a critique of his treatment of Hegel and modernity, see Pippin 1991.

25. Indeed, Habermas comes close to articulating a feature of what I shall call a dialogic narrative of the tradition in one of the comments he makes in praise of Parsons: "Among the productive theorists of society no one else has equaled Parsons' intensity and persistence in conducting a dialogue with the classics" (1987a, 200).

# CHAPTER FOUR

# Humanist and Contextualist Narratives

**D**espite the differences among those narratives of the sociological tradition I classify as positivist, pluralist, and synthetic, all three visions share one pivotal assumption. Without exception they assume that sociology takes its essential character from being a kind of natural science, thus resembling other sciences by pursuing purely cognitive goals in a cumulative and progressive manner. The positivist vision locates that progression in the increasing subordination of ideas about social phenomena to controlled observation. The pluralist vision locates sociology's progress in the flowering of a multiplicity of perspectives needed for analyzing something so complex as society. The synthetic vision locates a decisive advancement of sociology in the supersession of inadequate theoretical perspectives by a position deemed suitable for all future work. The originative expositions of these visions (Park and Burgess 1921; Sorokin 1928; Parsons 1937) appeared during the interwar years. The optimism they conveyed about sociology as a science waxed during World War II and continued to prevail for nearly two decades more. By the late 1960s, however, new moods were stirring, moods that gave rise to visions of the sociological tradition no longer dominated by the image of sociology as a progressive science.

## THE DERAILMENT OF "PROGRESSIVE SCIENCE" IN THE 1960S

Following World War II sociology made robust strides as a profession. Departments of sociology sprang up or expanded throughout North America, Western Europe, Poland, Israel, and Japan. The American Sociological Association nearly tripled its membership in the dozen years after 1948. An International Association of Sociologists was launched with éclat under UNESCO auspices in 1949. Government agencies and private groups funded sociological research on an unprecedented scale; sociologists came to play a role in public policy deliberations and judicial decisions. The rise in sociology's status as a professional enterprise reinforced the tendency of sociologists to secure their self-esteem by carrying out carefully crafted, narrowly focused, and rigorously executed pieces of specialized research. These changes drew sociologists increasingly far away from the broad historical perspectives, moral concerns, and intellectual ambitions that had animated the founders of their discipline—so far away, in fact, that some sociologists became uncomfortable with what appeared as unbalanced "scientism" and sought a view of sociology's past that paid greater attention to its extrascientific dimensions.

This shift of attention toward sociology's extrascientific aspects reflected a number of concurrent developments. For one thing, the societal context of sociological work altered during the 1960s, especially in the United States. A swelling sector of society under the poverty line in an age of growing affluence fueled new concerns about economic inequality. Independence for the states of black Africa fueled a growing disposition among members of American society to campaign against racial injustice. Concerns about the status of former colonies in the "Third World" generally stirred unprecedented waves of opposition to the United States' military engagement in Southeast Asia. The outpouring of new energy into egalitarian movements also activated movements of protest against obstacles to women's equal rights and against what were perceived as unjust restrictions on student rights within academic institutions.

These changes produced demands for sociologists to take principled stands on policy questions and to play a more activist role in solving social problems, demands that contradicted the spirit of ethical neutrality most sociologists associated with their claims to professional credibility. In turn, social activists, especially students, turned against what came to be labeled "mainstream sociology" for sidestepping such civic responsibilities. Indeed, they went on to accuse sociology not only of failing to criticize the status quo but even of complicity in sustaining the injustice and repressiveness of the established order by contributing refined techniques of manipulation and domination. Such accusations in turn led critics to point to factors like economic interest and political ideology as extrascientific influences on mainstream sociological work as well as to raise loud questions about the place of ethical considerations in the calling of sociology (Levine 1970).

Other significant changes took place in the cultural context of sociological work that had no obvious connection to the societal changes that underlay the ideological critiques. One of these changes occurred in the philosophical context of sociological thought. I refer to the growing disposition to accentuate the nonrational elements of scientific discourse, whether through emphasizing the constraints of language, as in the later Wittgenstein; the diversities of historical semantics, as with McKeon; the subjective component in scientific revolutions, as with Kuhn; or the aesthetics of scientific work, as with Feyerabend. These epistemological tendencies could be said to support pluralist accounts over positivist and synthetic ones, but to some extent they spilled out beyond cognitive pluralism to focus attention on the external determinants of scientific work. Although the enterprise of the natural sciences did not seem significantly affected by these philosophic developments, the always-vulnerable stance of those wanting sociology to function like a natural science weakened further when philosophers came to question the very plausibility of that model of science.[1]

Yet sociologists had no need to venture into the precincts of professional philosophy in order to find grounds for questioning the adequacy of purely internalist views of scientific work. Such questioning evolved as a logical extension of the discipline's own premises. As articulated by figures like Durkheim, Scheler, and Mannheim, to some determinate extent the forms and contents of knowledge depend on the social conditions and cultural milieu in which they appear. Merton's efforts to apply these perspectives began to bear fruit by the late 1950s, when his own work returned with renewed vigor to the sociology of science and cohorts of his students began to lend commitment and productivity to the subject. The sociology of knowledge gained new visibility at meetings of the World Congress of Sociology at Stresa, Italy in 1959, during which Merton turned the perspective of the sociology of knowledge/science onto sociology itself. His "Social Conflict over Styles of Sociological Work" (1961) was perhaps the first substantive scientific contribution to the sociology of sociology.

These changes in the social and cultural environments of sociology had the effect of deflecting the quest for its meaning into directions other than a neatly cricumscribed path of scientific progress. Some pursued the quest by looking at contextual factors to find the chief meaning of the tradition. For others it took the form of reconfiguring sociology as in some essential part a humanistic enterprise.

### THE SEARCH FOR MEANING IN THE CLASSICS

One effect of sociology's push toward rigor and respectability as a scientific profession in the postwar years was its studied inattention to

---

1. For an instructive account of how comparable ideological and epistemological issues got played out in the American historical profession during the 1960s and after, see Novick 1988.

texts that had provided the intellectual capital for launching the sociological enterprise. Sociologists acted as if under compulsion to avoid the classics, adhering scrupulously to the injunction from the Whiteheadian epigraph to Merton's widely influential book of essays first published in 1949: "A science which hesitates to forget its founders is lost"—ignoring both the context of the quote and Merton's own practice contradicting it. W. F. Ogburn captured the spirit of this aversion in a locally influential memorandum which circulated at the University of Chicago around that time. Ogburn recommended that sociologists abstain from scholarship on earlier texts and likened instruction on the work of earlier sociologists to teaching chemistry students about alchemy (1952, 3).

This spirit remained effectual so long as sociology's status as a progressive science remained unassailed. It remains alive in certain quarters today, as in more recent claims that "it is in our fundamental interest to deposit Durkheim and other [classics] of our science in historical museums" (Freese 1980, 14). But growing skepticism about scientific progress in sociology, along with lingering nostalgia, left some sociologists with a sense of uneasiness, a sense that there was more to their heritage than contemporary practice seemed ready to acknowledge. This malaise led to a striking renewal of interest in the classics.

The theme was broached in an evocative essay, "The Calling of Sociology," which Edward Shils published in 1961.[2] To be sure, Shils paid respect to the intellectual crispness sociology acquired by following "the scientific model." Thanks to the influence of science, sociologists were applying steadily improved techniques of observation and producing more comprehensive and finely differentiated theories. In at least one important respect, sociology had proven itself truly scientific: "it makes cumulative progress, revising and clarifying its foundations, extending its scope, unifying discrete observations into coherent patterns of observation" (1961, 1446).

---

2. This essay formed the epilogue to a magisterial two-volume collection of writings by classic authors, *Theories of Society*, which Shils coedited with Parsons, Naegele, and Pitts. Shils published a revised version of this essay in a book bearing its title (1980), which omits the portion of the essay discussed in this section; further comments on sociology as a humanistic discipline appeared in his important essay published the following year, *Tradition*. Although passages in these writings legitimate the view of sociology as a kind of humanistic discipline, Shils's own narrative depiction of the tradition sweeps beyond that into an account of broad cultural movements that includes sociology as but one of many voices. Accordingly, I classify Shils's narrative genre as contextualist and will discuss it in the following section.

Yet the section in which these words appeared was headed "The Progress of Sociological Theory and the Permanent Relevance of the Classics." Shils went on there to claim that in spite of sociology's scientific advances, both the older classics of political and social thought and the classics of modern sociology remain important objects for sociological attention. This was true for sociology, if not for economics and the natural sciences, and it was so for two reasons. Contemporary sociologists, owing in part to their virtues of contemporaneity and meticulousness, had failed to attain the levels of insight and understanding evinced by the classics. Yet even if this educational defect were to be remedied, sociologists would still need to heed the classics. This is because the classics afford access to certain primal experiences of social life that cannot be represented by abstract formulas but can only be apprehended through the revelation of deeply personal experiences by persons of exceptional sensibility and intellect. Classics provide "a continuous opportunity for contact with an enduring problem, with a permanently important aspect of existence, as disclosed through the greatness of an [individual] mind" (1447).

In the years after Shils wrote these words, fresh translations, editions, and secondary analyses of classic authors became one of the faster-growing industries within sociology. Between 1972 and 1978, for example, no fewer than ten full-length books were published on Émile Durkheim alone. Associations devoted to recovering the complete works of Durkheim, Simmel, and Weber came into being. In the late 1960s, Morris Janowitz experimentally introduced The Heritage of Sociology series to republish selected writings by classic authors; the series elicited so strong a response that he felt encouraged to commission some forty titles over the next two decades. This quickened activity reflected not only a revived interest but a serious reversal of judgment about the worth of the classic writings.[3]

3. It is worth noting that the recovery of the classic authors depended largely on efforts of scholars from other countries. Durkheim was ignored in France in the postwar years. It took the efforts of Parsons, Merton, and Lukes to restore his significant voice to world sociology; the six books on Durkheim just mentioned were all by anglophone writers. Weber and Simmel were similarly ignored in postwar Germany. It took the efforts of American scholars, Parsons especially but also Shils, Merton, Frank Knight, Reinhard Bendix, Benjamin Nelson, Gunther Roth, and many others (including Raymond Aron in France) to legitimate his acceptance in Germany. Similarly, only in the United States were sociologists taking Simmel seriously in the postwar years (Levine, Carter, and Gorman 1976). Conversely, the recovery of interest in early sociology and social theory at Chicago was due in good part to European scholars: Martin Bulmer and Dennis Smith in England, Hans Joas and Habermas in Germany.

It remained for Robert Nisbet to sketch a narrative vision for which such reappraisals of the classics provided the animating principle. *The Sociological Tradition* (1966) set out to recover the fundamental ideas of European sociology by viewing them as inspired responses to the breakup of the old order in Europe in the wake of the industrial and democratic revolutions. Nisbet identified these core ideas as community, authority, status, the sacred, and alienation. The creative articulation of these ideas took place in the work of a small number of eminent authors who wrote between 1830 and 1900 (he should have said 1920): Comte, LePlay, Tocqueville, Marx, Tönnies, Durkheim, Weber, and Simmel. Their ideas taken together, he wrote, "constitute a reorientation of European thought quite as momentous . . . [as that] reorientation of thought that had marked the waning of the Middle Ages three centuries earlier and the rise of the Age of Reason" (8). Nothing so rich or exciting had appeared in sociology since that time. Indeed, he advised, "We live, and we should not forget it, in a late phase of the classical age of sociology. Strip from present-day sociology the perspectives and frameworks provided by men like Weber and Durkheim, and little would be left but lifeless heaps of data and stray hypotheses" (5).

In this and subsequent writings over the ensuing decade, Nisbet deepened that vision by contrasting the productions of present-day sociologists with those of their illustrious predecessors. Contemporary sociology had become sterile, banal, and amoral, he charged. It was succumbing to the mystique of scientism, which celebrates proof over discovery, and misleads students by persuading them that a small idea abundantly verified has more worth than a large idea insusceptible to textbook techniques of verification (1976, 3, 17). Or else it was succumbing to an irrationalist kind of subjectivism, sacrificing the quest for objective truth to indulgent preoccupations with the self (1974, vi–vii).

All this stands in striking contrast to the classics of the sociological tradition. Classics distinguish themselves by continuing to speak meaningfully and pertinently over time and by serving as exemplars of what is truly important. The classics of sociology distinguish themselves by the moral aspirations that inform them and the artistic intuitions that shape them. According to Nisbet, the sociologists of the classical age never ceased to be moral philosophers. They worked with intellectual materials they could never have come upon were it not for the persisting moral conflicts of the nineteenth century. Each of the great ideas analyzed in *The Sociological Tradition* first appeared in the open guise of moral affirmation. Even when those concepts become secularized, "their moral texture is never wholly lost" (1966, 18).

What is more, those ideas came into being through processes like imagination, vision, and intuition—processes that have greater relation to the thoughtways of the artist than to those of the scientific data processor or technician. Indeed, it is this aesthetic element in their work that contributes so much of their value. For this reason Nisbet gives Simmel a privileged position in the gallery of sociology's classic authors, for Simmel was "in many ways the most imaginative and intuitive of all the great sociologists." He fully exhibits "that wonderful tension between the esthetically concrete and the philosophically general that always lies in greatness" (1966, 19–20).[4]

It is this aesthetic element, finally, that separates sociology from some of the physical sciences,[5] for there is a limit to what the contemporary student of physics can learn from reading even a Newton. But how different is the relation of the contemporary sociologist to a Simmel or a Durkheim:

> Always there will be something to be gained from a direct reading, something that is informative, enlarging, and creative. This is precisely like the contemporary artist's return to the study of medieval architecture, the Elizabethan sonnet, or the paintings of Matisse. This is the essence of the history of art, and why the history of sociology is so different from the history of science. (1966, 20)

And that history, for Nisbet, takes the shape of a downward-sloping curve. For however contemporary critics may assess the architecture, poetry, and painting of the twentieth century, Nisbet leaves no doubt that nothing in contemporary sociology comes close in value to the authors of his golden age. Precisely what positive science has tried so hard to eradicate—the moral coloration of sociological ideas and the subjective intuition of social realities—Nisbet considers to be the source of whatever was worthwhile in the sociological classics. They are to be

---

4. Responding to the same features of Simmel's work, Sorokin reached a diametrically opposed evaluation. "[Simmel's work] represents only the speculative generalization of a talented man. . . . Without Simmel's talent the same stuff would appear poor. Simmel's talent saves the situation, but only insofar as talent compensates for lack of scientific methodology. Under such conditions, to call the sociologists 'back to Simmel' . . . means to call them back to a pure speculation, metaphysics, and a lack of scientific method" (1928, 502 n. 60).

5. In his next major work in this vein, Nisbet would emphasize the aesthetic component in all science and so blur the distinction between art and science altogether (1976).

viewed, finally, as works of humanistic creativity. Their themes—the need for community and authority, the place of hierarchy and sacrality, and the scourge of modern alienation—are the selfsame themes to be found in the art and literature of the nineteenth century. To gain light on these matters one rereads Comte and Simmel the same way one re-reads Carlyle and Stendhal, for during that period of time "humanist and sociologist worked in very large measure through common understandings, perceptions, and even forms" (1976, 40).

Taking Nisbet's work as the archetypical expression of the humanistic approach to sociology's past, we may formulate its central features as:

*the assertion that early sociological writings were not essentially different from those of humanistic writers attempting to come to terms with the transformations of urban industrial society;*

*the perception that the most outstanding of these writings represent intellectual achievements of such an order that they merit continued reexamination in the manner of literary or philosophical classics;*

*an assessment that latter-day sociological work stands in comparison as intellectually trivial, aesthetically weak, and morally impoverished, and so represents something of a decline from sociology's earlier productions.*

This is a strong form of the humanistic narrative. Few other authors present it in so extreme a manner, but several offer what may be considered moderate forms of this kind of narrative, which stress only the first two of the above features. I count as humanist narratives those that distinguish sociology's development from that of other scientific disciplines by its having produced a body of classic texts that present-day sociologists must consult in order to function adequately.

In that vein, we can identify a number of sociologists who have represented the sociological tradition as a succession of enduringly valuable statements by its principal classic figures. Raymond Aron (1965–67) produced the first truly substantial study of this type, a panorama of the "stages" (*étapes*) in the development of sociological thought.[6] Aron traces those stages by artfully expounding the leading ideas of Montesquieu, Comte, Marx, Tocqueville, Durkheim, Pareto, and Weber. Although he does not provide a clear-cut sense of what he understands the stages to represent—indeed, Aron tells us he considers

6. Aron's work bears the title, *Les Étapes de la pensée sociologique.* The English translation, *Main Currents in Sociological Thought,* misses the overtone of historicity suggested by the French.

Montesquieu "much more of a sociologist . . . [and] much more 'modern'" than Comte (1:13)—he climaxes his story with Max Weber, whom he evidently regards as the greatest of all sociologists. At any rate, Aron concludes his discussion of Weber with words that celebrate him as a humanistic author: Weber is like "all great thinkers whose work is both so rich and so ambiguous that each generation reads, questions, and interprets it in a different way. . . . Weber's sociology might be more scientific but it would, I think, be less fascinating if it were not the work of a man who was constantly asking himself the ultimate questions . . . and who, thanks to an almost monstrous historic erudition, searched all civilizations for the answers to his own questions" (2:302–3). Contrasting his approach with what would be obtained if one were to expound the history of sociology like the history of a natural science—in the form of a gradual discovery of a body of proven propositions—Aron speculates, "If we employed such a method in the case of sociology, the consequence would be unfortunate, for there is great danger that each sociologist would write a different history of sociology" (1:1). But there should be readier consensus, he implies, regarding the outstanding figures in its history who could be called sociologists.[7]

Lewis Coser represented the tradition by portraying a dozen classic European and American figures as *Masters of Sociological Thought* (1971).[8] Along with biographical profiles and summaries of the gist of their thought, Coser illuminates the intellectual and social contexts of their work. However, in contrast to the contextualist accounts to be considered below, Coser treats those contexts as aids to appreciating the classic figures, not as clues to the tradition's essential character. His appreciation of that character expressed itself earlier in a collection of readings, *Sociology through Literature,* which he introduced by affirming that "the great traditions of sociology are humanistic"—supporting his claim that the trained sensibilities and creative imagination of novelists and poets provide rich sources of social insight, richer often than what hails from the standard procedures of current sociological research

7. Aron, of course, misjudged the ease of obtaining consensus on a canon of classic figures. Between Aron's list of seven and Käsler's fourteen classic figures, for example, only five—Comte, Marx, Durkheim, Pareto, Weber—are shared; 57 percent of Aron's classics are Frenchmen, 64 percent of Käsler's are Germans. Also, see the following note.

8. While Aron includes no American authors, and Käsler only one, Coser's original list of twelve includes four Americans. The second edition of his work in 1977 added three more American masters and a number of contemporary Americans in a chapter on recent trends.

(1963, 3). Coser leaves no doubt about the moral of his story. He displays an admonitory epigraph by Goethe: "What you have inherited from your fathers, you must earn in order to possess."

In 1976 Dirk Käsler produced a two-volume historical compendium, *Klassiker des soziologischen Denkens,* consisting of essays by specialists on a dozen classic sociological thinkers. Käsler insisted that the project be read as "a history of sociology," one suited to satisfy the practical need for constructing a viable collective identity for the discipline and for legitimating our own work today. While acknowledging that what identifies historical forerunners as classic authors are the needs of present-day sociologists, he goes on to specify some defining characteristics of classic sociological texts. They are works that possess a patent relevance both for the time in which they are written and for future generations. This accounts for their unsettling character and for the fact that they are inexhaustible, that is, not susceptible to bearing a permanent, "definitive" interpretation. The sociological classics remain valuable not for the valid propositions they may contain but for their capacity to stimulate fresh theoretical work, to disclose a problematic domain and/or to disclose a novel methodological approach. The dangers of reducing classic works to mechanical formulas or idolizing them as antiquarian monuments are to be avoided by viewing them as contributors to a dialogue in which contemporary sociologists continue to participate. Besides providing identity, legitimation, and ideas for present-day sociologists, Käsler suggests that the classics continue to hold exemplary value, not for containing eternal verities but for embodying standards of intellectual rigor that present-day sociologists ought to emulate (1976, 1:7–18).

The enduringly constitutive role of the classics in the history of the discipline was reemphasized in 1981 by Edward Shils in a lengthy essay on the significance of tradition in human societies. Although Shils criticized sociology for chronically neglecting so potent a component of human experience, he wryly observed that, despite sociology's emphasis on contemporaneity, sociologists retain a self-conscious attachment to the great figures from their own past. He went on to underscore the humanistic character of the discipline by arguing that in spite of its desire to be as scientific as possible, sociology, like the other social sciences except economics, is "more like philosophy and theology than . . . like the natural sciences"; and it derives its main themes not from independently developed techniques of investigation but from traditions grounded on its classic texts (1981, 137–40).

## THE SEARCH FOR MEANING IN THE MILIEU

Whereas humanistic narratives diverge from the three earlier kinds of narratives by holding that the classics of social theory contain insight and understanding unmatched by the productions of present-day scientific sociology, the narratives I designate as contextual find the cognitive dimension of sociological work itself to be subordinate in some essential respect to other kinds of orientations—ideological, sociopolitical, religious, aesthetic, or moral. Contextualist narratives of the sociological tradition have flourished since the late 1960s, due to the renewed popularity of Marxism and the growth of the history and sociology of science.

The Marxian perspective has tended to view all cultural productions apart from technology and language as formations that express the socioeconomic interests of the strata that produce them—as expressions, in other words, of their producers' class-based ideology. With the evident exception of claims made by Marxian authors themselves, representations of social reality that claim to be scientific are held to function either as self-deluding utterances that hide actual or potential exploitation from those who subscribe to them, or else as symbolic weapons used by apologists for a certain class to defend its interests.

Perhaps the first sustained narrative by a sociologist working within this perspective was Irving Zeitlin's *Ideology and the Development of Sociological Theory*, which appeared at the height of the worldwide student protest movements (1968). Zeitlin treated the sociological tradition not as the evolution of a scientific discipline in some form or other, but as a series of ideological responses to challenges posed by the progressive forces of modern history. In the pre-Marxian period, the challenge stemmed from Enlightenment rationalism; it was met by the reactionary responses of Bonald and Maistre, and by the conservative sociologies of Saint-Simon and Comte. Following what Zeitlin calls "the Marxian watershed," the preeminent figures in sociological theory—Weber, Pareto, Mosca, Michels, Durkheim, and Mannheim—developed their respective sociological ideas as counters in debates with the ghost of Karl Marx. Two kindred British narrators expressed the germinal idea of this approach in the mid-1970s, depicting sociology as an "ideological response to the major social and political struggles of the last 200 years" (Shaw 1975, 101) and, more concretely, as a bourgeois product natural to "the era between the bourgeois and the proletarian revolutions" (Therborn 1976, 144).

Interpretations of this sort had been adumbrated some decades before by the noted Marxist scholar György Lukács. In *Die Zerstörung der Vernunft* (1954 [*The Destruction of Reason*, 1981]) Lukács analyzed the vicissitudes of irrationalism in German thought, tracing the main lines of intellectual activity—from Schelling through Nietzsche and Simmel, from Tönnies through Max and Alfred Weber and Hans Freyer—by which sociology as well as philosophy allegedly promoted a reaction against reason and therewith paved the way for the ideology of Nazism. Lukács portrays Simmel as "the ideologist of imperialist rentier parasitism" (1954, 400).

A full-blown realization of the Marxist approach to the sociological tradition appeared in a 1977 textbook published in the German Democratic Republic. *Grundlagen der marxistisch-leninistischen Soziologie* by Georg Assmann and Rudhard Stollberg maintains that the most decisive factors affecting the development of scientific work, especially work in the social sciences, are the level of the forces of production and the character of the relations of production. Accordingly, the authors identify two contexts for the development of sociology: societies whose relations of production are socialist and those whose relations are capitalist. Marxist-Leninist sociology took shape as a "coherent, scientifically grounded theory that represents the interests of the working classes and mobilizes them to battle against the exploitative order of capitalism." In capitalist counties, "bourgeois sociology" arose as an apologia for capitalism "in the context of the confrontation of the bourgeoisie with the labor movement and with Marxism" ([1977] 1979, 10, 330).

This narrative then represents the sociological tradition (apart from Marxian texts) as so many stages in the development of bourgeois apologetics. It characterizes German sociologists by their anti-Marxian animus and their efforts to uphold the bourgeois class. It describes French sociology as a set of apologia for capitalism that promote a false sense of optimism. It notes the interest in elites displayed by members of the Italian school, but dismisses their work as a whole for their alleged associations with Fascism.

In the Assmann-Stollberg story, American sociologists carried less intellectual baggage than Europeans, so they needed to import their theories from Europe; but Americans did so unslavishly, with a dash of "shirt-sleeved, backslapping innocence." They strove to produce scientific solutions for managerial problems faced by the bourgeoisie and to sharpen public consciousness about these problems, always with the aim—not always conscious, to be sure—of "upholding a historically obsolete class structure" (387–91). *Grundlagen* concludes by profiling a few American sociologists—MacIver, Parsons, Merton, and C. Wright Mills. Parsonian formulations of 'status' and 'role' and the four-function schema serve to counteract impulses for change in the system, so it "was not accidental that Parsons long personified the model of a sociologist of the ruling class." Mills, by contrast, appears as the rare example of a scholar who began to transcend the limits of bourgeois sociology. Although Mills's reception of Marx was piecemeal and not deeply engaged, he did succeed in questioning aspects of American bourgeois sociology and calling sociologists to consider the broader historical contexts of personal and social phenomena, including sociology itself (392–404).

In 1970 an American follower of Mills, Alvin Gouldner, published a widely read contextualist narrative, *The Coming Crisis of Western Sociology,* which may be taken as a prime exemplar of this genre. Gouldner studied at Columbia in the 1940s, during the early years of Mills's tenure there, but he worked extensively with Merton, who confirmed and sharpened his lifelong interest in the sociology of knowledge. With his lustrous monograph, *Enter Plato* (1965), Gouldner initiated two decades of work on the social context of social ideas, culminating with a posthumously published analysis of the sociology of intellectuals and the historical context of early Marxism (1985). *The Coming Crisis* offered a diagnosis of the contemporary dilemmas of sociology and a plea for its reorientation. As we have seen, all such charters for action entail a more or less explicit narrative about the history of the field. Gouldner's was quite explicit: he proposed a "model of what happened . . . an outline for the history of modern Western sociology" (1970, 88).

Gouldner outlines four periods in the development of Western sociology, defined chiefly in terms of the theoretical syntheses that dominated each period: Sociological Positivism, in early nineteenth-century France; Marxism, crystallizing in the mid-nineteenth century; Classical Sociology, in Europe at the turn of the century; and Parsonian Structural-Functionalism, crystallizing in the United States in the 1930s. Gouldner's account begins with his claim that the eighteenth century witnessed the ascendance of a new ethos, one tied to the interests of the ascendant middle class and rooted in their replacement of older religious and aristocratic values by a belief that the value of persons and things is measured by their utility. The four central schools in the evolution of Western sociological thought then appear as so many responses to the fluctuating fortunes and ideological needs of the Western middle class.

Gouldner sees the Sociological Positivism of Saint-Simon and Comte as an ideological counterbalance to the individualistic utilitarianism of the commercial middle class: their doctrine attended to the social needs neglected by a society focused on individual utility. Its particular "social utility" consisted in providing new mappings of the societal landscape to replace the mappings of the old regime destroyed by the workings of the utilitarian ethos. Gouldner describes the proponents of this new sociological doctrine as members of marginal social strata—dying aristocrats, middle-class intellectuals hungry for recognition, and various stigmatized groups—and interprets their appeal for objectivity as "the ideology of those who are alienated and politically homeless . . . and of those who reject both the conventional and the alternative mappings of the social order" (103).

The next school of sociological thought, Marxism, emerged to complete the utilitarian revolution by overcoming the obstacle bourgeois property presented to a full-scale application of standards of utility. It introduced a "binary fission" into the sociological tradition, which persists to the present. In contrast to the "hierarchical" metaphysics of the positivists, Marxism was animated by a "romantic" metaphysics, an outlook that expressed opposition to the rationalism, materialism, and utilitarianism of the emerging middle class. Although the Romantic movement took shape as a reactionary, right-wing opposition to the middle class and its economic order, and came to influence later Academic Sociology by way of figures like Max Weber and George Herbert Mead, in the hands of Marx and his followers Romanticism folded into a working-class critique of the bourgeoisie. Whereas Comtean positivism and its descendant Academic Sociology provided an ideology for strata and societies that made the first breakthroughs into industrialization, Marxism became the sociology of underdeveloped regions, strata least integrated into industrial societies, and classes that sought but were denied their benefits.

Gouldner's discussion of the period of Classical Sociology focuses almost entirely on Durkheim and the refractions of Durkheimianism in British social anthropology. He makes no mention of figures like Tönnies, Simmel, Pareto, Tarde, and Cooley, and only passing references to Max Weber, even though he refers to thinkers of the Classical

Period in the plural and follows Zeitlin in identifying their "common polemical target" as Marxism (116). For Gouldner, Classical Sociology distinguished itself from Sociological Positivism by abandoning an evolutionary perspective and replacing it with comparative studies and a functionalist perspective, thus preparing the way for the hegemony of functionalism in twentieth-century sociology. For such a story, the centrality of Durkheim was essential: Durkheim "began the consolidation of sociology as a social science of the synchronic present, which came to culmination in contemporary Functionalism" (119).

The appeal of functionalism to a now-ascendant middle class was that it "served to defend existing social arrangements . . . against the criticism that they were based on power or force." It thus expressed a kind of "popular utilitarianism [which] served to draw a line between the parasitical idlers of the old regime and the hard-working middle class, whose new political claims it served to legitimate" (124). Sociology modeled on this functionalist approach never took hold in England, since it was inconsistent with the traditional, nonutilitarian mode of legitimation of the surviving English aristocracy, and since the relative weakness of socialism in England meant that functionalist sociology was not so badly needed as an antidote to Marxism. But British social anthropologists in England were drawn to functionalism because it abetted the colonial aspiration to view primitive societies dominated by European powers as lodged in a timeless present, available to pay taxes but not disposed to evolve toward political autonomy and economic modernity. The key spokesmen for this development, Bronislaw Malinowski and A. R. Radcliffe-Brown, not only provided this ideological service for the British Empire, but also formed the essential bridge between Durkheim and the sociology of the fourth period, that of "Parsonian Structural-Functionalism."

Just as Gouldner makes Durkheim central to his third period, so he treats Parsons as linchpin of his fourth period; the critique of Parsons comprises over half his sizable volume. Parsons's writings of the 1930s, both *Structure* and the essays on professions, reflected a Euro-American crisis of the international middle class. They took shape as responses to the Marxian seizure of state power in Russia and the international Great Depression. At a time when capitalist institutions faced a severe crisis of confidence, those writings functioned to bolster the position of the capitalist class, both by appealing to moral values as a basis for holding society together so as not to threaten the privileged with proposals to redistribute income and power, and by legitimating the business elite by likening their roles to those of professionals.[9] A bridge between European and American intellectual life, *Structure* imported European theorists as weapons in the campaign against Marxism.

Fissures induced by the Great Depression healed in the years after World War II, as American society was reknit by the war-induced solidarity and the satisfactions of affluence. Parsons accordingly shifted gears, playing down the energizing effect of moral values and playing up the socializing processes of a successful social system. His later emphasis on conformity with legitimate expectations fit the interest of the welfare state in securing the loyalty of deprived social strata. Under his theoretical guidance Academic Sociology began to flourish, as the United States used the social sciences to check the spread of movements friendly toward Marxism. Gouldner's contextualist narrative is outlined in Figure 3.

Gouldner then proclaims that a new period was emerging, one marked by the beginnings of dialogue between Marxism and Academic Sociology and by the decline and fall of Parsonian hegemony. The "entropy" of Parsonian theory reflected (1) the sensibilities of a younger generation oriented to new left politics and "psychdelic culture," sensibilities dissonant with the sentiments and assumptions embedded in the Parsonian synthesis; and (2) the requirements of a mature welfare state oriented to mobilization for justice and equality, values that Gouldner alleges could not be accommodated within the Parsonian scheme. Marxism, too, was undergoing a kind of crisis, appearing too conservative for social revolutionaries in the West while failing to provide Soviet leaders with the kind of social technology they needed to further their governance. In neither case was the rejection of functionalism or Marxism based on scientific considerations:

> The difficulties of the Marxian thesis concerning the "increasing misery" of the proletariat, or of the thesis about the polarization between capital

---

9. To sustain this interpretation Gouldner had to portray Parsons as hostile to welfare state programs of the New Deal, although Parsons was unambiguously a "staunch New Deal liberal" (Camic 1989; Parsons 1961; Mayhew 1982; Alexander 1983). He also had to ignore the work Parsons carried out prior to the Depression (see Camic 1991). And in suggesting that Parsons's "personal reality" of growing up among the genteel capitalists of New England rather than the "hog-butcher" elites of the Midwest rendered him more sympathetic to finding moral orientations in businessmen, he had to overlook the fact that Parsons spent his first sixteen years in Colorado.

| TIME | STATUS OF THE MIDDLE CLASS | SOCIOLOGICAL PERIOD | KEY FIGURES |
|------|---------------------------|---------------------|-------------|
| 1800–40 | Embattled against vestigial aristocracy | I. Sociological Positivism | Saint-Simon / Comte    Gans |
| 1840–80 | Viewed as oppressive | II. Marxism | Marx |
| 1880–1920 | National; embattled against Marxism | III. Classical Sociology | Durkheim Weber |
| 1910–30 | (colonial) | (transitional) | Malinowski Radcliffe-Brown |
| 1930–70 | International; entrenched and threatened | IV. Parsonian Structural-Functionalism | Parsons    Lukacs    Stalin |

Figure 3.  Gouldner's Historical Model of the Sociological Tradition

and labor—these and may other problems were long familiar to Marxists. This "disconfirming" evidence, then, cannot account for the modern interest of Soviet Marxists in Academic Sociology, any more than the recent shift in Parsonianism toward Marxism may be explained as a result of its own empirical difficulties or its failure to be supported by the facts. (1970, 450)

This passage alerts us to the first moral of Gouldner's story, which can be taken as the defining premise of the contextualist type of narrative: *shifts in the orientations of sociologists come about "largely for reasons exogenous both to the theory and research of sociology"* (370). Discussions about scientific method and logic constitute so much defensive posturing—Pareto might have called them "derivations"—concealing from sociologists their deep personal investments in the matters they treat. Sociologists begin to spin their theories under the prick of a disjunction between some perception of reality and some cherished value. The social function of grand social theories, Gouldner avers in one of his assaults against functionalism, is "to provide an anxiety-reducing reorientation" to the world (86). Functionalism does this by making the powerful seem useful hence good, and making the good seem historically potent.

Gouldner's narrative thus embodies and seeks to legitimate a vision of sociology that finds its value not in the quest for truth but in its enactment of some sort of moral ambition. The second lesson to be learned from his story, then, is that *sociologists should become aware of the assumptions and sentiments that undergird their enterprise*—an intellectual task he assigns to a "sociology of sociology." As a charter for future directions, however, that would seem to open the door to legitimating any kind of ideological pursuit. Registering some awareness of this point, Gouldner simply announces that he will present his own distinctive conception of this work by naming it "Reflexive Sociology." The mission of Reflexive Sociology is to help humans recognize the reality of the different levels on which they live and tie together the "loose ends" of their existence, an "effort at integration that was once the task of religion" (510). As for the content of this integrating worldview, Gouldner rejects not only all religious traditions but also traditional humanism (for its elitist distortions) and liberalism (for its commitment to seeking remedies for social problems without challenging essential societal premises). Instead, his Reflexive Sociology is to be radical, utopian, feisty, transformative, and rehumanizing, providing a counter to the "administrative sociology" that serves the capitalist (or state Marxist) status quo.

Themes invoked by Gouldner appeared in a number of other contextual narratives in the following decades. The notion that sociology's historic role was religious in character rather than just empirically cognitive informs a book by Robert Friedrichs published the same year as Gouldner's, as well as Arthur Vidich and Stanford Lyman's book on American sociology subtitled *Worldly Rejections of Religion and Their Direction* (1985). Friedrichs pointedly titled his book *A Sociology of Sociology* and not a *history* of sociology, yet his story begins in eighteenth-century Paris, and he claims that a discipline's history can illuminate current controversies over its "paradigmatic" base. Friedrichs locates the chief extrascientific dimension of the discipline in the "self-image" of sociologists rather than in the ideological needs of the bourgeoisie, and casts those self-images into two types: priests and prophets. The priestly sociologist tries to bring people in touch with a sense of the "real" by manipulating communal symbols; the priest is aloof, elitist, and objective, yet affirms the status quo. The prophetic sociologist, by contrast, is an actively engaged critic of society, one whose work draws inspirations ultimately from figures like Amos and Plato.

In the Friedrichs narrative, sociology "was born from the loins of prophecy" (1970, 69). It matured in this mode with the work of the reform-minded sociologists in the United States in the late nineteenth-

and early twentieth-centuries. Its nemesis was the doctrine of value neutrality, which an emerging sociological priesthood used to legitimate its claims to esoteric social knowledge organized around the "system" paradigm of the early 1950s. Its bible was Parsons's *The Social System*. Beginning in the late 1950s, the priestly stance and its attendant systems paradigm were challenged by a resurgence of prophetic demands tied to a counterparadigm based on conflict theory. Robustly expressing his view of the extrascientific telos of the discipline, Friedrichs argues that the systems paradigm must finally be rejected because it is at odds with the values of the Hebraic-Hellenic heritage. His story concludes with another pair of religious metaphors: he defines the "calling" of sociology by describing it as "witness" to an ongoing dialogue between the prophetic and the priestly modes.

Vidich and Lyman cover similar ground with an even more extended treatment of sociology as a vehicle for religious purposes. Their subject is American sociology, though they mention the formative influence of Comte on early American proponents of the field. Noting that sociology in the United States was originally inspired by Puritanism and later by the Social Gospel, they trace later developments of the discipline, from Lester Ward's "secular eschatology" and Sumner's secular Calvinism to comparable para-/post-Christian expressions at Harvard and Columbia, thence Chicago, and finally California. In each place they delineate the Protestant origins of American sociologists' sensibilities and ideas, finding them adherents to the notion of a "secular covenant" and professors of some sort of "sociodicy." Sociodicies amount to transformations of theodicies, doctrines designed to justify God's ways to man, by representing secular efforts "to justify the ways of society to its members" (1985, 281).

The past generation, however, has reneged on this historical mission. Comparable to Friedrichs's tale of a replacement of prophets by priests, but denying the successor sociologists any religious mantle whatsoever, Vidich and Lyman find the new orthodoxy of mainstream sociology sadly wanting: "The positivists and the functionalists have exchanged the promised utopia of a worldwide Christian community for the bloodless entelechy of a society-centered dynamic equilibrium." The moral of their story is that the need for sociodicy is greater than ever, yet one must look to currents outside the mainstream to find it:

The heterodox sociologists speak of an open-ended world, of existential phenomena, of the contingencies of history, and of the individual located

somewhere between freedom and determinism. From these hetero-
doxies flow the intellectual visions of a sociodicy yet to be developed for a
modern industrial society. (307)

The Gouldnerian theme of Romantic protest figured in two other
accounts from the late 1980s. In contrasting ways, Bruce Mazlish
(1989) and Wolf Lepenies (1985) identify protests against industrial
rationalism as the force that generates sociology. By profession a historian and not a sociologist, Mazlish nonetheless constructs a narrative of
the discipline intended to head sociology in a certain direction for the
future.[10] What interests Mazlish in the Romantic response is not, as
with Gouldner, its focus on the repression of the self, but its reaction to
the dissolution of human ties in the wake of the French and industrial
revolutions. Mazlish looks first at literary figures like Edmund Burke,
Thomas Carlyle, William Wordsworth, Elizabeth Gaskell, and George
Eliot, who voiced laments about the effects of those revolutions, interpreting these as laments about the breakdown of a connected world.
The sociological tradition, then, emerges with Marx, Engels, and
Tönnies, followed by Simmel, Durkheim, and Weber, as a series of efforts to provide acceptable diagnoses and treatments of those broken
connections by clothing them in the mantle of scientific plausibility.
For Mazlish, the most significant feature of sociology's history is its
transformation of the "sensibility" of the literary lamenters into a scientific idiom. In the process, sociologists produced greater understanding of society, albeit nothing that could qualify as possessing any
"scientific" validity. Indeed, they created powerful new myths of their
own: "that modern society is the scene of a breakdown in connections,
rather than a transmutation in their form" and "that the earlier connections were somehow 'better'" (253). Mazlish thus connects both the
substantive and the moral centers of the sociological tradition with the
notion of community. He applauds the tradition for emphasizing values
that balance those promoted by the enthusiasts for breaking connections—those who espouse liberation from the "chains" of premodern
social orders. The sociology he advocates would promote a kind of social humanism, balanced between devotion to individuality and to
community.

Where Mazlish sees sociology as giving voice to the Romantic pro-

10. Soon after, Mazlish would write that the "task of constructing a new sociology
for the twenty-first century is as daunting as it is challenging. It requires much prelimi-
nary argument about the nature of sociology" (1991, 1256).

test against rationalized society, Lepenies locates it largely on the rationalist side of that divide. For Lepenies, the intellectual conflict most salient to sociology's development was not individual liberation versus communal enmeshment, but the opposition between the Enlightenment espousal of cold rationality and the counter-Enlightenment celebration of the feelings. His luminous analysis, *Between Literature and Science: The Rise of Sociology* (1988; orig. *Die Drei Kulturen,* 1985), sees sociology as one arena in which this larger cultural struggle was acted out. Lepenies portrays sociology as a precipitate of that complex process by which scientific modes of intellectual work became differentiated from literary modes, such that a literary intelligentsia and an intelligentsia devoted to applying science to social phenomena vied with one another to offer the orientations most appropriate to living in industrial society. This struggle played out first in France and England, then in Germany; oscillation between scientistic and literary approaches continues to beset sociology even today.

The moral of the Lepenies narrative is muted, but discernible: sociology should own itself as a legitimate field between literature and science, an authentic third culture. If sociology abandons its affinity for natural science, it draws perilously close to literature and to an abandonment of reason that cannot be wholesome. However, sociology can never become a true natural science of society no matter how much it imitates the natural sciences. Worse, its unqualified scientific pretensions foster an "arrogant rationality" whose suppression of the affective life has tended to shunt emotional yearnings into cults of irrationality that have historically found expression in totalitarian ideologies.

A related critique of the scientistic pretensions of sociology appears in work by a historian on the rise of sociology, not in Europe but in the United States. In *The Origins of American Social Science* (1991), Dorothy Ross argues that American economics, political science, and sociology alike essentially express such national cultural traits as liberalism, pragmatism, "shallow historical vision," and technocratic confidence. Above all, American social science has constructed purportedly naturalistic models that in fact embody the values and the logic of the ideology of American exceptionalism. This national ideology, based on a sense of unique republican governance and economic opportunity, led early American social scientists to believe that their country was exempted from such modern European phenomena as mass poverty and open class conflict. Although civil war followed by rapid industrialization led social scientists to confront the possibility of a fate similar to that of the Old World, they constructed a counter-response in an attempt to find regular natural social phenomena "within and beneath history" that would enable them to escape such a destiny. In so doing, they came to embrace a scientism that proceeds in dangerous ignorance of historical differences and societal complexity.

In a number of essays written and revised over a span of two decades, Edward Shils has produced an uncommonly erudite, subtle, and multifaceted account of the growth of sociology (1980). One is hard put to classify it in terms of the ideal types I have been using. Shils evinces a positivistic appreciation of the unmistakable refinement of sociological methods; a pluralistic sense of the perduring diversity of traditions—national, epistemic, and ideological—and motley subject matters that constitute sociology's heritage; a synthetic sense of a unified orientation that dominates the field, protesters to the contrary notwithstanding, in the form of a common language and a common way of looking at society; and a humanist's appreciation for the transcending significance of the sociological classics. Nevertheless, following the criteria I set earlier, what distinctively typifies Shils's interpretation is his assertion that the central precondition and product of sociology was not its stated goal of producing a codified body of scientifically warranted knowledge, but rather "a general orientation." The orientation in question includes moral as much as cognitive elements, for the consciousness that dominates the social sciences rests on "deeper strata" of "sensibilities, ethical dispositions, animosities, and sympathies" (1980, 454). Their content reflects nothing less than a modern revolution in moral sentiments.

The institutionalization of sociology, Shils argues, required it to secure a place in the academic world, yet this place was bitterly contested. In the early decades of its academic life, sociology was both scorned by the tough-minded for its alleged lack of scientific rigor and the mediocrity of its intellectual achievements, and reviled by the humanists for its alleged degradation of the human spirit. Eventual acceptance in the academic hierarchy depended largely on its wider acceptance by the educated public, an acceptance based on practical interests that varied by country: in the United States, earlier in this century, by pressures to address social problems; following World War II, in England as a vehicle for social discovery and bohemian liberation; in France, as a rebound object for disillusioned Marxists; in Poland and the Soviet Union, as a critique of lifeless dogma and a declaration of the will to live in conviviality with one's fellows. Preeminently, however, what led the educated public to provide a critical threshhold of support for sociology, transforming it from a marginal and embattled field into an established, successful discipline, was the secular expansion of humanitarian sentiments in the modern world, a slowly but surely growing wish of moderns to understand one another and their societal homes.

Throughout the nineteenth and twentieth centuries, Shils avers, members of modernizing societies manifested a certain uplift in their moral capacities. They came to appreciate generic human qualities more deeply and to extend the universe of those to whom they ascribed these qualities. This cultivation of empathic sensibility formed the central precondition and primary product of the sociological tradition. It accounts for the emergence of the face-to-face interview as a primary technique of sociological research: more than a merely cognitive instrument, the interview, for Shils, is a venue of conviviality and rapport, an intrinsically moral engagement. The expansion of empathic linkage likewise informs the central theoretical orientation of the discipline, which affirms that "all human beings possess a quality which entitles them to the respect and consideration of their fellows" (1980, 15). So although sociology *could* become a science like any other, it is not and will never be a purely cognitive undertaking; in a fundamental sense it consists of a moral relationship between the human beings studied and those who study them. Insofar as sociology has been a vehicle for expressing ideological sentiments, it has conveyed not an apologia for the socioeconomic interests of an oppressive bourgeoisie but the humanitarian and antiauthoritarian orientations of modern liberalism.

Although the historic vocation of sociology—to serve as an organ of humanitarianism in late modern society—has been carried by the main stream of sociological activity, two deviant tendencies deflect from this mission. Sociologists have also given voice to some of the destructive countercurrents in the river of modern moral life, currents that manifest narcissistic, antinomian, antisocial, and frivolous attitudes. Two lines of sociological work reflect such alienative dispositions, one that views human subjects as manipulable objects, the other viewing the social order in an oppositional stance as a manifestation of radical evil. Regarded as modes of praxis, these dispositions take the form, respectively, of technological sociology, which serves as an unquestioning instrument of the ruling powers, and of oppositional sociology, which represents a tradition of irresponsible antagonism against the ruling powers. What Shils designates as consensual sociology embodies the historically appropriate calling for the discipline. Consensual sociology serves to modify the relationship between rulers and subjects by enhancing the sense of affinity between them and by raising the level of collective self-understanding: "Its task is the extension and elevation of the public life of society by improving the citizen's understanding of the collective life in which he is involved and by improving the quality of discussion among citizens" (1980, 92).

The authors whose narratives share the approach I call contextualist differ enormously in their interpretive perspectives. What makes them similar is not their sensitivity to the dependence of sociology on material, moral, and psychological resources from the discipline's environments. Such dependence is true for all the sciences, and awareness of it is not inconsistent with the emphases of the narratives that locate the essential character of sociology in its scientific mission. What specifically distinguishes the "contextualist" narratives is their emphasis on *some dimension of action outside that of pure investigation as essential in shaping both the aims of sociological work and the directions its cognitive work takes.* That extracognitive dimension has been located in several places: the ideological needs of a social class, the religious needs of a secular society, emotional yearnings stimulated by industrialization and urbanization, enduring traits of national culture, or the expansive moral aspirations of a humanitarian epoch. Because of such emphases, the contextualist narratives pay comparatively little attention to—when they do not denigrate or distort—the substantive content of sociological productions. At the same time they have enriched the discourse about sociology's mission by illuminating the cultural milieu of sociological work and the variety of practical roles sociology could be called on to fulfill.

# CHAPTER FIVE

# The Changing Need for Narratives

The fact that visions of the sociological tradition have changed a good deal over the past century provokes a number of questions. What do these changing narratives imply about the status of the classics? What do they tell us about the history of sociology? What do they suggest about how to envision the sociological tradition in the 1990s and beyond? These questions form the agenda for the present chapter.

## THE PROBLEMATIC STATUS OF THE CLASSICS

The period when humanistic visions of sociology came into being was also a time when the very question of whether sociologists should spend time reading their classics became a mater of open concern. While humanistic accounts of sociology were defending a privileged status for the classics, sociologists of other dispositions also found themselves paying renewed attention to their classical legacy. The more the discipline evinced an interest in reading the classics, however, the more problematic their status seemed; an upsurge of interest in the classics was hard to square with sociology's self-image as a natural science. Time and again, sociologists found themselves embarrassed to exclaim: physicists no longer read Newton, economists no longer read Adam Smith; why are we still reading our old classics? With becoming honesty, Robert Merton confessed at last: "I have long shared the reluctance to lose touch with the classics, even before finding a rationale for it"—and then went on to articulate a set of functions that justify continuing interest in "the classical works of sociology and presociology" (1968, 30).

The functions he had in mind concerned mainly the utility of classic writings for the prosecution of contemporary research programs. Merton promoted the classics as sources of information that later generations had not fully retrieved. As such, they might provide sharper formulations of hunches in progress as well as independent corroboration or disconfirmation of current ideas. Some dozen years later, Coser (1981) described this function more concretely by specifying the kinds of positive information the classics contained—data and phenomena previously obscure or ignored, concepts not fully appropriated, and unincorporated explanatory propositions.[1] Stinchcombe glossed the function generically by citing the classics as sources of "underexploited normal science" (1982, 8).

In short, the classics could readily be included as elements of a positivistic conception of sociology, figuring either as way stations in the advancement of the discipline as a mature science or as sources of data, concepts, and propositions of which positive sociology today might avail itself. Proponents of other perspectives would dispute this value, however, and champion the classics for other kinds of reasons. Thus, following a style of thought forwarded by Skinner (1969), scholars like Levin (1973) and Peel (1972, 1978) insisted that the meaning of social scientific concepts is bound up with the historic context in which they emerged. Rather than read the classics to discover timelessly valid materials for use in contemporary research, it is valuable to read them now in order to disclose the particularizing milieus that shaped the ideas contemporary sociologists naively inherit from them. Put otherwise, in the contextualist perspective the classics are seen not as scientific so much as *expressive* documents, revealing sources of information about the culture and conditions of the time and place where they were composed. Alternatively, the contextualist perspective can regard them as expressive symbols within the community of sociologists, performing ritual functions to represent collective solidarity within a dispersed and fragmented discipline (Levine 1981b; Stinchcombe 1982). In this view, Robert Alun Jones once suggested, the classic author becomes a collective representation for the profession, an "ancestral spirit . . . which both expresses and maintains the clan's sense of social unity" (1980, 209–10).

From the pluralist perspective, the classics are valuable for setting forth trenchant statements of the major alternate positions within the discipline. Stinchcombe (1982) identifies this as a "small coinage" function: referring to a particular classic forbear is a quick and inexpensive way to identify one's major intellectual allegiance. The pluralist values classics for offering expanded rationales of typical positions, a function that Galston articulated when writing about debates in political theory: "The contending parties make use almost exclusively of doctrines not of their own devising, doctrines that they have inherited

---

1. Coser also wrote a circumspect essay analyzing the inductivist manner in which Merton himself made use of the classics of European sociology (1975).

and of whose origin and meaning they are largely oblivious. . . . We must therefore undertake a genealogical or archaeological investigation of the contending doctrines that leads to their source, a point at which they are fully elaborated with complete awareness of their necessary premises" (1975, 26). One may also search the classics for alternative approaches in the face of current orthodoxies or stifling conventional wisdom. In this vein Morris Abrams had celebrated the classics of literary criticism, claiming, "a humane study that forgets its founders is impoverished . . . and progress in fact depends on our maintaining the perspectives and insights of the past as live options, lest we fall into a contemporary narrowness of view" (1972, 52). Alexander, meanwhile, observes that every major theoretical orientation has established its case through creative rereadings of sociology's germinal classics, and that shifts in orienting assumptions are typically legitimated either by revisionist readings of a classic or by replacing one classic tradition with another (1982, 2:3–4).

In contrast with the pluralistic defense of the classics that Alexander here mounts in pointed opposition to the more positivist defense presented by Merton,[2] Alexander's first reading of the classics led him, we saw, to a synthetic perspective on the sociological tradition. The synthetic perspective finds the classics important for having formulated the basic questions of the field and providing partial answers to them, answers whose successful synthesis can be charted by reconstructing the presuppositional routes the classic authors traversed. Thus earlier Alexander, following Parsons, searched the classics to establish the problems of "action" and "order" as *the* fundamental problems of sociological theory and to project the synthesis, which logically grew out of the classic statements, in the form of a "multidimensional" and "voluntaristic" theory of action. One can also construct narrower syntheses by seeing how they incorporate enduringly influential but partial statements by classic authors, the way Smelser grounded a base line theory of societal differentiation by synthesizing Spencer and Durkheim (1968, 243–51), or Parsons found inspiration and support for his ideas about internalization and social control by conjoining Freud and Durkheim (1981).

In quite different ways, then, positivist, pluralist, and synthetic readings of the classics find them valuably pertinent to current work at the

---

2. For his later, more elegant statement of the pluralist apologia for the classics, including a more extended critique of Merton, see Alexander 1987.

frontiers of scientific sociology. According to the humanistic perspective, however, their worth is not thereby exhausted. Murray Davis (1984) in fact argues that the continuing appeal of the classic authors cannot be explained by viewing them merely as forerunners of contemporary theories, methods, or concerns, nor as respondents to their particular time and place. Instead, he seeks to locate their appeal in qualities of the internal rhetorical structure of their writings. Davis concludes that the essential ambiguity and open-endedness of the sociological classics makes them more like classics in the humanities than in the natural sciences, and he subsumes them under the criteria Frank Kermode specified for literary classics: "an openness to accommodation which keeps them alive under endlessly varying dispositions [and] . . . a plurality of significances from which, in the nature of human attentiveness, every reader misses some—and, in the nature of human individuality, prefers one" (Kermode 1983, 44, 133).

This quality of intrinsic richness often commends the classics to commentators aligned primarily with other perspectives. Although Merton and Stinchcombe mainly adopt the positivist stance on the classics, Merton also hails the classics as exemplars of high-caliber intellectual work that function to elevate standards of taste and judgment (1968, 36), and Stinchcombe also praises the classics as nonreplicable touchstones of excellence that are especially suited to stimulate the intellectual development of students (1982, 4). Yet tension between positivist and humanist views of the classics persists. In a recent review essay, Gerald Platt attacks the opposition of scientific sociologists to the study of the classics, arguing that "absence of systematic discussions of the issues addressed by the classics and the continuous failure of 'scientific' sociology to provide either satisfying or substantial knowledge . . . undermines the legitimacy of the discipline" (1992, 428). For Platt, as for Nisbet, scientific professionals have trivialized the problems treated so luminously in the classics, to the extent that modern sociology "has lost connection with the impulses underlying its origins" (436).

It is thus apparent that growing affirmation of the continuing relevance of the sociological classics—regarding "direct and repeated encounters with the works of the founding fathers" an elementary test of sociological literacy, as Merton put it (1968, 30)—masks disputation about the grounds of that relevance. Granting the classics high contemporary status does not reduce the arbitrariness with which the sociological tradition is envisioned. Of course, the fact that any tradition consists of a limited set of given objects constrains the arbitrariness with which the past can be reconstructed (Shils 1981; Schudson 1989). For example, although there is wide variation regarding which past figures get selected as originative figures, it is difficult to imagine any history of the sociological tradition that does not devote some attention to the work of Émile Durkheim. Even so, because each of the types of narrative considered above interprets the significance of the classics in a distinctive way, the manner in which Durkheim's oeuvre has been interpreted differs radically from one type of narrative to another.

## READING DURKHEIM

In *The Flight from Ambiguity* I took note of the enormous variation in readers' opinions about what positions Durkheim actually espoused. Some found him a philosophical nominalist, some a realist; some a supporter, others a foe, of modern individualism; some an ardent secularist, others a mystical religionist. He was variously labeled a conservative, a liberal, and a socialist (1985a, 55–56).

To that array of interpretations we may now add the different views of Durkheim that derive from conceiving the sociological tradition in diverse ways. Positivist narratives look at classic writings with an eye to assessing their role in the advancement of sociology's status as an observational science. In this spirit, Park and Burgess represent Durkheim primarily as an exponent of one of the schools into which sociological thought was dispersed prior to "the period of investigation and research," the period of genuinely scientific work they saw sociology just entering. They call it the school of Social Realism. They cite mainly Durkheim's less empirical monographs, *On the Division of Labor in Society* and *The Elementary Forms of the Religious Life,* and their discussion focuses on his controversial conception of collective representations.[3]

By the time of John Madge's book, Durkheim's most empirical work—the analysis of suicide statistics—had long been translated into English and had become familiar to American sociologists through the mediations of Parsons, Merton, Lazarsfeld, and others. Ignoring Durkheim's other writings, Madge assessed his contribution solely

---

3. Their failure to draw substantially on *Suicide* was not due to its unavailability in English. Besides citing the *The Elementary Forms* heavily, they make repeated references not only to the then-untranslated *De la division du travail social* but also to a number of other untranslated papers, and once to *Le Suicide* itself.

from *Suicide*. For Madge, the 1897 monograph signally advanced sociology from dilettantism and speculation toward the condition of a mature science. It did so by introducing analytic concepts of heuristic value, such as social fact and anomie;[4] by establishing substantive propositions of such robustness that they would be upheld by studies of suicide a half-century later; and by pioneering such key methodological devices as the coefficient of preservation, ingenious statistical correlations, and the "indirect clue" or intervening variable.

Pluralist narratives, by contrast, feed on Durkheim's work for exemplifying a clear and distinct theoretical approach. This is not unlike the way Park and Burgess regard him, except that pluralists view Durkheim's approach as a more perduring constitutive component of the sociological enterprise and so pay more serious attention to the grounding and implications of his approach. Thus, Sorokin treats Durkheim as an eminent representative of the school of thought he terms sociologism. The basic tenet of this school, that the properties of human individuals derive from social interaction, was anticipated by such classic philosophers as Buddha, Confucius, Plato, and Aristotle. In the modern period, the basic outlines of sociologistic theory—including the assertion that psychological phenomena are to be explained by means of social phenomena, but not vice versa—were articulated by Comte and his Russian disciple, Evgeni de Roberty. Indeed, Sorokin credits de Roberty, along with Alfred Espinas, with producing formulations of the sociologistic doctrine clearer and superior to as well as prior to those of Durkheim (1928, 443).

While Sorokin does not find Durkheim powerfully originative as a theorist, he credits him for scrupulous attention to facts and for constructing interesting correlations in pursuing the sociologistic program. Durkheim substantiates the sociologistic doctrine by appealing to objective social conditions to explain increases in the division of labor, by showing that all the principal types of suicide are due entirely to social causes, and by elaborating sociologistic explanations of religious symbols and conceptual knowledge. Sorokin supplements this appreciative account of Durkheim and his school with vigorous criticisms of their stance as one-sided, exclusionary, and monopolistic, and the distinctive conception Durkheim contributes to this school, the notion of a collective mind exterior to individuals, Sorokin scores as "unjus-

---

4. On some problematic aspects of the appropriation of anomie by later sociologists, see Levine 1985a, ch. 4.

tifiable mysticism" (465–66). Martindale's treatment of Durkheim essentially follows Sorokin, except that he uses the term 'organicism' rather than 'sociologism' to designate Durkheim's holistic principles. Martindale also suggests that the project to combine organismic principles with positivistic methods inexorably led to a methodological crisis, a crisis that Durkheim gamely sought to surmount in *The Rules of Sociological Method*.

Of all the treatments of Durkheim lodged within narratives of the sociological tradition, those by Parsons and Alexander stand as the most exegetically intensive. Parsons, we saw, aspired above all to portray a process of theoretical convergence between Durkheim and Weber, authors who found their points of departure in two very divergent intellectual traditions. Parsons therefore considered it important to represent Durkheim in a way that documented his transition from an exclusive focus on adaptive factors to a position that embraced the efficacy of normative factors as well. The stages of Durkheim's journey then count as so many steps toward validation of the voluntaristic theory of action for which Parsons claims authority in defining sociology's future. Accepting this synthetic conception of sociology's development, Alexander portrays Durkheim in ways that differ from Parsons only marginally: he examines a broader selection of materials from the Durkheimian corpus, and lays greater weight on the more exclusively "idealistic" stance that Durkheim purportedly took in his later years. For Alexander, Durkheim's development shows a movement precisely in the opposite direction from that of Marx, starting from materialist premises and proceeding toward idealist ones. As a result, the mature writings of Durkheim and Marx lay out two parallel but fundamentally opposed lines of analysis, whose synthesis was effectively achieved among classic authors only by Max Weber.

In contrast to the narrative perspectives that scan Durkheim's work for its contributions to advancing the discipline of sociology, humanistic accounts emphasize Durkheim's roles as moral philosopher and social diagnostician. Aron, for example, finds the center of Durkheimian thought to be an apologia for rationalist individualism that nevertheless preaches respect for collective norms. Far from regarding Durkheim's books as documents of an evolving scientific orientation, as do Parsons and Alexander, Aron sees them simply as variations on this central humanistic theme. Nisbet similarly objects to the division of Durkheim's thought "into mutant and disconnected phases" (1966, 87). He finds all of Durkheim's works to be expressions of the "social metaphysic" that emerged early in Durkheim's career, along with a methodology that brought new dimensions of understanding to such matters as morality, law, contract, religion, and even the nature of the human mind. Nisbet searches Durkheim's texts for the wisdom he has to impart on such themes as sacrality, hierarchy, and modern alienation, and stresses Durkheim's preoccupation with the moral crisis of his time. Linking that preoccupation with the art and literature of the nineteenth century, Nisbet avers that no religious poet or novelist could have portrayed this crisis more eloquently than Durkheim (1976, 127).

Quite different interpretations, finally, appear in writings that stress the ideological context of Durkheim's thought. Thus Zeitlin—and, following him, Gouldner—treat Durkheim less as a scientific pioneer or classic author than as a defender of bourgeois class interests against the threat posed by the working-class movements of his time. Their hermeneutic project seeks to disclose the ideological intentions that inform the putatively scientific work of the master. Zeitlin reads Durkheim's lines to find expressions of "a conservative and authoritarian ideology that dominated his entire sociological system" (1968, 241), and Gouldner finds him sidestepping issues of progressive change by transmuting sociology into a "science of the synchronic present" (1970, 119).

Each of these narrative perspectives highlights selected features of Durkheim's oeuvre. At the same time, these stories constrain interpretation in ways that obscure and often distort Durkheim's work. Thus Sorokin, in reducing Durkheim to an exemplar of the sociologistic type, fails to grasp Durkheim's concern with individuality or to take note of his points of convergence with authors whom Sorokin placed under different categories. Bothered by Sorokin's biases, Parsons introduced others. He forced his picture of Durkheim into a framework set by the parameters of action theory (a discourse that actually never engaged Durkheim) and by his narrative need to demonstrate major presuppositional changes in the course of Durkheim's life. This led him to attribute only to Durkheim's later years positions he had held in his first major monograph, and to portray Durkheim as having abandoned other positions he never gave up.[5] Although Alexander's searching ac-

---

5. At one point Parsons admits he is taking poetic license in his treatment of Durkheim—"it is necessary to resort to a certain amount of construction and to put things somewhat differently from the way in which Durkheim himself did" ([1937] 1968, 400)—but even poetic license cannot justify interpretations like the notion that Durkheim only gradually came to understand constraint as "a system of sanctions at-

count attends to portions of Durkheim's oeuvre that Parsons neglected, his commitment to a similar narrative form amplifies Parsons's distortions. Thus Alexander entraps Durkheim in a materialist-idealist itinerary and so glosses his *Division of Labor in Society* as a tract that emphasizes "the mechanical power of material conditons" (1982, 2:160), while the work in fact poignantly depicts criminal norms as expressions of collective values and invites occupational specialists to devise new norms through creative interactions. Madge's exclusive focus on *Suicide's* methodology obscures the philosophical issues Durkheim pondered so intensely. Nisbet's account neglects the significance of Durkheim's methodological advances. Authors like Zeitlin and Gouldner scant Durkheim's science for different reasons, depreciating his work by reducing it to ideology.[6]

In the various ways they treat Durkheim, then, just as in the ways they select classics and define their role, different narratives pursue in diverse ways their sense of sociology's past as a key to legitimating certain directives for its future.

Can one do anything more than list this panoply of narratives as so many plausible alternative visions of the discipline? I believe so, for the order in which they appeared historically forms a story of its own. And if so, perhaps that story has a moral as well.

---

tached to normative rules" (463), that only later did he conceive ends and norms as "no longer merely individual but also social" (462), that after 1897 demographic factors "drop out of his work altogether" (327), that the notion of moral education appears only in his later work by that title, that the split between collective and individual components of the concrete individual gets made only later on, etc. More generally, as noted above (ch. 3, note 4), Parsons simply refuses to credit Durkheim's early concern with common norms and his later concern with social morphology.

6. So anxious is Zeitlin to portray Durkheim as an ideological partisan that, for example, he insists on representing him as a disciple of Saint-Simon gone astray toward the right wing, defiantly ignoring many passages where Durkheim avows his intellectual debts to Comte. Zeitlin glosses Durkheim's arguments against inheritance rights and favored treatment of the well-born as a "momentary concession" to Marx, a concessionary note to which, owing to Durkheim's incorrigibly conservative stance, "he never returns" (1968, 256–57); yet Durkheim continued to publish those remarks from his lectures on civic morals in successive editions over the next two decades. Zeitlin finds Durkheim so committed to the party of repression that he represents Durkheim, quite inaccurately, as one who never asked whether existing rules may be unjust or immoral, one who "transforms all individual values into egoism pure and simple," one who considered suicide worse than war (261, 258, 273). (Some of these tendentious glosses were deleted in the second edition of his book). Gouldner's reduction of Durkheim's sociology to an apologetic science of the synchronic present ignores the evolutionary and historical features that suffuse the Durkheimian oeuvre (see Bellah 1959).

## A HISTORY OF HISTORIES

The historical disciplines enjoy perpetual youth, Max Weber once wrote, because they are forever shifting the point of view they bring to problems. They do so because changing circumstances elicit concerns that demand new avenues of illumination from the past. Archetypal narratives of the sociological tradition emerged at historic junctures in which distinctive problems presented themselves to minds that were at once active and possessed of a keen sense of responsibility for articulating the collective identity of the discipline. One way to tell the history of sociology in this century is to parade the succession of histories that leading minds in the discipline constructed to define their current situation and orient future scholarship. I consider the following five texts to be the key archetypal narratives for such a history of sociology: Park and Burgess 1921; Sorokin 1928; Parsons 1937; Nisbet 1966; Gouldner 1970. Each was produced by a scholar of considerable stature; each evoked resonance throughout the discipline; each articulated a vision of sociology's past that was responsive to current issues confronting the field.

Park and Burgess produced *Introduction to the Science of Sociology* at a time when sociology was struggling to shed its image as a vehicle for social reform and social work, and to legitimate itself as an academic discipline clothed in the mantle of science. Their brief history of the field served the purpose of leading readers to conclude that the time was ripe to abjure the speculations of earlier sociologists and forward the work of scientific investigation. Each section of their book culminated with research ideas designed to steer the new waves of graduate students inclined to sociology in the years after world War I toward a commitment to no-nosense fact gathering. It does not matter that there is still no consensus regarding the theoretical questions that used to divide sociologists, they argued:

> Fortunately science does not wait to define its point of view nor solve its theoretical problems before undertaking to analyze and collect the facts. The contrary is nearer the truth. Science collects facts and answers the theoretical questions afterward. In fact, it is just its success in analyzing and collecting facts which throw light upon human problems that in the end justifies the theories of science. ([1921] 1924, 211)

A history of sociology that stressed its evolution into a rigorous empirical discipline was surely appropriate for those years when sociology needed to legitimate itself by producing a solid corpus of substantive research findings. Indeed, the period between the two world wars was crucial for its acceptance as an academic discipline. While much of the intellectual capital needed for launching the sociological enterprise was generated in Europe during the century after 1820, by the end of World War I sociology was established as a professional field mainly in the universities of the United States, and there somewhat precariously.[7] The emphasis Park and Burgess placed on fact gathering was congenial to the pragmatic American temper, and their history reassured generations of young sociologists that their endeavors were supported by the course of intellectual history.

Yet a history of the field that finally dismissed the theoretical controversies of its predecessors as irrelevant to current work could not long satisfy the intellectual curiosity of the most intelligent of its young devotees. There were works of stunning intellectual power in sociology's heritages, and they wanted to know about them in their own right, not as fore-stages to intellectually antiseptic research projects. Sorokin's great work of 1928 arose to challenge the adequacy of the Park and Burgess narrative. Sorokin brought theory back into the story of sociology, not as a prehistoric vestige but as an essential warp for the discipline. The problem was, so many theories had taken root in the evolving garden of sociology that it was essential to provide a map that ordered the various species and genera along with their historical filiations.

Sorokin's story, we saw, stressed the perduring pluralism of sociology's theoretical legacy. To some, this pluralism exhibited anything but a credible scientific discipline. The Parsonian narrative of 1937 arose to protest the vision that there are as many systems of sociological theory as there are sociologists, for that vision either "encourages the view that the only sound work in the social field is detailed factual study, without benefit of theory," or else "it encourages a dangerous irrationalism which lets go of scientific standards altogether, [maintaining] that sociology is an art, that what is valuable in it is to be measured by the standards of intuition and inspiration, that it is not subject to the canons of rigorous logic and empirical verification" (Parsons [1937] 1968, 774).

7. Harvard University did not establish a department of sociology until 1931. On the embattled status of sociology during the interwar period, see Shils 1961. Germany was the only other country where sociology had a firm foothold, and that was weakened, though by no means cut off, following the Nazi accession to power in 1933 (Rammstedt 1986).

For a few observers at the time, and for many more later on, the history of the tradition that Parsons presented in *The Structure of Social Action* itself formed a crucial episode in the history of the field. As Shils describes it:

> By the late 1930's, sociology presented a picture of disarray. In the United States, there was already in existence a disconnected mass of particular inquiries, with practically nothing in common except their lively curiosity about contemporary America and their aspiration toward observational discipline. . . . *The Structure of Social Action* was the turning point. It was this work that brought the greatest of the partial traditions into a measure of unity. . . . It redirected sociology into its classical path and, in doing so, it began the slow process of bringing into the open the latent dispositions that had underlain the growth of sociological curiosity. (1961, 1406)

Thus the histories of the interwar period served in different ways to legitimate the status of sociology as a scientific discipline, but also to orient members of the discipline toward future work in ways that embodied successively emerging conceptions of what it meant for sociology to function as a science. These narratives and their later manifestation proved adequate for a few decades, until depictions of sociology exclusively or mainly as a scientific discipline no longer satisfied the sociological community. In the course of the 1960s, sociology as a vehicle of progressive science got derailed.

Perhaps sensing some of that growing disaffection, Madge made a valiant effort to retell the positivist narrative in 1962. Concluding his grand review of key events in the evolution of scientific sociology, he cautioned, "We must be very circumspect in criticizing such developments" (1962, 567). But to little avail. Torrents of criticism flowed from the narratives that grew out of the 1960s.

Increased exposure to the classics impressed some sociologists with the discrepancy between what the classic authors had achieved and what contemporary workers were producing. It was no longer merely a question of "bringing theory back in," as Sorokin and Parsons, in different ways, had proposed. It was a yearning for the philosophical depth, moral commitments, and intuitive brilliance displayed by the classics at their best—precisely those qualities that scientific sociology, in all its guises, had tried to eradicate. Nisbet's efforts to recover the sociological tradition in 1966 and after gave eloquent voice to these yearnings. His narrative must thus be seen in dialectical opposition to all three of the earlier types of history.

Yet the activist temper of the 1960s combined with sociologists' increasing readiness to subject their own discipline to sociological analysis meant that the classics, too, would need to be examined in their pragmatic contexts. Contextualist narratives arose to challenge treatments that considered elements of the tradition, classic or contemporary, purely *sub specie contemplationis*. Contextualist narratives would insist on confronting the intrusion of various social and cultural needs into the work of sociologists, and would nudge that work in directions —ideological, religious, aesthetic, or moral—they found congenial. Goulder's *Coming Crisis*, however flawed and limned with ressentiment, notably combines the two chief dispositions of this genre: a search for the ideological dimension of sociology as a means to legitimate pursuit of some contemporary ideological yearning, and an application of the sociology of knowledge framework to the productions of the field.

The moral of this history of sociology told through its sequence of histories is threefold. For one thing, it suggests that the main narratives of sociology took the shape they did because of important functions they performed for the discipline appropriate to their time. Second, it encourages us to ask what vital problem current sociology faces and consequently what kind of history might be most suitable for the present juncture. Finally, this history of histories may itself offer ideas for how we might proceed to construct more timely narratives for the tradition.

In formulations offered some years ago in a paper, "On the Heritage of Sociology" (1985b), I suggested that the outstanding problem faced by current sociology might relate to the cries of crisis emitted by spokesmen for the social sciences since the mid-1970s. (I return to the diagnosis of this crisis in chapter 14.) My analysis cited the widespread perception that the social sciences in general, and sociology in particular, had become so specialized substantively and so fragmented ideologically that there was no identifiable core or consensus to provide a basis for genuine communication among their far-flung practitioners. At this point, my phrasing of the problem would add: there is no credible narrative today that the sociological community can embrace as a way to provide an energizing identity. For such a narrative to be acceptable, it would have to find ways to include the very disparate segments of the sociological community.

Anticipating this way of putting the matter, I went on to suggest that sociology's fragmented and anomic condition might be alleviated by fresh efforts to recover the sociological tradition, not by establishing a common set of beliefs for all to rally behind but by acknowledging the varied branches of present-day sociology as having descended from participants in a common conversation. I styled this way of construing the tradition dialectical. *Dialogical* seems to me now a better term. Since then, it has become apparent to me that what I was suggesting amounts to a new way of constructing a narrative for the sociological tradition. Others have also seen the need for such a narrative. In particular, rereading the account by Eisenstadt and Curelaru led me to think that *The Form of Sociology—Paradigms and Crises,* which had earlier lent itself to reading as a pluralistic narrative, could in fact be taken as broaching a kind of dialogical narrative, since its account of postwar sociology sees diverse approaches in confrontation with, and with occasional dialogical openings to, one another.[8]

## TOWARD A DIALOGICAL NARRATIVE

*If the sociological community needs a new narrative, what is wrong with producing a fresh version of one of the five types of narrative that have already been created?*

Although the earlier types of narrative remain instructive, each of them admits intellectual vulnerabilities that have become apparent over time. More important, none of them is inclusive enough to satisfy the contemporary need for an encompassing community of discourse. I provide support for these claims in chapter 14.

*Does that mean none of the previous types of narrative can provide points of departure for a new narrative?*

That depends. Certainly, each contains at least one assumption that should be retained in any future narrative:

1. the positivist assumption that the history of sociology does exhibit a progressive refinement of observational and analytic capabilities and a cumulatively developed body of findings;

2. the pluralist assumption that the universe of viable sociological approaches consists of an irreducible multiplicity of perspectives, principles, methods, definitions of subject matter, and statements of aims;

3. the synthetic assumption that agreement has been reached and can be reached on the relevance of certain basic terms, conceptions, and generalizations;

8. Personal communication from Professor Eisenstadt in 1993 made clear that he would like his account to be viewed as a dialogical narrative.

4. the humanistic assumption that the heritage of sociology contains much more than a body of replicable techniques, substantive findings, and theoretical analyses;

5. the contextualist assumption that historical contexts have shaped the character of sociological concepts and problems in profound, often subtle ways.

*Aren't you demanding the impossible? How can one go about constructing a narrative that encompasses all the previous narratives, salvaging what is viable of the old but offering a fresh entree, in a way that provides an umbrella for all participants in the community?*

The way was in fact suggested by our history of histories of sociology. We discovered what was vulnerable in each narrative type by examining the criticisms made of it by each later comer in the story. But those criticisms did not demolish the types for they continued to reproduce themselves in later incarnations. The history finds a place for all participants by showing how each type arose through critical engagement with the others and how each continues to occupy a place in the broader tapestry. This kind of story is what I shall call "dialogical" narrative.

*Isn't it presumptuous to claim that you are just now inventing the narrative that will supersede all previous narratives once and for all? Who do you think you are, Hegel?*

Not quite. It follows from my argument that other needs will arise in the future, requiring future generations to create more suitable narratives. And the narrative I am preparing to unfold in Part Two will exhibit only one version of the kind of narrative I consider appropriate to the present juncture. I must also waive a claim to complete originality, since although I arrived at this version of my narrative more than a dozen years ago, before analyzing the alternative approaches described in Part One, I later discovered that key features of it had been adumbrated by senior and more knowledgeable colleagues.[9] But perhaps my argument provides a usable response to the question left unanswered in the book on histories of scientific disciplines edited by Graham et al.: if histories serve the purpose of legitimating certain directions, how can one evaluate them as more or less valid?

9. Thus, on rereading "The Calling of Sociology" by Edward Shils I found a clear espousal of all five of the assumptions listed above. And, as just noted, on rereading Shmuel Eisenstadt's narrative I found an account of developments in postwar sociology —of differing traditions engaged in more or less open communication with one another— that prefigures what I am proposing.

*Supposing you are right that sociology needs a new history, and that this is the way to go about composing it. Isn't it parochial to find that need so important when the world is coming apart at the seams and needs the attention of sociologists on so many more urgent problems?*

Two responses. For one thing, what I have been saying is that the effectiveness of sociological activity, like any human endeavor, depends on a lively sense of self-understanding, an identity that juts out like the top of an iceberg from a foundation laid by a coherent narrative of one's past. So I believe that this history may help sociologists be more effective in dealing with their research on more topical matters.

But there is something else. When we get to Part Three, I shall argue that current tensions and dynamics within the sociological tradition are analogous to secular changes at work in society at large. Contemporary society has many new needs, among them a need for new kinds of charters for multicultural communities. New kinds of narratives must be constructed—and not just for sociologists.

If you think about it, you may recognize the narrative types we have considered as models that have been used in thinking about the histories of national communities or of the world system. The positivist narrative of sociology quite resembles a positivist history of human society: its institutions evolve, slowly but inexorably, toward forms based increasingly on the achievements of modern science and technology. The humanist narrative, by contrast, resembles traditionalist stories: the golden age of human achievement lies behind us, mankind's best hope is to recover the ideals and monuments of classical ages. Against these one-track histories, pluralist stories emphasize the diversity of human cultures, the irreducible otherness that gets reproduced, and should be openly acknowledged and cherished, generation after generation. The synthetic narrative has its counterpart in convergence theories, according to which initially diverse cultures find their way inexorably toward a common culture of modernity. Finally, the counterpart of contextualist histories may be found in various kinds of reductionist history, according to which cultural achievements of various sorts are understood in terms of some other basic explanatory factor, like relations of production or the will to power. Perhaps the dialogical model suggests new ways of constructing narratives appropriate for multicultural communities beyond the world of academic disciplines.

*All right, go ahead. What would a dialogical narrative of the sociological tradition look like?*

It proceeds from three assumptions. The first is that traditions are real cultural entities. They exist and they perdure.

Second, the components of any tradition are not discrete writings, or the oeuvres of individual scholars, but conversations, or dialogues. The elements of a tradition are never merely handed down; they are continually engaged with by contemporaries and successors. What is more, the parties to a conversation can themselves be clustered conversations: the larger tradition of sociology, for example, consists of a number of constitutive subtraditions engaged in dialogue with one another.

Third, the dialogues among traditions evince opposition, imitation, and progress. New subtraditions take shape in part through creative opposition to established subtraditions. At times they absorb ideas and accommodate criticism from those other traditions. This cumulative process of confrontation and absorption constitutes progress in the search for truth. It takes the form of a spiral

*You said that there may be more than one way to create such a dialogical history. What exactly will you set forth in Part Two?*

The social sciences contain two broad orders of tradition: theoretical and empirical. At least six discrete empirical traditions have entered the landscape of modern social science: the tradition of descriptive statistics stemming from seventeenth-century political arithmetic; that of community surveys pioneered in England in the nineteenth century; ethnographic reportage, formalizing the procedures of travelers and missionaries, advanced by Alexander von Humboldt and a number of nineteenth-century ethnographers; laboratory experimentation on the behavior of human subjects, pioneered by Wilhelm Wundt at Leipzig in 1879; analytic statistics, established in England in the 1890s by Galton, Pearson, and Fisher; and the tradition of the clinical interview, transformed by the work of Sigmund Freud.

In this work I confine my story to the theoretical traditions, seven in number. I define them primarily as national traditions, for two reasons. The originative figures of modern sociology mainly cite fellow nationals, as, for example, Halbwachs is likely to cite Rousseau; von Wiese, Simmel; Park, Sumner. More important, over the generations they reproduce what are palpably national characteristics. Moreover, when they engage in dialogue with parties from other national traditions, they do so, openly or by implication, in a more contrastive mode—as when Durkheim explicitly contrasts his French discipline with British and German traditions. Marx is the exception who illustrates the rule in its inverted form, for he constructs his theory in a pointedly antinational mode.

My assumption is that the originary focus of these contrasting national traditions is an effort to deal with problems generated by the secularization of moral thought. Here I follow the suggestion by Leo Strauss and others that moral philosophy originates when ancestral moral authorities are desacralized, thereby stimulating the quest for a secular grounding of morality. Their common ground is the search for a secure secular basis for *morality* that departs from an articulated view of *nature*. Where they differ among themselves, I shall attempt to show, is with regard to (1) how they view nature, and (2) how they view morality.

Each of the seven philosophic traditions that helped shape the modern social sciences, then, I define as expressive of a distinctive national culture. I present these traditions as constituted by a series of dialogues about the following three questions:

1. How can secular thought ground moral judgments? More concretely, how does a particular secular view of nature relate to some vision of a good society?

2. What is the source of human dispositions to act morally? What leads humans to counter tendencies to follow purely appetitive or expedient dispositions?

3. How are the facts of human experience and history to be constructed and explained?

If the last of these questions appears most familiar to us from the discourse of contemporary social scientists, it is the first two that most deeply engaged its founding figures. Questions about the grounding of morality, both in the sense of the grounding of normative criteria and in the sense of the location of human moral dispositions, were and remain closely tied to questions about how to describe and explain social phenomena. Examining the broad sweep of the sociological tradition in this dialogical perspective, we shall find evidence that despite noteable scientific progress in both the empirical and theoretical dimensions of the enterprise, the extrascientific concerns of the classics continue to flavor it in subtle ways, concerns that in turn reflect the specificity of certain national cultures in the evolution of the modern world.

*Aren't some risks involved in following such an approach?*

No account can do everything. My ideal-typical construction of tendencies of national traditions and my neglect of the empirical traditions

| CONCEPTION | ARCHETYPAL EXEMPLARS | SITUATION IN SOCIOLOGY | PROJECT | STATUS OF CLASSICS |
|---|---|---|---|---|
| Positivist | Park & Burgess 1921 | Methods of natural science now applicable to social phenomena | Promote use of scientific methods; legitimate positive sociology | 1) Way stations of naturalistic advance 2) Sources of unincorporated propositions and facts |
| Pluralist | Sorokin 1928 | Tower of Babel | Clarify theoretical differences; legitimate orientational pluralism | Exemplars of diverse approaches |
| Synthetic | Parsons 1937 | Unific paradigm now available | Explicate and legitimate the synthetic conception | Texts that raise problems and offer partial solutions |
| Humanist | Nisbet 1966 | Superficial consciousness | Sophisticate con-sciousness and legiti-mate study of classics | Texts of enduring intrinsic value |
| Contextual | Gouldner 1970 | Politicized climate | Promote ideological engagement; legitimate engaged social science | Expressive documents |
| Dialogical | (Eisenstadt 1976) Levine 1985b | Disciplinary community fragmented, anomic | Organize discourse; partially legitimate all the above | Parties to a conversation |

Figure 4. Conceptions of the Sociological Tradition

necessarily entail certain shortcomings. The former emphasis means that significant outliers in various traditions—Burke and Hobhouse in England, Tarde in France, Vico in Italy, Giddings in the United States —get short shrift. Cross-national connections are treated as significant, but in less detail than they perhaps deserve, and too little attention gets paid to synchronic cross-national developments. The concentration on explaining the various national sociologies that emerge in the 1880–1920 period means that substantive work from more recent decades receives little attention.

Perhaps more distressing, my focus on the philosophic orientations that undergird modern social science means that what are arguably the most important contributions of the sociological tradition—its rich array of interpretations and explanations of puzzling social phenomena—get overlooked. Yet it is precisely such contributions— from Tocqueville's explanation of the French Revolution to Weber's explanation of the persisting importance of religious sects in a modernized America, from Scheler's interpretation of the dynamics of ressentiment to Coleman's of the dynamics of community conflict, from Simmel's account of how different hierarchical structures affect personal freedom to Wilson's account of the worsening condition of the underclass in American and in West European cities—that make up the most valuable achievements of the sociological tradition. My gesture at repairing this omission, the overview of interpretations of modernity in the final chapter, remains no more than a gesture. It would take several books to compensate for this omission. I can only ask readers to keep in mind that the question of narrative frame only introduces the sociological tradition, it does not adequately represent it; and that there is no substitute for coming to grips with the substantive contributions of sociological authors, classic or contemporary.

Finally, I should mention that a focus on the origins of modern academic sociology requires one to attend only to West European and North American authors. A comprehensive harvest of the heritage of social thought and protosociology would cast a wider net and include authors from Eastern Europe, like Gumplowicz and Kovalevsky, and from other continents and epochs, like Buddha, Confucius, and Ibn Khaldun, not to mention more recent contributions to world sociology from many parts of Africa, Asia, the Middle East, Latin America, and the British Commonwealth.

*Could you sum up the argument of Part One in schematic form?*
No problem. See Figure 4.

# PART TWO

# Visions of the Future

## SEVEN TRADITIONS IN SEARCH OF A GOOD SOCIETY

Every nation has a moral philosophy that is in harmony with its character.
ÉMILE DURKHEIM

# CHAPTER SIX

# The Hellenic Tradition

The modern social sciences derive in good part from the great quest of Western philosophy to fashion a rational, secular social ethic. This quest originated in ancient Greece during the fifth and fourth centuries B.C. among thinkers who had become excited about the powers and possibilities of the human intellect. It proceeded from a wish to find substitutes for the two primordial bases of morality, custom and annunciation.

In prephilosophical cultures, a way of acting was generally considered good because it was endowed with the authority of a group's ancestral custom or the legitimacy ascribed to certain lawgivers. The quest of moral philosophy began with doubts about the authority of ancestors conjoined with efforts to articulate rational principles with which to justify ways. Citing texts by Plato and Aristotle, Leo Strauss describes their rational challenge to conventional justifications of morality as follows: "The primeval *identification* of the good with the ancestral is replaces by the fundamental *distinction* between the good and the ancestral; the quest for the right way or for the first things is the quest for the good as *distinguished* from the ancestral" (1953, 86; emphases mine).

Strauss further maintains that this quest turned out to be a search for what is good by nature as distinguished from what is good merely by convention.[1] Almost all the classical philosophers, he observes, came to support the distinction between those human desires that accord with human nature and so are good for people and those that destroy their humanity and so are bad, leading to "the notion of a human life that is good because it is in accordance with nature" (1953, 95). Accordingly, the arguments forged by Hellenic moral philosophy required

---

1. The word 'good' can be used for several Greek words, which have different associations with nature and convention. When good and bad stand for *dikaion* and *adikon* (just and unjust) or *kalon* and *aischron* (noble and base), Hellenic usage contrasted what is good by nature with what is good by convention. But the term *agathon* (contrasted with *kakon*) denotes and commends what is objectively good, and no one, Plato says, would accept something as *agathon* that was only good by convention (*Theatetus* 177d; Arthur Adkins, personal communication).

the prior discovery of the idea of *nature*. Aristotle describes this discovery as the originary work of philosophic thinkers, noting that the earliest philosophers began with questions about the movements of celestial bodies and the origins of the universe, and proceeded to speculate about the natural principles of all things, in contrast to the thinkers before them who discoursed about gods (*Metaphysics* 1.982b18, 983b6ff.). With the articulation of the idea of nature in natural philosophy, moral philosophy could then investigate the question of what is good by nature. Through this process, the authority of "nature" came to replace the authority of the ancestral.

This rationalizing process can be traced to the archaic period, to lawgivers like Solon and Cleisthenes, who attempted the rational promulgation of civic norms and constitutions. As a philosophic movement it began with a group of itinerant teachers of the fifth and early fourth centuries, men like Protagoras of Abdera and Thrasymachus. These Sophists, as they later came to be called, radically criticized old customs and superstitions, and turned the attention of philosophical inquiry from the natural cosmos to the moral problems of human life and society. Socrates and then Plato advanced the quest for a secular ethic by an unremitting effort to find rational foundations for the common conceptions of the good, albeit not without appreciation for the beneficent effect of ancestral custom (*Laws* 793aff.), therewith giving subsequent European philosophy its basic themes and problems. However, it was Aristotle (384–322 B.C.) who organized those problems into distinct categories and assigned them to separate disciplines. With his vision our story begins.

### PRAXIS AND THEORIA

Aristotle sought rational arguments to ground morality in treatises that laid foundations for what we have come to call the social sciences. The generic term Aristotle used for the disciplines they embodied was *epistemai praktikai*, the sciences of action (*praxis*). Their job was to investigate the grounds of good action. Aristotle subdivided the universe of practical knowledge along lines that pertained to particular domains of action. In Hellenic society, these domains were few in number. Essentially, Aristotle fixed on three: the domains of personal action, the household (*oikos*), and the city-state (*polis*).

The central questions of Aristotelian social science, then, can be formulated as: (1) what is the best way to organize personal lives? (2) what is the best way to organize domestic associations? and (3) what is the best way to organize inclusive communities? Aristotle made these domains of action the subjects of three distinct but related sciences: ethics (*ethike*), economics (*oikonomia*), and political science (*politike*). The disciplines differed because under nonideal circumstances the characteristics of good actions in these three domains differed—the good human being was not identical with the good citizen, nor the ways of good political rule the same as good household management. The disciplines were closely linked because finally they all dealt with the same subject matter: the right action for human beings.

When Aristotle came to articulate his own notion of the good life, he proceeded by considering the diverse views expressed in common opinion. He reports that the general run of people as well as persons of refined judgment agree that the highest of goods is a condition called *eudaimonia*. This pivotal term, often translated as happiness, might be rendered more truly as "a condition of feeling in fine spirit." In order to resolve the more controversial question of what constitutes *eudaimonia*, Aristotle appeals finally to the argument that *eudaimonia* involves something toward which other ends are subordinate and which is itself a self-sufficient end of action. This self-sufficient end for humans he locates in whatever is the distinctive function (*ergon*) of human nature, and that turns out to be neither possessions nor physical activities but a kind of mental activity, one in which faculties that involve a rational principle (*logos*) are exercised in accord with excellence (*arete*).

The discipline of ethics has the task of specifying this human good more concretely, and that becomes a problem of identifying the different kinds of human excellence whose attainment will promote the highest human good, *eudaimonia*. Aristotle divides these types of excellence, or virtues, into two broad categories. Those that simply exhibit the play of rational activity comprise the intellectual virtues; those that involve the subordination of appetites and desires to reason comprise the characterological virtues. The latter depend above all on the formation of good habits through regular practice. Characterological virtues —such as courage, temperance, and liberality—get instantiated in actions that follow a mean course between extremes, as courage is a mean between foolhardiness and cowardice. The intellectual virtues—which include intuitive understanding, scientific demonstration, and practical wisdom—are states of mind, acquired through proper teaching.

The analysis of the modes of distinctively human excellence forms the fundamental discourse of Aristotelian social science. It constitutes the central agenda of the discipline of character formation, as *ethike* might be translated. It obtrudes into the discipline of economics, which "attends to human excellence more than to the excellence of property which we call wealth" (*Politics* 1.1259b19). It becomes a matter of concern for the discipline of politics, since the aim of that knowledge, and the legislative actions it informs, is to make citizens good by developing their virtues (*Ethics* 1.1102a10, 2.1103b4). Although economics and politics must also attend to what is required for human associations simply to survive, the preeminent concern of those disciplines is what is required for humans to live well, in accord with excellence.

In the *Politics*, Aristotle considers the ambiguity of that criterion, noting that there are in fact four different meanings of 'best' (4.1288bff.). The best state could signify one that is conceived according to an abstract ideal; one that is considered best for human communities in general; one that is best for a particular community under given conditions; or one that, while in no sense ideal, is as good as can be attained under the circumstances. It is the province of a complete science to consider all four of these matters, an agenda Aristotle pursues in that treatise.

When we examine the strategy by which Aristotle worked out his answers to questions about the good life, however, the notion that they stem directly from his conception of nature runs into serious difficulties. In developing his notion of *episteme praktike*, Aristotle took pains to differentiate the properties of its subject matter from the properties of what he evocatively designated as "things that exist by nature." Inquiries about things that exist by nature belong to a special set of disciplines, the theoretical sciences (*episteme theoretike*), which Aristotle distinguished at every turn from the sciences of human action.[2] He made those distinctions, he insisted, because every science needs to limit its attention to a certain class of things in order to demonstrate their essential attributes.

With respect to their *subject matters*, while the theoretical sciences deal with things that exist by nature, practical sciences deal with a different class of things—*ta prakta*, things to be done. Actions do not occur by nature, they are made by humans (as are *ta poieta*, things produced, which form the subject matter of yet another group of disci-

---

2. Aristotle's theoretical sciences include the natural sciences, mathematics, and metaphysics. For his discussion of how they differ from one another, see *Metaphysics* 6.1.1025bff.

plines, the productive sciences [*epistemai poietikai*]). Things existing by nature, or natural substances, differ from human actions in two fundamental respects. Natural substances have an internal principle of change as, for example, a hen's egg evolves into a chick, or fire moves upwards. In the case of actions, however, the principle of change is external to them—in the will of the actor. (Similarly, in the case of things made, the principle of change is external to the object, in the mind and hand of its artificer.) What is more, the essential properties of natural substances are invariable—hen's eggs always turn into chicks, never into puppies—whereas human actions result from deliberate choice (*prohaeresis*) and so are variable. Aristotle asserts that fine and just actions, which form the subject of investigation by the sciences of action, "admit of much variety and fluctuation of opinion, so that they seem to exist only by convention, and not by nature" (*Ethics* 1.3.1094b15–16).

The sciences of action differ from the sciences of natural substances in their *methods* as well as in their subject matters. The methods employed in studying natural substances are twofold, induction and deduction. Through induction one proceeds to apprehend true generalizations: water becomes ice at a certain temperature, hen's eggs become chicks when hatched. Through deduction one proceeds to demonstrate the determinate consequences of those generalizations. Since ice is a solid, and solids have the property of hardness, at a certain temperature water acquires the property of hardness. The propositions of natural science take the form of necessary universals because the essential characteristics of natural substances are invariable.

For several reasons, the form taken by inquiry in the practical sciences diverges from that of physics. Since human actions are based on choice, not on natural necessity, their properties cannot be so securely grasped. What is more, because people differ so radically about what they consider good, inquiry into the direction of good action has to take into account the variety of opinions people hold. Finally, since the circumstances of right action differ so markedly from situation to situation, knowing what is best to do demands above all knowledge of particulars.

Methods geared to the demonstration of universal propositions are therefore out of place in the practical sciences. The appropriate method for determining the right course of action is what Aristotle called deliberation (*bouleusis*). Inquiry proceeds by examining and refining the diverse opinions people hold about an issue, and its successful resolution depends on traits of good character already possessed by the deliberating parties. Deliberative excellence involves the selection of worthy ends and the determination of suitable means by using sound reasoning in a moderate amount of time. The conclusions of deliberative investigation can never be expected to attain the levels of precision and certainty attainable by the natural sciences, and it is the mark of an educated person to realize this.

Another difference between the two kinds of sciences concerns the *faculties,* or cognitive capacities, needed to prosecute them. The generalizations of natural science come from exercising the mental faculty Aristotle referred to as intuitive reason (*nous*). Showing the logical consequences of those generalizations involves a capacity he called scientific demonstration (*episteme*). On the other hand, deliberations about the good life involve a different sort of mental ability, which he designated as *phronesis,* translated as practical wisdom or prudence. In deliberating about laws and policies, a special variant of *phronesis,* which he termed political wisdom (*politike*), is needed. In contrast to the states of mind that generate theoretical knowledge, *phronesis* is concerned with the "ultimate particular fact" (*Ethics* 6.114b14–22, 1142a23–28).

Finally, the *ends* or purposes for which the two kinds of science are pursued also differ radically. The motivation for studying natural substances is to understand the world, for the sheer aesthetic pleasure and for the relief from ignorance such understanding affords. By contrast, the reason one studies human actions is for the sake of learning how to act well and how to cultivate the dispositions that promote good action, which is to say, how to pursue the *aretai,* or excellences.

To understand anything fully—natural substance, deed, or artifact —Aristotle maintains that it is essential to examine it in four ways. One must know the material of which it consists, the form or shape that it takes, the agency that brought it into being, and the end toward which it is directed. Aristotle refers to these four ways of understanding objects as causes, and the four causes just listed he calls material, formal, efficient, and final causes. The dimensions along which he discriminated practical from theoretical sciences likewise exhibit this fourfold mode of analysis. Figure 5 schematizes this Aristotelian organization of the sciences.

## NATURE AND MORALITY

Despite his consistent efforts to differentiate the sciences of action from the sciences that deal with natural substances, there is nonetheless some sense in which Aristotle evidently attempted to establish his

| | THEORETICAL SCIENCES | PRACTICAL SCIENCES | PRODUCTIVE SCIENCES |
|---|---|---|---|
| SUBJECT MATTER (*Material Cause*) | Natural substances (*ta physei*) | Actions (*ta prakta*) | Artifacts (*ta poieta*) |
| METHODS (*Formal Cause*) | Induction of invariable causes and properties; deduction | Deliberation about variables and opinions | Techniques of construction |
| COGNITIVE FACULTY (*Efficient Cause*) | Intuitive reason (*nous*) and scientific knowledge (*episteme*) | Practical wisdom (*phronesis*) | Art (*techne*) |
| AIM (*Final Cause*) | To know | To act well | To make things |

Figure 5. Aristotle's Organization of the Sciences

notions of the good life and the good society by appealing to aspects of human life that exist by nature. It was indeed his position that "that which is good by nature is more worthy of choice than something whose goodness is not by nature" (*Topics* 3.1.116b11). To clarify this matter we need first to consider the ways in which Aristotle thought about nature.

In book 2 of the *Physics*, once Aristotle has established that the predicate "existing by nature" refers to things that have a source of change within themselves, he proceeds to examine various meanings of the term nature. At times, he notes, nature signifies the immediate material substratum of such things; at other times it signifies their form or shape; and yet another sense appears when it refers to the process of growth by which a thing's nature is attained. This array of meanings can be taken to represent the material, formal, efficient, and final causes. Just as Aristotle deems it essential to look for these four causes when one seeks a complete understanding of something, so it follows that one could apply the predicate "existing by nature" in each of these four ways.

### THE NATURAL AND THE ARTIFICIAL IN MODELS OF THE GOOD

The material substratum of objects can be either natural or artificial. The materials the artist works with are commonly artificial, for example, the dyed yarn of the weaver or the aluminum of the sculptor. Those artists could, however, work with naturally existing materials—

undyed wool or stumps of wood—but the resulting product would be artificial; on their own, those materials would never evolve into weavings or sculpted figures.

This configuration suggests a way to visualize Aristotle's conception of the place of nature in human virtue. He proceeds by identifying the virtues as parts of the soul (*psyche*), together with the passions and the faculties (*dynameis*). The passions (emotions like love, hate, grief, and joy) exist by nature; as we might say today, they are organismically grounded. They provide the motivational energies for action. The faculties, which are psychological capacities to experience those emotions —analogous, for example, to the faculty of sight as the ability to experience visual perception—likewise derive from organismic sources. (In addition to those faculties that animate emotional strivings, the natural faculties include other irrational faculties—the capacities for digestion, movement, and sense perception—and rational faculties—calculation [*logismos*] and thought [*dianoia*].)

In contrast to these naturally given components, the virtues (aretai) comprise states of character (*hexeis*) that come into being artificially, through teaching and directed practice. They consist of *good habits*. People can also form bad habits, however. Consequently, Aristotle observes, "none of the moral virtues arise in us by nature; for nothing that exists by nature can form a habit contrary to its nature." And then he adds, "Neither by nature, then, nor contrary to nature do the virtues arises in us; rather we are adapted by nature to receive them, and are made perfect by habit" (*Ethics* 2.1.1103a20–25).

As this formulation indicates, Aristotle holds that neither the formal nor the efficient causes of the virtues are naturally given. The appetites and desires are naturally given, but these are neither good nor bad in themselves; their moral quality appears only to the extent that they are modulated by proper habits. Although the form of characterological virtues—a disposition to act in ways that follow a moderate course between extremes—may on occasion appear in nature, a virtue only comes into being reliably through exercising instances of it. For example, courage comes into being by executing courageous acts. The efficient cause of the virtues is not a naturally given propensity but the practice of activities directed and reinforced by parents, teachers, friends, and legislators. To say that we are adapted by nature to receive the virtues means that the material potential for virtue is given by nature; to say we are made perfect by habit is to say that the forms of the virtues and the forces that produce them are artificial.

This is like saying that undyed wool provides naturally given material for the weaver to use in creating a beautiful rug. However, Aristotle also argues that human beings have an inherent disposition to perfect themselves by acquiring virtues, whereas wool harbors no disposition to turn into a rug. This argument suggests a second sense in which human virtues are natural—in their final cause. The end of human virtues—the end for which people seek to cultivate them—is to realize their generic essence. Since people naturally seek *eudaimonia,* and since *eudaimonia* comes from realizing a distinctively human activity, and since that activity consists of exercising a rational faculty, then the quest to shape one's natural desires in a way that accords with reason is the natural goal, or *telos,* of human *praxis.* For moral judgment at the individual level, then, Aristotle's formula is: the model of the good person is based on nature in its *material potentiality* and in the *goal* it aims at, while the particular *form* it takes and the *ways of achieving* it are not naturally given.

Aristotle's notion of the natural grounding of models of the good community exactly parallels his formula regarding the natural grounding of models of personal virtue. After declaring that the political community aims at the highest good for man, Aristotle initiates his quest to determine what this good consists of by examining how such communities come into existence. He identifies two forms of association that come into being naturally: the conjugal relation, for the sake of reproduction, and authority relations, for the sake of self-preservation. These two relationships combine to form the household (*oikos*), the partnership that comes about *kata physin,* in the course of nature, to satisfy everyday wants. Several households join together to form the village, a natural union formed to satisfy more than mere daily needs. Finally, a number of villages unite to form the city-state (*polis*). The *polis,* too, exists by nature, and that is so for three reasons: (1) human beings by nature are endowed with the faculty of speech, by which they are disposed to discourse about good and bad, a disposition they can express only in the political community; (2) the component units of the *polis,* households and village, exist by nature; and (3) the *polis* is the form of association toward which those units aspire, the culmination of their existence—and that makes it their end. In other words, with respect both to its material cause and its final cause, the political community, locus of the highest human good, exists by nature.

However, the forms these households take and the structures of the political communities they constitute are highly variable. Political structures vary with respect to the number, quality, and disposition of the governing and the subject strata. These variations are typified by different constitutions, themselves the product of human agency. Just as individual characters may be formed by good or bad habits, so political communities may be formed by good or bad regimes. Similarly, just as forms of character and processes of character formation result from human agency, both the formal and the efficient causes of states are man-made.

For Aristotle, then, a rational secular ethic gets grounded on nature *understood as a complex of goal-directed potentialities of both individuals and communities*. However, knowledge about the best forms in which to actualize those potentialities in order to attain those ends will have to come not from an examination of natures but from other sources.

## THE NATURAL AND THE ARTIFICIAL IN MORAL DISPOSITIONS

In Aristotle's philosophy, the questions of the grounding of normative criteria and the grounding of moral dispositions exist in the most intimate relationship. After examining his analysis of those dispositions, we shall reflect on that relationship.

Aristotle's complete analysis of moral dispositions emphasizes both their emotional and their rational dimensions. He defines the process of choice (*prohaeresis*), the site of morality and the essence of human agency, alternatively as "desiderative reason" (*orektikos nous*) or "ratiocinative desire" (*orexis dianoetike*) (*Ethics* 6.2.1139b5). The capacity for genuinely moral conduct exists when good reasoning is conjoined with good moral character.

From Aristotle's *Ethics* one can construct a sketch of the complex process by which human morality emerges during the life cycle. The process consists of four developmental stages, marked by the progressive development of psychic capacities and shifts in the relationships among them. Infants exhibit the flourishing of the vegetative part of the soul—nursing, digesting, and sleeping—and its dominance over the other, barely developed functions. In early childhood, the emotions get developed and take precedence over the merely vegetative functions. From childhood through young adulthood, the emotions get formed into good habits or moral virtues while the cognitive faculties get developed into scientific virtues—which take increasing prominence in the personality. Finally, in mature adulthood, practical reason—the last virtue to develop—comes into maturity and establishes full hegemony over the emotions and the appetites.

It is clear that Aristotle sees the ingredients of moral dispositions as partly natural, partly artificial. The material potentialities given by nature are twofold—the affective faculties and the rational faculties. Their actualization in the form of a moral adult is a natural goal of human life, for it leads to the goal of happiness, which all humans naturally seek. But the shaping of affects and the cultivation of reason does not occur by nature. These developments require inputs from other human agents, the socializing efforts of family, friends, and political institutions, and the educative resources of schools.

The ingredients for moral dispositions are widespread in any community. The potentialities for their development are universal and, since virtually everyone grows up in families and communities, those potentialities become actualized to some extent in most people. However, the fully mature, stable good person is relatively rare. It is no easy task to be good; knowing the right thing to do can never be indicated by universal rules alone, but always entails discerning what is appropriate in individual cases. Good action involves doing the right thing to the right extent at the right times toward the right persons, and doing so for the right motive and in the right way. That is why goodness is so "rare, praiseworthy, and noble (*kalon*)" (*Ethics* 2.6.1106b20–24; 2.9.1109a25–29).

It follows, then, that for Aristotle questions about normative criteria necessarily get intertwined with the question of personal morality. If the good is concerned with the production of good actions, and only persons with certain qualifictions can know what good actions are, then a central task in deliberating about the good must be to identify those who are properly qualified to take part in such deliberations. At the very least, it makes a great deal of difference—indeed it makes *all* the difference—if they have been brought up with proper habits from childhood. Self-indulgent persons are simply not candidates. It also makes a great deal of difference if they have had a fair amount of experience, and have a developed talent for practical deliberation. This point has profound repercussions for the agenda of the social sciences which Aristotle drew up.

## THE ARISTOTELIAN VISION

Aristotle's charter for the social sciences forms an integral part of his vision of the good life and the good society for humans. The central ingredients of good lives and societies are, first of all, the establishment of good habits in human beings and citizens during their formative years and, second, the exercise of practical wisdom respecting the particular circumstances of the varied decision-making situations actors confront. But although disciplined knowledge can never substitute for personal qualities in promoting goodness, ethical and political wisdom can be enhanced by certain kinds of knowledge, which the practical sciences uniquely provide.

As we have seen, the problems of practical philosophy are set by two natural givens, the organically grounded goals of human action—to live, and to live well—and the organically grounded energies, capacities, and associational forms with which humans might attain these goals. It is properly the province of a natural science to determine what those natural materials consist of. Aristotle undertook the task of investigating the natural foundations of personality development in *De Anima*, the natural science of psychology, by examining the parts of the psyche that are given by nature. It would be consistent with his principles to imagine a natural science of social forms, one that would similarly examine the naturally given forms of human association—a possibility that Aquinas once acknowledged. If knowledge of such natural givens were sufficient to guide action, then the knowledge base for the social sciences could take the form of a natural science, and the social sciences could be included among the theoretical sciences.

It is precisely where Aristotle deviates from viewing the criteria of good as wholly grounded in natural substances, however, that he opens the door to the construction of his distinctive practical sciences. What remains for *episteme praktike,* once the natural bases of the good life have been ascertained, is to determine the best forms of organization and the best ways to create and preserve them. The method for doing this is to examine what thinkers and communities have already said and done, and to deliberate about their models and procedures in open discourse that can finally yield not certain answers but suggestive ideas for continuing trial and inquiry.

If this is Aristotle's model for social science at the level of its most general principles, a second level of specification appears when we include his assumptions about what is needed for persons both to carry out that public discourse and to organize their lives and actions in social institutions: a combination of virtuous habits and developed deliberative capacities. When we get more specific than this—and attend to the particular virtues, associational domains, structural dimensions, and assumptions about gender-related and other kinds of personality traits

that Aristotle discusses—we reach the debatable and correctable substantive propositions of Aristotle's work. So much of the critique of
Aristotle has focused on these matters that his much more durable
ideas about the constitution of the social sciences have been obscured.[3]
I shall attempt to recover them now and set them forward in a systematic manner. The prescriptions of an Aristotelian organon for the social
sciences can be represented as follows:

a. circumscribe the universe of human action as its generic subject
   matter;
b. identify the various domains of action and specify their ends;
c. analyze the constitutive elements of each domain;
d. determine, in view of the specified ends, the best dispositions of
   those elements;
e. prescribe the socialization processes needed to promote those
   dispositions;
f. determine the best types of organization or regime for each domain, in view of the available human resources and the diverse
   meanings of 'best';
g. prescribe the social processes most likely to create and preserve
   those regimes;
h. specify the degraded or vicious forms those regimes are vulnerable to becoming.

Aristotle conceived the universe of action as including the properties
and phenomena of human life that humans do not share with plants
and animals. These include the capacity for choice, or purposive conduct; the movements of animals, he thought, are mere reactions to sensory stimuli.[4] Related to choice is the uniquely human possession of
rational faculties. Human action, moreover, is characteristically mediated by symbolic forms. Animals possess voice, which enables them
to indicate pleasure and pain, but only humans possess the power of
speech, which enables them to communicate about the expedient and
the inexpedient, the just and the unjust, and the like. Only humans,
finally, can develop themselves in accord with excellence and, relatedly,

3. However, for a thoughtful attempt to redeem even the apparently most egregious
of Aristotle's substantive doctrines—those having reference to property, slavery, youth,
and women—see McKeon 1978.

4. Aristotle's comments on choice (*prohaeresis*) vary; sometimes the word refers to
the selection of means, sometimes to ends, sometimes to both. Interestingly, Max Weber,
whose conception of action (*Handeln*) resembles Aristotle's shows similar ambiguity in
his use of *zweckrational* ("purposive") conduct.

can experience pleasure, not just as a discrete target for instrumental action, but as a supervening sensation that they feel when they attain excellence.

The diverse domains of action get organized around their distinctive purposes. The domain of personal action, studied in ethics, is oriented to organizing personal lives so as to promote *eudaimonia*. The domain of the household, studied in economics, pursues the goals of mundane subsistence and of cultivating the powers of its members. The domain of the polity, studied in political science, pursues the goals of defense and subsistence for its constitutive households and villages, and the achievement of justice and the promotion of the virtues among all its citizens.[5]

The constitutive elements of the personality are its motives and faculties. The best way to shape them is by creating habits that give actors control over them, and by cultivating the various intellectual faculties. The ideal configuration of the personality is to have appetites and passions expressed in ways that conform to guidelines stipulated by practical reason. The constitutive elements of associational domains are their role sets and the resources available to them. In the Hellenic household, for example, these included the role sets of husband-wife, parent-child, master-slave, and master-inanimate possessions. Aristotle's treatment of the *polis* included only the division between rulers and ruled; other roles, of course, could be specified in a more differentiated analysis. The best way to orient the incumbents of these roles is to see that they attend to the proper responsibilities of their domain. In the household, for example, a man should manifest different concerns toward children as their father than toward his wife as her husband, and he should be able to acquire, preserve, improve, and properly utilize property. The responsibilities of the head of a *polis* differ from those of the head of a household, and rulers should discharge them in ways that attend to the welfare of all its members, not just one or a few. For each domain, one should set forth the optimal path of socialization to cultivate those dispositions, as Aristotle went on to prescribe the ideal course of education for citizens in his *Politics*.

---

5. That Aristotle conceived the sciences of economics and politics as different in subject matter but parallel in form is indicated by such lines as: "The differences between economics and politics correspond to the differences between the two kinds of community over which they preside. . . . Politics shows us how to build up a *polis* from its beginning, as well as how to order rightly one that already exists, so economics similarly tells us how to acquire a household and then how to conduct its affairs" (*Oeconomica* 1.1.134a1-9).

Besides attending to socialization practices, the other main focus of prescriptive work for Aristotelian social science concerns the regime, or organizational structure, best for each domain. One acquires a fund of such models from two sources. On the one hand, one reviews the available teachings about the best regime, as Aristotle reviewed the models proposed by Plato, Phaleas, and Hippodamus. On the other hand, one carries out a comparative examination of the regimes of different communities, as Aristotle examined the constitutions of more than 150 different communities with an eye to finding exemplars of excellent regimes and data about the sources of regime stability. One asks what is the best conceivable regime, what types are best suited for the general run of humanity, and what is best for different kinds of communities according to their size and socioeconomic makeup. When analyzing these optimal forms, one also specifies the kinds of perversion or degradation to which each form is vulnerable. In addition, one considers what to prescribe in communities with such serious deficits that no good regime is possible, only the lesser of various evils. The comparative examination of different communities should then also include some generalizations about processes that have been successful in creating and dissolving various regimes, and in supporting and preserving them.

Finally, since all these disciplines deal with human action, and since their concerns are interrelated—collective domains are concerned with the cultivation of individual powers, and personal domains include dispositions to promote the welfare of the associations individuals affiliate with—the relationship among the disciplines dealing with action may be indicated by saying that they are separate but interrelated.

Obviously, Aristotle's own realization of this organon for the social sciences is far too elementary for contemporary purposes. One conspicuous shortcoming of his corpus concerns the range of associational domains it considers. A social science suitable for analyzing complex societies of the modern era has to include disciplines dealing with business, industry, religion, education, medicine, states or provinces, federal governments, international regimes, and other institutional domains. Its structural parameters would have to be expanded a good deal, and a good number of its substantive propositions revised or refined. Thus differentiated, however, there is no reason why such a contemporary social science could not be elaborated following Aristotelian principles. It would tell us about the properties of human action generically and then the properties of action in these diverse associational domains. In every discipline, its object would be one and the same: to arrive at prescriptive suggestions for ways to socialize their members into optimal moral habits and reflective competences, and for ways to structure the relations among their constituent parts so as to achieve survival, justice, and the optimal achievement of its purposes.

So understood, there is something deeply attractive in Aristotle's vision of the good society and the kind of social science needed to promote it. Why did the modern social sciences not evolve along its lines? That question must be addressed in the chapter that follows.

# CHAPTER SEVEN

# The British Tradition

Scholars of diverse persuasions regard Thomas Hobbes (1588–1679) as the central foundational figure for modern social science. Leo Strauss described the political philosophy of Hobbes as "the first peculiarly modern attempt to give a coherent and exhaustive answer to the question of man's right life, which is at the same time the question of the right order of society," and hailed him as "the first who felt the necessity of seeking, and succeeded in finding, a *nuova scientia* of man and State. On this new doctrine, all later moral and political thought is expressly or tacitly based" (1936, 1). Sorokin named Hobbes as the first of a brilliant group of philosophers who created "'The Social Physics' of the seventeenth century, which, at least in its plan and aspirations, has not been surpassed by all the mechanistic theories of the nineteenth and twentieth centuries" (1928, 5). Parsons identified Hobbes as founder of the utilitarian tradition, one who "saw the problem [of order] with a clarity which has never been surpassed, and [whose] statement of it remains valid today" ([1937] 1968, 93). I now go further and advance the claim that all the philosophical traditions that undergird the disciplines of modern social science—anthropology, economics, political science, and psychology as well as sociology—consist of elaborations, revisions, or replacements of the Hobbesian conception of social science.[1]

## THE HOBBESIAN ASSAULT ON ARISTOTLE

The full import of Hobbes's achievement cannot be grasped without setting it in a context of dialogical confrontation with Aristotle. This is not to say, of course, that Aristotelian views of practical philosophy held sway in Europe for two thousand years until Hobbes came along. Aristotle's corpus was virtually forgotten for three centuries after his death. When it did come to light in the first century B.C., it aroused

---

1. Recent scholarship has tended to play down the originality of Hobbes by situating his thought in a general movement of ideas in that period. This does not, however, diminish the centrality of Hobbes as a point of reference in the tradition.

opposition from the practical-minded Romans and later from Christian thinkers. Aristotle's writings did not even get translated into Latin for more than a millennium after their rediscovery, and then largely through the introduction of his texts by the Arab scholar Averroes. The *Politics* arrived in the West by a different route, from Byzantium, and was translated at the request of Aquinas in 1250. Aristotle's political ideas gained currency through their use as support for republican ideas in the Italian city-states of the early Renaissance, most notably in the work of Marsilius of Padua. Only by the fourteenth or fifteenth century could one identify Aristotle as the authoritative voice of secular European moral philosophy, but then that is when the quest for a secular ethic began in earnest.

The critique of Aristotle as the preeminent authority in secular, moral, and political thought may be said to have begun with Machiavelli's declaration that guides to action should no longer be based on the "imagined republics and principalities" of the past but rather on the hard-nosed truth about how human beings actually live. It was consummated by Hobbes's full-scale effort to erect a secular ethic on wholly new philosophical foundations in the 1640s.

This was no work of a rebellious youth. Until his early forties Hobbes stood faithful to the philosophy of Aristotle, a stance reflecting his classical education at Oxford and a young adulthood devoted to classical literature. Prefacing his first publication—a translation of Thucydides in 1628—Hobbes affirmed the common sense that "Homer in poesy, Aristotle in philosophy, Demosthenes in eloquence, and others of the ancients in other knowledge, do still maintain their primacy: none of them exceeded, some not approached, by any in these later ages" ([1843] 1966, 8: vii). The following year, however, Hobbes experienced what has been described as an intellectual "conversion" during a visit to France: there he tasted geometry for the first time. Euclid offered him a powerful new entree to truth. On a later visit to the continent, which included a pilgrimage to Italy to visit Galileo, he became attracted to the latter's audacious views that motion is the natural state of bodies and that bodies continue in motion to infinity unless impeded. These views contradicted the Aristotelian doctrine that rest is the natural state of bodies. Hobbes also embraced the Galilean notion that the natural universe consists of a vast field of atomic motions, replacing Aristotle's conception of natural phenomena as a collection of substances constituted by essential qualities and ends. Applying these ideas of Galilean physics to psychological phenomena led Hobbes to challenge Aristotle. In his *Little Treatise* (1637) he reinterpreted sensation in terms of the interaction of external bodies with sense organs. He went on to develop a view of human action as impelled by unlimited desires and perpetual motion rather than tending toward a state of rest and fulfillment.

Moved by the promise of geometric method and mechanistic psychology, Hobbes aspired to use the ideas of this new science to transform all of moral and political philosophy. These new ideas brought him to the point where he regarded the political and ethical teaching of Aristotle (though not the latter's work on biology and rhetoric) as "the worst. . . that ever was" (Aubrey 1949, 255).[2] His project was to take the form of three treatises—first on the body, then on man, and last on the state. Upset by the growing civil strife in England in the late 1630s, however, Hobbes proceeded to draft the last treatise first, hoping to use forceful new modes of argument to persuade his fellow citizens to obey the law, and thus put the finger on lawless killers and conspirators by refuting the vicious doctrine that it is all right to rebel against kings. In due course he completed the entire project.[3]

Much has been made—and rightly so—of the significance of Hobbes's new substantive moral doctrines. Attention to his work has generally concentrated on his secular reasons for justifying the absolute authority of political sovereigns, albeit in discussions that tend to ignore the moral constraints Hobbes imposes upon sovereigns at the same time he exempts them from legal restraints. Strauss (1936) has also argued that the truly revolutionary feature of Hobbes's moral philosophy lay in its displacement of the elitist ethic found in Aristotle's celebration of the aristocratic virtues of magnanimity and valor by an egalitarian ethic that championed the virtues of justice and charity. However, for the story of the sociological tradition I am telling, what must be stressed is the new set of principles Hobbes devised for shaping a discipline of practical philosophy. We can best consider those prin-

2. The point gets expanded in the *Leviathan:* "And I believe that scarce any thing can be more absurdly said in naturall Philosophy, than that which now is called *Aristotle's Metaphysiques;* nor more repugnant to Government, than much of that hee hath said in his *Politiques;* nor more ignorantly, than a great part of his *Ethiques*" (ch. 46, par. 11).

3. The treatise on the state appeared first as *Elements of Law* in 1640; it was circulated in manuscript form and not published until 1650. Hobbes published an expanded version of part of the *Elements* in Latin as *De Cive* in 1642, which he later reworked and published in English as *Leviathan* in 1651. The treatise on the body, *De Corpore,* appeared in 1655 and the treatise on man, *De Homine,* in 1658 (although it was not translated into English until 1972).

ciples by contrasting them with the Aristotelian principles Hobbes was replacing.

## NATURE

Like the Greeks, Hobbes sought to construct a purely secular rational ethic, and to do so on the basis of what is natural. His laws of morality turn out to be "laws of nature." To be sure, he also referred to these laws as commands of God, possibly to protect himself against charges of atheism, but the logic of his arguments flows quite independent of any theological strictures.[4] Nevertheless, what Hobbes understands by "nature" differs so radically from Aristotle's *physis* that this shift in metaphysical assumptions radically transforms the whole program of moral philosophy.

Where Aristotle considered nature to be the essential quality of something in a universe of substances which tend toward rest, Hobbes came to view nature as an inherent force which directs the world, in a universe of atoms existing in perpetual motion. Like Aristotle, Hobbes regarded human passions—the appetites—and human faculties, like reason, as natural phenomena. Unlike Aristotle, Hobbes thinks they exhaust the universe of natural human phenomena. The human world is constituted as a great field of interacting impulses, just as the mechanical world is constituted as a great field of interacting atoms, and their force is so strong that they perturb the workings of the only other natural phenomenon humans evince, reason. Analysis of these interacting motions, based on the natural propensities of atomic individuals, constitutes the alpha and omega of Hobbesian social science.

For Hobbes, the primary motions were twofold: "a perpetual and restless desire for power after power" (*Leviathan,* ch. 11, par. 2), and the avoidance of violent death, which proceeds from "a certain impulsion of nature, no less than that whereby a stone moves downward" ([1642] 1972, 115). The first impulse derives from the uninhibited expression of various natural appetites; the interaction of individuals animated by this desire for power produces an anarchic condition, the

---

4. "Though Hobbes does not provide us with a political theory free of theology, there is nothing essential missing when the theology is taken out. . . . He also makes it clear that God requires nothing of men which they would not require of each other if there were no God. Atheists, no less than other men, can discover that the laws of nature are rules which it is every man's interest should be generally observed, and have as powerful a motive for creating the conditions in which it is most likely that they will be observed" (Plamenatz 1963, 21, 16).

war of all against all. This condition in turn activates the second natural impulse, self-preservation. This impulse aligns with reason and motivates men to covenant among themselves to instate a sovereign who can impose civil peace. The Hobbesian model can be diagrammed as shown.

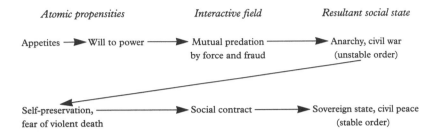

*Atomic propensities*     *Interactive field*     *Resultant social state*

Appetites ➤ Will to power ➤ Mutual predation ➤ Anarchy, civil war
                              by force and fraud        (unstable order)

Self-preservation, ➤ Social contract ➤ Sovereign state, civil peace
fear of violent death                        (stable order)

Hobbes restricts what is natural in humanity to a field of strong appetitive forces and a relatively feeble faculty of reason. This eliminates two other phenomena that Aristotle also assumed to be natural: the propensity of substances to actualize their potential in a certain direction, and the tendency of humans to organize themselves in enduring associations. Discarding the latter assumption makes the polity entirely a work of art, not a natural formation. Discarding the assumption that humans have a natural tendency to actualize themselves toward the good means that analysis can focus only on the presumed givens of human conduct, not on imagined ideal end states.

Semantic shifts can take one of three forms: a shift in the generic meaning of the concept, in the identification of phenomena that get described by the concept, or in the qualities associated with the concept. The way the meaning of 'nature' changed from Aristotle to Hobbes is so momentous because shifts of all three kinds take place simultaneously. Hobbes replaces the classic notion of nature as signifying the essential quality and character of something with the more abstract sense of an inherent force that directs the world. As applied to human phenomena, he withdraws the attribution of natural from social formations and thereby restricts it to individual human behavior. Further, he specifies as natural primarily the self-regarding appetites and secondarily the faculty of reason, eliminating individuals' developmental ends, which Aristotle had regarded as inherent in their nature. So momentous a complex of shifts had ramifications throughout the philosophy of Hobbes and of those influenced by him. Not least of these ramifications were the associated shifts in conceiving the relation between theory and practice.

## THEORY AND PRACTICE

Throughout his systematic treatments of moral and political philosophy, Hobbes based his expositions on the ideas and methods of natural science. Since it was the power of geometric argument that originally had inspired these analyses, geometry provided the model he sought to emulate in constructing his sciences of man. In a moment of enthusiasm for the model, he exclaimed: "Were the nature of human actions as distinctly known as the nature of *quantity* in geometric figures, the strength of *avarice* and *ambition,* which is sustained by the erroneous opinions of the vulgar as touching the nature of *right* and *wrong,* would presently faint and languish; and mankind should enjoy such an immortal peace that . . . there would hardly be left any pretence for war" ([1642] 1972, 91).

There were three respects in which Hobbes can be said to have tried to make moral philosophy like mathematics. As the above passage indicates, one was to employ distinct and univocally defined terms for discourse, in marked contrast to Aristotle, who acknowledged the plenitude of meanings that commonplace terms about action bore and sought to incorporate those diverse meanings in discourse about the good. Another was an attempt to suggest a calculus for representing quanta of good and evil, about which more will be said below. A third was to employ rigorous deductive reasoning, following what he described as Galileo's resolutive-compositive method. This method reduces political phenomena to their elements—the propensities of individuals—and then reconstitutes them through logical deduction. Thus Hobbes made the deductive aspect of natural science—what Aristotle called *episteme,* or scientific demonstration—the constitutive method of his practical philosophy. In all three respects Hobbes turned his back on Aristotle's dictum that one should not expect the kind of certainty one gets in mathematics from investigations concerning human action, and thereby erased one of the boundaries between theoretical and practical knowledge that Aristotle had drawn.

He similarly collapsed the Aristotelian divide between the subject matters of the two branches of philosophy. Natural science dealt with the motions of bodies, so likewise the sciences of man dealt with the motions of bodies. Not action for the sake of some good purpose, but action as the playing out of so many natural impulses comprised his practical subject matter. The point of practical philosophy for Hobbes was to follow the vicissitudes of these natural motions and to align reason with them at junctures where natural equilibria were being reset. This approach to practical philosophy made it consist of nothing other than *applied theory*. And since natural bodies were now understood as consisting of atoms in motion, not as substances actualizing their potential forms toward some end, the forms and ends of human action could be disregarded. Hobbesian practical science no less than Galilean physical science eliminated the search for formal causes and final causes by directing attention exclusively to the search for material and efficient causes.

## GROUNDING MORALITY

Hobbes, like Aristotle, projects a vision of the good society that at the same time theorizes about the source of human moral dispositions. For Hobbes, however, the good society does not deal with arrangements for realizing the highest potentialities of humans, but rather restricts itself to the ways and means of creating a state free from warfare. The practical problems for Aristotle were twofold: how to go on living and how to live well; for Hobbes, just living at peace suffices.

Logically, this agenda for practical philosophy gets set by assuming that practical wisdom consists of the applied theory of nature. Criteria of the good then derive from affirming the naturally given needs and rights of individual human actors. Since Hobbes's theory of the natural human condition holds that the free play of human appetites leads inexorably to the war of all against all, the central dilemma of action must be to secure a stable equilibrium or order. The touchstone of morality becomes obedience to the laws of an absolute sovereign. Moral laws are laws of nature, the first of which is to seek peace, but to provide defenses for oneself in the absence of peace. Since morality gets channeled exclusively into a concern for survival and stability, the touchstone for personal morality becomes a disposition to abide by the laws and manners of civil society, and therefore "all the virtues are contained in justice and charity" ([1658] 1972, 70). Such laws of nature are defined as the dictates of right reason: they are inexorable consequences of aligning natural reason with the passion for self-preservation.

The secular ethic propounded by Aristotle involved a complex mixture of ingredients: realized potentials for excellence, voluntaristic decisions, proper use of language, public discourse, well-constituted societies, wise laws, suitable habits, and satisfied appetites. From this complex Hobbes abstracted one element—the satisfaction of natural desires—as the cornerstone of his entire ethical edifice. He proceeded to transform moral philosophy by adopting a new method based on geometry and mechanics; he developed a new view of nature, based on a conception of atomic elements in motion; and he devised a new way of posing the question of morality, based on resolving the dilemma posed by free play of natural appetites. In so doing, he constructed a framework of assumptions that were to undergird the major philosophical efforts to construct sciences of human phenomena in Britain for the next three centuries. At the same time, he stripped moral philosophy of a number of Aristotelian assumptions—about the natural character of social associations, the importance of voluntarism for moral judgment, the disjunction between theoretic science and practical knowledge, the natural bases of goal-directed potentialities, the social importance of well-qualified elites, and the probabilistic character of moral judgments—that thinkers in other traditions would struggle for centuries to restore.

## THE LOYAL OPPOSITION: BRITISH CRITICS OF HOBBES

Although Hobbes's writings do acknowledge a human capacity for benevolence, what is theoretically central in his system is the human striving for self-aggrandizing power—as in his point that "man surpasseth in rapacity and cruelty the wolves, bears, and snakes that are not rapacious unless hungry and not cruel unless provoked, whereas man is famished even by future hunger" ([1658] 1972, 40). Due to this disposition of human nature, the unconstrained expression of natural impulses inexorably produces an intolerable state of mutual predation.

Perhaps most readers of Hobbes would echo the judgment of Pogson Smith: "He offers us a theory of man's nature which is at once consistent, fascinating, and outrageously false" (1909, ix). The intellectual landscape of the two centuries after Hobbes is strewn with trenchant refutations of this theory. Those refutations—in Britain, France, and Germany—form the points of departure for notions that undergird the modern social sciences.

Subsequent writers in England and Scotland were quick to challenge many of Hobbes's bold substantive statements. They criticized his views on political authority as well as his image of human nature, and focused on societal problems other than that of civil security. In virtually all cases, however, *they retained the basic principles for erecting a social science that Hobbes had laid down.*

One can schematize the Hobbesian principles in the form of postulates that provide one set of answers to the three questions posed at the end of Part One. To the question of how the facts of human experience are to be constructed and explained, Hobbes responds with what may be called the **Postulate of Methodological Individualism:** *Social phenomena are best explained by analyzing the propensities of the individual actors that constitute them.*

To the question of how secular thought can provide a rational grounding of moral judgments, Hobbes responds with what may be called the **Postulate of Normative Individualism:** *Normative judgments are best grounded rationally by appeal to the naturally given needs and rights of individual human actors.* Practical wisdom thus amounts to the direct application of theoretical knowledge to moral questions.

To the question about the source of human moral dispositions, Hobbes responds with what may be called the **Postulate of Natural Individual Morality:** *Human moral orientations derive, directly or indirectly, from natural propensities inherent in all human beings.*

Later writers in the British tradition of social thought characteristically accepted all three of these postulates while challenging Hobbes on one or another point regarding the particular contents they might embody. For a half-century or so after Hobbes, these writers—principally Locke, Shaftesbury, and Mandeville—lived in England. For the century thereafter, they flourished in Scotland, forming that remarkable cluster of figures who created what is known as the Scottish Enlightenment. Following the century of Scottish ascendancy, the tradition reverted to England. Figure 6 presents a genealogical outline of the British tradition of social theory. It depicts not merely a number of thinkers who lived in Britain, but *a network of participants in a transgenerational dialogue who constituted a real tradition by virtue of documented connections with one another.*

The process of revising Hobbes's conclusions in a framework of debate loyal to the postulates he set forth began with a group of philosophers known as the Cambridge Platonists and with John Locke. Although Locke did not explicitly engage with Hobbes in the self-conscious way that Hobbes criticized Aristotle, Hobbes affected Locke's thought both by giving him a target to attack and by offering him the mode of thinking by which to carry out that attack.[5] Adhering to what I have called the postulates of Methodological Individualism and Normative Individualism, Locke followed the example set by Hobbes of making the rights of individuals the cornerstone of his moral and political philosophy. However, in a stance more in keeping with the values of British political culture, which stood for curtailing the powers of sovereigns, Locke endeavored to refute the Hobbesian defense of political absolutism. In so doing, he introduced two notions that would guide centuries of British revisionism: that the human animal manifests socially benign dispositions, and that human selfish dispositions can have socially benign consequences. These notions were taken up by two writers who, though mutually antagonistic, both reflected Locke's influence: the Earl of Shaftesbury and Bernard de Mandeville.

## THE SHAFTESBURY AMENDMENT

Anthony Ashley Cooper, Third Earl of Shaftesbury, is known chiefly for a collection of essays published in 1711 under the title *Characteristicks of Men, Manners, Opinions, Times, Etc.* An elegant writer more than a systematic thinker, he gains importance in our story for crystallizing one of the two main lines of revision of Hobbesian thinking. Educated privately by Locke, who was a close friend and physician of his grandfather, the first Earl of Shaftesbury, he went on to elaborate two of Locke's humanistic themes: the importance of political freedom for the improvement of mankind, and a view of humanity as relatively benign in character. The latter theme is developed through a pointed attack against Hobbes's emphasis on the selfish cast of human nature, an attack supported by his identification of a number of self-transcending passions or affections, such as love, sympathy, and friendship. Shaftesbury traces them to a "social feeling" or "associating inclination" that appears naturally strong in most people. Against Hobbes he defends the natural bases of sociability by arguing that the very disposition to establish conventions presumes social sentiments: "faith, justice, honesty, and virtue, must have been as early as the state of nature, or they

5. "The word 'Leviathan' occurs in [Locke's] *Second Treatise,* and there are phrases and whole arguments which recall the Hobbesian position, and must have been intended in some sense as comments upon them. Moreover, the thinking of Hobbes was of systematic importance to Locke and enters into his doctrines in a way which goes much deeper than a difference in political opinion. . . . He seems to have been in the curious position of having absorbed Hobbesian sentiments, Hobbesian phraseology in such a way that he did not know where they came from: his early reading, never repeated, perhaps; or other men's books and the general discussion of Hobbes; or both" (Laslett 1960, 81, 85–86).

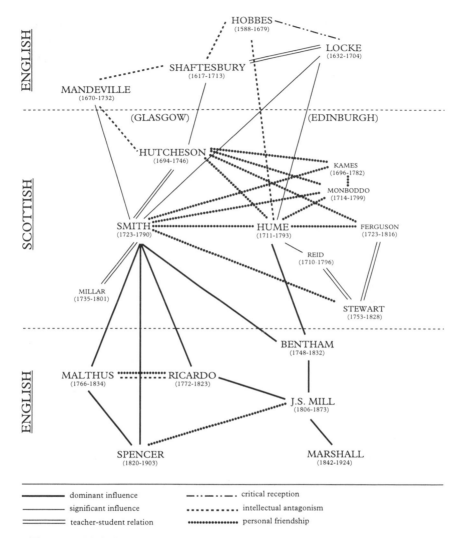

Figure 6.  Links in the British Tradition

could never have been at all" ([1711] 1900, 1:72–75). He also makes reference to a naturally given moral sense, which he likens to a sense for right proportions in the tuning of musical instruments—a sensibility that disposes one to find enjoyment by expressing natural social affections and prudential self-affections in the right proportions, and to shun unnatural affections like cruelty and malice (1:258–93).

Whereas Locke had sought some rapprochement of moral philosophy with Christian theology by placing the source of morals in the will

of God, Shaftesbury, though a spirited deist, championed a purely secular basis for his ethical notions. Shaftesbury not only defended human
nature against its disparaging depictions by writers like Hobbes, he celebrated nature itself as the source of all value,[6] which earned him acclaim as "the first moralist who distinctly takes psychological
experience as the basis of ethics" (Sidgwick [1886] 1954, 190). His approach was pursued by the moral philosophers of the Scottish Enlightenment, who used the notion of a moral sense to ground moral
philosophy strictly on the basis of psychological facts. But his position
was also seized to be made the butt of one of the keenest wits in England.

## THE MANDEVILLE AMENDMENT

Like Hobbes, Mandeville believed that coercive authority was essential
to civil order, observing, for example, that a hundred equal men "under no Subjection, or Fear of any Superior upon Earth, could never live
together awake Two Hours without Quarreling" ([1714] 1924, 1:347).
However, Mandeville followed Locke in placing his analytic emphasis
on the problem of commercial prosperity rather than on the problem of
civil order. In the commercial domain, man's selfish dispositions produce socially advantageous consequences; according to the subtitle of
*The Fable of the Bees,* Mandeville's most famous creation, they produce
*Private Vices, Publick Benefits.* For example, vicious traits like vanity,
envy, and love of luxury motivate people to buy goods and thereby
stimulate the economy. Deceitful practices of buyers and sellers alike
lubricate trade; even criminals serve to keep locksmiths in business and
circulate wealth. Society is held together by public morality, to be sure;
but public morality springs from the vain and hypocritical behavior of
egoists eager to gain public approbation, and therefore "Moral Virtues
are the Political Offspring which Flattery begot upon Pride" (1:51).

Mandeville assumed that all natural human propensities were exclusively oriented toward the satisfaction of self-regarding appetites. In
defense of this thesis he later took up cudgels against Shaftesbury, regarding whom he quipped: "The attentive Reader . . . will soon per-
ceive that two Systems cannot be more opposite than his Lordship's
and mine. His Notions I confess are generous and refined . . . What

6. "O glorious nature! supremely fair, and sovereignly good! . . . O mighty nature!
Wise substitute of Providence! . . . I sing of nature's order in created beings, and
celebrate the beautys which resolve, in thee, the source and principle of all beauty and
perfection" ([1711] 1900, 2:98).

pity it is they are not true" (1:324). Mandeville placed more stock in human artifice than in human nature, and found the incremental accumulation of experience over long historical periods crucial for developing the human skills that generate material prosperity. He invoked the doctrine of the division of labor as a principle essential for this development. This enabled him to explain the development of mankind from an originally savage state to its modern constructive capacities without recourse to an optimistic view of human nature, a position that Mandeville may have reached through his search for arguments with which to counter Shaftesbury (Horne 1978, 41).

However pronounced the oppositions among Hobbes, Shaftesbury, and Mandeville, from a more distant perspective one cannot fail to be struck by similarities among their underlying analytic schemas. This is evident if we cast their models in the form of figures, and compare them with that of Hobbes shown above.

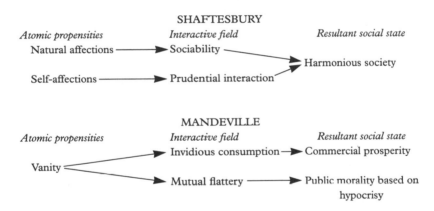

Abstracting from the particular contents of these formulae, we find in each of them the basic tenets of *atomic naturalism,* a term useful for designating an ideal type that represents some core assumptions of British social theorists. Nearly all of them proceed from an assumption of certain propensities located within individuals, propensities that are naturally grounded, universally distributed, and followed in some calculating manner. From these propensities they derive the notion of a social field constituted by kinds of interactions produced by individuals so disposed; they culminate with a conception of a relatively stable order analogous to that of mechanical equilibrium produced by the aggregation of those social interactions.

Taken together, Hobbes, Shaftesbury, and Mandeville articulated the British tradition's three variant presuppositions regarding the individual-society nexus:

1. natural human propensities are essentially selfish and produce destructive consequences unless coercively checked;

2. natural human propensities are essentially selfish, but they produce positive social consequences; and

3. natural human propensities include dispositions toward social affection and moral sensibility.[7]

Over the next two centuries British social theorists used these presuppositions to construct systematic discourses and academic disciplines. One practical impetus behind their work was a need to valorize the dispositions required for a commercial society, as Mandeville had done, while yet upholding some sense of human life as oriented to the realization of virtue, as in the tradition of civic humanism. Addressing this challenge became the distinctive mission of a subtradition known as Scottish moral philosophy. Its father was an Irish Presbyterian teacher, Francis Hutcheson, who returned to the University of Glasgow (his alma mater) as professor of moral philosophy in 1730. Five years before, Hutcheson had staked out his place in the trangenerational dialogue by declaring on the title page of his first publication that his would be a work "In Which The Principles of the late Earl of Shaftesbury are Explain'd and Defended, against the Author of the *Fable of the Bees.*" Indeed, the wish to combat what he saw as the misguided doctrine of natural egoism became the driving force behind much of Hutcheson's work, starting with letters to newspapers against Hobbes and Mandeville and continuing for two decades. In Hutcheson's view, the doctrine that held the principle of self-interest to be the spring of all human action simply did not stand up to the evidence: "This scheme can never account for the principal actions of human life such as the offices of friendship, gratitude, natural affection, generosity, public spirit, compassion. . . . In like manner this scheme can never account for the sudden approbation and violent sense of

---

7. These assumptions inform what Elie Halévy identified as the three logically distinct doctrines used by utilitarian thinkers to reconcile individual interests with the general utility or public interest—the doctrines, respectively, of the artificial identity of interests, the natural identity of interests, and the fusion of interests. Although these positions appear somewhat contradictory, all three are present in some form in every utilitarian doctrine ([1901–4] 1966, 13–18).

something amiable in actions done in distance ages and nations" ([1728] 1971, 117–18).

In addition to upholding Shaftesbury's claim that, besides self-interest, humans exhibit naturally sociable and benevolent affections, Hutcheson followed Shaftesbury in locating the disposition to make moral judgments in a naturally given faculty, the moral sense, and in making the exercise of that faculty the touchstone of moral judgment. Moral judgment thus represents an autonomous phenomenon; it cannot be reduced to self-interest, as with Hobbes and Mandeville; to the will of God, as Locke maintained; or to self-evident truth, as with rationalists like Gilbert Burnet. Errors in moral judgment get corrected by providing the moral sense with more accurate information regarding the consequences of an act for the general welfare. With this notion Hutcheson found a way to relieve the discomfort produced by Mandeville's formula of "private vices, public virtues"; for if an action, however motivated, was conducive to some sort of public benefit, then Hutcheson's utilitarian formula would indicate that it must not be considered a vice, but morally good.[8] He thereby found a way to reconcile the principle of self-love (which Mandeville had found so crucial for commercial society) with virtue.

Hutcheson also aimed to impart scientific rigor to moral philosophy. The title page of his first essay on morality advertises an "Attempt to Introduce a *Mathematical Calculation* in Subjects of Morality." That essay included a Newtonian formula that likens benevolence to the force of gravitation and so makes the strength of benevolence inversely proportioned to the distance between people ([1725] 1971, 220). It also sets forth a standard for measuring the goodness of an act—"the moral evil, or vice, of a given action, is as the degree of misery, and the number of sufferers; so that action is best which accomplishes the greatest happiness for the greatest number" (177)—a standard elaborated in his *System of Moral Philosophy* (1755), which includes a chapter on how to calculate the morality of actions. Thus, however much Hutcheson aimed to refute Hobbes by defending the irreducibility of human passions for the public weal, he reproduced Hobbes's scientific project by claiming to rid the subject of morality of its usual causes of error—"the

---

8. Hutcheson did make a distinction, however, "between actions materially good that regardless of motive, benefited the public and acts formally good that were public benefits resulting from virtuous motives" (Horne 1978, 90).

confusion of ambiguous words"—and by making moral analysis a matter of quantifying the desires and aversions of individual actors.

David Hume continued the project by applying the Newtonian method of experimental science to Hutcheson's observations about the human mind and the moral sense. Although Hume may seem to have undermined the quest for a rational secular ethic by separating judgments of fact from judgments of value, he reintroduced it by making a rationally discernible natural faculty the basis for all moral judgments, a faculty that operates by identifying what is good with the production of pleasure and the avoidance of pain. Hume advanced the utilitarian tradition beyond Hutcheson's formulation of the greatest happiness principle by analyzing its anthropological grounding in a natural sentiment of approbation of things that are useful to society. "It appears to be a fact," he argues in his *Enquiry Concerning the Principles of Morals,*

> that the circumstance of *utility,* in all subjects, is a source of praise and approbation; that it is constantly appealed to in all moral decisions concerning the merit and demerit of actions; that it is the sole source of that high regard paid to justice, fidelity, honour, allegiance, and chastity; that it is inseparable from all the other social virtues, humanity, generosity, charity, affability, lenity, mercy, and moderation; and, in a word, that it is a foundation of the chief part of morals, which has a reference to mankind and our fellow creatures. ([1751] 1975, 221)

A student of Hutcheson and friend of Hume, Adam Smith applied their ideas to questions of economic productivity and moral order. Known in his lifetime chiefly for *The Theory of Moral Sentiments* (1759), which extended the doctrines of innate social sentiments and moral sensibilities and erected a coherent theory of morality upon the analysis of sympathy, Smith gave a powerful boost to the social sciences through his other masterwork, *An Inquiry into the Nature and Causes of the Wealth of Nations* (1776). Both Smith's definition of the nature of a nation's wealth and his analysis of its causes reflect the premises of atomic naturalism. The wealth of a country, he argues, is to be measured not in terms of the amount of bullion in its treasury but in terms of the quantity of goods produced each year divided by population. This measure of annual gross national product per capita registers the number of possessions enjoyed by all individuals in the society, at the time a revolutionary way to register a nation's wealth.

The sources of that wealth Smith identifies as twofold, the level of productive skill in the workforce (treated in book 1) and the ratio of productive to unproductive laborers (treated in book 2). The level of

productivity in the workforce is a function of the extent to which productive capacities are specialized, for specialization promotes manual
dexterity, efficiency, and inventiveness. Specialization flows from the
division of labor, which in turn gets promoted to the extent that a market exists for specialized products. Although the extent of the market
depends on infrastructural factors like transportation, what ultimately
accounts for markets is a natural human disposition—the propensity to
trade one thing for another.

The other main factor responsible for high productivity is the pro-
portion of the workforce actually engaged in productive labor. This in
turn depends on the quantity of capital stock available to finance enterprises that can employ workers. The amount of capital accumulation in
turn depends on a natural human disposition to save, based on "the
desire of bettering our condition, a desire which . . . comes with us
from the womb, and never leaves us till we go into the grave" ([1776]
1976, 1:362).

Left to themselves, these two naturally grounded dispositions—to
better our condition through trade and through savings—are sufficient
to lead any society to wealth and prosperity. Other natural propensities
account for the cohesion of communities. The natural disposition to
admire rank, distinction, and preeminence accounts for stable social
hierarchies while a disposition to revere general rules upholds the ob-
servance of societal norms. The human capacity for sympathy together
with the naturally powerful wish for approval accounts for the moral
order in society.[9] The logic of Smith's sociology follows the same pattern we witnessed above in Hobbes, Shaftesbury, and Mandeville:

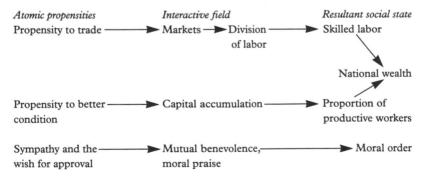

9. Smith was so committed to explaining social formations by natural propensities
that he engaged in such naturalistic pursuits as studying the behavior of birds. For an
illuminating account of Smith's naturalism and its grounding in the naturalistic theology
of Hutcheson and other British predecessors, see Brown 1994.

Natural individual propensities not only provide Smith with the principles by which social phenomena are to be explained; they also serve as the grounding of human morality and of criteria for defining the social good. Smith repeatedly praises nature for her unerring wisdom ([1759] 1982, 218, 222, 226).

The good becomes known through "what, in particular instances, our moral faculties, our natural sense of merit and propriety, approve or disapprove of" (159). The chief objects of moral approbation are those laws that safeguard the rights of individuals: their life and persons; their property and possessions; and their personal rights, or what is due them from the promises of others (84). Beyond this, the efficacy of natural dispositions in promoting public weal indicates that government should undertake only what individuals cannot accomplish on their own—national security, administration of justice, and certain public works—and otherwise observe a principle of laissez-faire, so that "the obvious and simple system of natural liberty establishes itself, [such that] every man, as long as he does not violate the laws of justice, is left perfectly free to pursue his own interest his own way, and to bring both his industry and capital into competition with those of any other man" ([1776] 1976, 2:208).

## FROM UTILITARIAN PHILOSOPHY TO SOCIAL SCIENCE

Thanks to his eighteenth-century critics, the simplified psychology expounded by Hobbes turned into a colorful palette of human motivations. Later writers presumed a rich variety of motives that drive the human animal. Thus Adam Ferguson—sometimes called the "first sociologist"—observed that war may come from misunderstanding and error as well as from intention to injure; social bonding from acquaintance, habit, dislike of solitude, fellow feeling, sexuality, fear of injury, esteem, memory, moral support, and the like; virtuous actions from such diverse factors as public reputation, religion, legal sanctions, and personal conscience ([1792] 1973, 177).

An empirically rich human psychology such as Ferguson offered, however, frustrated the penchant to simplify that sought abstract generalizations of wide scope. An avowed disciple of Smith and Hume, Jeremy Bentham revived Hume's Newtonian ambitions in his effort to design a scientific calculus with which to reform human conduct and institutions. To be sure, Bentham acknowledged a wide variety of operative motives—hunger and sex, love of reputation and love of power, desire of amity and wish for money.[10] At one point he alludes to a Shaftesbury-like typology of social, self-regarding, and dissocial motives. Yet all these dispositions can be subsumed under the broad category of desires to avoid pain and pursue pleasure—or happiness, as he alternatively styles it. In the opening words of his most famous work, *An Introduction to the Principles of Morals and Legislation,* he claims:

> Nature has placed mankind under the governance of two sovereign masters, *pain* and *pleasure.* It is for them alone to determine what we ought to do, as well as to determine what we shall do. On the one hand the standard of right and wrong, on the other the chain of causes and effects, are fastened to their throne. ([1789] 1948, 1)

Bentham formulates this foundational thought as the principle of utility: the principle that both accounts for the patterns of human conduct and assesses every action according to its apparent effect in promoting the happiness of the party whose interest is in question. Bentham hastens to add that the only parties whose interests can be so considered are individual persons. These robust assertions express Bentham's commitment to the postulates of atomic naturalism. The Postulate of Normative Individualism appears in his framing the criterion of ethical judgment in terms of the happiness of individual actors. Methodological individualism appears in his statement that the community is a fictitious body composed only of its individual members— and his lampooning the notion of a body politic as a metaphor through which "poetry has invaded the domain of reason" (1843, 2:306)—and thus the interest of the community is no more than "the sum of the interests of the several members who compose it" ([1789] 1948, 3). Following that assumption he proposes that the pleasures and pains of individuals be measured with respect to seven variables—their intensity, duration, degree of certainty, propinquity, fecundity, purity, and the number of persons affected by them.[11]

---

10. In 1817 he even published a comprehensive *Table of the Springs of Action,* which listed dozens of human motives and hundreds of terms for describing them.

11. Bentham's prescription for calculating the general tendency of any act is first to calculate the value of each distinguishable pleasure and each pain the act produces initially. Then one calculates the value of each pleasure and each pain produced secondarily (their respective fecundity and impurity). Next one sums up all the values of the pleasures and pains so as to get the good or bad tendency of the act for the individual person. One repeats this process for each person whose interests appear to be affected, arriving finally at a balance indicating the general good/evil tendency of the act with respect to the total community of individuals concerned ([1789] 1948, 30–31).

In advocating this quasi-mathematical procedure Bentham believed he had managed to treat moral questions in a properly scientific manner. Indeed, he was probably the first person to use the phrase "social science" in English, eagerly translating the term *ciencia social,* which a Spanish editor had used in titling a selection of Benthamite writings.[12] His formulations stimulated a number of efforts that eventuated in the distinctively British contribution to social science in the course of the nineteenth century.

Although Bentham attracted little attention for some decades after *Principles* appeared, the utilitarian doctrine was developing alongside and independent of him, fast becoming "the universal philosophy in England" (Halévy [1901–4] 1966, 153).[13] Bentham finally became well known thanks largely to James Mill, who did much to publicize Bentham's views and bring them to the political arena. Through Mill, Bentham also came to exert some influence on David Ricardo, whose *Principles of Political Economy and Taxation* was the first British treatise on political economy in four decades after *The Wealth of Nations,* although its systematizing approach and progressive history reflected Mill's influence more than Bentham's, and its substantive emphases moved in directions inspired more by Thomas Malthus's ideas about population and rent. Concluding his career as a member of Parliament, Ricardo applied the Greatest Happiness principle in speeches that defended the aggregate interests of all the consumers in English society.

James Mill also conveyed Bentham's teachings to his son John Stuart, who in 1823 organized a discussion group in London under the name of the Utilitarian Society. Developing ideas that in part grew out of those discussions, the younger Mill went on to devote a number of publications to topics in utilitarian philosophy. Although he became highly critical of Bentham's simplistic views on human nature and morality, he gave credit to Bentham for being the first to bring the method of science to the art of legislation: "he was the first who attempted regularly to deduce all the secondary and intermediate principles of law, by direct and systematic inference from the one great axiom or principle of general utility" ([1833] 1969, 10).

12. *Espiritu de Bentham: Sistéma de la ciencia social,* ed. Toribio Nuñez (Salamanca, 1820). See Baker 1964, 224.
13. Of the currency of utilitarian thinking during this period Halévy adds: "Reformers were forced to speak the language of utility if they wanted to make their opinions accepted or even understood by the public to which they were addressed." Even Burke, whose views were so much at odds with the Benthamite Radicals, "took his stand on the principle of utility in order to develop a traditional philosophy" (154).

*A System of Logic* expressed J. S. Mill's own conviction that social reforms and political action should be based on scientific knowledge, not on custom, authority, or revelation, and included a seminal section on how to construct a credible social science. Mill proceeds by identifying a variety of methods that had been successfully employed in the natural sciences, including five different methods of experimental inquiry developed in chemistry and the abstract deductive method of geometry. Owing to the enormous complexity of social phenomena, none of those methods is suitable for the social science, or sociology, as he begins to call it. In rejecting the geometric method, which deduces certain consequences from singular assumptions, Mill cites both Hobbes and Bentham as misguided practitioners, since they mistakenly assume that single motives—mutual dread and the pursuit of worldly self-interest, respectively—can be taken as the causes of societal phenomena. Geometry affords no room, he notes, for what constantly occurs in the domain of mechanics: the existence of conflicting forces, of causes that counteract or modify one another—conditions that regularly obtain in human affairs. The concrete deductive method of *physics,* which allows the deduction of all the causes that conjointly produce a given effect, thus recommends itself for sociology.

While criticizing Hobbes and Bentham for their simplistic psychologies, Mill nevertheless retains their underlying Postulate of Methodological Individualism. Indeed, he presents one of its classic formulations:

> Men . . . in a state of society are still men; their actions and passions are obedient to the laws of individual human nature. Men are not, when brought together, converted into another kind of substance, with different properties: as hydrogen and oxygen are different from water, or as hydrogen, oxygen, carbon, and azote are different from nerves, muscles, and tendons. Human beings in society have no properties but those which are derived from, and may be resolved into, the laws of the nature of individual man. ([1843; 8th ed. 1872] 1987, 65)

In addition to endorsing the concrete deductive method of physics, Mill also exhibits the Postulate of Methodological Individualism when he embraces the ancillary "inversive deductive, or historical method." In this mode, sociology's task is to ascertain empirical laws of society from the study of history and then to connect these deductively with the laws of human nature.

Mill concludes his tome on logic by considering the relationship between theory and practice. For Mill the relationship is clear-cut: theorems of natural science provide the grounds of every rule of practice. Art simply supplies an end to be attained; science provides the proposition that specifies what actions must be taken to attain that end. To be sure, the setting of ends in art is altogether a different order of intellectual activity from that of science, which can only assert matters of fact such as existence, coexistence, succession, and resemblance. In purely physical science there is little temptation to mix the two by determining what ultimate ends are to be pursued. Those who treat of human nature and society, however, invariably claim to proclaim those ends: "*They always undertake to say, not merely what is, but what ought to be*" (141; emphasis mine). To entitle them to do so, Mill avers that a complete doctrine of ends is indispensable. In the *Logic* he alludes to such a doctrine—one that justifies the greatest "happiness of mankind" as the ultimate practical principle ("or rather," he adds in a phrase that to my knowledge has never been picked up by any non-Buddhist utilitarians, "of all sentient beings")—and proceeds to develop it systematically elsewhere.

In *Utilitarianism* (1861) and *On Liberty* (1859), Mill advanced eloquent defenses of the main principles of Normative Individualism. Expostulating on utility, or the Greatest Happiness principle, he argued, against Bentham, that the pursuit of happiness entails some discrimination among pleasures, since those who have experienced higher intellectual and moral pleasures can ascertain their superiority as sources of happiness over the lower pleasures. This also leads to Mill's version of the Postulate of Natural Individual Morality: nobility of character and well-cultivated faculties come about through the individual's natural pursuit of pleasure, since selfishness and mental indolence are prime causes of unhappiness in human life. Extending his advocacy of individual well-being into the political domain, Mill defends the maximum extension of personal liberty, not just on the Smithian grounds that it promotes the economy or the Shaftesburyan grounds that it promotes human progress, but also on grounds that freedom to express one's own opinion and to select one's own plan of life promotes individual well-being.

The product of two centuries of transgenerational dialogue in England and Scotland, the utilitarian philosophy issued in two major streams that contributed to the constitution of modern social science. Their foundational texts were the work, respectively, of the preeminent neoclassical economist Alfred Marshall and of Herbert Spencer, arguably the greatest English sociologist.

Although Spencer is known as an early spokesman for the theory of evolution and conceived his sociological work as an application of cosmic evolutionary principles, he viewed his project mainly as a way to provide a rational foundation for ethics at a time when traditional religious bases for ethics no longer commanded adequate support.[14] A decade before Mill published the essays on liberty and utilitarianism, Spencer's first major work, *Social Statics,* adumbrated such an ethical code (albeit still in a deistic idiom). Certain points, however, raise questions as to whether Spencer's ideas still fit the postulates of atomic naturalism identified among the utilitarian philosophers. Spencer not only faults utilitarian philosophy for illogically presupposing that everybody has an equal right to happiness, he proceeds by attacking the assumption of a universal human nature held by his British predecessors. Since the primary ontic reality is flux rather than constancy, since nature in its infinite complexity is ever changing, it is absurd to maintain than human nature is uniform and to use its putatively constant properties as a basis for projecting a moral code. Nothing is more evident than "that mankind vary indefinitely, in instincts, in morals, in opinions, in tastes, in rationality, in everything" ([1850] 1972, 7).

Such comments appear to have led some readers to infer that Spencer was a foe of utilitarianism. Piqued by such readings, Spencer told his friend J. S. Mill that he objected to being considered an opponent of utilitarianism, and that in fact he did regard happiness as the ultimate end of morality (Mill [1861] 1969, 258). Indeed, this belief could not be more clearly expressed than in passages where Spencer affirms happiness as the final goal of all human striving, from which he deduces his first principle of ethics: since happiness consists in the exercise of all human faculties and since the complete exercise of those faculties requires liberty, therefore "every man may claim the fullest liberty to exercise his faculties compatible with the possession of like liberty by every other

14. In his preface to the first volume of *The Principles of Ethics* in 1879, Spencer wrote that from the time of his first publication in 1842, "my ultimate purpose, lying behind all proximate purposes, has been that of finding for the principles of right and wrong in conduct at large, a scientific basis. Now that the moral injunctions are losing the authority given by their supposed sacred origin, the secularization of morals is becoming imperative. Few things can happen more disastrous than the decay and death of a regulative system no longer fit, before another and fitter regulative system has grown up to replace it" (v–vi).

man" ([1850] 1972, 16). With this argument, Spencer joined the two planks associated with the mature position of normative individualism, the principles of utility and of liberty. But he also went on to introduce a new way of considering those principles by linking them with the dynamics of social evolution.

Besides the variability he insists upon, Spencer finds a universal constant at work in the various adaptations humans have made to different living conditions: the propensity to adapt oneself toward fitness for surrounding circumstances. With this in mind Spencer sketches a longterm evolution of human character, from an earlier stage marked by repressive political institutions oriented toward warfare to a modern civilized stage in which industry and commerce get pursued largely through voluntary associations. Adaptive fitness to the former state entails an egoistic kind of character, which gets socialized through repressive social institutions; in industrial societies, repressions get lifted as moral controls become internalized and human character becomes essentially altruistic. The evidence for this includes such distinctive modern tendencies as the growth of charitable societies, opposition to capital punishment, funds for emigrants, the milder treatment of children, even societies to prevent cruelty to animals.[15] In this evolutionary perspective, Spencer preserves the principles of individual happiness and liberty by translating them from criteria appropriate to a universally constant human nature to the climactic ends of a progressive humanity. In his hands, natural science has produced a social ethic by supplying the biological criterion of "non-adaptation of constitution to conditions" (8) as the root of all evil and by discovering the law governing the evolution of human character toward a state of perfect morality.

Even if Spencer has thereby reconciled the Postulate of Normative Individualism with a perspective of historical evolution, another of his theoretical innovations would seem to threaten the other main assumption of the British tradition, that of methodological individualism. For

15. Awareness of these tendencies did not prevent Spencer from commenting on the gross sins of his time, including "the felonies that fill our prisons, the trickeries of trade, the quarrelings of nation with nation, and of class with class," etc. He simply cited these as instances of the failure of humans to complete their process of adaptation to the social state. He also spoke of regressions into barbarism when people partially adapted to the social state get placed in circumstances that call forth their old propensities. In later decades, when international developments seemed more ominous, he predicted that "there is a bad time coming, and civilized mankind will morally be uncivilized before civilization can again advance" (1972, 19–20, xxxvii).

Spencer's sociology took from biology not only the notion of evolutionary change but also the model of the organism. In a turnabout from Bentham's dismissal of the body politic metaphor as misleading poetry, Spencer argued not just that society is like a biological organism but that society really *is* an organism. Using this notion, he introduced into sociological theory the germinal concepts of social structure, societal function, and systemic equilibrium that would later figure as bastions against the claims of methodological individualism.

Here again, Spencer's roots in British thought reached too deep for him to abandon its individualistic premises. In lines that could have come from Ferguson or Smith, Spencer maintained that the complex structure of modern industrial organization arose "under the pressure of human wants and activities [w]hile each citizen has been pursuing his individual welfare, and none taking thought about division of labour." The study of sociology would best proceed by realizing that in society as elsewhere "the properties of the units determine the properties of the whole they make up" and so it is to the intellectual and emotional qualities of individuals one must look in order to explain the extent to which persons even cohere in social aggregates (1972, 54, 97–99).

Bringing together the assumptions of methodological and normative individualism, then, Spencer voices his enduring conviction, already in the first defense of his proposal to view societies as essentially parallel to biological organisms, that societies also differ seriously from organisms inasmuch as it is their constituent units, not the corporate body, that maintain consciousness. He shrank from drawing the analogy between animal brains and society's central regulative organs; there is no "social sensorium," he would put it later. So "this is an everlasting reason why the welfare of citizens cannot rightly be sacrificed to some supposed benefit of the State; but why, on the other hand, the State is to be maintained solely for the benefit of citizens" ([1860] 1972, 60).

If Spencer emphasized the part of the Hobbesian program that treated social phenomena as compounds built from natural individual processes, Marshall's work represents a culmination of work directed to abstracting some of those processes and rendering them in mathematical form. Hobbes introduced a strain toward mensurability in the British tradition with his rules for comparing the magnitudes of different goods:

> If good and evil be compared, other things being equal, the greater is that which lasts longer, as the whole is to the part. And, other things being equal, that which is stronger, for the same reason. For larger and smaller

differ as greater and less. And, other things being equal, what is good for more is greater than what is good for fewer. For the more general and the more particular differ as greater and less. ([1642] 1972, 53)

Hutcheson followed suit, not only with his Greatest Happiness formula, but with a chapter of rules for computing the virtuous quality of actions and of the affections that motivate them.[16] Later writers directed such moral arithmetic less to the assessment of virtues and more to the raw matter of pleasures and pains. By the nineteenth century the passion for metric precision was aimed almost exclusively at egoistic motivations. Bentham remarked that the individual's passion for pecuniary gain was the one most given to calculation. Halévy takes this to signify that Bentham's wish to establish morals as an exact science led him to isolate in the human soul that feeling which seems to be the most easily measurable and, consequently, in his search for finely calibrated legal sanctions, to focus on egoism as the predominating influence on human actions. This is why, he observes, "political economy, the 'dogmatics of egoism,' is perhaps the most famous of the applications of the principle of utility" (Halévy [1901–4] 1966, 15).

For someone so astute as J. S. Mill, this assumption of pecuniary egoism was justifiable if understood only as a convenient abstraction that made it possible for economists to examine a neatly investigable slice of human life.[17] As the century wore on, some economists moved

16. For example: "Where kind affections alone are the springs of action, the good effected by any agent is as the strength of these affections and his ability jointly. The strength of affection therefore is directly as the good effected, and inversely as the abilities; or, in plainer terms, when the good done by two persons is equal, while their abilities are unequal, he shows the better heart, whose abilities are smaller. . . .

"Now a temper is certainly so much the better, the more susceptible it is of all sweet affections upon smaller causes, especially those of the generous kind, provided it entertains proportionally warmer affections where greater causes appear. . . .

"Prospects of private advantage then only abate the moral beauty of an action, when 'tis known by the agent, or justly presumed by others, that without this selfish motive the agent would not have done so much good." (1755, 238, 244, 246).

17. "Political Economy. . . concerns itself only with such of the phenomena of the social state as take place in consequence of the pursuit of wealth. It makes entire abstraction of every other human passion or motive, except those which may be regarded as perpetually antagonising principles to the desire of wealth, namely, aversion to labour, and desire of the present enjoyment of costly indulgences. . . . The science then proceeds to investigate the laws which govern these several operations, under the supposition that man is a being who is determined, by the necessity of his nature, to prefer a greater portion of wealth to a small in all cases, without any other exception than that constituted by the two counter-motives already specified; not that any political economist was ever so absurd as to suppose that mankind are really thus constituted, but be-

by the strain toward mensurability tended to lose track of the empirical contexts of their formulations. The Oxford economist F. Y. Edgeworth wrote *Mathematical Psychics* (1881) to celebrate the possibility of translating the hedonic quanta of utilitarian ethics into the language of mathematics. Stanley Jevons at Manchester described the struggle for existence in Benthamite terms as a "calculus of pleasure and pain," and his theory of economics as purely mathematical in character; he "turned out of his focus every aspect of economic life which was not reducible to the jigsaw precision of his scheme" (Heilbroner 1961, 149). Jevons turned his mathematizing penchant toward innovative techniques of constructing price index numbers, but also toward a novel manner of representing value. The first Englishman to write about marginal utility theory—which holds that, for purposes of price determination, the utility (use value) of every unit of a given commodity equals the value of its least important or "last" unit use—he proceeded to deduce the utility-maximizing allocation formula for the consumer, the foundational notion for subsequent neoclassical theorizing.[18]

In contrast to Jevons, whose work met little acceptance during his lifetime, Alfred Marshall won acclaim as the foremost economist of his time. The first few decades of twenties-century economics have been described as the "age of Marshall" and later developments glossed as extensions and countermovements to his influence (Corry 1968, 25). Before Jevons and others published their work on marginal utility theory, Marshall was expounding comparable ideas in lectures at Cambridge; his written presentation of these ideas appeared only in the *Principles of Economics* in 1890, in which he straightened out some inconsistencies in Jevons's theory of value.

In that monumental textbook Marshall included a section on the growth of economic science. Its key names are figures from the British tradition: Smith, Bentham, Ricardo, Mill, and Jevons. Marshall considers economists from other countries only briefly and then as "followers and . . . critics" of British economists. While expressing high regard, in particular, for the historical scholarship and social zeal of

---

cause this is the mode in which science must necessarily proceed." ([1843; 8th ed. 1872] 1987, 90)

18. Other pioneers of marginal utility value theory included Carl Menger of Austria and Léon Walras of France, whose contributions Jevons acknowledged in a masterly survey of the field in a preface to the second edition of his *Theory of Political Economy* in 1879.

German scholars, he concludes with a cautionary note that recalls the moral of his story: broad learning and reforming enthusiasm should not be allowed to weaken what, appealing to Spencerian biological imagery, he calls "a firm backbone of careful reasoning and analysis" ([1890; 8th ed. 1920] 1930, 769).

The firm backbone of British social science stemmed from efforts to imitate the metric precision and logical rigor of physics. Marshall maintained that economics does its work by establishing accurate measures of human satisfaction. Utility is correlative to desires, which cannot be measured directly, only indirectly by the outward phenomena to which they give rise. For economics, the measure is to be found in the price a person is willing to pay for the satisfaction of his desire. And so, "although it is true that 'money' or 'general purchasing power' . . . is the centre around which economic science clusters; this is so, not because money or material wealth is regarded as the main aim of human effort . . . but because in this world of ours *it is the one convenient means of measuring human motive on a large scale*" (22; emphasis mine). Although measuring motives this way is not perfectly accurate—if it were, "economics would rank with the most advanced of the physical sciences and not, as it actually does, with the least advanced"—still the measurement is close enough to let experienced persons make fairly good predictions (26).

Even so, Marshall repudiated the tendency to let the development of economics be driven by mathematical manipulations. He insisted on connecting the abstractions of his discipline with empirical realities, and minimized his formal use of mathematics—in any event questioning whether much has been gained from using complex mathematical formulae (84)—out of a fear that equations omit or distort too many factors. Above all, he emphasized the ethical mission of the discipline. For example, he considered the eradication of poverty its central moral responsibility. A major reason he developed utility theory was to create powerful tools for welfare economics, and although his welfare economics supported the classical view that a regime of free markets maximizes welfare, he modified that doctrine to admit the point that redistributing income from rich to poor would increase total satisfaction. Asserting that the economist like every one else must concern himself with the ultimate aims of man, at one point he declared that the supreme aim of the economist was to discover how the capacity for unselfish service can be developed most effectively (9). Elsewhere he celebrated the energetic exercise of human faculties as the very aim of life itself (cited in Parsons [1937] 1968, 141). Indeed, throughout his work

Marshall stressed the importance of the system of "free industry and enterprise" for the cultivation of the higher human virtues, as Parsons so trenchantly made clear.

Marshall's science of human action clearly exhibits all three postulates of atomic naturalism. It represents social phenomena as aggregations of measurable individual wants and defines collective achievements as the outcomes of individual energies. It employs normative criteria based on a calculation of what promotes the maximal satisfaction of those wants. And in its analysis of human virtue it exhibits the Postulate of Natural Individual Morality, finding ideal character traits like entrepreneurial energy and honest industry to be an outgrowth of activities pursued both from a wish to satisfy those wants and from a natural desire to excel in the exercise of one's faculties.

## THE BRITISH LEGACY

The British social theorists listed in Figure 6 form an unbroken transgenerational conversation that spans two and a half centuries. Its participants held widely divergent political ideologies, from the centralism of Hobbes to the libertarianism of Spencer, from the radicalism of Bentham to the cautiousness of Marshall. They pursued a wide range of substantive interests: far from attending to the problem of civil order like Hobbes, as Parsons's account of utilitarianism suggests, the others focused on such diverse problems as increased commerce (Mandeville), human psychology (Hume), living standards (Smith), legal reform (Bentham), population pressure on resources (Malthus), distribution of wealth (Ricardo), and the enhancement of liberty (Mill and Spencer). Far from subscribing to a common model of action—a model that depicts actors as oriented toward the instrumentally rational pursuit of selfish interests, as Parsons argued—some of them, like Hobbes and Hume, stressed the primacy of the emotions while others, like Bentham and Jevons, emphasized man's calculating powers, and still others, like Smith and Mill, treated rational and affective dispositions with equal seriousness. They included many, like Shaftesbury, Hutcheson, Smith, and Mill, who celebrated the power of social sentiments and of moral ideals, as well as Hobbes, Mandeville, and Bentham, who highlighted human egoism, and Spencer, who supposed an evolution of human character from egoism to sociality.[19] On the face

19. Camic (1979) notably advanced this critique of Parsons on the utilitarian tradition.

of it, British moral philosophy consists of one long string of disputations. What could be more biting than Mandeville's attack on Shaftesbury, more robust than Hutcheson's rebuttal of Mandeville, or more edifying than John Stuart Mill's respectful but devastating critique of Bentham?

Yet all these thinkers were united behind the quest for a humane secular ethic. Such an ethic would express the more pervasive values of British culture, in which the touchstone of morality was maximizing individual satisfactions. They were also united behind the ideal of using the new atomic view of nature and the methods for its study professed by modern physics as a launching pad in that quest. Just as Hobbes took inspiration for his new science from Galilean physics, so his successors were inspired by Sir Isaac Newton. At the close of his *Optiks*, Newton wrote: "If natural Philosophy in all its Parts, by pursuing this [analytic] Method, shall at length by perfected, the Bound of Moral Philosophy will be also enlarged" ([1730] 1979, 405). The temptation to heed this challenge and become the Newton of the moral sciences was irresistible for generations of British thinkers. Since Newton's ideas were taught in Scotland before it became permissible to teach him in England, the challenge was taken up first in Glasgow and Edinburgh. After men like Hutcheson, Hume, Smith, and Ferguson had tried their hand at it, Englishmen like Bentham and Mill retrieved the project, and Spencer essayed a single field theory for the entire universe.[20]

So considered, Hobbes's successors remained true to his program of grounding normative and empirical analyses on the natural properties of individuals. Except for Mandeville, they all proppounded a worldview that both endorsed dispositions needed for commercial-industrial society and championed virtues of character. Writers like Ferguson, J. S. Mill, Spencer, and Marshall even managed to restore one feature of the Aristotelian philosophy that Hobbes ignored and more narrowly hedonic philosophers like Bentham appeared to exclude: the assumption that cultivating higher human virtues is essential to happiness. The British celebration of individual efforts also produced numerous incisive analyses of complex societal formations as the unintended consequences of spontaneous individual actions. The foundational statements for modern sociology thus included principles of atomic

---

20. One of Spencer's contemporaries likened his sociological writing to Newton's *Principia,* and predicted that, as with the earlier opposition to Newton's law of gravitation, resistance to Spencer's ideas would fade within a generation (Spence 1897, 27).

naturalism so reworked that they could enter the mainstream of twentieth-centruy sociology, as we shall see below.

Viewed from a distance, then, the noisy disputes of the British tradition consist of nothing so much as a continuous set of variations on themes enunciated by Hobbes. Yet those themes also constituted a refrain to be challenged, no less recurrently, by participants in the transnational dialogue from France and Germany.

# CHAPTER EIGHT

# The French Tradition

**W**ritings of the British moral philosophers were well known to intellectuals in France and in Germany during the eighteenth century. Voltaire did much to popularize Newton and Locke. Diderot translated Shaftesbury. Condillac worked with Locke's epistemological notions, as Condorcet did with Hume's. Quesnay followed Locke and Hume in propounding the principles of individualistic capitalism based on natural laws. Helvétius served as the conduit through which the utilitarian notions of Hume reached Bentham. Kant has been credited for being one of the few contemporary readers of Hume's *Treatise of Human Nature* to have understood it fully; he lavished praise on Shaftesbury and Hutcheson as well as Hume. Herder waxed ecstatic over Shaftesbury. Yet in neither country did the atomic naturalism of the British philosophers take root in ways that would orient sociology along lines they had projected. Instead, their ideas came to serve as foils against which French and German philosophers would react and move in radically different directions for grounding a social ethic and modern sociological thought.

## MONTESQUIEU AND ROUSSEAU

The great theme French thinkers would oppose to the British idealization of natural individuals was the ideal of society. The Baron de Montesquieu can rightly be taken as progenitor of this theme in French thought. Later theorists in the tradition—Rousseau, Comte, Durkheim—would name him as the seminal inspiration for the modern science of society.[1] Montesquieu, too, promoted the notion that by himself he had fathered something original, referring to his masterwork

---

1. Rousseau referred to Montesquieu as "the one man of modern times who was capable of calling this great [social] science into being" ([1762] 1979, 458). Comte observed that "Montesquieu must have the credit of the earliest direct attempt to treat politics as a science of facts" ([1822] 1974, 157). Durkheim averred that Montesquieu made "our science" aware of its subject matter, its nature and method, and laid its groundwork (1960, 2).

*De l'esprit des lois* (1748) as *prolem sine matre creatam,* an offspring created without a mother (Lepenies 1988, 1).

Montesquieu challenged Hobbes on every major point of his doctrine. Since humans are always born into a society and never encountered outside of society, he argued, it is meaningless to talk about the origin of society and government, as Hobbes had done, by analyzing the raw dispositions of individual actors. Moreover, self-interest cannot be a sufficient basis for human institutions, so the possibility of good government depends on moral socialization and the inculcation of civic virtues. Finally, there can be no universal touchstone for morality; rather, what is morally appropriate must depend on a society's particular circumstances—its physical milieu, its customs, its ideas about life, its informing spirit.

Although Montesquieu became known as a follower of Locke and a champion of "English" notions like liberty, toleration, and constitutional government, his treatment of those notions rested on distinctive positions.[2] Thus, freedom does not stand as an absolute value derivable from the properties of human nature and related human rights. Rather, freedom is a social fact: it depends on favorable environmental conditions and social customs, and manifests itself as a right to do only whatever the laws permit. And social dispositions do not stem, as British critics of Hobbes and Mandeville would argue, from naturally given social sentiments and moral sensibilities, but from socially instilled attitudes, beliefs, and habits.

One can thus find in Montesquieu's writings, albeit expressed in a literary mode and often analytically imprecise manner, the core notions of the French tradition, which subsequent thinkers in that tradition would develop more pointedly. We can usefully formulate the positions in question by contrasting them with the postulates of the British tradition outlined above. To the question of how the facts of human experience are to be constructed and explained, Montesquieu adumbrates what may be called the **Postulate of Societal Realism:** *Society is a supraindividual phenomenon with determinate properties not reducible to individual propensities.*

---

2. Montesquieu's attachment to the ideal of liberty only came after his visit to England in the years 1729–31. Earlier, expressing sentiments Comte would echo a century later, he had belittled the advantages that free peoples hold over others and showed disdain for popular disputations and the fashionable infatuation with freedom of speech (Shackelton 1961, 284).

To the question of how secular thought can provide a rational grounding of moral judgments, Montesquieu adumbrates what may be called the **Postulate of Societal Normativity:** *Normative judgments are best grounded rationally by determining what enhances societal well-being.* This can be known through the investigations of intellectual experts, so practical wisdom amounts to the application of theoretical knowledge about society to moral questions.

To the question about the source of human moral dispositions, Montesquieu responds with what may be called the **Postulate of Societal Morality:** *Society is the source of moral sentiments and habits, which it instills through institutions like the family, education, religion, and government.*

Jean-Jacques Rousseau has been described as "the first great thinker to pass under the spell of Montesquieu" (Peyre 1960, xv). However, if subsequent writings in the French tradition are to be viewed as a more or less continuous refinement of Montesquieu's social thought, then to some extent Rousseau must be seen as an aberration or retrogression. That was how Comte viewed him. For Rousseau reverted to the Hobbesian way of beginning the quest for a social ethic by speculating on how humans live in an imagined state of nature anterior to forming a social order.

For Rousseau, as for Hobbes, society is *not* a natural entity. But in contrast to Hobbes, Rousseau's *homo* in the state of nature is a benign, self-sufficient creature who can survive very well without civil society. Few writers in the Western tradition can match the sincerity and depth with which Rousseau depicts the "natural goodness" of man (Melzer 1990). Nevertheless, Rousseau's natural man does not possess a *moral* sense. Both morality and reason can develop only in and through society. Accepting Montesquieu's argument that humans require moral socialization in order to live together sociably, Rousseau grounds that argument on a priori speculation rather than on appeals to observed societies.

In his famous essay on the social contract, Rousseau draws a number of distinctions between the properties of human life in the state of nature and in civil society. In chapter 8 of book 1, "On the Civil State," Rousseau lists a number of changes in the human condition that come about when people pass from the natural state into the civil state. Humans in the state of nature are marked by instinct, physical impulse, inclination, stupidity, and animality, whereas in civil society these traits are replaced, respectively, by justice, morality and duty, reason, intelligence, and full humanity. Man's natural condition exhibits liberty limited solely by force, and slavery to the appetites, whereas in the social state humans acquire civil liberty, which is limited by the general will, and moral liberty in which they enjoy self-mastery by virtue of obeying laws they themselves collectively legislate. What is more, in nature possessions are secured by force, in civil society through ownership of a positive title. In his chapter "On the Legislature" in book 2, Rousseau adds that the establishment of society under laws transforms each individual from being self-sufficient, solitary, and independent into a dependent yet integrated and moral being.

*Reculer pour mieux sauter.* If from the point of view of developing positive sociology Rousseau has regressed into pure speculation about the human condition in an assumed state of nature, he has withal provided an unprecedentedly precise analysis of the societal component of human functioning. In doing this he sharpened Montesquieu's key pronouncements about the nature of society.[3] For one thing, Rousseau refined Montesquieu's notion of a society's general spirit (*esprit général*) by developing the idea of a general will (*volonté générale*), which enabled him to draw a distinction between 'aggregation' and 'association,' and to describe the general will as sui generis and not derivable from aggregating private wills (*volonté de tous*). He formulated the theorem of emergent levels, which later French writers would employ repeatedly, defining society as "a moral entity having specific qualities distinct from those of the individual beings which compose it, somewhat as chemical compounds have properties that they owe to none of their elements" (cited in Durkheim [1892] 1960, 82).

Second, Rousseau articulated the principles of the existential and normative primacy of the collective will. Montesquieu held that laws are based on customs and manners, political structures on climate and societal conditions. Rousseau translates this into the proposition that government functions as an agent of society, commissioned to do the bidding of the will of the people. And he affirms the moral superiority of the collective body over individual interests by calling the intrusion of private interests into public affairs "evil," and asserting that "whatever breaks up social unity is worthless" ([1762] 1987, 55, 99).

---

3. Rousseau himself implied that part of his mission was to sharpen some of Montesquieu's formulations, when he observed of the latter that "this great genius often lacked precision and sometimes clarity" ([1762] 1987, 56).

In spite of Rousseau's idealized view of the human condition in a state of nature, his quest for a social ethic thus culminates in a conception of *societal well-being as the preeminent value*. He declares the social order to be a "sacred right that serves as a foundation for all other rights." He proposes to diagnose the "health of the body politic" by assessing the extent to which public opinions are harmonized and private interests are subordinated to the public interest. Another diagnostic criterion is the extent to which a state's citizens become populous and multiply, so he includes "count, measure, compare" in his advice to future social scientists looking for an objective indicator of societal health (17, 81, 67).

## FRENCH CRITICS OF ROUSSEAU

At first the ideas of Montesquieu and Rousseau did more to shape political ideologies than to build a social science. Montesquieu's linkage of checks and balances with political democracy guided the framers of the United States constitution, while Rousseau's *volonté générale* inspired the makers of the French Revolution.[4] Before Durkheim could redefine them as ancestors of French sociology, the tradition would have to be thickened.

Just as in Britain the postulates of atomic naturalism accommodated widely diverse views about human nature, so in France the postulates of what I shall call societal essentialism went along with views of man that diverged sharply from those of Rousseau. In the wake of the French Revolution such views burst forth in writers who took issue with Rousseauan assumptions and the revolutionary doctrines associated with them. These writers tapped a deeper vein of thought in the French tradition in which man was viewed as an essentially weak and sinful creature. Montaigne in his *Essays* (1580) and La Rochefoucauld in his *Maxims* (1665) had painted man as essentially vain, stupid, self-deceiving, and vicious—reflecting strands of Augustinian moral thought embedded in the Catholic tradition. The preeminent post-revolutionary writers in this vein, Louis de Bonald and Joseph de Maistre, reaffirmed the role of Catholicism in counteracting essential human immorality. Bonald attacked Rousseau's starting point of the

4. Prerevolutionary pamphleteers like the Abbé Sieyès, National Assembly delegates deliberating on the rights of man, and engineers of the Terror alike espoused simplified versions of Rousseau's teachings. For a superb review of recent literature anent the long-debated question of Rousseau's influence on the Revolution, see Starobinski 1990.

self-sufficient individual by arguing that only society and its traditions, anchored in language, can give individual life any reality; to regain social health, postrevolutionary France would have to return to a unified political system (monarchy) and a single set of religious beliefs (Roman Catholicism). Describing himself as a spiritual twin of Bonald, Maistre actually pushed this line of thought to ferocious extremes. Maistre dwelt on the incurably wicked and corrupt nature of man, which made absolute authority indispensable. He ridiculed contractarian views, which assume that individuals know what they want. For Maistre, humans not only have no clear sense of what they want; they are propelled by unlimited strivings and irrationally destructive and self-immolative urges. What is more, individuals cannot articulate their needs before entering society, for the very language they need to do so comes from society. Similarly, contracts presuppose an elaborate network of social conventions and a complex social apparatus of enforcement. Society is as ancient as man, and adequate human functioning requires the fusion of the individual in a society that is sustained by a common religion and coercive authority. Individualist strivings to pursue imagined rights or needs can only atomize the social tissue.

For his radical opposition to social contract theories, in relation to Rouessau Maistre has long seemed like nothing but an antagonist. Indeed, Maistre derides Rousseau's concept of the legislator as intolerably confused, rebuts his conception of law, ridicules his belief in the sovereignty of the people, and calls his maxim that man was born free a "foolish assertion" (1971, 101, 120, 123, 143). In the words of his prime British translator, "Maistre saw Rousseau as one of the arch-villains of his century of villains" (Lively 1971, 44). Nevertheless, these robust differences arise on top of a foundation of common understandings. As that same commentator goes on to observe:

> Yet . . . Maistre shares many basic assumptions and emotional attitudes with Rousseau. . . . His ultimate object, like Rousseau's, was to resolve the conflict between man's self-will and his social nature, to release the capacity for virtue frustrated by existing civilization, to reestablish a state of harmony lost through the persistent exercise of self-will. . . . [This] required the willing subordination of men to authorities whose moral justification consisted, in the last resort, not in what they aimed at, but in the unity they enforced. . . . Both were more anxious abut the moral quality of communal life than about the source of sovereignty, and both judged that moral quality by the degree of emotional, unreasoned involvement in the community felt by the individual. (Lively 1971, 44, 42)

Whereas Maistre like Rousseau took a dim view of the prospects of modern society—Maistre posed as the last defender of a high civilization about to perish while Rousseau revered Geneva as one of the last embers of freedom in a darkening world—other critics of Rousseau took a more positive view of the prospects of humanity in the age of reason and science. These included the Marquis de Condorcet, an exemplary philosophe who played a prominent role in the Legislative Assembly of the Revolution. Following his denunciation by Jacobins in 1793, Condorcet fled into hiding in Paris, where he capped a lifetime of struggle to erect a precise social science with an ebullient sketch of mankind's future. That *Esquisse,* often regarded as the philosophical testament of the eighteenth century—bequeathing to the nineteenth century its animating notion, the idea of progress—celebrates the progressive liberation of humans from the scourges of nature and social bondage through the unfolding of human capacities to observe accurately and reason soundly.

Through schemes of public education and a journal coedited with Abbé Sièyes as well as his own publications, Condorcet had devoted his life to promoting the application of scientific method to human phenomena—most notably, the procedures of mathematics, including a calculus of probabilities. Condorcet embraced Rousseau's notion that individuals should submit their actions to the decisions of the general will, and like Rousseau sought a way to institute a system that would rationalize collective decision making for the public good. However, he departed from Rousseau's model of radical democracy, both by arguing for the legitimacy and indispensability of representative institutions and by defending the need for qualified elites to produce rational public decisions. These departures reflected his view of the general will as a vehicle for expressing the truth discoverable by reason rather than as an expression of moral right based on collective will (Baker 1975, 229–31, 243). More generally, he departed from Rousseau in affirming the value of reason and its progressive cultivation as a liberating force in human history. Condorcet hailed the emergence of "social mathematics" as a critical factor in the progress of humanity.

Henri de Saint-Simon, a marginal supporter of the Revolution, admired both Condorcet and Maistre. He shared the humanitarian rationalism of the philosophes—their espousal of scientific progress and their attacks on religious dogmas for suppressing the masses. At the same time he rejected their wholesale critique of medieval political and religious institutions. Siding on this matter with Maistre, who in turn evoked Rousseau and Montesquieu, Saint-Simon held that some sort of common faith was essential to sustain social solidarity and that moral beliefs had to be in accord with societal conditions. Thus, while harsh on past ecclesiastical abuses—he indicted as "heretical" all popes and cardinals since the fifteenth century for supporting the Jesuit order and the Inquisition, and condemned Protestants for their allegedly inferior morality, faulty forms of worship, and false creed—Saint-Simon affirmed the positive role of the medieval Church in promoting political unity and intellectual and social vitality.[5]

Proceeding from convictions about the need for social harmony, the role of ideas in promoting it, and the superiority of science and industry over theology and militarism, Saint-Simon evolved a vision of the good society that inspired generations of his countrymen. Like most Enlightenment thinkers his social ethic rested on the conviction that the good society must be in accord with what is natural in human life. From physiology, he derived the notion that this entailed a society based not on the principle of equality but on the natural inequalities of people.[6] The way he divided up different human capacities changed. What endured was his belief in the need for social elites and for sincere deference to citizens with superior qualifications—thanks to which the society of the future would be free of class conflicts and would sanction a greatly reduced role for coercive authority and governmental action. In the feudal order these superior strata took the form of religious and military elites; in the modern era those would be replaced—gradually, to avoid the horrors of revolution and sudden change—by men of science and leaders of industry.

Given how much credibility the theologians had lost in the eighteenth century, it was important now for savants to provide a new social bond. They could do so following the trajectory of intellectual development along which each of the natural sciences had progressed, from a

5. These indictments actually appear in Saint-Simon's final work, *New Christianity*, where he broke with his earlier rationalism to affirm the revealed character of Christianity and announced that, in "fulfilling a divine mission [to recall] nations and kings to the true spirit of Christianity," the voice of God was now speaking through his mouth ([1825] 1952, 114–16).

6. Saint-Simon adapted Bonald's and Maistre's thesis that at bottom humans desire not to achieve equality with those of higher status but to express themselves in roles they were born into; in other words, people naturally desire to express their intrinsic physiological aptitudes. These aptitudes included different functional capacities—divided among knowing, willing, and feeling—as well as different levels of ability (Manuel 1962, 126–27).

conjectural to a positive, or empirically grounded, basis of reasoning. Saint-Simon reproached scientists for losing themselves in mindless accumulation of isolated facts and urged them to create a general theory that could unify all scientific knowledge. Indeed, Saint-Simon became impatient with any scientific work that was not immediately directed to practical objectives, one of the grounds of his later rupture with Comte.[7] Concurring with Bonald on the importance of "systematic unity," he rejected Bonald's proposal that it be based on the concept of deism in favor of the concept of universal gravitation (1952, 18).

Following Saint-Simon's death in 1826 his chief disciples declared that the task of the future consisted in reconciling the ideas of Maistre with those of Enlightenment rationalists like Voltaire and Condorcet (Berlin 1990, 62). This task their leader had of course already initiated. He had resolved the opposition between Maistre's claim of the human need for hierarchy and the philosophes' rejection of old privileges by positing a need for new elites based on scientific and industrial capabilities. He had reconciled Maistre's respect for historical context and the philosophes' belief in progress by viewing the work of earlier periods as historically appropriate contributions to the long-term development of humanity. Yet his last-minute reversion to revealed religion doubtless made some followers believe he finally reneged on the commitment to rationalism that led him earlier to describe deism as an outworn belief. This crucial reconciliation was to be achieved by Saint-Simon's young associate of seven years, Auguste Comte.

## SOCIETAL ESSENTIALISM

In chapter 2 I considered Comte's prehistory of sociology; it is time now to examine his social ethic and related sociological ideas. Those ideas took shape through a remarkable synthesis of diverse strands of the French tradition up to his time, as Figure 7 suggests. Comte drew significantly on Montesquieu, Turgot, Condorcet, Bonald, Maistre,

7. Saint-Simon promoted technological progress as well as expanded social organization. "The philosophy of the eighteenth century was critical and revolutionary, that of the nineteenth will be inventive and organizational" was the motto of an encyclopedia of scientific knowledge he envisioned. Saint-Simon's thinking inspired cadres of engineers, including the first men to work on the Suez Canal as well as advocates of a federated Europe. The editor of Saint-Simon's *Oeuvres Choisies,* Lemonnier, founded a League of Peace from which sprang the idea of the League of Nations (Saint-Simon [1952] 1964, xxi, xxxiii, xliii).

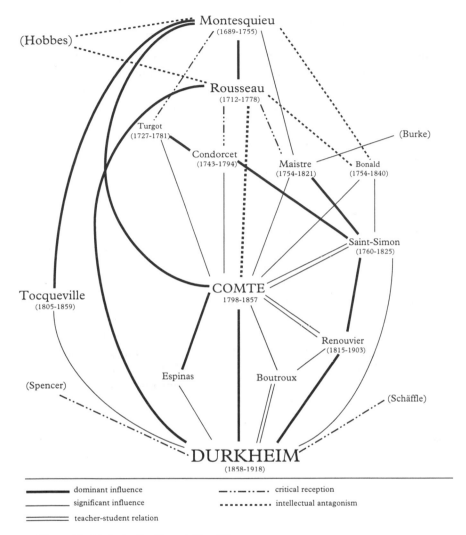

Figure 7. Links in the French Tradition

Saint-Simon—even Rousseau, possibly. From Montesquieu he took the aspiration to promulgate laws of societal functioning; from Turgot and Condorcet, the vision of human progress powered by the perfection of man's rational faculties; from Bonald and Maistre the importance of societal integration and moral regulation; and from Saint-Simon the conception of new forms of temporal and spiritual elites to replace the old.

One might conjecture that at some point he absorbed from Rousseau the theorem about emergent organizational levels. It appears that Comte did not get that idea from Saint-Simon. This is noteworthy, since Comte shared virtually every other major assumption with Saint-Simon. Indeed, except perhaps for Marx and Engels or Dewey and Mead, there has scarcely been any collaboration in the history of Western social theory so intimate as that between Saint-Simon and Comte.[8]

Saint-Simon recruited the impecunious nineteen-year-old Comte as his secretary in 1817, becoming his mentor and patron as well as employer. With Comte's aid he published a series of periodicals devoted to proclaiming the virtues of the coming industrial order. Although Comte gratefully absorbed much from his benefactor for some years, he began to chafe as the relationship wore on. The break came in 1824, over issues that were largely psychological, programmatic, and proprietary.[9] Yet there was one important substantive question on which they diverged, a divergence that came more sharply into focus as Comte forged his system of positive philosophy. Saint-Simon assumed the only truly certain knowledge was mathematical, an assumption Comte would criticize as "metaphysical." In that spirit Saint-Simon advocated a unified theory of all phenomena based on the law of gravity; Saint-Simon appealed to such a theory to ground his new religion for humanity, which he called "Physicism." Yet his problem—how to reconcile Condorcet's rationalism with Maistre's religionism—was not thereby solved. Universal gravitation scarcely provided an object capable of eliciting the sentiments of philanthropy that Saint-Simon required to animate his reorganized European society. This embarrassment comes poignantly to the fore in his 1808 essay on science when Saint-Simon, after invoking the concept of universal gravitation as lynchpin for the new scientific system "*and consequently for the new religious system,*" goes on to argue that the idea of God is defective and should not be used in

8. "During [Comte's] formative period it is no more possible to separate the proprietary rights of Saint-Simon or Comte from their common store of ideas than it would be to perform the same task for Marx and Engels" (Manuel 1962, 259).

9. Comte resented Saint-Simon's continued assumption of a tutelary position as he approached his mid-twenties. And Comte became disturbed by his aging master's mental condition—the intellectual stagnation, the apparent turn toward theology, the pathetic suicide attempt. The two also had different views about how to implement the positive program: Saint-Simon wanted to apply his epochal discoveries to contemporary affairs without delay, while Comte believed it necessary first to secure firmer intellectual foundations by completing the new synthesis of positive knowledge. Tensions came to a head in jurisdictional quarrels over the publication of Comte's seminal essay of 1822, "Plan of the Scientific Operations Necessary for Reorganizing Society," which incited Saint-Simon to cut him off.

the physical sciences. Then he adds, "but I do not say that it should not be used in political affairs, at least for a long time; it is the best means yet discovered for motivating high-minded legislative dispositions" (1859, 1:211, 219). The chasm between what Saint-Simon's political community needed in the way of common beliefs and what his physicalist science could produce was unbridgeable—so much so that he finally turned to a fervent theism to anchor his social faith.

One of Comte's main contributions to the running dialogue of the French tradition was to bridge that remaining chasm between Condorcet and Maistre—between the rational imperatives of modern science and the emotional imperatives of societal order. He did so by establishing a series of claims regarding the objects of scientific study and the intellectual procedures for studying them. Opposing Saint-Simon's quest for a universal science unified under physics, Comte held that the essence of positive science was its subordination of rational propositions to empirical facts, and that observations had to respect the distinctive features of different types of phenomena. Rather than essay something so "chimerical" as explaining all phenomena by a single law like the law of gravity, Comte made it the task of positive philosophy to coordinate *different* laws pertaining to different orders of phenomena.

The master thought of Comte's schematization of the sciences is this:

> All observable phenomena may be included within a very few natural categories, so arranged as that study of each category may be grounded on the principal laws of the preceding, and serve as the basis of the next ensuing. This order is determined by the degree of simplicity, or, what comes to the same thing, of generality of their phenomena. Hence results their successive dependence and the greater or lesser facility for being studied. (1974, 44)

Following this principle, Comte proceeds to divide all natural phenomena into two classes—inorganic and organic bodies. Inorganic bodies then get ordered, according to the principle of increasing complexity and decreasing generality, into celestial bodies, masses, and molecules—the subject matters, respectively, of astronomy, physics, and chemistry. Organic bodies similarly divide into individual organisms and species. The sciences that study any of these bodies become positive to the extent that they relinquish the futile search for ultimate causes, whether finding them in spirits or in abstract notions, and rely

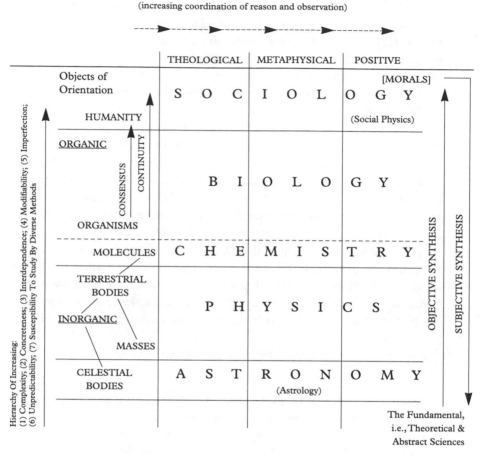

Figure 8. Comte's Theory of Knowledge

instead on the search for empirically ascertainable laws of coexistence and succession. Human knowledge approaches this positive condition one science at a time, beginning with the science of the most general and least complex of the phenomena, astronomy, and moving in order up the hierarchy, as in Figure 8.

Due to this uneven development of the sciences, there is a chronic tendency for proponents of well-established sciences to explain higher-order phenomena in the terms appropriate for lower ones: for mathematicians to absorb mechanics into calculus, for physicists to absorb chemical phenomena, for chemists to absorb biological into chemical terms, and, finally, for biologists to make sociology a mere corollary of their science. Comte called this tendency materialism; today we would more likely call it reductionism. Accordingly, each of the sciences has to undergo a long struggle against the encroachments of the one preceding it. The time had finally arrived for sociology to complete this struggle and reveal social phenomena as subjects to invariable natural laws not reducible to those of biology or any other simpler science. This meant that in addition to the inanimate and organismic phenomena, which for Saint-Simon exhausted the phenomenal universe,[10] there was yet another, more complex order of reality whose facticity could be established and whose properties, like those of other orders of phenomena, could not be reduced to those lower in the hierarchy of beings. That reality was society.

How did Comte's positive schematization of the sciences solve the Saint-Simonian question of faith? It did so in part by making the whole question of God's existence obsolete. Although atheism had been useful during the metaphysical period for removing the last vestiges of theological belief, now it prolongs the metaphysical stage by seeking new solutions of theological problems instead of setting them aside as utterly futile. Since humans can never penetrate the mystery of the essential cause that produces phenomena, the only meaningful type of knowledge to seek is that which establishes laws about the behavior of phenomena. Further, the negative spirit of atheism has greater affinity with anarchy than with union at a time when society needs to move toward an organic, solidary state.

Instead of belief in God, what can provide the cement for modern society is the idea of humanity. That idea represents no theological or metaphysical speculation, but a being whose properties can be determined. If its ultimate cause cannot be known, its reality can be demonstrated by the fact that it exhibits lawful regularities. Its reality thus justified, humanity can serve henceforth as an object for religious devotion in a positive polity. Comte's positive philosophy thus eliminates theology, as Voltaire and Condorcet wanted, but retains religion, as Bonald and Maistre wanted.

The Postulate of Societal Realism serves as the key building block for Comte's social science and his social ethic. Comte articulates it in its classic form, arguing that "society is no more decomposable into indi-

10. "There are no phenomena which are not either astronomical, chemical, physiological, or psychological" (Saint-Simon [1952] 1964, 21).

viduals than a geometric surface is into lines, or a line into points" ([1848–51] 1875, 2:181). The master concept of the science that studies this supraindividual phenomenon is *consensus,* defined as the interconnectedness of all parts of the social system. Comte took the concept of consensus from biology, but took pains to distinguish its manifestations in human society from those in biological organisms, since the former uniquely admits *historical* linkages, that is, the gradual and continuous influence of generations upon each other. With this notion in mind, Comte formulates the governing principle of social science as follows:

> Without extolling or condemning political facts, science regards them as subjects of observation: it contemplates each phenomenon in its harmony with coexisting phenomena, and its connection with the foregoing and the following state of human development; it endeavors to discover, from both points of view, the general relations that connect all social phenomena—and each of them is *explained,* in the scientific sense of the word, when it has been connected with the whole of the existing situation, and the whole of the preceding movement. (1974, 473)

Once the reality of society as a phenomenon subject to static and dynamic laws has been established, a remarkable transformation takes place in human thought—a transformation manifest in Comte's own transition as he moved from the *Course in Positive Philosophy* to the *System of Positive Polity.* The superiority of the theoretic function now gives way to the superiority of the practical.[11] "It is our business," Comte had advised, "to contemplate order, that we may perfect it (1974, 461)." The hierarchical arrangement of natural phenomena established through the objective method gives way to a new, inverted order-

---

11. From his first publications, Comte diverged from Saint-Simon by insisting on the distinction between theoretical knowledge and practical knowledge, and the need to constitute the latter as an application of the former. In the *Course,* Comte judged theoretical knowledge superior not only for providing a necessary foundation anterior to practical knowledge, but also regarding the dignity of its subject matter: "However great may be the services rendered to industry by science . . . we must never forget that the sciences have a higher destination still . . . that of satisfying the craving of our understanding to know the laws of phenomena. To feel how deep and urgent this need is, we have only to consider for a moment the physiological effects of *consternation,* and to remember that the most terrible sensation we are capable of is that which we experience when any phenomenon seems to arise in violation of the familiar laws of nature" (1974, 40). In the *Positive Polity,* he reversed this ranking, stressing the contribution of positive philosophy to practical life and submitting that "it leads at once to an object far higher than that of satisfying our scientific curiosity; the object, namely, of organising human life" ([1848–51] 1875, 1:46).

ing of phenomena based on what Comte calls the subjective method. This subjective synthesis begins with a new discipline now placed at the top of the old hierarchy, the science of morals. Morals provide systematic guidance for humans based first on attachment to the whole of humanity and to the progressive course of its development. These practical commitments henceforth direct the problems to which specialists in each of the sciences should devote their attention.

These notions indicate the way Comte links the Postulate of Societal Realism with the Postulate of Societal Normativity. Normative judgments are to be based on what enhances societal well-being, and that can be known through a science that determines the normal conditions of order and progress. This assumption, in turn, is linked with the Postulate of Societal Morality, in that the moral dispositions needed to secure social order have to be instilled by social institutions—most notably, the family, which cultivates the social affects of "attachment" and "veneration," and religion, which cultivates the love of humanity. In Comte's view, then, society is "essential" in three senses: the term refers to a real being with essential properties, it is required as an object of attachment in order to establish moral guidelines, and it is necessary for instilling the moral values needed to sustain the social order.

## THE FRENCH DISCIPLINE

Due to the eccentric cast of his religion of humanity and his odd personal and intellectual conduct, Comte was ridiculed and largely forgotten for decades after his death in 1857.[12] Yet half a century later his ideas had become enshrined in one of the most powerful bodies of thought to enter the foundations of modern social science, the sociology of Émile Durkheim. That is suggestive evidence of the tenacity of national traditions and their capacity to wash out idiosyncratic expressions.

Some of Comte's ideas reached Durkheim through Émile Boutroux, his teacher at the École Normale, who favored Comte's emphasis on the irreducibility of different levels of phenomenal reality, and through the widely influential writings of Charles Renouvier, one of Comte's students at the École Polytechnique, who inspired Durkheim with an

---

12. The comment by Hippolyte Taine, often alleged to be a follower of Comte, is typical: "[Comte's] mind seems in all respects to be absolute, exclusive, narrow, vigorously and irrevocably immersed in its own evolution, confined to limited horizons and to a single conception" (quoted in Simon 1963, 130).

uncompromising rationalism and a determination to submit the domain of morality to scientific study. Durkheim may also have been exposed to the activity of Comte's erstwhile disciple Émile Littré, who organized a sociology society while Durkheim was in secondary school. He was also exposed to Comtean ideas through German authors, especially Comte's erudite disciple Albert Schäffle. More directly consequential for his science of sociology was Alfred Espinas, an outspoken follower of Comte, whose dissertation on animal societies offered an exemplar for the naturalistic study of social organization. For considering social consciences "among the highest realities" and "society [as] a concrete living thing" (quoted in Deploige [1911] 1938, 125) and for studying social facts in order to construct a rigorous science of them, Durkheim felt that Espinas's book constituted the very first serious achievement of scientific sociology (Lukes 1972, 84). Espinas in turn was able to provide major support for Durkheim's sociological project by establishing the special chair, in pedagogy and social science, that brought Durkheim to Bordeaux in 1887.

Even so, Durkheim's absorption of Comtean notions reflected not just the continuing efforts of supporters to keep the master's vision alive, but also the resonance of Comtean themes with French intellectuals' widespread disposition to take literally the metaphor of society as a body. This, together with his sheer intellectual brilliance, helps account for the ascendancy of Durkheim and his school over intellectual competitors like Gabriel Tarde and René Worms, both of whom shared certain Comtean notions but rejected, on different grounds, the core concept of societal essentialism.[13] Although this disposition was fortified by reactions against the French Revolution, it had already appeared before the Revolution, as in Diderot's definition of morality as

13. Clark defends Tarde's own brilliance and the superiority of his positions over Durkheim's in many instances, but argues that his work suffered because it "was out of harmony with the dominant intellectual temper of the time" (1968, 508). Specifically, Clark makes reference to Tarde's values of spontaneity and disengagement, in contrast to Durkheim's Cartesian rationalism and engagement (1969, 7–18). But the central substantive divergence between the two hinged on the question of methodological individualism versus societal essentialism. It seems fair to say that Tarde's nominalism was out of harmony with Durkheim's milieu as well. While Tarde was fairly isolated socially, Worms, like Durkheim, was heavily involved in institutionalizing sociology by founding a journal, a social science library, a Paris society of sociology, and the Institut international de sociologie. However, Worms failed to galvanize an intellectual following, in good part because he abandoned Comte's tenet that society has sui generis properties that cannot be found at the organismic level of reality. On Comtean strains in Tarde and Worms, see Simon 1963; on the institutional ascendance of Durkheim, see Clark 1973.

that which is "conductive to the survival and cohesion of the body so-cial" (Proust 1962, 338). Foucault has expressed the matter vividly: for the fantasy of the king's body the French came to substitute "the idea of a social body constituted by the universality of wills . . . a social body which needs to be protected, in a quasi-medical sense" (1980, 55). Throughout the nineteenth century French of all ideological hues agreed in finding the social order threatened with dissolution by the noxious growth of individualism.[14] This concern for protecting the health of the French body social was intensified by the national demor-alization that set in following the defeat of France by Prussia in 1871.

Thus Durkheim's formative years were spent in an intellectual and political milieu that both encouraged him to cultivate the Comtean doctrines of societal essentialism and promised him a responsive ambi-ence for them if he did the job well. In any event, Durkheim's appro-priation of Comte turned into one of the most productive instances of dialogue in the history of Western social theory. For if it is true, as Evans-Pritchard once remarked, that "there is little of general meth-odological or theoretical significance in [Durkheim's] writings that we do not find in Comte if we are earnest and persevering enough to look for it" (1970, 19)—indeed, Durkheim himself always freely acknowl-edged the influence (Lukes 1972, 68)—this was by no means a matter of rote replication. Not only did Durkheim provide trenchant support for Comte's doctrines, but on a number of issues he transmuted Comte's positions in nontrivial ways.

14. The summary description of this situation by Steven Lukes is worth citing at length: "The theme of social dissolution was a pervasive one in nineteenth-century French thought. . . . It was taken up, with differing emphases, by conservatives, Catho-lics, Saint-Simonians, Positivists, liberals, and socialists. All agreed in condemning *l'odi-eux individualisme*—the social, moral, and political isolation of self-interested individuals, unattached to social ideals and unamenable to social control; and they saw it as spelling the breakdown of social solidarity. For some it resided in dangerous ideas, for others it was social or economic anarchy, a lack of the requisite institutions and norms, for yet others it was the prevalence of self-interested attitudes among individuals. It was variously traced to the Reformation, the Renaissance, the intellectual anarchy conse-quent on the 'negative' thought of the Enlightenment, the Revolution, to the decline of the aristocracy or the Church or traditional religion, to the Industrial Revolution, to the growth of capitalism or democracy. Almost all, however, agreed in seeing it as a threat to social order—whether that order was conceived of in a traditionalist and hierarchical manner, or as an organized technocracy, or as essentially liberal and pluralist, or, as the socialists envisaged it, as an ideal co-operative order of 'association' and 'har-mony'. . . . In short, Durkheim's notions of 'egoism' and 'anomie' were rooted in a broad and all-pervasive tradition of discussion concerning the causes of imminent social disintegration and the practical measures needed to avoid it—a tradition ranging from the far right to the far left" (1972, 195–98).

Regarding issues related to the Postulate of Societal Realism:
1) Durkheim agrees with Comte that society represents a sui generis, nonreducible natural reality; but he
   a) advocates the study of societies and clusters of social facts, not generic "society" or humanity;
   b) inserts the domain of psychology between that of the biological study of organisms and the sociological study of societies.
2) Durkheim agrees with Comte's precept that society like all other phenomena should be studied in a positive manner, eliminating uncontrolled speculation; but he
   a) criticizes Comte's practice for being at odds with this standard, calling him metaphysical and dogmatic, and rebuking his sociology as a "science . . . brought to a conclusion with its foundations barely laid" (quoted in Lukes 1972, 69);
   b) dismisses Comte's rejection of the scientific search for causes and couches his own program in terms of a search for social causes; and
   c) frames sociological explanation in terms of efficient and final causes instead of following Comte's holistic method of explaining social phenomena in terms of the totality of current and preceding conditions.

Regarding issues related to the Postulate of Societal Normativity: Durkheim agrees with Comte that the theoretical determination of normal societal states can provide diagnostic standards for practical action and that one of the major criteria of societal health is the presence of adequate social solidarity, but he
1) disagrees with Comte that in modern industrial societies solidarity should be based on an extensive body of common beliefs and the suppression of individual freedoms of expression. Instead, he argues that in modern societies functional diversity requires moral diversity, and that the modern cult of the individual provides the only system of beliefs that can ensure the moral unity of such a society;
2) also rejects Comte's model of a single evolutionary trajectory for all of humanity in favor of an evolutionary model like a tree, with branches heading in divergent directions, each of which possesses its own characteristic standard of morality.

Regarding the Postulate of Societal Morality, Durkheim supports Comte's notion that social institutions like the family, government, and religion are important for inculcating morality, but dismisses Comte's notion that certain social dispositions are instinctually based. In this he reverts to a more Rousseauan position of finding a radical duality in human nature: purely egoistic dispositions grounded in the natural organism opposed by moral dispositions that come only from society. Indeed, Durkheim filled the biological side of human nature with potentially insatiable appetites that without regulation would lead to pathological extremes like suicide.

Durkheim similarly qualifies Comtean positions with respect to a number of more particular propositions. For example, he accepts Comte's association of the division of labor with population growth, but holds that Comte has mistaken a cause of the division of labor—demographic growth—for one of its consequences. Durkheim agrees with Comte that the division of labor produces mental overspecialization and moral parochialization, but he does not agree that this thereby diminishes societal solidarity. Moreover, he considers impossible and undesirable Comte's prescription that such differentiation be balanced through societal organs that produce consensus. Durkheim also agrees with Comte that certain intuitively bad phenomena may be socially beneficial, but Comte sees this only as the cost of progress while Durkheim sees socially disfavored phenomena, like crime, as an inherent part of social order.

In these and other ways, Durkheim refined the relatively crude formulations of Comte and set the stage for twentieth-century sociology. Yet there is no mistaking the central rhetorical thrust of his life's work. As I argued in a previous publication (1985a, 67–68), his major monographs can be viewed as efforts to demonstrate the validity of what I have identified as the three grand postulates of the French tradition of social theory. The Postulate of Societal Realism was clearly the enveloping theme of *Suicide,* which begins by identifying an explanandum, suicide rates, as constituting a type of fact that represents, both in its constancy and its variability, distinctive properties that can be identified only at the societal level of analysis; and concludes by asserting the demonstrated superiority of explanations that adduce strictly social causative factors.

The Postulate of Societal Normativity formed the rhetorical focus of *The Division of Social Labor.* Holding that the principal objective of every science of life is to define and explain normal states and to distinguish them from pathological states, Durkheim sought in his first substantive monograph to address the question whether or not high levels of specialization were morally acceptable. He did so by asking if the division of labor contributes to the well-being of society, and if those phenomena associated with the division of labor that are commonly considered objectionable represent normal or pathological conditions. Durkheim aimed in that work to demonstrate that moral questions could be treated in a superior manner through a positive science that would examine types of societies and determine their normal and pathological states.

The Postulate of Societal Morality formed the more general theme of Durkheim's last monograph, on religion, as of a number of related writings from his later years, in which he came to argue that just as society provides the object to which religious symbols ultimately refer and the forces that predispose humans to create and revere such symbolism, so society constitutes the reference point of moral beliefs and sentiments and the agency for inculcating them in otherwise nonmoral organisms.

In addition to bringing the themes of the French tradition to a kind of climactic expression, there are other respects in which Durkheim may be said to represent a summation of the French tradition. For one thing, he performed a kind of civic role by providing recognition for virtually all the participants in the transgenerational dialogue listed in Figure 7. For Montesquieu, Rousseau, Saint-Simon, and Comte, he wrote much to celebrate them as contributors to the French tradition.

What is more, he repeatedly identified the body of work that led to sociology as a specifically French creation. In an official report of 1895, he asserted that sociology could develop only where two conditions obtained—an intellectual dissatisfaction with simplistic conceptions and a disposition to apply scientific method to complex objects—and those conditions existed only in France. In an article for the *Revue Blue* in 1900 he declared: "To determine France's part in the progress made by sociology during the nineteenth century is to review, in large part, the history of that science. For it is in our country and in the course of this century that it was born, and it has remained an essentially French science" (1973, 3).

Finally, in a way that is surely exemplary for the story I am attempting to relate here, he sometimes clarified and defended his positions by contrasting them with divergent positions held in British and German philosophy. That practice introduces a new dimension to my narrative: the dynamics of transnational dialogue.

## A TALE OF TWO TRADITIONS

In their quest for a social ethic the key figures of the British tradition evinced a recurrent disposition to view the good life as one in which individual needs and rights were maximally satisfied and the good society as one that secured the greatest amount of such satisfactions for the greatest number. By contrast, the key figures of the French tradition linked the good life with the incorporation of socially transmitted moral dispositions and the good society as one that exhibited a maximum degree of solidarity. These divergent moral conceptions were embedded in differing models of social reality. The British models typically derived the properties of governments, markets, and communities from the propensities of individual actors, while French thinkers typically found the notion of the "abstract individual" a brazen distortion and imagined a societal whole with essential properties of its own—a whole that in fact was needed to complete the phenomenal reality of individual actors.

These differences between the two traditions are not easily reducible to differences of ideology. They stand compatible with conservatism or progressivism, rationalism or irrationalism, totalitarianism or libertarianism. Thus, Hobbes and Rousseau have both been viewed as proto-totalitarians, but Hobbes anchors his glorification of the sovereign on considerations of individual interests, decisions, and rights while Rousseau glorifies the sovereign on grounds of the need to promote social existence and moral virtue. Similarly, Spencer justifies an individualistic ideology on grounds of the inherent needs and claims to liberty of actualizing human beings, whereas Durkheim's defense of liberty reflects his sense that individualism is the ethos most appropriate for cohesive urban-industrial societies, that it expresses collective values centered on the cult of the individual, and that centralized political structures are essential to guaranteeing individual liberties.[15]

The divergent postulates that underlie these persisting differences were honed and deepened in the course of centuries of mutual confrontations between British and French social theorists. Figure 9 schema-

---

15. Durkheim showed himself aware of the fact that he and Spencer could agree on the triumph of modern individualism but otherwise diverge radically: "Like [Spencer], we have stated that the place of the individual in society, from being originally nothing at all, has grown with civilization. But this indisputable fact has presented itself in a completely different light than to the English philosopher, so much so that in the end our conclusions are in contradiction to his, more than echoing them" ([1893] 1984, 141).

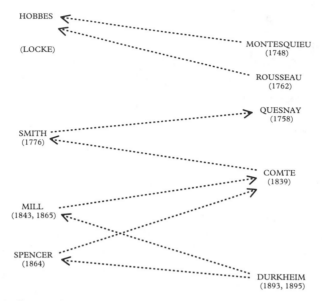

Figure 9. Interactions between British and French Authors

tizes a selection of those cross-Channel conversations. I now represent some of their contents.

## MONTESQUIEU AGAINST HOBBES

The germinal confrontation appears in Montesquieu. Points made in the *Persian Letters* anticipate what Montesquieu later argued more extensively: that men are always born into a society and that it is therefore meaningless to discuss the origin of society and government; that self-interest is not a sufficient basis for human institutions, as Hobbes had asserted; and that the possibility of good government depends on education and example, in short, on civic virtue.

## ROUSSEAU AGAINST HOBBES

To a number of readers, it has seemed that Rousseau wrote the *Second Discourse* for no other purpose than to refute, point by point, the *Leviathan*'s argument regarding the human condition in the state of nature (Melzer 1990; Plattner 1979). Rousseau's arguments in the *Social Contract* include the point that the state does not come into existence through a contract among individuals but on the basis of a commission from the communal will (book 3, ch. 1), and that if the state is to be effectual, it must rule on the basis of the consent of the governed, not through force (book 1, ch. 3).

## SMITH AGAINST QUESNAY

Reversing the direction of argument, Smith initiated a century-long harangue against the French penchant for overregulating individual members on behalf of the social body with his mannered critique of the physiocrat François Quesnay:

> Some speculative physicians seem to have imagined that the health of the human body could be preserved only by a certain precise regimen of diet and exercise. . . . Experience, however, would seem to show, that the human body frequently preserves . . . the most perfect state of health under a vast variety of different regimens; even under some which are generally believed to be very far from being perfectly wholesome. But the healthful state of the human body . . . contains in itself some unknown principle of preservation, capable either of preventing or of correcting . . . the bad effects even of a very faulty regimen. Mr. Quesnay, who was himself a physician, and a very speculative physician, seems to have entertained a notion of the same kind concerning the political body, and to have imagined that it would thrive and prosper only under a certain precise regimen. . . . He seems not to have considered that in the political body, the natural effort which every man is continually making to better his own condition, is a principle of preservation capable of preventing and correcting, in many respects, the bad effects of a political economy, in some degree both partial and oppressive. ([1776] 1976, 2:194–95)

## COMTE AGAINST SMITH

Comte returns the compliment in his first systematic exposition of sociology, which includes pointed criticisms of the assumptions of political economists. Although Comte expresses admiration for the scholarship and wisdom of the "illustrious philosopher" Smith himself, he castigates Smith's would-be successors for getting caught up with metaphysical abstractions instead of appropriating his fertile exploratory approach. They also present misleading abstractions by presuming to isolate the economic phenomena from the intellectual, moral, and political context of society, past and present. But Comte's more general criticisms appear to apply to the Smithian discipline as a whole. Political economy accounts for the division of labor, a conspicuously societal fact, in terms of the pursuit of individual advantage. Perhaps worst of all, in the practical sphere it "systematizes anarchy":

it sets up as a universal dogma the absence of all regulating intervention whatever as the best means of promoting the spontaneous rise of society; so that . . . this doctrine can respond to urgent practical needs only by repeating that systematic negation. Because it perceives a natural tendency in society to arrange itself in a certain order, not seeing in this a suggestion of an order to be promoted by social arrangements, it preaches an absence of regulation which, if carried out to the limit of the principle, would lead to the methodical abolition of all government. . . .

One of the cases of inconvenience inherent in every industrial improvement [is] its tendency to disturb . . . the mode of life of the labouring classes. Instead of responding to the legitimate and urgent protests produced by this disruption of our social order as symptoms demanding attention from true social science, our economists can do nothing better than repeat, with pitiless pedantry, their barren aphorism of absolute industrial liberty. Without considering that all human questions, practically regarded, are reducible to mere questions of time, they venture to reply to all complaints that, in the long run, all classes, and especially the one most injured on the existing occasion, will enjoy a real and permanent amelioration—a reply which will be regarded as derisive as long as man's life is incapable of being indefinitely lengthened. (1974, 448–49; translation modified)

## MILL AGAINST COMTE

By the middle of the nineteenth century differences between the two traditions could be explicitly noted. As the British came to be associated with doctrines celebrating individual needs and natural competitive processes, so the French became associated with doctrines stressing the preeminent needs for moral regulation and societal integration. John Stuart Mill's stance toward Comte expresses this opposition, dramatically so since Mill initially bestirred himself to champion Comte's positivist methodology. Writing in 1843, Mill concluded his analysis of the forms of inductive logic used by positive scientists with a brief for doing social science with the inverse deductive, or historical, method. Although Mill deferred to Comte as authorizing this procedure, he in fact substituted for Comte's holistic methodology one based on individualist premises: taking properties of human nature (or nationally shared character traits) as explananda of states of society. This represented precisely the kind of reductionism that Comte's sociological method was set out to oppose!

In his 1865 essay on Comte, however, Mill was less deferential. By this time he could not conceal his aversion to the societal normativity that Comte and the French tradition espoused:

> Novalis said of Spinoza that he was a God-intoxicated man: M. Comte is a morality-intoxicated man. Every question with him is one of morality, and no motive but that of morality is permitted. The explanation of this we find in an original mental twist, very common in French thinkers, and by which M. Comte was distinguished beyond them all. He could not dispense with what he called "unity." It was for the sake of Unity that a religion was, in his eyes, desirable. . . . To this theme he continually returns, and argues that this unity or harmony among all the elements of our life is not consistent with the predominance of the personal propensities, since these drag us in different directions; it can only result from the subordination of them all to the social feelings, which may be made to act in a uniform direction by a common system of convictions. . . . The *fons errorum* in M. Comte's later speculations is this inordinate demand for "unity" and "systemization.". . .
>
> The strangest part of the matter is, that this doctrine seems to M. Comte to be axiomatic. That all perfection consists in unity, he apparently considers to be a maxim which no sane man thinks of questioning . . . May it not be the fact that mankind, who after all are made up of single human beings, obtain a greater sum of happiness when each pursues his own, under the rules and conditions required by the good of the rest, than when each makes the good of the rest his only object, and allows himself no personal pleasures not indispensable to the preservation of his faculties?
>
> This brief abstract gives no idea of the minuteness of M. Comte's prescriptions, and the extraordinary height to which he carries the mania for regulation by which Frenchmen are distinguished among Europeans, and M. Comte among Frenchmen. It is this which throws an irresistible air of ridicule over the whole subject. ([1865] 1969, 336, 343)

### SPENCER AGAINST COMTE

A year before Mill published this critique of Comte, Herbert Spencer took pains to publicize his "Reasons for Dissenting from the Philosophy of M. Comte." Vexed by the effort of a certain French critic to show the influence of Comte on English writers—Mill, Buckle, and Spencer himself—Spencer laid out a series of propositions held by Comte, followed in each case by his own contrasting propositions. He concludes that although he agrees with Comte on a number of matters pertaining to the common beliefs of scientific thought of the age as well as on sundry minor matters, like use of the name 'sociology' and the need for a new order of scientific generalists, he found himself "diametrically opposed to M. Comte in everything distinctive of his philosophy" . . . ([1864] 1968, 19). These matters include Comte's ideal of subordinating individuals to extensive moral regulation through political and social hierarchies, which Spencer opposes with the ideal of minimizing external constraints and maximizing spontaneous cooperation. Spencer also rejects Comte's setting up the collective life of society as the Supreme Being worthy of worship: it is a Finite Knowable, whereas individuals have come to regard the Infinite Unknowable as the proper object of religious sentiment.

### DURKHEIM AGAINST MILL

The century concludes with a series of critiques of British authors by Durkheim: implicit in the case of Mill, explicit regarding Spencer. Durkheim objects to Mill's position in his *Rules of Sociological Method,* where he rejects the assumption in Mill's *Logic* that social phenomena can be explained by identifying them as consequences of individual motivations. For Durkheim, social facts can be explained only by other social, that is, supraindividual, facts. Consequently, he rejects both of the deductive methods Mill prescribes, which entail deduction from psychological propensities. On the other hand, his own methodological prescriptions favor use of what Mill called the chemical method, which Mill ruled out for sociology owing to the complexity of social phenomena.

### DURKHEIM AGAINST SPENCER

Durkheim delivers a series of salvos against Spencer's Postulate of Methodological Individualism,[16] concluding that "thus we should not,

16. "Spencer states that 'a society, in the sociological sense, is formed only when, beside juxtaposition there is cooperation'. We have just seen that this alleged axiom is the opposite of the truth. On the contrary, it is evident, as Auguste Comte says, 'that cooperation, far from being able to produce a society, supposes necessarily its spontaneous establishment beforehand'.

The Utilitarians . . . supposed that originally there were isolated and independent individuals who thus could only enter into relationships with one another to co-operate, for they had no other reason to bridge the empty gap separating them, and to associate together. But this theory, which is so widely held, postulates a veritable creation *ex nihilo.* It consists, in fact, of deducing society from the individual. But we possess no knowledge that gives grounds for believing in the possibility of such a spontaneous generation." ([1893] 1984, 219, 220) as does Spencer, present social life as the mere resultant of individual natures alone, since, on the contrary, it is rather the latter that emerge from the former" ([1893] 1984, 286). One particular domain where Durkheim repeats this criticism concerns the explanation of religion. Durkheim rejects Spencer's individualistic hypothesis that religion originates in the individual's fear of the dead; instead, he favors a sociologistic interpretation that derives religious forms from the creativity of a collectivity ([1895] 1982, 126–27; [1912] 1965).

Durkheim is equally critical regarding Spencer's Postulate of Normative Individualism: "Whatever efforts Spencer might have made to overhaul utilitarianism, his fundamental postulate is still formulated in the same way as that of the utilitarians, holding that the objective of morality is the advancement of the life of the individual and that the good and the useful are synonymous terms" (1887, quoted in Giddens 1972, 90).

Durkheim's dialogues with Spencer, then, take a form rather different from his dialogues with Comte. With Comte, Durkheim agreed on basic postulates while criticizing a number of specific applications, producing more precise and differentiated formulations in the process. By contrast, despite areas of substantive agreement with his counterpart across the English Channel, Durkheim confronted Spencer's positions as views stemming from an alien tradition.

He took much the same stance regarding the very different tradition across the Rhine. This was so in spite of enthusiasm for German thought at the outset of his career. Durkheim's first publication was an admiring review of a book by Schäffle, and the report of his visit to Germany in 1885–86 breathed with appreciation for the achievements of German social science, philosophy, and academic life generally. By the outbreak of World War I, he had come full circle. Not only did Durkheim indict the German government for provoking the war by inciting Austria to attack Serbia and otherwise fomenting hostilities, but he went on to interpret the militaristic outlook behind the German war effort as expressing a peculiar sort of public mentality. Although it evinced a touch of idealism, this martial mentality appeared pathological: it embodied a state of mind he described as "a morbid hypertrophy of the will, a sort of mania of voluntarism [une sorte de manie de vouloir]" (1915, 44). Well before the war, however, Durkheim had taken pains to distance himself from German philosophies of morality and the state that rested on such exalted views of human will. Early on he came to criticize certain assumptions of German moral philosophy, questioning the value of freedom as a principle for grounding ethics and looking instead to organic societal norms as brakes on the ambitions of pure will. We turn now to consider the formidable tradition that evolved the other set of views so alien to the French sociologist.

# CHAPTER NINE

# The German Tradition

## KANT'S TRIPLE REVOLUTION

N o one in the history of Western philosophy pursued the quest for a rational secular ethic with more feverish intensity than did Immanuel Kant (1726–1804); no one since Hobbes altered the course of that quest more profoundly. In transforming the field of moral philosophy Kant introduced ideas and themes that inspired a library of seminal works of German social science.

Like some of the French authors who came to reject atomic naturalism, Kant began his career under the influence of British thinkers. Awed by Newton's achievements, Kant focused his early work on the sciences of nature. He lectured at the University of Königsberg on physics, mathematics, and physical geography, and wrote extensively on cosmology and natural philosophy. In the 1760s Kant still accepted the British assumption that Newtonian science could provide grounds for a credible ethic. He praised Shaftesbury, Hutcheson, and Hume for having made the most progress to date in the search for the first principles of all morality. During his fifties, however, Kant became increasingly troubled by the challenge a thoroughgoing Newtonian determinism posed to ethics, which led him to develop a new approach to philosophical questions through the *Critique of Pure Reason* and the *Critique of Practical Reason.*

In these writings Kant viewed himself as producing an intellectual revolution no less momentous than that of Copernicus. In effect, he begot not a single but a triple revolution. For one thing, Kant overturned the notion that all the concepts needed to represent natural phenomena could be derived simply by observing external events. Instead, he insisted that our understanding of phenomena is necessarily conditioned: it must be structured by forms of intuition and categories of understanding supplied by human subjects in order to represent the things they observe.

Second, he introduced a separation between domains defined by two radically different perspectives, the world of nature and the world of freedom. The former is a world of appearance, or phenomena, the latter a world of supersensuous reality, which he called noumena. For

Kant, the world of freedom, not that of natural phenomena, constitutes the ground of morality. Thus, for his third revolution Kant became the first secular philosopher in the West to reject the possibility that criteria for the good are to be grounded on the natural properties of living creatures.

With his critiques of the 1780s, Kant staked out a position more expressive of the worldview of German religious culture, which, owing to a deeply rooted strain of pietism and the teachings of Martin Luther, maintained an opposition between the constraints of nature and the experience of inward freedom and righteousness.[1] Where French social philosophers rejected the 'atomic' but kept the 'naturalism,' Kant went further and rejected the naturalism. He located the good not in the expression of natural inclinations but in the performance of duty, which he defined as compliance with moral laws that individuals rationally and freely construct for themselves. He defined virtue neither as the expression of a natural sensibility nor as the acquisition of socially instilled habits, but as the capacity and resolved purpose of free agents to resist natural opponents of the moral disposition within them.

Kant rejected the notion that morality could be based on nature for a number of reasons, some having to do with the shortcomings of the sciences of nature and some having to do with the shortcomings of nature as a principle of morality. Like Hobbes and Comte, Kant strove to exploit the resources of modern rationality to secure a foundation for moral judgments that could overcome partisan bickering and the temptations of evil. But Kant could not agree with Hobbes, Comte, and their followers that natural science provided the model for achieving this secure basis. For one thing, Kant believed that a credible ethic had to be absolutely and unconditionally valid, and the only kinds of knowledge relevant to action that natural science can provide are conditional. Natural science can indicate the most effective means to attain a given

1. Luther emphasized that "man has a twofold nature, a spiritual and a bodily one" and characterized the inner person as righteous and free. He held that no external thing has any influence in producing either righteousness or freedom, or unrighteousness or servitude. Consequently, Luther argued that good works do not make a good person, but that a "person himself [must] be good before there can be any good works, and that good works follow and proceed from the good person" (1957, 7, 24). Pietism was a form of Christian religiosity that opposed both ecclesiastical establishments and orthodox intellectualism with an emphasis on inner experience, feeling, participation, and introspection. It became organized as a religious movement in Germany in the seventeenth century, although it stems from attitudes that have been attributed to medieval German culture.

end, but the utility of that knowledge is conditional on commitment to the end in question. With respect to the determination of ends, natural science can indicate what empirical ends motivate human actions, but these ends vary so much among different peoples and circumstances that knowledge of them cannot provide a secure universal standard.

In the course of searching for an unconditioned and universal moral standard in his *Grundlegung* (1785), Kant fixes on a good will as the only conceivable thing in the world that can be called good without qualification. When he enquires into what constitutes a good will, Kant proposes that acting in accord with a good will entails conforming to duty for its own sake. Through appetitive and egoistic impulses nature continuously throws up temptations to avoid acting in accord with duty. What is more, even when nature prompts one to perform deeds of a generous sort, that does not make the actions moral, since they have not been executed for the sake of duty. Kant furthers depreciates nature as a ground for morality by viewing it solely as the arena of deterministic causality, whereas the only secure basis for morality, a good will, requires the agency of human freedom to provide the kind of laws that alone can be formulated by a rational being and followed for their own sake. Natural philosophy, moreover, can never demonstrate the existence of freedom nor document the existence of a good will, the reality of which must be assumed in order to carry out ethical actions.

As a result of these considerations, Kant produced a secular ethic rooted in the proposition that achieving the good requires nature to be transcended and in the assumption that both the need for this transcendence and the means of attaining it derive from the distinctive properties of the human subject. In one guise or another, Kant's theme of the transcending subject became foundational for all subsequent German moral philosophy.

In creating a radical disjunction between the domains of nature and of moral value, Kant further introduced a novel mode of conceiving the relation between the theoretical and the practical. Instead of viewing theoretical understanding as a way to identify a set of human natural potentials whose actualization formed the agenda for a distinctive discipline of practical philosophy, as with Aristotle, and instead of regarding practical knowledge as a straightforward application of principles and propositions established by theoretical disciplines, as with the British and French social theorists, Kant constructed the disciplines of practical philosophy as wholly independent of and separate from the disciplines of theoretical philosophy.

Kant's radical distinction between the worlds of nature and freedom and his insistence that the good is to be attained through a process in which nature is somehow transcended gave expression to thoughtways so deeply embedded in German culture that his ideas were embraced and reworked by hundreds of German philosophers and poets.[2] His articulation of the irreducible reality of a conscious and self-determining subject became the leitmotif of authors in the German tradition. This motif can be discerned in the otherwise dramatically contrasting productions of Kant's onetime student, Johann Gottfried von Herder.

### HERDER'S ROMANTIC REVOLUTION

Herder studied with Kant before the latter issued his epochal critiques. Thus was it possible for Herder to evince sincere devotion to his professor at Königsberg yet strike off on a different path.[3] It is hard to imagine two more sharply divergent philosophical expressions than those of Kant and Herder. Where Kant enthroned reason, Herder extolled sentiment. Where Kant erected universal standards of morality and justice, Herder espoused cultural relativism. Where Kant made the individual a source of cognitive forms and ethical laws, Herder depicted the collectivity as a matrix of form-giving creativity. Where Kant's argument was precise and logical, Herder's style was evocative and flamboyant.[4]

Even so, Herder no less than Kant celebrated the distinctive capac-

---

2. By the early 1790s, Kant had become a major cultural force in Germany. A decade later, nearly three thousand separate pieces on him had been published. Even Goethe, whose work pointed in a different direction, eventually came to find Kant's critical writings congenial. The poet Hölderlin called Kant the Moses of the German nation (Sheehan 1989, 182; Ermarth 1978, 40).

3. "I have had the good fortune to know a philosopher. He was my teacher. . . . No cabal, no sect, no prejudice, no desire for fame could ever tempt him in the slightest away from broadening and illuminating the truth. He incited and gently forced others to think for themselves; despotism was foreign to his mind. This man, whom I name with the greatest gratitude and respect, was Immanuel Kant" (Kant 1963, xxviii).

4. Herder's defection from Kant's philosophical approach was all too apparent to his erstwhile mentor, well before Herder issued a "Metakritik" chiding Kant for trying to separate reason from the other human powers. In a review of the first part of Herder's *Ideen,* Kant observed that Herder failed to present "a logical precision in the definition of concepts or careful adherence to principles, but rather a fleeting, sweeping view, an adroitness in unearthing analogies in the wielding of which he shows a bold imagination. This is combined with the cleverness in soliciting sympathy for his subject—kept in increasingly hazy remoteness—by means of sentiment and sensation" (Kant 1963, 27).

tity of human beings for freedom and reason.[5] Herder contrasts humans with other animals, who are "stooping slaves" possessing souls not ripened into reason and thus condemned to the service of imperious instincts. Humans stand upright; they are free to examine and to choose. Although they are endowed with instincts like other animals, they suppress these instincts as they mature and acquire reason. Their capacity for inner dialogue evinces a marvelous "self-created inner sense of the spirit" (1969, 141). Even when man abuses his liberty, he remains a king.

However, while Kant found himself logically constrained to represent the voluntarism of human subjects by strictly separating the domain of freedom from that of nature, Herder simply placed reason and freedom within the domain of nature itself (thus making himself vulnerable to charges of a contradiction between his strong naturalistic determinism and his notion that one can and should resist natural impulses and natural forces). He casts it as a law of nature that "man is a free, thinking, and creative being" (153), and muses "how much it seems Nature hesitated before entrusting . . . the great gifts of reason and freedom . . . to such a feeble, complicated, earthly creature as the human" ([1784] 1887, 146). During the years when Kant was laying the foundations for an uncompromisingly antinaturalistic ethics of practical reason, Herder was making a revolution of a different stamp.

Kant located the capacity to transcend brutish instinct in the exercise of the faculties of reason. While Herder, too, appreciated human reason, he considered the expression of sentiment to be the prime medium of human transcendence. He describes human feeling as one of man's greatest organic advantages, the source of invention and art and a far greater inspiration for our ideas than we suspect. Among the gifts nature conferred on humans for the expression of feeling, Herder especially noted the gift of song, available to children and the simplest of peoples. The free and spontaneous forms of self-expression fulfill the true demands of human nature.

5. Isaiah Berlin writes: "Although a great intellectual gulf divides Kant from Herder, they share a common element: a craving for spiritual self-determination as against half-conscious drifting along the streams of uncriticized dogma (whether theological or scientific), for moral independence (whether of individuals or groups), and above all for moral salvation." Berlin relates this shared emphasis on the life of the spirit, which alone liberates humans from the bonds of the flesh and of nature, to the inward-looking tradition of the Pietist movement, which was especially strong in East Prussia where Kant and Herder grew up (1976, 152).

What is more, for Herder these forms are not the work of individual persons but the creations of an integrated community. They appear above all in the language of a people—the embodiment of its historical experience, its whole heart and soul—as Herder was one of the first Europeans to argue (in a prize-winning essay of 1770). Specifically human creative expressions also appear in a people's music and art, in their myths and religious forms. The ensemble of these cultural expressions Herder designated as the *Volksgeist,* the spirit of a people.

Since every culture or historical period possesses a unique character, Herder held that efforts to analyze such phenomena as combinations of uniform elements or to subsume them under universal rules tended to obliterate precisely those crucial qualities that constitute them, as the generalizing science of a Montesquieu grotesquely demonstrated.[6] From this perspective, the quest for a universal standard of value must seem futile. What appear to be excellent achievements worthy of universal emulation occur only as embedded in a particular configuration. Thus, "because Athens had exquisite orators, it does not follow that its form of government must likewise have been the best possible, or that because the Chinese moralize so excellently, their state must be a pattern for all others. . . . Each [culture] bears in itself the standard of its perfection, totally independent of all comparison with that of others" ([1784] 1968, 100, 98).

Overturning Enlightenment commitments to the ideal of the rational individual beholden to universal standards, Herder thus evoked a vision of the good based on a set of collective expressions of sentiment that manifest an aesthetic integrity. Humans achieve the good life by living in natural units, true, but do so in societies that transcend the limits of natural circumstance by having created a harmonious shared culture. Central to the ethic he propounded, then, was an injunction to respect and indeed cherish the differing cultures manifested by different peoples. This led Herder to a precocious critique of European imperialism for its repression of less civilized peoples. Indeed, it led him to be critical of political repressiveness in all forms. Herder became an ardent foe of absolutism, no matter how enlightened; more generally, he expressed a certain antagonism to the modern state. How ironic that the philosopher who did so much to popularize Herder's notion of the

6. "Three wretched generalizations! . . . the history of all times and peoples, whose succession forms the great, living work of God, reduced to ruins, divided neatly into three heaps. . . . O, Montesquieu!" (Herder 1969, 217).

*Volksgeist,* Hegel, should have been the chief proponent in modern political theory of the state as the historical medium of transcendence.

## FROM KANT TO HEGEL

Nineteenth-century German social thought begins with a series of efforts to ground an ethic on the distinctive creative properties of the human subject—and so it ends. In both periods the legacies of Kant and Herder had to be reckoned with. For all their differences, the two men shared a set of assumptions distinctive of the German tradition, which can be represented in terms similar to those I have used for the British and the French traditions. To the question of how the facts of human experience are to be constructed and explained, they respond with what may be called the **Postulate of Subjective Meaning:** *Human phenomena can best be understood by grasping the meanings with which actors imbue their actions.* This entails a method of understanding that in principle diverges from methods used for understanding natural phenomena. For Kant, this was the direct grasp of the self's own legislative activity through *Vernunft,* the faculty of practical reason, which he contrasts with *Verstand,* the faculty used for understanding and explaining natural phenomena. For Herder, it was a method of sympathetic imagination, *Einfühlung,* which he contrasts with the methods of abstraction and objectification used in the natural sciences.

To the question of how secular thought can provide a rational grounding of moral judgments, they respond with a **Postulate of Normative Self-determination:** *Normative judgments are to be grounded not through some agency external to actors but through codes that free human agents, as individuals or collectivities, promulgate for themselves.* This entails a prescription of unconditional respect for the free expressions of other human agents, which Kant formulated as a categorical imperative and Herder as the only moral absolute.

To the question about the source of human moral dispositions, they respond with a **Postulate of Subjective Voluntarism:** *Human moral orientations derive from a distinctive human capacity to identify and make choices between good and evil.*

While Kant and Herder thus articulated the German longing for an ethic centered on the nature-transcending qualities of self-determining subjects, their writings contained enough apparent contradictions to busy generations of thinkers in ever new departures from their philosophies. The first major philosopher to address those contradictions was Johann Fichte, who sought to rescue Kant's philosophy from the error he believed the master had committed in separating a metaphysics of freedom from a metaphysics of nature. Fichte's search for an uplifting secular ideal had led him to Kant's ethics of duty, which he translated into an injunction to achieve increasing freedom through growing loyalty to one's spiritual ideals. Since the effort to realize one's ideals requires a world of objects on which to act, a primal moral will brings into existence the phenomenal world as a field needed for the self-objectification of moral activity. In holding that the ego must posit a non-ego, nature, for its essential field of operation, Fichte sought to complete the Kantian project by locating the noumenal "thing-in-itself" within the transcendental activity of the human mind. Where Herder had overcome the nature-freedom divide by making reason and freedom special "gifts of Nature," Fichte overcame it by making nature an externalization of human spirit: history thus became the story of the continuous struggle of human ideals against the pressures of natural instincts.

Considered the leading philosopher in Germany by the late 1790s, Fichte deeply influenced his young colleague Friedrich von Schelling, who joined him at the University of Jena. Schelling gradually worked himself free from Fichte's subjective idealism, arguing not only that the world of nature is just as real and important as the world of the ego but even that nature gives rise to consciousness, as Herder had held. Even so, Schelling held fast to the Fichtean commitment to voluntarism, maintaining, in words famous among his contemporaries, that "the beginning and end of all philosophy is—freedom."

Schelling's philosophy thus replaces the concept of ego as supreme principle of philosophy with the concept of natural force. In the *Philosophy of Nature* (1797) Schelling argued that mechanical, chemical, electrical, and vital forces were different manifestations of the same underlying cosmic force, a "pure activity" that continuously seeks to realize itself. He later constructed a theory of stages of knowledge: from sensation, to perception, to reflection, to will. For Schelling, human will becomes the visible, self-conscious part of one world understood as creative energy; before man, spirit slumbers; in man, nature attains consciousness. The real is the rational process of the world developing toward its realization in the final, unified expression of ultimate truth, and it is possible to know the world by tracing reflectively the logical process through which nature and history move. Self-determination is the primary condition of all consciousness. The process of history consists of the development of human self-determination through the gradual realization of law, culminating in a sovereign world federation of all sovereign states in which all people will be citizens.

Along with Fichte, Schelling gave his friend G. W. F. Hegel ideas that could be used to bridge the gap between Kant and Herder. Following Kant, Hegel perceived a stark opposition between the domains of nature and spirit (*Geist*). "Nature," he writes, "exhibits no freedom in its existence, but only *necessity* and *contingency*" (*Philosophy of Nature*, §214); spirit, by virtue of its self-consciousness and containing its being within itself, is essentially free. Nature is cyclical and endlessly repetitive, whereas spirit is progressive and continually innovative. Although reason exists in nature, it is not self-conscious but "petrified intelligence," he says quoting Schelling (*Logic* §24); through spirit humans differ from animals, not just by thinking but by the capacity for self-conscious thought. Hegel's lifelong effort was to find a more plausible way to connect the domains of nature and freedom than he thought Kant had done. He did so by looking at the problem as a matter of *historical development*.

Although Kant's quest for a credible ethic was pursued through metaphysics, not historical analysis, he set the stage for Hegel's project with his brief musings on history in the "Idea for a Universal History from a Cosmopolitan Point of View." Kant published this essay in 1784, soon after he had worked out his new philosophical position. Appalled by the record of human history—a tableau of vanity, folly, malice, and destructiveness—Kant wonders if nature might hold some larger plan or purpose for a species whose story otherwise appears to be full of idiocy, signifying nothing. He proposes that while the human animal is distinguished by possessing reason, this faculty cannot possibly be developed in the short life span nature allots humans; full development of their rational capacities would require an unreckonable series of generations. To achieve this end nature relies on the mutual antagonism of people—their "unsocial sociability," a disposition to associate with and then to oppose one another. Unremitting social conflict first awakens humans from laziness so that they develop their powers; it eventually perfects their self-discipline by creating a universal civic society under the rule of law. Although Kant offers this view of the ultimate destination of humanity in a regime of reason and freedom as "a consoling view of the future," he cautions that the means nature provides for reaching that destination are unmistakably immoral: "everything good that is not based on a morally good disposition, however, is nothing but pretense and misery" (1963, 25, 21).

In searching for a way to save human freedom from naturalistic determinism, Kant thus made a certain gnawing tension foundational to German moral philosophy. One is required by a categorical imperative to act autonomously—on the basis of moral laws derived from one's own rational activity—yet no amount of searching one's acts or those of others can determine whether that condition has been attained. Worse, the inspirational idea that mankind may attain a more ethical condition in the future rests on a view of history that seems to sanction absolutely proscribed immoral deeds in the present.[7] This is nothing if not a recipe for despair.

Kant's essay arguably served as a template against which Hegel came to stake out his own historicizing philosophy.[8] In his "Idea for a Universal History" Kant had openly invited some philosophical successor to resolve the mystery about history's plan, for which he was merely supplying a clue, to play Newton to his Kepler (1963, 12). Hegel happily accepted the invitation, although he finally imitated Kant in referring to his own attempt to discern the grand design of history as merely Keplerian (1988, 68). In approaching his solution Hegel incorporated a number of notions from his contemporaries, including Herder's notion of the *Volksgeist* and the ideas of Fichte and Schelling about a historical evolution of *Geist* that culminates in the rule of law.[9]

Like Kant, Hegel admits that inspection of the ordinary course of human events is demoralizing, that history is a "slaughter-bench, upon which the happiness of nations, the wisdom of states, and the virtues of individuals were sacrificed" (24). And again like Kant, Hegel discerns in history a latent purpose—the progressive realization of humanity's capacities for reason and freedom—and argues that the means of attaining this purpose are not the moral intentions of individuals but selfish interests and social strife. Finally, Hegel also holds that the

---

7. The predicament resembles that of the Calvinists portrayed by Max Weber: no matter what good deeds they perform, they can never know whether or not they have been chosen to be among the elect who will be saved.

8. In *Kant and the Problem of History*, Galston (1975) persuasively argues that Hegel's view of history resulted from modifying a few of the principles that informed Kant's.

9. Fichte's ideas about alienation and dialectics also figured significantly in Hegel's system.

culmination of the drama of history appears at the attainment of universal freedom, which comes about not through unbridled license but through obedience to self-made laws.

In setting forth these views, Hegel sought to eliminate the contradictions that had troubled Kant and his readers. He did so, first, by challenging Kant's notion that man's sensuous nature is morally suspect and contains no constructive forces. Hegel followed Herder in acclaiming the passions as the prime creative force in human experience. He called them the woof of the vast tapestry of world history, the driving energy that alone makes possible the realization of reason. He followed Herder (and Fichte and Schelling) in finding nonrational expressions—such as myths, images, and religions—to be part of the process of self-expression whereby human nature realizes itself. He also departed from Kant, following Herder, in considering the agents of human self-realization in history to be not individuals but peoples, and he used Herder's metaphor of the organic development of peoples as a way to subordinate considerations of individual morality and happiness (even though his *Philosophy of Right* insists on the individual's right of subjective satisfaction as the distinguishing feature of modernity). Hegel departed from Herder, however, in his attitude toward the nation-state. Where Herder had located human transcendence in culture and waxed critical of the state for its repressive stance toward culture, Hegel—leaning on Fichte and Schelling—held that culture reaches full bloom only where it has advanced to the developmental stage of forming a state.

With these alterations in Kant's philosophy Hegel attempted to resolve the moral dilemma posed by Kantian philosophy. He overcomes the nature-freedom dualism both by subordinating nature, as a fundamentally deficient mode of being that has its substance outside itself, to human freedom, and by affirming the natural passions as the efficient cause of reason and freedom in history. He downplays qualms about individual morality by denying that morality is the highest thing in the world, and acknowledges circumstances where asserting that formally immoral means have served the great end of human progress. He justifies this by contesting the assumption that Kant's formal morality and reason constitute an eternally valid standard for morality on grounds that morality cannot be alleged to exist outside of history. Instead, Hegel historicizes reason and morality. That is, he argues that reason and morality take shape through a process of unfolding over time, that a person's ethics reflects that of their people (*Volk*) at a certain stage of development, and that morality is fully realized only in the modern state in which freedom achieves full objectivity. In rejecting both Kant's universalistic morality, which stands over against reality, and Herder's relativized morality, which is tied to particular cultural formations, Hegel provides a third way. He views all historical moral configurations as stages on the way toward a universally binding ethic that becomes valid only when it becomes real—at the culmination of the historical process.

With his conception of objective mind, Hegel succeeded in synthesizing two of the major movements of the previous half-century of German thought: the German Enlightment idea of the state as the encompassing community that realizes the morality of its members, epitomized in Kant's notion of the jural order, and the idea of what came to be known as the German Historical School, with its discovery of the common spirit (*Geist*) of a community. The Hegelian synthesis dominated German philosophy for a full quarter-century after the defeat of Napoleon in 1815. In the decade after Hegel's death in 1831, Hegelians of varied hues staked out diverse positions in defense or emendation of the master (Toews 1980). The breadth and intensity of his hold on the German intellectuals of that time has often been compared to a religious movement.

### . . . AND BACK TO KANT

By the middle of the century, however, Hegel's influence had begun to wane. The stage was set for another powerful intellectual movement that proceeded under the banner "Back to Kant." The banner was unfurled by a twenty-five-year-old philosopher at Jena, Otto Liebmann, in a book (*Kant und die Epigonen*, 1865) whose every chapter, critical of prevailing philosophical positions—realism, empiricism, and transcendentalism as well as Hegelian and other idealisms—concluded with the refrain "Kant must be returned to."

Hegel's philosophy became discredited for several reasons. His reputation as *the* philosopher became tarnished when bitter dissension broke out within the ranks of his followers in the decades after his death and intensely anti-Hegelian figures, like Schelling and Schopenhauer, became popular.[10] The ascendance of empirical natural science led to

10. Schelling's relations with Hegel and Fichte, personally and intellectually, were complex. Schelling and Hegel (and the poet Hölderlin) had been students together at Tübingen in the early 1790s, where they converted to Kantianism and shared an enthusi-

an increasing repudiation of Hegel's idealistic philosophy of nature, one of whose proponents had evoked ridicule by defining diamond as "quartz which had achieved self-consciousness" (Willey 1978, 25). Hegel's moral philosophy came to disquiet those who found his enthronement of the political and the historical a source of unacceptable ethical relativism. His appeal as a political philosopher waned after 1848, when liberals inspired by Hegelian ideals of a state based on law (*Rechtsstaat*) became disillusioned by the suppression of the reform movement at Frankfurt, and again after 1866, when Bismarck's defeat of Austria at Königgratz confirmed the hegemony of the Junker aristocracy and triggered an upsurge of cultural chauvinism associated with Hegel's emphasis on nationalism.

A number of intellectuals thus came to embrace Kant over Hegel in the hope of using Kantian philosophy both to reconnect science and philosophy and to return to a universalistic ethic. Such an ethic would help overcome both ethical relativism and the growing gulfs between social classes and between Germany and Western Europe. Beginning with figures like the physicist Hermann Helmholtz, who blamed Hegelianism for the estrangement between science and philosophy and advocated a return to Kant's epistemology, and the political activist Friedrich Albert Lange, who found Hegel a regression to scholasticism and used Kant's ethics to ground his quest for political freedom and social justice, Kant's ideas underwent a revival that continued unabated through the rest of the century. The 1870s witnessed a rapid expansion of academic courses on Kant all over Germany, more than quadrupling in several universities (Köhnke 1986, 315). By that time Hegel was considered terminally obsolete, a condition described with characteristic color by Nietzsche: earlier there was "a fine bumper crop of green Hegelian corn standing in the fields. But now that harvest with its disappointed hopes and promises has been ruined by the hail and all the ricks stand empty" ([1874] 1990, 224).

---

asm for the promise of the French Revolution. Schelling to conveyed his enthusiasm for Fichte to Hegel. Fichte brought Schelling to Jena, where Hegel arrived a few years later. Hegel tried to clarify the difference between the philosophies of Fichte and Schelling in an essay that would precipitate a break between the two protagonists. Hegel's *Phenomenology of Mind* of 1807 borrowed more heavily from Fichte than from Schelling, while Schelling increasingly distanced himself from Hegel; eventually the two men became antagonists. In 1841 Emperor Frederick Wilhelm IV appointed Schelling to lecture at Berlin in order to get rid of "the dragon seed of Hegelianism." Attending his inaugural course were four students who in different ways came to challenge the Hegelian legacy: Kierkegaard, Bakunin, Engels, and Burckhardt.

Even so, thanks to the efforts of Wilhelm Dilthey and others, toward the end of the century Hegel as well as Herder enjoyed a new round of appreciation. Together the three seminal thinkers provided the ultimate source of the philosophical ideas that oriented German sociology when it emerged as a credible discipline around the 1890s, ideas that in fact inspired a number of disciplines that bear a distinctive German stamp—interpretive cultural anthropology, phenomenological sociology, philosophical anthropology, introspective and psychoanalytic psychologies, and the sociology of knowledge.

## CONFIGURING THE GERMAN TRADITION

In their role as agenda-setting sociologists early in this century, Georg Simmel and Max Weber appear as the German counterparts to Durkheim. However, the role played by Durkheim as codifier and spokesman for a national tradition of social thought was in Germany taken by Dilthey. Dilthey wrote probing essays on German cultural traditions. Like Durkheim, Dilthey exerted himself to recover and enhance the visibility of earlier participants in the transgenerational dialogue that prefigured modern social science.[11] Hailing Kant as the hero who revolutionized German thought, he helped to prepare a new critical edition of Kant's writings. He published an exemplary biography of Schleiermacher, and later a volume on Hegel—based on previously unknown texts—which did much to revive Hegelian studies in Germany. Dilthey repeatedly noted that the tradition of idealism and philosophy of mind was "the foundation of German national culture" (Ermarth 1978, 38). What is more, in bringing certain themes of the German tradition to a kind of climactic expression, he held them up as broaching a distinctive kind of scholarship that needed to be counterposed to the intellectually dangerous sociologies stemming from France and England—those of Comte, Mill, and Spencer, in particular. Thus, he argued that "only from Germany can a *genuinely empirical* procedure come to replace the biased dogmatic empiricism [of J. S. Mill]" and praised the "specifically German conception of historical development that showed the

11. In courses on German philosophy and essays on Kant, Goethe, Schopenhauer, and Nietzsche, Simmel also played this role to some extent. However, in contrast to Durkheim and Dilthey, Simmel did not construe those authors as forerunners of a nationally distinctive approach to social science. Dilthey's scope was also enormously inclusive. Besides the works mentioned in this paragraph, Dilthey wrote essays on Goethe, Fichte, Schelling, Schopenhauer, Trendelenburg, and many others.

falsity of those total sociological systems [of Mill, Comte, etc.]" (cited in Belke 1971, lvi–lvii). This set the tone for a custom of portraying German social science as an embodiment of superior ethical qualities.[12]

Of the traditions that laid philosophical foundations for modern social science, the German tradition was the most complex, as Figure 10 makes clear. Through somewhat separate transgenerational linkages, the analysis of human subjectivity was pursued along several different pathways, most of them emanating from Kant.[13] Thus, while nearly all authors in the German tradition emphasize ways in which human subjects can and should transcend ordinary natural processes, they do so by construing the subject in different ways. One construction features the subject as *creating meanings* that, in contrast to natural phenomena, ask to be understood. A second emphasizes the ways in which human knowledge about any phenomenon gets organized through *using a priori categories.* A third celebrates the capacity of human subjects for *acting willfully.*

UNDERSTANDING THE EXPRESSIVE SUBJECT

Dilthey focused his attention on the Kantian pathway that led *to* experience. Indeed, the term for lived experience, *Erlebnis,* formed the bedrock on which Dilthey sought to erect a distinctive approach to the social sciences—the *Geisteswissenschaften,* or disciplines concerned with mind. One proposition informed this enterprise: *to understand the meaning of an actor's experience requires a special kind of cognition, which contrasts with that used in the sciences of natural phenomena.* Dilthey called this cognitive mode *Verstehen,* or understanding. Dilthey's entire lifework has been described as an effort to provide the philosophical vindication of *Verstehen* (Ermarth 1978, 243).

Diverse intellectual streams emanating from Kant, Herder, and

---

12. Thus German economists like Gustav Schmoller came to extol the discipline they called *Volkswirtschaftslehre* for its humane focus in contrast to the crass materialism of "Manchester economics." The methodological doctrines of German sociology would be described as having emerged "from the deepest powers of the German spirit" to culminate in "an accomplishment of the highest ethical significance" (Freyer 1923, 2).

13. Dilthey appreciated some of this complexity. In certain passages, for example, he observes that Kant influenced developments in two opposed directions—one that led to the phenomenological understanding of experience, and one that led away from experience toward pure idealism (1921 4:47, 281; cf. Ermarth 1978, 39). But idealism itself took different forms, as critics of Dilthey, notably Windelband and Rickert, were to emphasize.

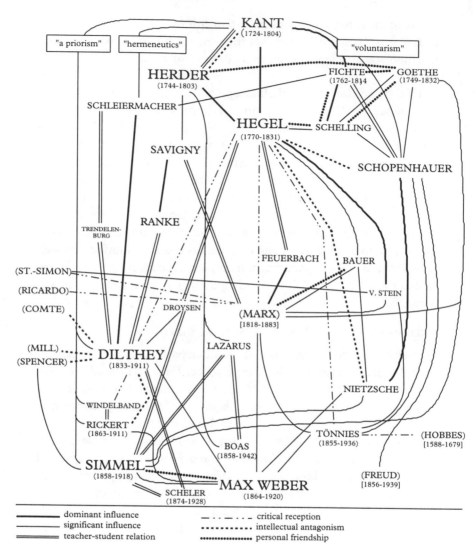

Figure 10.  Links in the German Tradition

others had repeatedly broached the notion of *Verstehen* without, Dilthey thought, giving it firm philosophical foundations. One stream was the hermeneutic tradition. The discipline of hermeneutics was pioneered by two outstanding philologists, Friedrich Ast and Friedrich August Wolf. Ast sought to grasp the spirit (*Geist*) of antiquity through close attention to the language of its literary production, and viewed the process of understanding that language as a reproduction of the creative process. Wolf defined the aim of hermeneutics as that of grasping an author's thoughts as he would have liked them to be grasped, and considered a talent for empathizing with others' thoughts to be a requisite for practicing this art. Other forms of hermeneutics were cultivated in other disciplines, such as theology, which interpreted the meaning of biblical scriptures, and jurisprudence, which interpreted the meaning of legal documents. In a famous course of lectures at Berlin in 1819, the theologian Friedrich Schleiermacher sought to move beyond these specialized hermeneutic disciplines and develop a general hermeneutics as a generic art of *Verstehen*. Schleiermacher tried to illuminate the "mysterious process" through which a listener divines the meaning of a speaker's string of words, depicting it as a process of re-experiencing the speaker's mental processes. This process links any particular utterance to the larger whole of which it is a part—through a two-way linkage he called the "hermeneutic circle"—and assumes an intuitive leap of understanding. After Schleiermacher's death, the project of developing a general hermeneutics languished until it was recovered by Dilthey, who seized his predecessor's conception as a weapon with which to defend human experience against reductionist and mechanistic approaches of naturalistic social science. Dilthey judged that Schleiermacher was the only one of Kant's successors who had held fast to Kant's analytic method, offering not metaphysics but a phenomenology of consciousness.

Dilthey may have been introduced to the contrast between *Verstehen*, the method used by historians, and *Erklären*, the method of explanation used in natural science, by the historian Johann Droysen. Droysen was arguably the first to articulate the famous distinction between *Verstehen* and *Erklären*, although he had been schooled to appreciate the method of *Verstehen* both by his teacher Hegel and by critics of Hegel who belonged to what was known as the Historical School. The German Historical School took its ultimate inspiration from Herder, who not only formulated the intellectual ideal of grasping the distinctive *Gestalt* of a particular culture or historical period but also described the special method needed to do so as involving a process of sympathetic imagination. A succession of distinguished historical scholars—most notably, Barthold Niebuhr, Friedrich von Savigny, and Leopold von Ranke—flourished in Berlin in opposition to the orthodox Hegelians, searching for the expressions of *Geist* not in a higher world of abstract ideas but in a concrete world of particular historical formations. The cognitive procedure favored by this school has been described as that of "immediate intuition" (Ermarth 1978, 57).

Dilthey had studied with Ranke at Berlin, where he absorbed Ranke's passion for the aesthetic appreciation of historical particulars. But Dilthey faulted the Historical School for being indifferent to questions of theory and method. His own effort to supply a philosophical basis for intuitive understanding began with a prize-winning essay of 1860, before he had left theology for philosophy, in which he hailed Schleiermacher as "the Kant of hermeneutics." The formula Dilthey used again and again to represent his methodological commitment was "We explain nature, we understand mind." His continuous elaboration of this formula extended over two long phases. In the first period, marked by the monumental *Introduction to the Human Sciences (Geisteswissenschaften)* of 1883, Dilthey developed his goal of grasping the feeling and imaginative life of the whole human being. He proposed to address "the great problem of the relation between the order of nature and freedom" much as Kant had: by leaving it to natural science to examine the natural processes that underlie the psychophysical life, and proceeding to grasp the facts of human purposiveness through an independent set of disciplines privileged to grasp "undistorted reality, [which] only exists for us in the facts of consciousness given by inner experience" ([1883] 1976, 166, 161). His emphasis here was on carrying out a kind of empathic psychology. In Dilthey's second phase, marked by a multivolume work on the historical world in 1906, he shifted to a concern with the objective expressions of experience. His formula became tripartite: Experience-Expression-Understanding. Here, too, Dilthey opposed the merely naturalistic understanding of the physical facts of human life with a call for understanding the productions of the human spirit, now not through psychological insight but through grasping the mind-created cultural structures that possess patterns and laws of their own.

Dilthey's heroic efforts to consolidate the German tradition behind a non-naturalistic kind of social science paved the way for a good deal of twentieth-century German sociology. Another stream of the hermeneutic channel flowed more directly from Herder through the originative figures of German anthropology, including Wilhelm von Humboldt, Adolf Bastian, Moritz Lazarus, and Heymann Steinthal. Humboldt was a broad-gauged humanist from whom Dilthey drew considerable inspiration. Besides playing a key role in founding the University of Berlin, where so much of the hermeneutic tradition got developed,[14] Humboldt wrote essays that featured understanding of historical experience as a crucial means for cultivating human personality. Like Herder, Humboldt emphasized that true knowledge of humanity relies on deep intuitive faculties, a "divining faculty" (*Ahndungsvermögen*) and an ability to see connections (*Verknüpfungsgabe*). He outlined a plan to develop a comparative anthropology designed to study the moral character of different human types, which inspired later advances in German ethnology. Lazarus and Steinthal played a key role in that development, not least through their pioneering journal devoted to the psychology of cultures (*Zeitschrift für Völkerpsychologie und Sprachwissenschaft*), which flourished in the 1860s and 1870s. Lazarus significantly influenced some key figures who studied with him at Berlin, including both Simmel and Boas. Thanks to Boas, the Herder/Humboldtian notion of intuiting the genius of a culture's distinctive configuration though careful study of its language and an irreducible process of intuitive understanding became central to much of later cultural anthropology.

RECOGNIZING THE COGNITIVE SUBJECT

Dilthey defended the need for a science of human experience that differed fundamentally from sciences of nature in that humans alone could symbolize meaning and thus be understood by fellow humans in ways nonhuman phenomena could not. A number of neo-Kantian philosophers centered in the province of Baden agreed that the human sciences differed fundamentally from natural science, but placed the source of that difference not in its subject matter but in the type of cognitive interest pursued by the scholar.

Wilhelm Windelband is commonly associated with the core statement of this position. In a famous address delivered upon assuming the rectorate at the University of Strassburg in 1894, Windelband reconfigured the way natural science should be distinguishing from disciplines concerned with human history. The hallmark of the natural sciences, he argued, is their method and intention—to formulate general laws—which he called a nomothetic intention. By contrast, historical disciplines look not for general laws but for single, nonrecurring realities. They pursue what he called an idiographic intention, a search

14. The scholars who studied and/or taught at the University of Berlin included Schleiermacher, Fichte, Hegel, Schopenhauer, Trendelenberg, Savigny, Ranke, Droysen, Bastian, Lazarus, Dilthey, Simmel, Weber, Buber, and Scheler.

for singular and unique facts that are important to the inquirer because they embody significant values. Windelband's student Heinrich Rickert, who succeeded him at Heidelberg, can be said to have built his career elaborating that point. Rickert went on to articulate and defend the cultural values associated with the methods of science and history, respectively. Although both Windelband and Rickert passionately adhered to Kant's notion of the free will, their commitment to voluntarism took the form of stressing the repercussions of differing types of value interests for cognitive forms.

## ANALYZING THE VOLUNTARISTIC SUBJECT

During the years when Windelband was working to restore the prestige of philosophy and reaffirm the enduring relevance of Kant, a more strident type of voluntarism was being promulgated by Friedrich Nietzsche. Nietzsche brought to culmination the strand of thought running from Fichte to Schopenhauer that stressed the subject's sheer self-determination. Fichte had translated Kant's doctrine that moral action rests on autonomy into an emphasis on the strenuously voluntaristic character of moral action. For Fichte, placid routine activity and self-contented stagnation form the archenemies of morality. This notion fed into later social science through two channels. One channel stressed the moral quality of persons who create themselves through deliberate choices and so developed the theme of the voluntaristic individual. The other channel developed the theme of voluntaristic social formations. This led to typologies of historical periods and social states that culminate in states of advanced voluntarism.

The theme of the voluntaristic individual appeared throughout Fichte's writings, founded, as we have seen, on the basis of Kantian antinaturalistic ethics. But it was also stressed by those, like Goethe, who found in nature a source of inspiration for human values. Goethe championed the ideal of creating unique selves through the right kind of cultivation (*Bildung*)—an ideal close to Schleiermacher's definition of the task of every human being as that of fashioning and consolidating his own individuality. Identifying with Goethe's naturalistic interests, Schelling opened a new road to voluntarism by linking the notion of will with natural phenomena, making human will continuous with the other kinds of energies in the cosmos.

Like Hegel, Arthur Schopenhauer felt all these philosophic influences in his youth. He idolized Goethe, studied with Fichte (and Schleiermacher), pondered Schelling. Yet he responded by charting a course radically different from Hegel's, even thought it his mission to repair the damage done to philosophy by the contorted language and mystifying schemes of Hegel and his followers. In the early work that presented his essential thought, *The World as Will and Representation* (1818), Schopenhauer reaffirmed Kant's doctrine that true knowledge of the ultimate nature of the external world is forever inaccessible to humans. Then, however, he turned his focus on the one thing humans truly can know: their own will. Although Schopenhauer followed Schelling in naturalizing the will—he referred to human will as "Nature at the highest grade of its self-consciousness" ([1818] 1958, 1:276)—he nonetheless saw life not as a process of progressive realization of rational will but as the unbridled play of blind instinct and brute force. In Schopenhauer's cosmos the intellect figures largely as a medium for illusions stimulated by the unconscious will. The road to transcendence requires humans to detach themselves from this endlessly futile and frustrating assertion of wills. He likened the mass of mankind to puppets, pulled by the wires and strings of nature and the world-as-will, and saw escape from this state of unfreedom only through the exertions of exceptional persons—moral heroes who had the insight to recognize the universal operation of the rapacious will to live and the courage to liberate themselves from it.

At twenty-one Nietzsche was set to embark on a promising career as a philologist when he chanced upon Schopenhauer's opus. From the very first page, he confessed in a seminal essay nine years later, he knew he would hearken to every word in the book ([1876] 1990, 169). What excited Nietzsche so much about Schopenhauer was the latter's uncompromising honesty in the pursuit of truth. In going beyond his master, Kant, Schopenhauer taught Nietzsche how to be independent.[15] In turn, Nietzsche went beyond his master, Schopenhauer. Where the latter, resonating with the Vedantic philosophies of India, found the phenomenal world a senseless clashing of wills from which relief could come only from an effort of mind leading to ascetic abnegation, Nietzsche evolved an ethic of robust assertion of the will. Nietzsche formulates for all humanity a doctrine of personal self-creation, and he celebrates culture as a source of inspiration for such transcendence,

---

15. Indeed, Nietzsche celebrates Schopenhauer for having voluntarily created himself as a *genius,* through a continuous struggle in which Schopenhauer displayed a "monumental effort of will, first against his contemporaries, then against his enemies, and finally against himself," a feat that arguably inspired young Nietzsche to mold himself as a genius (Pletsch 1991, 173–81).

through formative teachers who function as genuine liberators, revealing one's "true original meaning and basic stuff . . . something fettered and paralyzed and difficult of access" (166). In his mythic character Zarathustra Nietzsche depicts a heroic teacher who rejects disciples and sends them off to pursue their own ends. He stresses the dangers of a conventionally naturalistic interpretation of humans, calling Darwin's doctrine that humans are basically like other animals "true but deadly," and viewing man as "necessary in order to redeem nature from the curse of animal existence" (194). Nietzsche's influential call for self-perfection through strenuous efforts to become one's own true self climaxed a century of German preoccupation with the problem of how human subjects can transcend the common determinants of life.

But the German tradition also harbored ideas that involved a social or collective manifestation of voluntarism. This notion, too, was advanced by Fichte, who depicted the arduous struggle of reason over instinct as taking place through a succession of historical epochs. Fichte identified a sequence of five stages in this process. History began with an epoch of unreflective conduct, leading to a period of repressive laws, which was followed by a period of antiauthoritarian defiance. This rebellious stage gave way to the consensual acceptance of rational law, which was succeeded by a culminating epoch of spiritual humane fulfillment. Fichte believed that Germany in his time was about to lead the world through a transition into a culminating epoch of freedom.

Endorsing this general theme, Hegel outlined the progress of freedom through history as a process in which humanity evolved from complete unfreedom to a state where one is free, then to a state where some are free, and finally to a state where all are free. One strand of early German sociology took shape as an effort to translate Hegel's abstract philosophic depiction of this process into a sociologically plausible account of actual societal developments. Thus Lorenz von Stein, whom some have called the first sociologist, substituted actual historical states for Hegel's idea of the state: for Hegel's idea of the progress of universal reason (*Weltgeist*) he substituted the notion of the increased diffusion of educational opportunities throughout various sectors of society.

Ferdinand Tönnies similarly hailed Hegel's achievement in demonstrating the historical necessity of rational modern structures: civil society and the state. At the same time Tönnies faulted Hegel for presenting a vague and obfuscating view of social life and for propounding the idea of a unilineal development toward perfection. In seeking to correct these shortcomings Tönnies attempted to bring persons back into the picture and to uncover "the real relationship between individual will and social groups," which Hegel had "blotted out" ([1912] 1971, 27). It was a constant feature of Tönnies's sociological vision, he once noted, to "see in the entire historical development since the Middle Ages the gradual setting free of rationalism and its increasing dominance as inherently necessary processes of human mind as will" ([1932] 1971, 6). The most seminal formulation produced by Tönnies set the stage for nearly all subsequent German sociology. This took the form of a schema that represented a succession of two major societal types. As is generally known, this schema comprises the type called *Gemeinschaft*, which bases organization on common qualities such as kinship, territory, language, and religion, and the type called *Gesellschaft*, which organizes people on the basis of formalized criteria through contracts and constitutions. What is not so generally known is that Tönnies actually represented these two societal types as the outcomes of two types of social *will*—a point of departure he reached from his study of Schopenhauer. The former expresses an unreflective, spontaneous will that is close to natural inclinations. The latter expresses a deliberate, reflective, calculating kind of will in which human voluntarism attains a much higher grade.

## MORAL CRISES AND SOCIOLOGICAL FOUNDATIONS

One effect of the Copernican and Newtonian revolutions in natural science, we have seen, was to challenge ethical outlooks based on theological and Aristotelian philosophies. In Britain and France this challenge was met by recasting the philosophical bases of ethics through positions aligned with the assumptions of natural philosophy. In Germany, however, the ascendance of natural science was experienced in part as a threat to human inwardness and moral self-determination, leading to the supposition that post-Newtonian ethics would have to protect the freedom of the human subject by positing some sort of transcendence of the nonhuman natural order.

The philosophies of Kant, Herder, and Hegel articulated this tension in ways that subsequent German social science could never forget. All three had struggled to find ways to protect the sense of human dignity and freedom against threats posed by rising tides of naturalistic explanation and natural determinism. In the course of their struggles, they produced three archetypal solutions that became channels for later German social thought. Kant transcended nature by locating morality in a sphere that operated independent of the domain of nature. Herder transcended nature as a domain of instincts by identifying human language and culture as creative capacities through which nature reached a higher level. Hegel portrayed the route whereby humanity overcame nature over the course of world history by subordinating it to *Geist*.

German universities of the nineteenth century provided a hothouse for the growth of positivistic natural science, a development that posed a continuously nagging threat to the Germanic commitment to inwardness and subjective freedom. Kant's private misgivings about Newtonian determinism became a widely shared cultural angst. While Mill and Spencer could blithely discount the logic of the "free-will metaphysicians" who opposed a naturalistic social science (Mill [1843; 8th ed. 1872] 1987, 22–28; Spencer 1961, 33–35), Windelband would exclaim that freedom of will was the "greatest brain-racking problem of modern humanity, one which torments the minds of the very best thinkers" (1884, 211). This torment was part of what fired Dilthey's enormous effort to lay foundations for a non-naturalistic science of humanity; Dilthey confessed that "the great crisis of the sciences and European culture which we are now living through has so deeply and totally taken possession of my spirit that the desire to be of some help in it has extinguished every extraneous and personal ambition" (Ermarth 1978, 15).

All together, German social thinkers came to identify five different grounds of opposition to Anglo-French naturalistic ethics and social science. (1) In the wake of the hermeneutic subtradition, they rejected its perspective on humans as objects to be studied from the outside in favor of a method that attended to the subjective meanings of actors. In the wake of the a priorist subtradition; they rejected both (2) a strictly inductivist epistemology in favor of one that stressed the constitutive work of the knower, and (3) the premise that practical directives could be grounded exclusively on theoretical propositions, in favor of a sharp distinction between empirical and normative domains. In the wake of the voluntarist subtradition, they rejected both (4) a deterministic metaphysics in favor of one that explicitly protected space for free human agency, and (5) the tendency to analyze social formations in strictly naturalistic terms in favor of taxonomies that made room for consciously constructed associations.

Max Weber is generally considered the conduit through which these philosophic positions were transmitted into modern social science.

The first three of these positions are best known through terms made famous by Weber as, respectively, the doctrines of *Verstehen,* of value relevance, and of ethical neutrality. Although all those doctrines were articulated earlier and more originatively by Weber's senior colleague Georg Simmel, both men were basically engaged in the common process of adapting the legacies of German antinaturalistic moral philosophy for the purpose of grounding a modern approach to social science.

## THE REQUIREMENT OF *VERSTEHEN*

Whether they theorize about it or not, most German sociologists have paid a good deal of attention to the inner meanings of individual actors and cultural strata. Simmel theorized about this matter a good deal, arguing in his *Problems of the Philosophy of History* that historical knowledge uniquely preserves the meanings and motivational context of human experience. It does so by securing an "immanent" understanding of the inner life of historical actors, an understanding not different in principle from the way one understands an everyday acquaintance. Even actors at some cultural remove are intelligible through this process: "One does not have to be a Caesar to really understand Caesar, nor another Luther in order to comprehend Luther" ([1907] 1978, 65; 1977, 74).

Weber critically incorporated the main lines of Simmel's arguments, stating that by far the most developed logical analysis of a theory of *Verstehen* had appeared in Simmel's work (1922, 21; Levine 1985a, 97). In his programmatic statements about sociology, Weber made the process of *Verstehen* fundamental to what he considered sociology's mission: the interpretive understanding of social conduct to which actors have ascribed a subjective meaning. Although Simmel did not explicitly extend the methodological principle of *Verstehen* from history to sociology, his sociological analyses in fact attend to the phenomenology of actors' experience—what it feels like to be engaged in relations of conflict, gratitude, secret societies, or dyadic intimacy.

## THE REJECTION OF INDUCTIVISM

Fundamental to the epistemologies of Simmel and Weber was the assumption that scholars necessarily bring certain categories and concepts into inquiry a priori. Simmel's essay on the philosophy of history sought to refute the doctrine of historical realism—the notion that the historian should represent historical events as they actually occurred. History, for Simmel, was one of those great formative categories—like philosophy, art, science, religion, and common sense—that the human mind must employ to make sense of the contents of experience and through which all of those contents can be organized to form a "world." There is no history as such, Simmel stressed, only particular kinds of history, which take their character from the specific a priori categories any historian employs. To reject historical realism in favor of acknowledging the a prioris of historiography is emancipatory. Although man, as something known, is made by nature and history—a hapless product of deterministic laws and forces—nevertheless man as knower makes nature and history. Simmel dedicated his treatise on the philosophy of history to "the general objective of preserving the freedom of the human spirit—that is, form-giving creativity" over against historical realism in the same way he argued that Kant had done with respect to naturalism. Elsewhere Simmel discusses other options for cognizing human experience—in the perspectives of the individual, of society, of objective culture, or of humanity (1971, ch. 3).

Although Weber did not philosophize much about the matter, he accepted the general neo-Kantian premise regarding a priori categories as a matter of course, for the most part following Rickert's leads. Weber formulated the concept of cognitive interest to represent ways in which the concerns of knowers operate to construct perspectives from which they can investigate objects, and he used the Rickertian concept of value relevance (*Wertbeziehung*) to signify the ways in which the values of investigators affect their cognitive interests.[16]

THE SEPARATION OF FACT FROM VALUE

Perhaps the most crucial way the thinkers of the German tradition of social theory opposed the British and French traditions lay in holding that naturalistic science was not suitable for grounding ethical directives. This position got expressed most forcefully in Simmel's early work, *Introduction to the Science of Ethics (Einleitung in die Moralwissenschaft)*, published in two volumes in 1892–93, at the same time as

---

16. In a famous passage on the subject, Weber expressed his awareness that specialized scholarship for the most part attends to the analysis of data as an end in itself without assessing the relationship of that data to ultimate ideas of value. "Indeed, [specialized scholarship] will lose its awareness of its ultimate rootedness in the value-ideas in general. And it is well that should be so. But there comes a moment when the atmosphere changes. The significance of the unreflectively utilized viewpoints becomes uncertain and the road is lost in the twilight. The light of the great cultural problems moves on. Then science too prepares to change its standpoint and its analytical apparatus and to view the streams of events from the heights of thought" (1949, 112).

Durkheim's *Division of Labor*. Just as Durkheim did in introducing his monograph, Simmel asserted a need to abandon the abstract approach of previous philosophical ethics by undertaking empirical investigations of the ethical creeds by which humans actually live in society. However, where Durkheim claimed that such investigations could provide a more reliable basis for rational ethics, Simmel insisted that facts and values represent two utterly different worlds, such that a positive science of ethics could have no practical moral value.

The better-known formulation of this position appears in Weber's essay on ethical neutrality (*Wertfreiheit*) in the social sciences, which contains his forthright rejection of naturalistic metaphors as a source of normative criteria. Similarly, his magisterial "Science as a Vocation" insists that scholarship can provide no basis for adjudicating differences among value positions, positions their advocates must uphold in the form of an unending battle of the gods.

## THE POSTULATE OF NORMATIVE SELF-DETERMINATION

In Fichte's hands, Kant's principle of finding the ethical in adherence to universal laws determined through one's own rational powers got transformed into an admonition simply to act in accord with ideals one had voluntarily chosen. The pursuit of this theme reached its apex in Nietzsche's dictum "*Werde, was du bist*" ("Become what you are")—an injunction to transcend mere animal passivity and realize true humanity by boldly manifesting one's uniquely personal, freely chosen goals. This injunction was much on the mind of both Simmel and Weber, who recognized it as an ethical prescription and as an empirical variable.

Simmel's subscription to the Nietzschean dictum remained latent throughout much of his career, but he gave it full philosophical articulation in his late essay "Das individuelle Gesetz."[17] Simmel argues there that the categorical imperative must not take the form of a universal maxim, because universals are external to the ethical person and not an expression of the individual's own authentic being. If moral obligation is to be based on self-determined principles, it should not express some external content but should grow from the roots of each person's

17. Simmel published the essay in *Logos* in 1913, then enlarged it as chapter 4 of his *Lebensanschauung* in 1918. Simmel's law of the individual looks like nothing so much as a formalization of Nietzsche's counsel: "What until now have you truly loved, what has raised up your soul, what ruled it and at the same time made it happy? Line up these objects of reverence before you, and perhaps by what they are and by their sequence, they will yield you a law, the fundamental law of your true self" ([1874] 1990, 166).

own life experience. This individualized ethics implies that one's moral imperative does not remain fixed for all time, but changes in accord with the integration of emerging ethical decisions. In consequence, "the responsibility for our entire history lies in the emerging duty of every single action" (1918, 243).

Out of his principle of scholarly restraint, Weber refused to articulate a reasoned defense of any ethical position. Yet his practice recurrently contradicted this principle. By temperament a prophet, Weber could never refrain from insinuating his advocacy of what was in fact a heroic ethic of self-awareness and self-determination (Levine 1985a, ch. 8). He felt that the calling of scholars and scientists was best justified by the contributions their work makes to enhancing human self-consciousness. He belittled the human tendency to submerge decisions about ultimate values under the surface of everyday routines, and urged that "every important decision, indeed life as a whole, *if it is not to slip by like a merely natural process* but to be lived consciously, is a series of ultimate decisions by means of which the soul, as in Plato, chooses its own destiny, in the sense of the meaning of what it does and is" (1978, 84; emphasis mine).

## THE EMPIRICAL ANALYSIS OF VOLUNTARISM

The extent to which persons are free to choose their own actions and develop themselves in accord with their unique individualities comprises the most significant dependent variable in Simmel's widely ranging essays on social phenomena. It is central to analyses of the four main topics he treated systematically: social differentiation, money as a general medium of exchange, the dynamics of culture, and the modern metropolis.

The theme pervades Simmel's first sociological monograph, *On Social Differentiation* (1890). Here, again, comparison with Durkheim is instructive. Where Durkheim analyzed socially produced individuation chiefly with an eye to its consequences for social solidarity and personal morality, Simmel treated the transformative relaxation of various jural and customary constraints chiefly as a process leading to self-determination and individual fulfillment. This took the form, for example, of replacing collective responsibility for crimes with the notion of individual liability, and replacing relatively compulsory patterns of group affiliation based on accidents of birth and propinquity with voluntary associations, which create more individualized constellations of a person's group affiliations.

Simmel's analyses of the effects of a monetarized economy focus largely on its implications for personal freedom and individuality. The use of money as a general medium of exchange advances the emancipatory processes Simmel had treated in *On Social Differentiation*. By enlarging a person's sphere of social relations through an expanded market and by enabling those relations to be limited to a precise, specific exchange, money promotes the freedom of individuals from external social constraints. What is more, by making it easier to engage in voluntary associations organized about particular interests, and by providing a general resource fully submissive to the will of an ego, money enhances the freedom to express one's unique individuality. It further enhances the freedom to be one's true self by serving as a means to differentiate between the subjective center and the objective performances of a person.

On the other hand, in *The Philosophy of Money* Simmel's analysis becomes more complex and less sunny than in the earlier work.[18] He attends now to ways in which money also has the effect of impeding the growth of genuine individuality, thereby manifesting his more mature position that the most basic feature of the modern order is its capacity to differentiate and promote opposed characteristics. For example, he describes ways in which persons are debased by having their personal qualities translated into monetary terms.

Much of Simmel's analysis of the threats to individuality in the modern period relate to what he considers the oppressiveness of "objective culture." For Simmel, the primordial sense of culture refers to the process whereby the powers of the human individual are perfected by taking in purposely created external objects. These external things that promote the fulfillment of individual personality Simmel designates as objective culture, using the term subjective culture to mean the measure of development thereby attained. One major line of Simmel's interpretation of modernity concerns the imbalance between these two cultural dimensions—the fact that modern humans suffer from a sense of being surrounded by an innumerable number of cultural elements they can neither assimilate nor ignore. All the above strands of interpretation are woven together in Simmel's remarkable essay "The Metropolis and Mental Life" ([1903] 1971), which he introduces as an

18. This is not to say Simmel radically changed his outlook at the end of the 1890s. Central themes of *The Philosophy of Money* already appear in his 1889 paper "Zur Psychologie des Geldes," while certain early pessimistic points—e.g., the intensification of inner conflicts due to increased intersection of social circles—do not appear later.

inquiry into the specifically modern conditions that bear on the struggle of individuals to maintain their autonomy and individuality in the face of overwhelming forces of social organization, technology, and cultural tradition.[19]

Weber, too, produced an array of sociological analyses that focus on the level of voluntaristic action as a primary variable. In one of his first typological ventures, the 1913 essay on categories for a *verstehende* sociology Weber distinguished among associational forms by the extent to which they involved voluntary agreement. His most famous taxonomy, that of the forms of social action, distinguishes them explicitly in a hierarchy of ascending voluntarism—from traditional habitual action that is animal-like in character to the highly deliberate kind of action he called instrumentally rational (*zweckrational*). Weber used a similar kind of typology to classify the various grounds for upholding legitimate authority. More generally, Weber's leitmotif for the comparative analysis of culture and history is the question of what favors the rational construction of social and cultural phenomena. His most famous plaint about modern society concerns the constriction of individual voluntarism by the inanimate forces of capitalistic production and the animate mechanisms of bureaucracy.

Behind those constricting forces, however, Weber identified deep historical cultural innovations involving the progressive embodiment of human rational will. That is to say, Weber represented objectified forms of rationality in bureaucratic organization and capitalistic forms of production as conflicting with the new dimensions of subjective rationality and freedom opened up by modern science and law (Levine 1985a, chs. 7–9). This analysis parallels Simmel's depiction of tragic conflict between subjective and objective culture, and his belief that the struggle to maintain personal freedom and individuality in the face of supraindividual social and cultural forces gives rise to the "deepest problems of modern life." Preoccupation with this tension by thinkers like Simmel and Weber may be said to reflect the fact that the opposition between individualist and collectivist themes, sustained between the British and French traditions as two different forms of naturalism, played out in Germany as two different forms of voluntarism. Kant had

19. These Simmelian themes are further elucidated in Levine 1981b and 1991a. Even in other substantive essays, Simmel at times used the sphere of personal freedom as a significant dependent variable. For example, his essay on super- and subordination considers the effects that different structures of domination have on the personal freedom of subordinates.

celebrated the voluntarism of the individual subject, Herder and Hegel that of the collective subject. Where Hegel finally subordinated individual agency to an unfolding collective *Geist*, Simmel and Weber saw the interaction between these two manifestations of human creative agency as constituting a tragic struggle.

Throughout, Simmel and Weber maintained positions that put them in continuing opposition to the naturalistic traditions developed in Britain and France. For all the differences in their sociological agendas, they both subscribed to the Postulates of Subjective Meaning, Normative Self-determination, and Subjective Voluntarism.[20] It was the genius of both scholars to provide enduring syntheses of the three subtraditions emanating from Kant, which I identified above. The philosophic foundations they provided for the social sciences include doctrines about *subjective meanings,* which necessitate a distinctive *methodology of empathic understanding;* assumptions about the *a priori categories of knowing subjects;* belief in the *irreducibly distinctive character of practical judgment;* and emphases on *human agency, both as a normative ideal and as a crucial variable for sociological analyses.* The formidable German defense of subject-oriented assumptions against Anglo-French support for naturalistic assumptions originated one of the persistent fault lines in modern social science.

20. For overviews of their sociological programs, see Bendix 1977, Käsler 1988, and Kalberg 1994. See also Levine 1981a for Weber; for Simmel, see Spykman 1925, Dahme 1981, and Levine 1981b.

# CHAPTER TEN

# The Marxian Tradition

A lthough some earlier German thinkers had accepted particular ideas from British or French authors, Karl Marx was probably the first theorist to identify significantly with key features of all three traditions. The journey by which he sought to integrate them in the decade after 1836 counts as one of the most turbulent and consequential episodes in the history of ideas—turbulent in how fast and often he changed his point of view, consequential in having engaged the three traditions just after they had spawned broad ideological movements.

In England by the early 1820s, James Mill was flourishing as leader of a movement devoted to implementing the utilitarian principles codified by Bentham, in good part through mobilizing a political party that became known as the Philosophical Radicals. Aspiring to be a "reformer of the world," John Stuart Mill founded the Utilitarian Society, a small group convened to discuss Benthamite principles, in 1822. A few years later, the eminent mathematician Olinde Rodrigues founded a movement to promulgate the teaching of Saint-Simon. Centered in Paris, the Saint-Simonians proselytized throughout Europe—organizing meetings, circulating journals, sending missions to the working classes. Fourier and Proudhon inspired other streams of what came to be called a socialist movement. In the early 1830s, the Hegelian movement captured the allegiance and energies of numerous German intellectuals. Whether oriented to individual interests and rights as in England, collective solidarity and well-being as in France, or the claims of ideal spirit as in Germany, all of these ideologists embraced the challenge of using reason not just to ground a secular ethic but to galvanize the reconstruction of society. Rarely have philosophical ideas been so directly linked to public activism as during Marx's early years—a linkage he would forge all the more tightly in the red-hot embers of his social passion.

## MARX'S CROSS-NATIONAL ITINERARY

The career of young Marx took the form of a journey across Western Europe that was at once physical, affective, and cognitive. Moving from

Trier to Berlin, thence to Paris, finally to London, Marx experienced a series of emotional shifts of allegiance as well as a broadening of intellectual horizons.

The scion of renowned rabbis, Karl Marx grew up as a believing Lutheran after his father Heinrich had him converted at the age of six.[1] As an adolescent Karl embraced the Kantian liberalism as well as the national patriotism of his father. In an essay written for school, "Reflection of a Young Man on the Choice of a Profession," he declared that one's choice of vocation should be steered by two considerations, "the welfare of mankind and our own perfection"—general ideals current at the time, to be sure, but also the two indeterminate duties specified in Kant's *Metaphysics of Morals*. From classical German idealism Marx absorbed the ideal of a realm of human freedom which transcends a world of merely natural occurrences—an ideal he would subsequently transfigure repeatedly but could never abandon.

After a carousing year at Bonn Marx transferred to the University of Berlin to study law, but felt drawn instead to pursue philosophical questions. At first he did so by constructing what he called a "metaphysics of law" modeled on Fichte. He produced a system that, though differing from Kant in matters of detail, he described as "bordering on the Kantian . . . in its fundamental schema." Dissatisfied by the effort, he wrote his father, "Once more I realized that I could not make my way without philosophy. . . . I wrote a new basic metaphysical system [but] upon its completion I was again forced to recognize its futility and that of my previous endeavors" ([1837] 1967, 45).

Throughout this period Marx "was greatly disturbed by the conflict between what is and what ought to be, a conflict peculiar to idealism" (42)—an idealism, he noted, he had nourished with Kant and Fichte (46). Annoyed by continuing philosophical frustrations, Marx abandoned these guides and renewed his quest. "A curtain had fallen, my holy of holies had been shattered, and new gods had to be found." He sought them by "seeking the Idea in the real itself. If formerly the gods had dwelt above the world they had now become its center" (46). This

---

1. Marx's mother came from a Dutch line of rabbinic families, which included a renowned professor at the University of Pavia. His paternal grandfather had been rabbi at Trier; his paternal grandmother descended from a number of distinguished rabbis, including the rector of the Talmudic university at Padua. In order to escape the harsh edicts against Jews imposed by the Prussian regime that liberated the Rhineland from Napoleon, Karl's father Hirschel converted to Protestantism and changed his name to Heinrich the year before Karl was born. Only after the death of his own mother could Heinrich bring himself to have the children converted also.

meant converting to the philosophy of Hegel (which previously he had disdained) and associating with the young Hegelians of the Doctors' Club.

What drew Marx from Kant to Hegel was apparently Hegel's ability to anchor the realm of human freedom in the vicissitudes of human history. Hegel found a way to ground the notion of a transcendental Ought that was so pronounced in Kant and Fichte. He did this by connecting human transcendence to a process of unfolding of the World Spirit triggered by the inexorable interplay of human passions. Along the way, we saw, Hegel displaced Kant's concern for individual morality to a peripheral position, conceiving modern state constitutions and religious doctrines to be the highest embodiment of reason and freedom instead.

By the time Marx encountered the teachings of Hegel, Hegel's followers had formed contesting factions. The main line of division among them is often defined by reference to Hegel's famous aphorism: "What is Rational is Real; What is Real is Rational." Conservative followers of Hegel emphasized the second clause, interpreting Hegel to mean that the contemporary historical circumstances of the Prussian state and its Protestant Christian religion formed the pinnacle of the evolution of reason and freedom. For them the philosopher's task was simply to show the rational character of the world and thereby reconcile thought with reality. The "Left" Hegelians stressed the former clause, holding that grasp of the truly rational provided a basis for mounting a critique of contemporary reality. They argued that the reality of certain conditions depended on the extent to which those conditions formed a rational totality. In this view, reason could dictate the need for radical transformation of given institutions, not accommodation to them.

It was this active, critical version of Hegel's philosophy that Marx broached in his dissertation of 1841. He argued that the appropriate task for philosophers, following the climactic culmination of speculative philosophy in Hegel, was to transform spirit into energy, into an expression of *will* that would have impact on a reality still devoid of spirit. In 1843 he described this task as "unrestrained [*rücksichtslose*] criticism of everything existing": criticism must neither shy away from drawing troublesome conclusions nor shun conflict with the powers that be. Such criticism is to work by clarifying human consciousness. The objects it should address include religion and science on the theoretical side and, on the practical side, the political state in all its modern forms (Tucker 1978, 13).

With this formula, Marx committed himself to a project of criticizing the social world that would direct the rest of his life. After using Hegel to complete his critique of Kant, he found in Feuerbach a means to launch a critique of Hegel. Feuerbach had argued that religious conceptions consist of the alienated representation of real human needs projected onto constructed symbolic objects. By analogy, Marx argued in 1843 that Hegel's idealized conception of the state was nothing other than the projection of a longing for social solidarity within atomized civil society onto a mythical, metaphysical plane. "The state is an abstraction. The people alone is what is concrete" (Tucker 1978, 18). Thus he made it his task to invert the Hegelian conception in order to focus on the "genuinely active elements" of the state: families and civil society (16).

At this point Marx believed that human emancipation could no longer be viewed either as the attainment of autonomy through individual adherence to self-determined moral maxims, as with Kant and Fichte, or, following Hegel, as the triumphant ascendance of World Spirit manifest in the centralized state and universal religion. Individual and collective forms of idealism alike were imaginary projections based on deluded consciousness about true human needs. Consequently, a concrete agency must be found to mediate the transcendent leap into the realm of human freedom. Once he had used Feuerbach's type of criticism to overthrow what he came to regard as Hegel's mystifications, Marx proceeded to debunk Feuerbach on the basis of a more thoroughgoing "materialistic" conception of history.

After exhausting the resources of the German tradition in looking for the decisive agency of human emancipation, Marx turned to France. In 1843 he taught himself French and began avidly reading the Paris socialists—Fourier, Proudhon, Dézamy, Cabet, Leroux. He had already been exposed to French ideas in Germany—in his hometown of Trier, where he doubtless encountered representative followers of Saint-Simon; in a book by Moses Hess (1837), whose combination of secularized Jewish messianism and French socialism introduced key ideas of Fourier, Saint-Simon, and Babeuf; and in Lorenz von Stein's analysis of the socialist movements in France (1842), a work that mediated Marx's entree into the French tradition and from which he may have borrowed the notion of the proletariat (Lobkowicz 1967, chs. 15, 19). Toward the end of 1843 Marx journeyed to Paris to coedit a journal, the *Deutsch-Französische Jahrbücher*, whose aim was to promote a synthesis between French political reality and German philosophy. In

Paris Marx devoured French writings unavailable in Germany, became close to radical philosophers like Fourier, Bakunin, and Proudhon, and associated with class-conscious artisans and craftsmen.[2]

In an essay (published in the *Jahrbücher* in 1844) written to introduce a critique of Hegel's *Philosophy of Right,* Marx signaled both his discovery of a historical agent for universal emancipation in the proletariat and an allegiance to the social themes of the French tradition. If in 1842 he had expressed himself as a German nationalist mildly skeptical about the French, the following year he became an anti-German Francophile. In this pivotal piece, Marx narrows his critical mission. The criticism of religious beliefs is completed; the task is now to criticize political conditions, indeed to overturn them. Criticism now becomes "not a lancet but a weapon . . . it aims not to refute but to destroy" (Tucker 1978, 55). The resources of philosophers cannot produce the revolution that seems called for. A modern political revolution requires the mobilization of an entire social class, one that undertakes from its particular situation a general emancipation of society. Yet Germany has produced no class with sufficient generosity of spirit to identify itself with the popular mind, let alone one that possesses the logic, insight, courage, and clarity needed to confront the social status quo (63). What, then, is to be done?

France pointed the way. There, Marx writes, every class of the population is *politically idealistic* and considers itself to represent the general needs of society. And in France the proletariat has emerged as successor to the bourgeoisie—as that class whose revolutionary strivings can be undertaken on behalf of the entire society. The one hope for emancipation in Germany is to form a working class on the French model. This would be a proletariat that has a universal character because its sufferings are universal, a class "which can only redeem itself by a *total redemption of humanity*" (64).

With his concluding peroration—"*the day of German resurrection* will be proclaimed by the *crowing of the Gallic cock*" (65)—Marx affirmed the social movement in France as the grand agent of emancipation for which he had been searching. The French also gave him a notion he

2. In an August 1844 letter to Feuerbach, Marx wrote, "You would have to attend one of the meetings of the French workers to appreciate the pure freshness, the nobility which bursts forth from these toil-worn men." Elsewhere that year he wrote that whenever French socialist workers assemble, their gathering turns before long to aimless camaraderie and then "the brotherhood of man is no mere phrase with them, but a fact of life" ([1844] 1975, 355, 313).

could use to replace the Hegelian ideals of World Spirit and the state: the Saint-Simonian ideal of panhuman society, shortly to be glossed as "associated humanity" (*gesellschaftliche Menschheit*). Saint-Simon's associationism lubricated the way from Hegel to socialism. Both Saint-Simon and Hegel had been critical of the Enlightenment for its hyper-rationalism and its destructive individualism, yet unlike the conservatives who shared that critique they expressed optimism and a belief in progress. They also viewed history as proceeding in a dialectical manner, whereby positive periods necessarily alternate with negative, critical periods. With all that as common ground, the French social thinker helped Marx shift from the Germanic glorification of the state to seeing the state as an instrument subordinated to human society, and from an ethos of dutiful subordination to an ethos pitched to fraternal solidarity.

Even so, the French tradition lacked resources for guaranteeing the redemptive triumph of the proletariat with the same certainty that Hegel had attributed to the salvific achievement of the modern state. To Marx's dismay the French prophets of social reconstruction could appeal only to the power of ideas. Socialists like Proudhon rejected the bourgeois economic world developing around them in favor of an egalitarian utopian communal order. The Saint-Simonians accepted the bourgeois economic order. They believed that with the French Revolution the last great conflict between social classes had occurred, and all that remained was to organize the new order by converting people to a secular religion of humanity.[3] Marx wanted to abide by Hegel's approach to realizing the ideal of emancipatory transcendence. This involved a scenario that eschewed idealistic moral strivings in favor of affirming an inexorable process of historical development. Consequently, Marx needed to find a way to affirm the achievements of bourgeois capitalism as foundational for an emancipated society without relying on the sway of moral ideals. He could only avoid appealing to utopian ideals by construing the transformations he desired as outcomes of scientifically grounded laws of historical change. In the search for such laws, he turned to the British tradition.

In 1844 Marx began to acquaint himself with English economics in greater depth—thanks mainly to Friedrich Engels, whose view of eco-

---

3. Recall that Saint-Simon had called finally for a "new Christianity." Even so, the phrase "scientific socialism" was apparently first used, circa 1845, to describe Saint-Simon's position (Hayek 1952, 155, 167).

nomics as the decisive force in history appeared in a *Jahrbücher* article Marx found impressive. And so, half a year after composing the article that compared France with Germany, Marx added a third nation to his repertoire. In an essay for the newspaper *Vorwärts* he named the English the "economist" of the European proletariat, joining the Germans as its theoretician and the French as its politician (Tucker 1978, 129).

Marx deepened his grasp of British political economy following his move from France in 1845, first to Brussels and then to England, where he spent the rest of his life. However, the key elements of his agenda were in place by the summer of 1844. He articulated them in unpublished writings that would become known as the *Economic and Philosophic Manuscripts of 1844* (hereafter EPM). In prefacing this work he announced his intention to issue a critique of several practical domains—law, ethics, politics, etc.—in a series of distinct, independent pamphlets. As it turned out, Marx never got around to publishing those critiques. Instead, he devoted himself ever after to working out the main subject of EPM, a critique of political economy. This critique appeared in five installments—the *Outlines for a Critique of Political Economy (Grundrisse)* of 1857–58; the *Contribution to the Critique of Political Economy* of 1859; and the three volumes of *Capital: A Critique of Political Economy* published in 1867 and (posthumously) in 1885 and 1894.

In the EPM Marx affirmed the basic premises of British political economy. This meant acknowledging the positive achievements of the new, commercial-industrial order and accepting the labor theory of value articulated by Adam Smith and David Ricardo. Ricardo's iron law of wages—that the tendency of population to increase up to limits set by the means of production provides a virtually unlimited supply of labor that can be employed at a constant real wage—helped him find a basis for predicting the coming triumph of the proletariat. From the ideas of British economists—on the propensities of actors to pursue individual interests in a market situation, and on the dynamics of profit, wages, and rent and the unequal social distributions that they generate—Marx sought to develop a theory that could demonstrate how

> the worker sinks to a level of a commodity and becomes indeed the most wretched of commodities; that the wretchedness of the worker is in inverse proportion to the power and magnitude of his production; that the necessary result of competition is the accumulation of capital in a few hands

. . . and that the whole of society must fall apart into the two classes—the property-*owners* and the propertyless *workers*. (Tucker 1978, 70)

In December 1847 Marx gave a series of lectures, later published as *Wage Labour and Capital,* which presented the core of the theory he would elaborate in later critiques of political economy.[4] In pursuit of their respective individual interests, capitalists exchange wages for the labor power of workers; capitalists compete among themselves for profits, leading to increasingly efficient production through the increased division of labor and mechanization of production; increased productivity leads to increased competition among workers, such that their work becomes more repulsive and their wages decrease. With this formula, Marx was positioned to show how natural laws governing the behavior of individuals interacting in a market cause the progressive immiseration of the propertyless workers, placing them in such desperation that they must join forces to overthrow the bourgeois capitalist order and therewith propel humanity into its redeemed condition.

### THE MARXIAN SYNTHESIS

By the time Marx embarked on his own vision quest, thinkers of the British, French, and German traditions had crystallized their views along two lines of opposition. As we have seen, the opposition between the core postulates of the British and French traditions hinged on the issues of methodological and normative individualism versus societal realism and normativity. The opposition between the German and the two other traditions hinged on the issue of voluntarism versus naturalism. Within the German tradition, the individual-societal opposition took the form of the contrast between Kant's individualism and the *Volksgeist* theories of Herder and Hegel. The antinomies in question can be represented as in Figure 11.

The process by which Marx successively confronted these different positions can be visualized as a clockwise movement around this figure beginning with the upper right cell. At each stage he held onto a core commitment but substituted features taken from the new position for one or more secondary beliefs. Marx's core commitment was arguably to the Kantian notion of securing human dignity through the transcendence of merely natural determinisms. This commitment emerges as

---

4. Some of his specific views regarding wage labor would change in his later writings.

| | | PRINCIPLE OF RATIONAL ETHIC | |
| :---: | :---: | :---: | :---: |
| | | NATURE | FREEDOM |
| *LOCUS OF REALITY AND VALUE* | INDIVIDUALS | Atomic Naturalism<br>\*\*\*\*\*\*\*\*\*\*\*\*\*\*\*\*\*\*\*<br>Smith<br>Ricardo (1844–) | Individual Voluntarism<br>\*\*\*\*\*\*\*\*\*\*\*\*\*\*\*<br>Kant<br>Fichte (up to 1837) |
| | SOCIETIES | Societal Naturalism<br>\*\*\*\*\*\*\*\*\*\*\*\*\*\*\*\*\*<br>Saint-Simon (1842–43) | Collective Voluntarism<br>\*\*\*\*\*\*\*\*\*\*\*\*\*\*\*<br>Hegel (1838–41) |

Figure 11. Marx's Journey Across the Three Traditions

one of the most constant themes throughout his life's work.[5] It appears in the language of EPM about the human essence and in *The German Ideology* on the division of labor:

> Animals produce only under the domination of immediate physical need, while humans produce even when free of physical need and truly produce only in freedom from such need. (Tucker 1978, 76; translation modified).

> The division of labour offers us the first example of how, as long as man remains in natural [*naturwüchsig*] society . . . as long, therefore, as activity is not voluntarily [*freiwillig*], but naturally [*naturwüchsig*], divided, man's own deed becomes an alien power opposed to him, which enslaves him instead of being controlled by him. (160)

It appears in the *Grundrisse* a dozen years later, when Marx describes what will happen when the basic human need to be active finds satisfaction in work that is no longer slave labor, serf labor, or wage labor: "The external aims become stripped of the semblance of merely external natural urgencies, and become posited as aims which the individual himself posits—hence as self-realization, objectification of the subject, hence real freedom" ([1857–58] 1973, 611).

5. Marx's lifelong devotion to the ideal of human freedom illustrates the truth he formulated so eloquently in his youth, even though his subsequent turn to historical materialism would appear to contradict it: "Ideas won by our intelligence, embodied in our outlook, and forged in our conscience are chains from which we cannot tear ourselves away without breaking our hearts; they are demons we can overcome only by submitting to them" (1967, 135).

It appears in Marx's final production, volume 3 of *Capital:*

> The realm of freedom actually begins only where labour ceases to be determined by necessity and external expediency. . . . Freedom in this field can only exist when socialized humanity, the associated producers, rationally regulate their material interchange with Nature, bringing it under their communal control instead of being ruled by it as by a blind force. (Tucker 1978, 441; translation modified)

And it appears in the writings of Engels, Marx's alter ego, whose rapturous account of human liberation following the communist revolution concludes with the perfectly Kantian image of humanity's ascent from the kingdom of necessity to the kingdom of freedom.[6]

One can characterize Marx's journey, then, as a continuing effort to anchor the quest for transcendent freedom in worldly realities. The first stage of this journey involved an effort to ground the process of attaining freedom in the dynamics of human history, when Marx embraced the Hegelian story of history as the progressive unfolding of freedom through collective development. In making this move, he sacrificed the Kantian principle of individual ethical self-determination as the source of morality.

Seeking then to ground the way to collective emancipation in the strivings of some concrete social class identified with the general needs of society, he embraced the French ideal of associated humanity and their conception of social classes as historical agents. In the process, he sacrificed the Hegelian principles of collective enactment of law as the source of morality and matured self-consciousness as the marker of collective freedom.[7] This completed his fateful transfiguration of the Ger-

6. "With the seizing of the means of production by society, production of commodities is done away with, and, simultaneously, the mastery of the product over the producer. . . . Then for the first time man, in a certain sense, is finally marked off from the rest of the animal kingdom, and emerges from mere animal conditions of existence into really human ones. The whole sphere of the conditions of life which environ man, and which have hitherto ruled man, now comes under the domain and control of man, who, for the first time becomes the real, conscious lord of Nature, because he has now become master of his own social organization. The laws of his own social action, hitherto standing face to face with man as laws of Nature foreign to, and dominating him, will then be . . . mastered by him. Man's own social organization, hitherto confronting him as a necessity imposed by Nature and history, now becomes the result of his own free action. . . . *It is the ascent of man from the kingdom of necessity to the kingdom of freedom.*" (Tucker 1978, 715–16; emphasis mine)

7. Marx's declining interest in the value of consciousness may be discerned in a shift in the way that he characterized the human species. In the EPM, he asserted that "the whole character of a species . . . is contained in the character of its life-activity; and free,

man concept of freedom: freedom no longer signified autonomy in the sense of subscription to moral laws of one's own (individual or collective) making, as in Kant or Hegel, but freedom to produce for one's own needs in a manner of one's own choosing.

Seeking to ground the attainment of universal emancipation through the ascendance of the proletarian class, Marx embraced the ideas of British political economists on the labor theory of value and the dynamics of profit-seeking individuals interacting in the marketplace. Although he retained the notion of social determinism insofar as he held that social conditions shape the form and content of individual interests and the means of realizing them (1973, 66), in the process he bypassed the arguments of French social realists about properly societal interests, including society's needs for regulation and integration and for qualified elites to satisfy those needs.[8] At the same time he rejected the British notions of natural moral propensities and individual rights.

The method by which Marx sought to integrate the three traditions, then, can be described as one of *progressive substitution*. His final synthesis combined Kant's notion of self-determination, Hegel's notion of collective historical development, French notions of associated humanity and social classes, and the British conception of the competitive pursuit of individual interests in the marketplace. Since it drew effectively from a variety of appealing philosophic traditions, this method of synthesis produced an ideological formula that proved powerfully seductive to intellectuals.[9] Nevertheless, although Marx made a heroic effort to bring those diverse traditions together, he cannot be said to have provided a stable resolution of the oppositions among them. Indeed, his synthesis bequeathed a gaping contradiction between the postulates of naturalism and voluntarism, and actually discarded assumptions about the role of morality and sentiment in human action

---

conscious activity is man's species character." "Conscious life-activity," he added, "directly distinguishes man from animal life-activity" (Tucker 1978, 76). But the following year, in *The German Ideology* (1845), he rather belittled the idea of making consciousness the distinguishing feature of the quintessentially human: "Men can be distinguished from animals by consciousness, by religion or anything else you like. They themselves begin to distinguish themselves from animals as soon as they begin to *produce* their means of subsistence. . . . What [individuals] are, therefore, coincides with their production, both with what they produce and how they produce. The nature of individuals thus depends on the material conditions determining their production" (150).

8. Marx came to rail against the idea of conceptualizing "society" as an abstraction counterposed to the individual (Tucker 1978, 86).

9. On the special ideological appeal of Marxism to intellectuals, see, for example, Aron 1957 and Feuer 1969.

that all the other traditions had shared. Before examining these issues, let us examine one other aspect of his synthesis.

## THE FUSION OF THEORY AND PRAXIS

In yoking the traditions of naturalism and voluntarism, Marx also fused two intellectual spheres that previous thinkers had contrasted in different ways—the spheres of theoretical knowledge and practical philosophy.

Recall that Aristotle had regarded practical philosophy as different from and largely independent of theoretical science. The practical sciences differed from theoretic sciences in their subject matters, principles, aims, and methods. Hobbes and his followers sought to overcome what Aristotle thought was endemic to practical knowledge, a probabilistic approach tied to the vagaries of public deliberation, by securing for practical knowledge a solid foundation in theoretic truth. For most of the modern naturalists, priority went to theoretic knowledge secured by the methods of modern natural science, so that practical knowledge became the application of that theoretic knowledge. When Kant came to believe that the determinism of theoretic knowledge robbed humans of their dignity and freedom yet failed to provide a sufficiently secure basis for practical understanding, he tried a different tack. Kant posited that practical philosophy could proceed on the basis of pure speculative reason, in a manner that reaffirmed the marvelous supposition of human freedom and autonomy, leaving to theoretical philosophy the radically different task of understanding the marvels of the natural world.

Marx's remarks on this issue suggest a position that diverges from all of those just mentioned. To begin with, he reworked the concept of the practical so that it no longer signified anything like what Aristotle or Kant had meant by the term. In lieu of Aristotle's notion of praxis, which related to the process of deliberate choice in action, Marx shifted its meaning to what Aristotle had meant by *poesis,* or making, that is, a form of activity that relied on *techne,* or art. Ignoring Kant's conception of the purely practical as relating to the formulation of moral duties, he restricted the term to what Kant had meant by the *technically* practical. *For Marx a practical problem no longer referred to choosing the right course of action, but concerned rather how to produce objects geared to satisfying human wants.*[10]

10. For a pioneering discussion of this issue, see Lobkowicz 1967.

In one of his more famous lines, Marx suggested that philosophy had a single point and that point was to change the world (Tucker 1978, 145). With that he denied any justification for an independent body of theoretical knowledge, just as his appeals to abolish the division of labor aimed to undo the separation of intellectual from practical activity. The direction for changing the world was to be dictated by the promptings of human sensuousness. Scientific socialism, the medium of human positive self-consciousness, "proceeds from the *practically and theoretically sensuous consciousness* of man and of nature as the *essence*." For Marx the idea of separating theoretical knowledge from the requirements of praxis introduces an element of alienation of cognitive activity from its only genuine basis in human sensuousness. Science is valid "only when it proceeds from sense-perception in the twofold form both of *sensuous* consciousness and of *sensuous* need." Theory and practice are unified because both proceed from a single source and address a single aim: human sensuous experience. Ultimately the science of humanity will be fused with natural science, and "there will be *one* science" (Tucker 1978, 90–93).

## SOME CONTRADICTIONS OF MARXISM

As an effort to integrate traditions of thought that sought to provide a secular rational grounding for morality in ways that became foundational for modern social science, Marxism generated three sorts of contradictions. Rather than ground a principle of morality either in nature or in the transcendence of nature, Marx in effect offered a normative orientation based simultaneously on natural determination and the transcendence of nature, all the while denying he was providing any normative guidelines at all. Rather than locate the sources of human moral dispositions either in the properties of some natural phenomena or in a distinctive human capacity for self-determination, Marx dispensed with a specifically moral component in his model of fully realized human nature, thus contradicting the apt consensus of virtually all other social thinkers about the salience of moral dispositions (in spite of wide variations in how they account for them). Rather than formulate such an ethic in ways that affirmed the sympathetic understanding of existing national societies, the Marxian tradition was antinational in orientation and, more generally, disposed to discount the role of sentiment in action, thereby contradicting both the facts about the growing salience of nationalism during his lifetime and since as well as the consensus of most other social thinkers about the salience of human sentiments.

## THE MORALITY OF EMANCIPATORY NATURALISM

From Kant and Fichte, and doubtless from his Lutheran upbringing, Marx absorbed a yearning to transcend merely natural processes understood as a complex of external determinants. Nevertheless, his attraction to positive science, joined with a lively compassion for suffering humanity, propelled him to address the human condition in ways that did not rely on moral exhortation. His rhetoric thus often shifted to that of a fervent naturalist. Ridiculing Proudhon's ideals such as justice and mutuality, he asked what we would think of a chemist who used ideas like "affinity" instead of studying the actual laws of molecular changes (cited in Lukes 1985, 7). Prefacing the first edition of *Capital,* Marx professed a Newtonian ambition: nothing less than "to lay bare the economic law of motion of modern society" (Tucker 1978, 297).[11]

Marx generally used 'nature' to refer to processes of external determination that allowed no room for human will; he contrasted 'natural' (*naturwüchsig*) with 'voluntary' (*freiwillig*). Along with Engels he maintained that all human history up to his time had been governed by such natural processes. At the same time, their repeatedly expressed aspiration was to see humankind catapulted toward an order in which self-determination replaced that natural determination. Tension between these two beliefs has confused generations of Marxists. Should the principle of right action be to act in accordance with laws of nature? If so, then one foregoes the opportunity to act in accord with Marx's professed ideal of self-determination. Should one act in accord with the principle of nature-transcending freedom? If so, then one risks acting in ways that ignore the constraints of nature.

Apart from the ontological problems involved in accounting for the transition from a determinate to an indeterminate condition, Marx's synthesis produced a doctrine that offers no coherent grounds for moral action in the historical present. Indeed, in contrast to the British, French, and German traditions, which in their different ways provided intellectual resources for justifying the protection of human rights, Marx and Engels implicitly belittled the whole effort. Early on they criticized notions such as the injunction against stealing and the right to free speech as so many bourgeois prejudices that serve to cloak class interests (Tucker 1978, 482). One of Marx's last utterances described

11. Lenin affirmed this aspect of Marx's thought when he lauded Marx for treating "the question of communism in the same way as a naturalist would treat the question of the development of, say, a new biological variety" (cited in Lukes 1985, 21).

discussions about right (*Recht*) as ideological nonsense and trash (531). As Steven Lukes has summarized the matter:

> Marxism has from its beginning exhibited a certain approach to moral questions that has disabled it from offering moral resistance to measures taken in its name; in particular . . . it has been unable to offer an adequate account of justice, rights, and the means-end problem, and thus an adequate response to injustice, violations of rights, and the resort to impermissible means, in the world we must live in. (1985, 141)[12]

## THE REJECTION OF MORAL DISPOSITIONS

A major concern of each of the traditions we have reviewed up to this point has been to identify the source of a human moral disposition or faculty. Some, like Hobbes, locate it in a calculative faculty inherent in human nature. Others, following Shaftesbury, locate it in biologically grounded social sentiments and moral sensibilities. Some like Montesquieu and Rousseau, locate it in habits instilled by the agents of society. Kant located it in the self-determining operations of pure practical reason, and Hegel identified it with subordination to collectively instituted legal norms. Aristotle provided a complex conception that located morality in natural potential, social training, habituated character, intellectual capacity, and deliberate choice.

What distinguishes the Marxian approach to this problem is the way in which it discredits the entire question. In his selective appropriation of elements from the various traditions, *Marx in each case rejected the accounts of the source of genuine moral dispositions without substituting a fresh account of his own.* For Marx, what moral philosophers describe as admirable moral faculties or ideas are but tendentious beliefs in service of a class struggle. Thus, in *The German Ideology* Marx and Engels derided Kant's notion of the good will as an expression of "the impotence, depression and wretchedness of the German burghers . . . whose whitewashing spokesman he was" (1965, 206ff.). Late Engels summarized their position by saying that since all moral creeds are the product of socioeconomic conditions and since society has historically been organized through class antagonisms, "morality has always been class morality; it has either justified the domination and the interests of the

---

12. Lukes further observes that the tendency to dismiss moral talk as dangerous ideological illusion, rendered anachronistic by the discovery of the laws of economic development, was broadly characteristic of most followers of Marx and Engels, including Kautsky, Lenin, Trotsky, and even a number of "neo-Marxists" (24–25).

ruling class, or, ever since the oppressed class became powerful enough, it has represented its indignation against this domination and the future interests of the oppressed" (Tucker 1978, 726). Since moral notions serve only as vehicles for exploitative or insurgent class interests, once the classless society arrives humans will no longer have need for them.

## THE REJECTION OF NATIONALITY

Marx was one of the first to stress the practical context of intellectual activity and the influence of national traditions in particular. He produced a number of telling insights into what would come to be called national character. Yet his theories of human action and societal development failed to embrace the play of national identities. In *The Communist Manifesto* (1848) he and Engels claimed that the proletariat had become denationalized: "Modern industrial labour, modern subjection to capital, the same in England as in France, in America as in Germany, has stripped [the proletariat] of every trace of national character" (Tucker 1978, 482). Despite sympathy for national liberation movements in Ireland and Poland late in his life, it is fair to say that Marx accorded little room to sentiments of nationalism in his forecasts of the future. Although some Austrian Marxists as well as Lenin would later evince a new appreciation of national groupings, the logic of Marx's original position was spelled out in Rosa Luxemburg's 1908 essay on the national question when she declared that "in a class society, 'the nation,' as a homogeneous political entity, does not exist" (Anderson 1995).

It is difficult not to see in Marx's avoidance of such issues a deep ambivalence about his own ethnic and national identity.[13] Given that he began his career as a positively self-identified German, how did that ambivalence emerge? One account would link it with political developments in Prussia in the early 1840s. At twenty-four he seems still to have been a sincere German nationalist aligned with his father's patriotism. His allegiance was shaken by two developments. On the one hand, social disruptions following Prussia's steps toward economic

---

13. One expression of his ambivalence toward being German appears in a letter to Engels about the recently completed manuscript of *Capital:* he comments that the work's architecture "is a triumph of German science, something an individual German can avow since it is in no way *his* merit, but belongs more to the *nation*. All the more happily, since otherwise it is the *silliest nation* under the sun" (cited in Mazlish 1984, 149). This is gentle compared to the fiercely anti-German sentiments he expressed elsewhere.

modernization—emancipation of peasantry, dissolution of guilds, and unprecedented population increase that outstripped economic growth—led to a concentration of impoverished people that both excited the sympathies of young liberals like Marx and alarmed the Prussian aristocracy. On the other hand, the traditionalist aristocracy had become increasingly hostile to liberal reforms in the 1830s, increasing the hold of conservative forces in the government and the universities. This resurgent conservatism thwarted the academic careers of Left Hegelians and led to the censorship and suppression of their newspapers.[14] Marx, like his comrades, felt doubly betrayed: by the promises of Hegelian idealism that had led them to think that the Prussian state would embody constitutional liberalism, and by the repressive actions of the authorities themselves. This sense of betrayal produced an intense need to repudiate the legacy of German idealism altogether. Marx became further alienated when Prussian authorities persuaded the French government to expel him from France at the beginning of 1845 and later issued a warrant for his arrest. The following year Marx gave vent to a burst of anti-German sentiment in the tract written with Engels, which represented German idealist philosophy as nothing but an ideology and in the process caricatured German national character.

The sense of betrayal experienced by Marx and his Left Hegelian colleagues has seemed to some a sufficient explanation for that representation (Mah 1987). However, Marx's biography exhibits certain features that strongly suggest deeper-lying personal motivations were also involved. Marx experienced chronic difficulties in establishing stable social ties; again and again he exhibits a pattern of attachment followed by repudiation. He quickly turned against most of his erstwhile German and French colleagues. He spent most of his adult years living in a country where he was triply alienated—from English society, from fellow radicals, and from the workers movement. His distancing, moreover, took the form not of passive withdrawal but of chronic combativeness. As Tucker put it, Marx "wrote as though his pen were dipped in molten anger" (1978, xxxviii). He polemicized against all the traditions from which he borrowed, not just those of Germany. These traits inform the intellectual profile we have identified: a lifelong agenda de-

14. Marx's older colleague Arnold Ruge was expelled from Halle in 1841, and the following year Bruno Bauer was expelled from Bonn. What triggered Marx's decision to move to Paris in 1843 was his resignation as editor of the *Rheinische Zeitung* when the Prussian government suppressed it after Czar Nicholas I protested Marx's editorial phillipics against Russia.

voted to critique and revolution rather than inquiry, and a mode of synthesis I have called progressive substitution, which depends precisely on a succession of attachments and repudiations.[15]

Whatever the underlying dynamics, Marx's alienation from the European nations of his day, conjoined with a fiercely combative temperament, disposed him to reject all allegiances to national orders and to construe social classes and the dialectical pattern of their large-scale conflicts as the only really significant social historical reality. More generally, as has been observed repeatedly, Marx detested emotionalism of every kind and "systematically under-estimated the influence of such non-rational forces as nationalism, and religious and racial solidarity," with the result that the Marxian tradition displays a "peculiar incapacity . . . to account for ethnicity, nationalism, regionalism, religion, and other identity-constituting cultural phenomena (other than as illusory, ideological products of class societies)" (Berlin 1978, 22; Lukes 1985, 76). Marx assumed a model of human action in which not only moral dispositions but also affective ties have little place. He therefore contradicts the consensus of all the other traditions regarding the role that emotionality plays in human conduct. Marx knew many of the other authors we have considered—Hume, Smith, and Mill; Montesquieu, Rousseau, and Saint-Simon; Kant, Herder, and Hegel—yet turned his back on exploration of factors in human action other than the instrumentally rational pursuit of sensuous interests.[16]

The intellectual tradition founded by Marx and Engels may now be represented in the format I have used for the other traditions as follows. To the question of how the facts of human experience are to be constructed and explained, it responds with what may be called the Postulate of Dialectical Materialism: *Human phenomena can best be understood by analyzing how the rational pursuit of individual*

15. This focus on Marx's personality may seem excessive. However, although the Marxian tradition contains a wide array of internally contested positions, like other traditions considered in this book, it bears the imprint of a single personality more than any other tradition save that of Aristotle. For an evocative introduction to these issues, see Mazlish 1984. My own sense is that Marx's ambivalence toward his German identity and his aversion to ethnicity and nationalism ride on a deeper complex of feelings about his family's Jewish identity, a matter that lies beyond the scope of this study.

16. In Weberian terms, Marx rejected traditionality, affect, and value rationality as significant dimensions of action, leaving humans essentially oriented only by instrumental rationality. Parsons pioneered this approach to understanding Marx by calling him a utilitarian, without realizing that those who were properly called utilitarians generally did not neglect the role of sentiment (see chapter 7 above).

*interests gets shaped by the conflictual yet progressive evolution of the means of production and the social relations of production.*

To the question of how secular thought can provide a rational grounding of moral judgments, it responds with a **Postulate of Evolutionary Determination:** *In lieu of normative judgments, scientific analysis provides indications of the objectively appropriate actions for a given historical period.*

To the question about the source of human moral dispositions, it responds with a **Postulate of Class-determined Morality:** *So-called moral faculties are simply ideological apologia for the repressive or insurgent interests of particular classes in historical periods. In a classless society humans will need no distinctly inculcated moral faculties.*

Of the many problematic predictions in the Marxian oeuvre, the forecast of the end of alienation and social inequality in a classless society became a major point of reference for the sociological tradition that arose next—largely in the shadow of Marxism, in sunny Italy.

# CHAPTER ELEVEN

# The Italian Tradition

The arrival of Marx quite altered the sociological tradition. In the nineteenth century his impact on the transgenerational dialogue was exceeded only by Darwin's theory of evolution. Although certain accounts exaggerate the role played by Marxian thought, there is surely some truth in Gouldner's claim that after Marx world sociology divided into two separate streams, Marxian and non-Marxian, and in Zeitlin's claim that much of Western sociology has involved a nontrivial degree of critical dialogue with the ghost of Marx. In Britain, France, Germany, and the United States, that dialogue directed attention to substantive issues but did little to set the basic tone of their social theories. In the case of Italy, however, confrontation with Marxism helped to stimulate certain foundational notions. The most consequential Italian contribution to the sociological tradition thus appears late on the scene: it is post-Marxian. Paradoxically, however, this contribution draws on a longer trajectory of history and culture than any other for its ultimate sources of inspiration.

## FROM ROME TO RISORGIMENTO

The search for a secular social ethic in Italy may be said to begin with Niccolò Machiavelli (1469–1527). Like Hobbes in Britain, Montesquieu in France, and Kant in Germany, Machiavelli originated the part of his country's cultural tradition that became foundational for modern sociology. He, too, believed he was providing a fresh departure for thought about human affairs: he "resolved to open a new route, which has not yet been followed by anyone" ([1532] 1950, 103). Unlike those other authors, however, and certainly unlike anything to come in upstart America, Machiavelli's new route took directions from cultural sources more than a millennium old—from his country's roots in ancient Roman civilization.

This was so in three senses. Most of the writers he borrowed from—Livy, Tacitus, Valerius Maximus, Frontinus, Polybius, Plutarch—were classical Romans. The historical exemplar he appealed to as a model for the good society was the Roman Republic. And his own thinking was shaped by participation in a kind of life that was directly continuous with the practices for which ancient Rome had become most famous: the active governance of city-states.

Machiavelli was not and did not aspire to be a philosopher in the manner of the other seminal authors. Both in their impressionistic and diffuse style of exposition and in their practical intent his writings evince not systematic theory but the views of a man whose middle years were spent shaping civic policies, fulfilling diplomatic missions, and mobilizing militias. He did so on behalf of his home republic of Florence, one of several city-states to take shape in northern Italy during the Middle Ages, along with Verona, Padua, Siena, Milan, Lucca, Pisa, and others.

Many of these cities were governed by assemblies of burghers known as *parlamenta,* unique in Europe of the time and the earliest exemplars of modern political democracy. To some extent these civic associations were modeled on the government of Venice. Founded as an asylum for refugees from the barbarian invasions of the fifth century, who hoped to salvage as much as possible of the glory that was Rome, Venice was the sole region in all of Italy whose population and traditions were continuous with ancient Roman life. And central to those traditions was the Virgilian notion that what distinguished Rome's empire from all earlier empires was the Romans' capacity for administration. This theme gets celebrated in the lavish murals of Siena's city hall, one side of which depicts an effective regime under which peasants, merchants, artists, and clerics enjoy productivity, well-being, and harmony, the other showing the effects of poor governance in poverty, misery, and civil strife. Machiavelli used the experience of ancient Rome to inspire and press his case for a view of human life and society that stressed the necessity of *competent rulership.* No theme could be more calculated to contradict the Marxian belief in radical egalitarianism.

Although the writings of Machiavelli that adumbrate a secular social ethic took the form of tracts designed to help princes and councilors practice the political craft,[1] they embody ideas that generations of readers have taken to comprise a coherent system of social thought. The moral anchorage of that system is the conviction that the security and well-being of the community represents the supreme value for man, so that considerations of individual welfare and personal morality get subordinated to the collective good. The collective good can be ad-

---

1. In addition, Machiavelli was an accomplished poet, playwright, and historian.

vanced through proper knowledge of the ways collectivities function. This is not a matter of wishful thinking but of careful determination of lawful regularities on the basis of impartial observation and detached analysis of historical instances. Societies are natural bodies, just like plants, animals, and individual humans, and so their properties can be ascertained by proper naturalistic study. Their well-being requires special understanding of their natures, which means examining the experience of successful political bodies from the past.

Collective well-being cannot be achieved simply by allowing the free play of individual instincts, for the latter are unreliable at best and likely to produce chaos at worst. In Machiavelli's book, humans are ungrateful, fickle, lying, hypocritical, fearful, shortsighted, grasping creatures. Personal dispositions must be shaped and controlled by astute leaders and sound social arrangements, such as giving ample recognition to meritorious citizens, opening careers for those ambitious to gain glory and honor, and ensuring that citizens know the legal consequences of their actions. Properly molded, citizens could manifest the *virtù* of the disciplined, courageous, and self-sacrificing citizen—exemplified by ancient republican Romans—needed to promote the welfare of the political community.

Thus far, Machiavelli's ideas run parallel to those we have found in the French tradition. They fit nicely under what we described above as the Postulates of Societal Realism, Societal Normativity, and Societal Morality. But in representing these postulates, Machiavelli introduced a set of ideas that turned the Italian tradition toward a distinctive version of Societal Essentialism. The writers of the French tradition, from Montesquieu and Rousseau through Durkheim, believed that social forces were needed to turn the human animal into a moral creature, but they trusted properly socialized actors to conduct themselves in a moral manner, enjoy the blessings of social solidarity, and be responsive to leaders who embodied their common ideals. Although there are moments when a harsher note appears, as when Comte discusses a need for elites to discipline and manipulate the masses, it forms a minor strain that virtually disappears by the time of Durkheim. That strain became the focal point for Machiavelli and the thinkers he came to influence.

Because Machiavelli combines so sharp a vision of collective well-being with so dim a picture of human nature, he places particular emphasis on the tactics rulers must use to accomplish their mission. Not only must they not shrink from using force but, since force is integral and essential to the political art, they must become truly proficient at it. Virtually alone among the great figures of Western social theory, Machiavelli included analyses of warfare in his repertoire. Rulers must be as fearsome as lions, Machiavelli advises, and—the memorable simile continues—as cunning as foxes. They should manipulate their subjects with ingenious incentives. Effective rulers also must promulgate ideas that induce followers to obey them. This includes promoting attractive images of themselves that need not be truthful; whatever it takes to do so, the ruler should seem to be full of mercy, integrity, and humanity. Above all, the ruler should appear as a man of religion. What is more, religion can play a critical role in promoting political solidarity by unifying the masses and vivifying their morale. The point of the good society for Machiavelli is not to move ever closer toward an ideal human condition, but to achieve whatever balance can be attained at a given time, protecting the interests of one's collectivity through the effective leadership of competent rulers. This process will run its natural course in the form of ever-recurring cycles. The concepts of ruling elites, force, legitimating ideologies, and cyclicality give Machiavelli's social theory its distinctive bite and distinguish a theoretical position we may designate as hierarchistic naturalism.

Although Machiavelli's ideas received much attention (if not often careful study) from writers in other countries,[2] they did not immediately stimulate a recognizable tradition of Italian thought. To be sure, several writers of genius appeared here and there in the succeeding centuries. The broad-gauged Neapolitan scholar Giambattista Vico approached the Hobbesian problem of order with a *Nuova Scientia* (1725), which pioneered the empathic study of cultures and included such characteristically Italian themes as a focus on ruling strata, nonrational action, and historical cycles. In 1764 the Milanese jurist Cesare Beccaria produced a brilliant *Essay on Crimes and Punishments,* which applied a utilitarian calculus of pleasures and pains to the subject of penal theory and galvanized a wave of penal reform all over Europe. In the early nineteenth century, figures like Gian Romagnosi and Roberto Ardigò produced Comte-like treatises adumbrating a positive science of societal phenomena, and later in the century Cesare Lombroso pioneered positivistic analyses of criminal behavior.

2. Expectably, French writers like Mably and Rousseau found particularly congenial Machiavelli's emphasis on the efficacy of a collective spirit, which is more than an aggregation of individuals wills.

Nevertheless, works of this sort functioned as isolated statements, not as part of an emerging national tradition. In other countries, writers like Locke and Smith, Montesquieu and Rousseau, Herder and Hegel were buoyed up by tides of national development; their ideas became aligned with men engaged in promoting the power, wealth, and glory of modern nation-states. The very success of the city-state structure that nourished Machiavelli delayed Italy's entrance into the vortex of nation-building.[3] What is more, the conquest of Florence by forces of Emperor Charles V a few years after Machiavelli's death precipitated an epoch of political and cultural decline. Its most degrading feature was the subordination of most of Italy to external powers—France, Spain, and Austria. Only three and a half centuries later, once the stirrings for independence inspired by Enlightenment humanism became coupled with renewed pride in the legacy of Roman civilization, did Italian social thought surge with its distinctive take on the problems that elsewhere had stimulated modern sociology. And for that endeavor, as for much of the sentiment that informed the nationalist stirrings known as the Risorgimento, Machiavelli's ideas helped to set the stage.

## CELEBRATIONS OF ELITES

The first major figure of modern Italian social theory was a Sicilian, Gaetano Mosca (1858–1941). Although Mosca devoted himself to governmental matters—he taught constitutional law at Palermo, Rome, and Turin, and served in the Italian government during most of his career—in the *Elementi di scienza politica* (1896), translated as *The Ruling Class,* he broached a more general theory of society. Where

3. As a distinguished Italian scholar once wrote of Italy's failure to follow the other European countries in the growth of modern nationhood, "There is no reason why this process was abortive in the country we call Italy, or the reasons are too many." But he continues, likening that process to the formation of a new set of celestial bodies from a disintegrating sun, the Roman Empire: "Metaphorically one can say that those fragments of the split sun which circled in the immediate neighborhood of what was left of the sun itself were under such emanations of energy, both centripetal and centrifugal, that they could not settle down into a new partial unity and were fated to revolve around Rome in an incandescent and nearly chaotic condition." He also goes on to fault the Italian elites for being captivated, under the influence of Dante, by the Roman universal idea in ways that hampered their ability to create a modern unified nation (Borgese 1938, 32, 34). Less poetically, Cochrane attributes the Florentines' failure to mobilize other Italian districts to join them in a coalition against the invader to their narrow civic pride (1973, 9).

Machiavelli had offered a mere handbook based on the narrowly circumscribed historical knowledge available in the sixteenth century,
Mosca said he would offer a genuinely scientific account of the constant tendencies in human society by means of sound analysis of the
historical facts about various nations.

Using the idiom of societal naturalism, Mosca formulates as the first
and most obvious truth about all "political organisms" their tendency
to divide into two classes, a class that rules and a class that is ruled.
Taking this formulation with serious consistency leads Mosca to eliminate two other political forms that had been identified by Aristotle and
Montesquieu, monarchy and democracy. What appear to be regimes
governed by the one or the many are in fact always under the rule of the
few. Ostensible monarchs require a class of agents to see that their orders are carried out. Ostensible mass rule requires an organized minority to discharge the functions of governance; "otherwise all
organization, and the whole social structure, would be destroyed"
([1896] 1939, 51).

Ruling minorities secure their power by their effectiveness and by
the propagation of beliefs. They are effective to the extent that they are
organized: an organized minority is irresistible as against any single individual of the majority. They are perceived as effective by virtue of
possessing or appearing to possess certain qualities prized by their
society—material, intellectual, even moral qualities. But what sustains
their rule above all is the propagation of doctrines that bind the loyalty
of the masses. Gradual persuasion can accomplish this, but the quick-
est way to establish an idea is through force. Mosca ridicules the notion
that force cannot establish beliefs in a population and marshals a number of historical instances to prove his point (190–92). Even so, in populous societies that have attained "a certain level of civilization," ruling
classes always attempt to valorize their superior status by appealing to
moral and political considerations. In earlier times this "political formula" was religious or supernatural in character; in modern times it
appears as a rational doctrine, such as "the will of the people." In neither case do these political formulas correspond to scientific truths. But
they fulfill a deep need in man's social nature, and it is doubtful whether
a society can hold together without one of these "great superstitions."

The social scientific advantage of the concept of the ruling class lies
in its ability to serve as a diagnostic tool to identify types of society.
What has been called Mosca's Law states that the "type and level of
civilization vary as ruling classes vary" (xix). Ruling classes vary accord-

ing to the extent of their control of various "social forces"—socially influential qualities such as money, land, military prowess, religion, education, manual labor, or scientific training. A regime's stability can be measured by calculating the ratio between the social forces it represents and those arraigned against it. Stability, however, is a mixed blessing, for the usurpation of power by a group that imposes its will universally through force produces tyranny and a lowered level of civilization. For Mosca the good society is one where diverse constellations of social forces coexist in a kind of equilibrium. Such a benign balance emerges when aggressive social forces are held in check, not by other defensive forces but by what Mosca calls "juridical defense," consisting of custom, morals, institutions, and constitution. Standing armies provide one aspect of this schema by disciplining and making socially productive the combative elements in populations.

Fundamental to Mosca's theory is the proposition that established elites tend not only to maintain themselves in power but to transmit their positions to their children: all ruling classes tend to become hereditary in fact if not in law. This tendency is opposed by the fact that from time to time societies feel the need for capacities different from those possessed by the current ruling class. For example, if a new source of wealth develops, if an old religion declines or a new one is born, if different kinds of knowledge become important, then dislocations take place as the ruling class gets challenged by those who evince the newly desired kinds of capacities. Members of a ruling class lose strength when they cease to find outlets for the capacities that brought them to power, when they can no longer render the social services they once did, or when their talents and services lose importance in their social environment. Indeed, Mosca suggests, "The whole history of civilized mankind comes down to a conflict between the tendency of dominant elements to monopolize political power and transmit possession of it by inheritance, and the tendency toward a dislocation of old forces by an insurgence of new forces; and this conflict produces an unending ferment of endosmosis and exosmosis between the upper classes and certain portions of the lower" (65). Changing the naturalistic simile, Mosca also likens the oscillation between phases of closed, stationary ruling classes and phases of dislocation and renovation of ruling classes to air masses that alternately settle through inertia and move about due to the unequal distribution of heat. Thus, although Mosca sees a long-term secular improvement in levels of civilization, what he outlines as the primary dynamic in history takes the form of an ever-recurring cycle. Driving home the societal naturalism that informs his entire analysis, Mosca asserts that what philosophers call free will has had and perhaps will always have little or no influence in hastening or delaying any phase of this cycle.

Like Mosca, Vilfredo Pareto (1848–1923) aspired to replace illusionary approaches to social thinking with a discipline built like the natural sciences—to construct a system of sociology, he said, on the model of celestial mechanics, physics, and chemistry. He came to this mission late in life. Trained as an engineer, Pareto worked for two decades as a corporate manager and consultant until he turned toward economics and began to profess the subject at Lausanne in 1893. Both his theoretic ideas and political views changed rapidly in the ensuing decade.

Pareto's thesis at Turin Polytechnic, *the Fundamental Principles of Equilibrium in Solid Bodies,* provided the guiding conception for his later work in social theory. Through four major books, from his lectures in political economy of 1896 to his treatise of general sociology of 1916, he probed the configurations of forces that produced equilibria in social systems. Although he started out as an atomic naturalist, curious to see how far he could go in using the assumptions of British economics to account for human phenomena, he quickly concluded he could not go very far. Just as real bodies with only purely mechanical properties do not exist, so real persons governed only by motives of pure economics do not exist. Although concrete phenomena cannot be immune from the laws of pure mechanics or pure political economy, their behavior cannot be accounted for by exclusively mechanical or economic forces ([1896] 1966, 107).

Pareto found it necessary to supplement the understanding of human social systems in terms of the rational satisfaction of individual desires in three ways. For one thing, he came to stress the prevalence of "nonlogical" forms of behavior. In a way Hume would have applauded, he argued that the greater part of human action springs from passional elements that make reason their slave by concocting various beliefs to justify them—a point little understood in Pareto's time, but familiar today as the notion that ideologies get constructed in order to rationalize emotional commitments. Although these sentiments cannot be observed directly, their effects can: the actions to which they give rise and the religious and moral beliefs through which they find verbal expression.

In addition to supplementing a psychology of interests with that of sentiments, Pareto proceeded to distinguish a collective level of human reality not reducible to individual phenomena, thereby entering the ranks of the societal essentialists. He did so by conceptualizing the social system as a reality consisting of complexes of interdependent forces and by identifying the phenomenon of social utility, or "utility of a community." In pure economics, only the utilities of individuals can be calculated and a community cannot be treated as a person, but since society has to be considered "as a complex whole, as a system, as an organism," in sociology "a community . . . can be considered, if not as a person, then at least as a unit" (1966, 103, 255). So, the scientific indefensibility of nonlogical beliefs does not matter, because they have some social utility: "for the good of society [it is not desirable] that the mass of men, or even only many of them, should consider social matters scientifically" (150).

Pareto further transcended atomic naturalism by identifying certain structural features of social systems, most notably their organization through elites and the cyclical character of their changes over time. All societies have aristocracies, groups identified by virtue of their superiority in different domains of activity. Elites are characterized by the type of nonrational beliefs they espouse. Pareto classifies the constant elements of such beliefs into six classes, two of which he treats most extensively: Class I beliefs are speculative and innovative; Class II beliefs are traditionalist. Remarkably, Pareto describes ruling elites oriented in these two ways in the same metaphoric terms used by Machiavelli, lions and foxes. The lions hold Class II sentiments and constitute governments that rely chiefly on physical force and religious sentiments. The foxes hold Class I sentiments and constitute governments that rely chiefly on persuasion, intelligence, and cunning. Over time, the composition of any elite alters as it comes to be confronted by members of the lower strata. A governing elite may fend off a revolution by creaming off the top elements of the counterelite, co-opting them into its ranks. Alternatively, rigid defensiveness by lions will preclude such upward mobility until a revolution explodes against them, or an insurgent counterelite of lions will take advantage of the humanitarian weaknesses of an elite of foxes and displace them.

The same types of beliefs appear in the domains of economic and cultural activity. Class I economic elites tend to be speculators and entrepreneurs, looking for new combinations, sources of innovation in ways of doing things. Class II elites are typified by rentiers and their retainers, those who live in routine ways on the basis of fixed incomes. In the domains of art and intellectual activity, Class I dispositions express skepticism, Class II dispositions express faith. What all three domains illustrate is the circulation of elites, which Pareto identifies as one of the primary ineluctable laws governing the life of societies. It is so not because of changing societal needs and values, as Mosca argued, but because of the one-sided character of each orientation, which sooner or later gets exhausted and invites replenishment by the other. The cycles by which they rotate constitute the principal deployment of internal forces that maintain the dynamic equilibrium of social systems.

It is difficult to pin down Pareto's views of the good society. He began as an enthusiastic liberal—a champion of free trade, parliamentary democracy, pacifism, reason, and progress. Yet while he excoriated both socialism and protectionism as ideologies, he came to argue the indispensability of ideologies for social systems. The ambiguity of his position appears in the fact that many have associated Pareto with support of Fascism—party intellectuals loudly celebrated him as a protofascist—whereas others maintain that he rejected Fascism and was unhappy about accepting a seat in the Italian senate, which Mussolini thrust upon him in the last year of his life (1966, 28). What seems consistent in his mature position is a sense that (a) the good society requires competent elites to maintain public order, secure independence, and increase wealth; (b) those elites must be able to use force to maintain their position if necessary; but (c) they must be subject to checks and balances that will restrain them from oppressing and exploiting those under their tutelage.

Mosca and Pareto began their sociological journeys from markedly different points of departure—Mosca from generalizing the dynamics of elite displacement he discovered in Taine's analysis of the French Revolution, Pareto from generalizing the dynamics of mechanical system equilibria and from transforming the economistic conception of action. The two of them arrived at conceptualizations of social phenomena that are in many respects similar. The evidence supports the notion that they did so independently, despite disputes over priority in discovering the circulation of elites theorem. Less apparent but no less remarkable is the fact that, despite their differences in intellectual objectives, they evolved postulates that replicate in all essentials the postulates professed by Machiavelli.[4]

4. So, to a certain extent, did their junior colleague Scipio Sighele, who wrote extensively on sex, crime, and politics. Sighele's social psychology stressed the irrational character of interpersonal relations, with special focus on suggestibility and complicity. Like Machiavelli, Sighele noted the salutary consequences of military force in human history,

Like Machiavelli, Mosca and Pareto subscribed to what I called above the theoretical position of hierarchistic naturalism. Like the French variant of societal realism, they hold that collectivities possess properties that cannot be reduced to the propensities of individuals: Pareto's utility of a community, Mosca's social evaluations of social services. But their most important systemic proposition concerns the indispensability of ruling elites and the inexorability of the circulation of elites.

Finally, like Machiavelli, Mosca and Pareto (as Michels later)[5] aspired to produce tough-minded naturalistic accounts of social phenomena. They tried not to judge the morality of particular actions; "we refuse to discuss whether an act is just or unjust, moral or immoral," Pareto insisted (1966, 173). Yet also like Machiavelli their work was informed by a consistent vision of the good society and by a mission to fulfill deep ethical commitments. They entertained a notion of a collective good to which individual well-being—indeed, individual morality—could acceptably be sacrificed. Their good society was maintained by a ruling elite that did not shrink from using force or from disseminating unscientific myths to promote social cohesion. Their mission was to destroy the illusions they thought had hampered realistic political analysis and action. Foremost among those illusions were the doctrines of Karl Marx.

## MARX IN ITALY

Mosca and Pareto were forging their sociological ideas at a time of two major political developments in Italy: the experiment with a national legislature and the mobilization of workers and intellectuals under a socialist banner. Shortcomings in the former were feeding the latter. In response, key features of the thought of Mosca and Pareto worked to defuse the appeal of Marxian socialism.

Mosca assaults Marx's doctrines both on scientific and on moral grounds. Regarding the Marxian assumption of economic determinism, he observes that numerous profound structural changes have oc-

---

the role of forceful leaders in shaping public opinion, and the need to promote patriotic sentiments. Sighele's 1891 tract on crowds analyzed them as vulnerable to base impulses and demagoguery, anticipating by a few years Le Bon's famous book, *The Crowd*.

5. Michels avowed that one of his aims was to demolish "some of the facile and superficial democratic illusions which trouble science and lead the masses astray" (1949, 405).

curred in human societies without simultaneous changes in their systems or relations of production. At several points Mosca faults Marxian interpretations of historical facts for being tendentious and misleading. For example, he notes that in *Das Kapital* Marx refers to laws that curbed wages, like the English Statute of Labourers of 1349 and a comparable French ordinance of 1350, as evidence that "the rising bourgeoisie made use of the state in order to regulate wages, in other words, in order to keep them down to a level that was convenient for holding the workers in the desired degree of subjection." However, Mosca notes that 1348 was a year of the Black Death, in which populations had fallen off seriously and wages were rising sharply, and cites contemporaneous provisions that fixed maximum prices for bread, grain, cloth, and rent. These considerations support the counterargument that rulers were probably attempting to use these laws to mitigate serious economic disturbances due to sudden jumps in the prices of commodities and labor ([1896] 1939, 304 ff.).

Mosca criticizes the "doctors of socialism" for declaring that most human imperfections and social injustices currently being committed result not from ethical traits natural to the human species but from the present bourgeois organization of society (288). This assumption feeds into the expectation that a reorganization of society can elevate the mean moral level of an entire people, whereas the dispassionate study of historical facts indicates that such moral transformation can only be achieved to a limited extent, and that when it has taken place, this is because the wills of those holding power have been curbed and balanced by others who hold positions of absolute independence from them. As for the distribution of immorality in the populace, Mosca observes that parasites, exploiters, and exploited exist in all social strata.

Mosca also disputes the kinds of predictions Marxists make about the future. Although we cannot be sure of what is going to happen, we can be sure of *what is never going to happen,* and that is a collectivist regime which admits full popular participation and satisfaction and in which the strong will be less overbearing and the weak less oppressed. Since all societies require organized minorities to manage them, in a collectivist society the administrators of the social republic would possess unprecedented and unconstrained power: "Under collectivism, everyone will have to kowtow to the men in the government. They alone can dispense favor, bread, the joy or sorrow of life. One single crushing, all-embracing, all-engrossing tyranny will weigh upon all" (285). Mosca declares that his "whole work" stands as a refutation of

Marx's assumption that the establishment of collectivism will inaugurate an era of universal equality and justice (447).

Despite such failures to represent the laws of social life accurately, Mosca argues that Marxian doctrines would have some merit if they produced some practical effect in improving the moral and material conditions of the majority of the people. Instead of furthering equality and social justice by promoting toleration and brotherly love, however, they foment hatred and violence. Passages in the Marx-Lassalle correspondence like "the thing to do now is instill poison wherever possible" indicate that socialist doctrines thereby "offer the lower passions too vast and fertile a field in which to multiply and spread in a rank growth" (307). What is more, in opposing patriotism Marx seeks to undermine the chief source of moral and intellectual cohesion in the societies of contemporary Europe (479–82).

Pareto's encounter with Marx shows a more complicated line of development. In his first book Pareto showed sympathy for Marx's account of class struggles as an expression of class interests. While he never ceased to be appreciative of Marx for uncovering the phenomenon of "spoliation," his position began to shift as a result of reflecting on the astonishing popularity of Marxism in Italy in the 1890s. How could it be, he wrote his friend Pantaleone, that so many of Marx's propositions that were demonstrably false could be regarded by the best youth in Italy as a "new gospel" worth sacrificing their lives for (1966, 11, 21)? By the time of *Les Systèmes socialistes* (1902) he had come to represent the chief contemporary conflict as a struggle not between bourgeoisie and proletariat but between two elites each trying to pursue its respective advantage by manipulating mass support. Pareto's *Trattato di sociologia generale* has been described as a "gargantuan retort" to Marx, in which he denatures Marxism by making Marxian propositions mere special cases of much more general phenomena (1966, 77). In that treatise Pareto faulted Marx both for subscribing, like other economists, to a theory of action that ignored motivational factors other than interest, and for proclaiming in the guise of science what was in fact just another illusory ideology. Marx, claimed Pareto, progressively abandoned the domain of science "in favour of excursions into the domain of romance" ([1916] 1935, I, §830).

Although Mosca and Pareto aimed to discredit Marxian assumptions and sentiments, the hierarchistic naturalism they represented came to affect even those who lingered under the spell of Marx. Mosca's most noted disciple, Robert Michels, was born and educated in

Germany but taught at the University of Turin where he became close to Mosca; later he taught at Rome and Perugia. In his twenties Michels became active in the socialist movement, resulting in his exclusion from an academic career in Germany (to Max Weber's dismay). A passionate activist sympathetic to the syndicalism of Georges Sorel, Michels became frustrated by what seemed the lethargic state of the labor movement and the way in which calculations of parliamentary advantage dominated party life and discouraged bold steps toward Marxian socialism. Although Michels represented the Italian Socialist Party at a party congress in 1907, he left the party soon after and began to work out his critique of the party and of trade unions.

Michels wrote on a wide range of sociological topics, but his major work remains the monograph that issued from that critique, translated as *Political Parties*. In that work Michels formulated his famous Iron Law of Oligarchy: that large organizations inexorably manifest oligarchic tendencies, notwithstanding their commitment to democratic values. These tendencies stem less from psychological factors than from organizational exigencies. The need for rapid decisions in sizable groups and for full-time specialists able to discharge complex tasks requires a stable group of qualified leaders. Although they may have a commitment to democratic values, these leaders then perpetuate a de facto oligarchical rule, producing the "domination of the elected over the electors." This dynamic gets abetted by the habits of the majority of people, whom Michels, like Mosca and Pareto, views as too apathetic to organize themselves and too submissive toward those in leadership positions. Confronting head on the Marxian belief he once cherished—that the proletarian transformation of private property into state property would put an end to all class antagonisms—Michels concludes that "we are led by an inevitable logic to the flat denial of the possibility of a state without classes" ([1915] 1958, 383). Following this disillusioning analysis Michels eventually joined the ranks of those elitist Italians who became antidemocrats, even moving toward a position sympathetic to Fascism in the early 1920s.[6] This was the very time, ironically, when Mosca was beginning to voice stronger support for representative government and opposition to Fascism.

In at least four respects, then, the core doctrines of classical Marx-

---

6. As Juan Linz observes, Michels did not seem to realize that it makes a difference whether leaders are displaced by elections, in which the majority decides who shall lead, or by death or violent revolution (1968, 267).

ism were challenged head on by the thinkers of the Italian tradition. In place of a thoroughgoing economic reductionism, which dismissed political forms as derivative of the structural relations of production, Italian theorists emphasized the signal importance of political forces in their own right. Instead of prophesying an era of social equality in which the distinction between rulers and ruled would be abolished, they proclaimed the critical necessity of a governing class that would not shrink from using force. Instead of dismissing philosophical and moral doctrines as mere by-products of social conflicts—doctrines for which there would be no need in a classless society—they stressed the powerful human need for ideologies of some sort to provide direction and social coherence. Finally, instead of viewing history as an inexorable unfolding of progressive developments culminating in a transcendent condition, they saw history as oscillating in developmental cycles marked by the unending circulation of elites.[7]

The tenacity of these themes in Italian social thought appears most strikingly in the case of Antonio Gramsci (1891–1937). In contrast to Mosca, who became a liberal democrat, and Michels, who became sympathetic to Fascism, Gramsci remained to the end a committed Marxist. Yet the variety of Marxism he developed was one that attacked followers of Marx for holding precisely the Marxian tenets I just listed. In thus modifying some of the most vulnerable aspects of Marxian doctrine, he rendered it more appealing for the generation of social scientists that would attempt to restore attention to Marx in the decades after World War II.

As Figure 12 suggests, Gramsci's intellectual genealogy is complex. Like Marx himself, Gramsci turned to the doctrine of dialectical materialism following a period of involvement with German idealism.[8]

---

7. With just a touch of self-consciousness, a young Italian scholar has recently composed a fresh interpretation of the history of Italian sociology that represents it in the form of cultural cycles, "in the manner of Vico—as sociological currents and countercurrents [corsi e ricorsi sociologici]" (Burgalassi 1990, 2, 19).

8. At a later point Gramsci even likened his historic role to that of Kant. In late nineteenth-century Italy, German idealism exerted more influence on social theory than perhaps in any other country. The border between Hegelian and Marxian ideas was readily crossed. The man who has been called the first Marxist in Italy, Antonio Labriola, matured in the Hegelian school at Naples before going on to profess Marxist philosophy in Rome. There he exerted much influence on the young Benedetto Croce, who in turn subsequently disavowed Marxism to become a neo-Hegelian. Through Croce and his contemporary Giovanni Gentile, whose philosophy of "actual idealism" laid particular stress on subjective agency and later provided intellectual support for Italian Fascism, Hegelian ideas came to dominate much of Italian intellectual life.

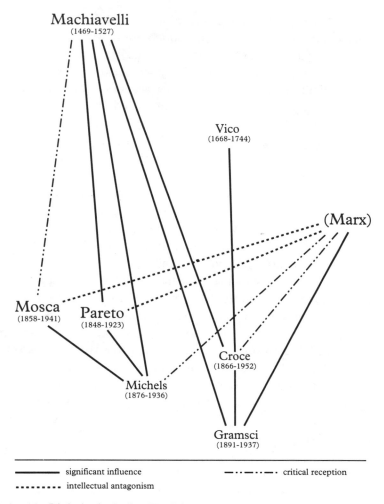

Figure 12.  Links in the Italian Tradition

Gramsci's mature ideas took shape in the city of Turin, where he went from his native Sardinia to attend the university during the years just before World War I. Following a strong initial interest in languages and linguistics, he came under the influence of a professor of literature who followed Benedetto Croce. Even after becoming a leader in the socialist movement Gramsci called Croce "the greatest thinker in Europe at this moment [1917]" (Cammett 1967, 47, 18), and later described his whole generation as followers of Croce's movement for moral and intellectual reform.

A prolific author and editor, Croce stood as the dominant figure in Italian culture throughout the first half of the twentieth century. Oriented by Vico, whom he did much to recover, as well as by contemporary Italian Hegelians, Croce carried out a lifelong battle on behalf of human voluntarism against materialist and positivist interpretations of history—a battle that included lifelong opposition to the discipline of sociology. For Croce, reality is historical, history is the development of spirit, and spirit is freedom: reality thus is *History as the Story of Liberty,* as one of his books is titled. The spirit is one, but it is divided into four distinct domains or forms: the theoretical dominions of art and logic, and the practical domains of economics and ethics.

Events radicalized Gramsci away from Croce's philosophy. Arriving at Turin sympathetic to socialism out of humanitarian protest against wretched living conditions in Sardinia, he affiliated with the increasingly militant labor movement of Turin, center of the Italian automobile industry. His involvement quickened due to the stimulating comradeship of party meetings, debates over Italy's entrance into the war, the February 1917 revolution in Russia, and finally the great uprising of Turin workers "for peace and bread" in August 1917. Gramsci's deepening commitment to socialism during the war years led him to the study of Marx, Engels, and Lenin and to a leadership role in the movement. In 1921 Gramsci was a key figure, along with his college friend, Palmiro Togliatti, in bolting the Socialist Party to found the Italian Communist Party. After a few years in the Soviet Union representing that party, he was elected to the Italian Parliament on the communist slate in 1924. When the Fascist Party outlawed all opposition parties two years later, Gramsci was arrested and sentenced to prison in order, the prosecutor said, to "stop this brain from working for twenty years." Instead, his mind entered a period of feverish productivity, filling thousands of pages in what became known as his prison notebooks.

Gramsci's conversion to Marxism led him to reject some key tenets of Croce's philosophy. He rejected Croce's Hegelian idealism by inserting a floor of materialist causation under the vicissitudes of intellectual history.[9] He also rejected Croce's pointed separation of aesthetics from history and practical activity, linking aesthetics to praxis in ways that would inform his highly original writings on popular culture during the prison years.

9. Croce and Gramsci have sometimes been called the Hegel and Marx of Italian philosophy.

Even so, Croce remained a constant factor in Gramsci's thought. In effect, he used Lenin's notions of revolutionary activity and the dictatorship of the proletariat as a lever with which to insert Crocean ideas of voluntarism into the framework of Marxist thought. This stance enabled him to hail the Bolshevik Revolution in Russia as a "Revolution against [Marx's] *Capital*," for he viewed Lenin's revolutionary achievement as an affirmation of voluntaristic action and political organization against the mechanistic determinism and economic reductionism of Marx's classic. As he wrote later, the claim of historical materialism that all fluctuations of politics and ideology can be explained as expressions of the structure of economic relations must be contested as "primitive infantilism," a point he would later support with reference to Marx's concrete political and historical writings (1971, 407). Gramsci thus seems never to have abandoned Croce's assumption that guiding ideas are essential agents in historical change.

Moreover, Gramsci began to appreciate the very fact of Croce's preeminence in Italian national culture. This exemplar stimulated Gramsci to develop what has often been considered his most distinctive theoretical construction, the notion of hegemony. As Gramsci evolved his usage of this term, it departs from Croce's concept of the"ethico-political" to represent a domain of political, cultural, and moral leadership. As one expositor of this complex and ambiguous notion has suggested, Gramsci's hegemony includes three major components: *structured class inequality,* since hegemonic processes operate through social relations of dominance and subordination; *consent,* since dominant classes must justify their claims to intellectual and moral leadership as well as control the state's coercive apparatus; and *contestation,* since the rule of all elites—even that of a presumptive proletarian dictatorship—involves a continuous process involving challenges, breakdowns, and transformations (Eley 1984, 462–63). One may connect Gramsci's projection of political oscillations even under communist rule with his views on the periodic ascendance of moral leaders from lower strata in earlier European periods. This represents a version of the cyclical view of history that Vico had propounded and that, we have seen, was prominent in the ways that Mosca and Pareto viewed history.

In asserting the dignity of the political sphere, the importance of qualified rulers, the need for leaders to promulgate moral ideas with which to secure consensus and integrate society, and a cyclical view of historical change, Gramsci adapted Marxian thought to the fundamental postulates of the Italian tradition. No less than the opponents of Marxism like Mosca and Pareto, he drew sustenance from the ancestor of modern Italian social thought, Machiavelli. In his prison notebooks Gramsci observes that Machiavelli took the important step of identifying the political domain as salient in its own right. He set a model for the goal of attaining an integrated social order in Italy by advocating direct appeals to the masses and a national militia composed of peasants as well as city folk. The author of *Il Principe* was likewise exemplary for realizing both the significance of decisive, forceful action and the truth that force alone cannot produce viable leadership without the attachment of the people. Gramsci also took note of his national heritage by describing the Italian revolutionary classes as a repository of Italian cultural values and ultimately "full heir to everything that was valuable in the traditions of their country" (cited in Williams 1960, 596).[10] For all his commitment to Marxist internationalism, Gramsci posed a dramatic contrast to Marx by celebrating as well as expressing distinctive features of his own national tradition.

## AN ITALIAN PARADOX

For all their differences, the diverse writers we have considered display a remarkably consistent profile. Machiavelli, Mosca, Pareto, Michels, and Gramsci all wrote in reaction against what they considered misleading myths and illusions about social reality. They pursued what they identified as a new, realistic, scientific approach to human history, which they hoped would rescue their contemporaries from illusory notions. They sought to counter idealistic appeals to morality, whether those of religion or secular ideologies, by appealing to the stern realities of human social life—the problematic character of human motives, the need for hierarchy, and the imperatives of force—while noting the crucial role of consensual beliefs in sustaining a viable political authority.

Central to all of their teachings were two notions: that the good of the individual should be subordinated to the good of the collectivity, and that the good of the collectivity depends crucially on capable leaders ensconced in a hierarchical structure. Drawing on the Italian experience of a politically apathetic and deferential peasantry as well as on Rome-inspired traditions of vigorous leadership, they sought to le-

---

10. For additional analyses of Italianate influences on Gramsci, see Garin 1958 and Nairn 1982.

gitimate and stimulate the activation of competent elites, elites who were resolute enough to use force as needed. They encouraged such elites to make use of symbolic devices in order to maintain their position and promote social unity. Although the Italian writers gave these symbols different names—political formulas, derivations, ideologies, myths—they were remarkably constant in their assumption that *the good society required a belief system that was to a nontrivial extent nonscientific.*

The Italian tradition, therefore, culminates in a great paradox. Inspired by a quest for the good society based on the findings of scientific reason, it concludes that the majority of people must be guided if not manipulated by acquiring beliefs that run counter to science. Under the very different historical circumstances of the New World, precisely the opposite position got developed across the Atlantic.

# CHAPTER TWELVE

# The American Tradition

The most distinctive feature of the American sociological tradition may be its resolutely empirical character. This feature can be detected early on. Consider what foundations for social science appeared in Western Europe around 1790, a century before the hothouse decade of the 1890s that produced the decisive works of modern sociology. England saw works by Bentham and Malthus that paved the way for utilitarian and Darwinian sociologies, and Scotland the *Principles of Moral and Political Science* by Adam Ferguson, often called the father of modern systematic sociology. France saw key formulations by Condorcet, Bonald, and Maistre, which inspired the great syntheses of Saint-Simon and Comte. Germany saw Kant's *Critique of Practical Reason* and Herder's *Reflections*, the seminal works behind German idealist traditions of social science. By contrast, the most notable comparable event in the United States at that time was the national census of 1790, which counts as the first periodic census in the world.[1]

To acknowledge its empirical cast is not to say that American sociology was not propelled by ethical concerns. If anything, early American sociologists wore their moral concerns more conspicuously on their proverbial shirtsleeves than anyone else. Those moral concerns followed two directions. One stemmed from the secularized Unitarianism of Emerson and the New England Transcendentalists, who, revolting against the greed of America's political and business leaders, denounced slavery, imperialist expansionism, and cultural philistinism. The other sprang from Protestant religious commitments through what was called the Social Gospel—the late nineteenth-century movement of reconstituted Puritanism that promoted good works through canvassing social woes. The 1890s—the formative decade for sociology in the United States as elsewhere—witnessed an explosion of such ills, stemming from the combined effects of mass immi-

---

1. This is not to minimize the intellectual achievements of figures like Madison, Hamilton, and Jefferson. However, their thought did not become part of a continuous tradition that fed into the foundations of modern sociology. On the discontinuity between the psychological and social philosophies of the Founding Fathers and those of the later pragmatists, see Wiley 1995.

gration, rapid urbanization, and industrial exploitation. Religious and secular orientations alike fed passionate engagement with these problems. They inspired the social survey movement, akin to muckraking journalism, which typically promoted social reform through compiling statistical correlations of disease, poverty, and housing conditions. Thus, those who sought to enlist emerging social science for the purpose of moral struggles concurred in viewing the hallmark of science as *induction from observed facts*.

Because of the atheoretical appearance of American sociology, it seemed to figures like Sorokin and Parsons, who sought to "bring theory back in," that they must look to Europe for the kinds of intellectual productions that would bring full respectability to the discipline in the United States.[2] Nevertheless, American sociology was steeped in theory from its very beginnings (Hinkle 1980), and it is surely not true that the quest for a rational secular ethic that stimulated the philosophic foundations of European sociologists had no American counterpart. The pragmatist movement played that role with éclat.

### FROM KANT TO PEIRCE

During the decades when creative scholars started to appear in the United States, Germany provided their training grounds. German universities attracted some nine thousand Americans between 1815 and World War I, mostly in the last decades of the nineteenth century. Eminent moral philosophers and sociologists studied there, including William James, Josiah Royce, George Herbert Mead, James Hayden Tufts, Albion Small, William Graham Sumner, W. I. Thomas, and Robert Park. American social philosophy took shape largely in response to stimulation from the teachings of the German tradition. Yet just as John Stuart Mill embraced Comtean positivism only to transmute its sociological approach into a form of methodological individualism, so American theorists transmuted Germanic idealism into doctrines bearing the stamp of their own distinctive cultural traits—and thereby produced what many would embrace as a philosophy taken "almost as our American religion" (Coughlan 1973, 161).

Charles Sanders Peirce (1839–1914) has often been described as

2. Even so, Sorokin, unlike Parsons, showed himself conversant with the major figures of American sociology, such as Ward, Sumner, Ross, Cooley, Thomas, Park, and Burgess. For a suggestive interpretation of why Parsons chose to ignore certain American authors pertinent to his project, see Camic 1992.

the one authentic genius and originary figure in American philosophy.[3] Peirce's philosophical focus was epistemological rather than ethical, yet his work proceeded from strong ethical concerns and carried profound ethical implications. The tradition that took the name he invented did much to articulate a social ethic and an intellectual charter for American social science. While Peirce did not study in Germany, his point of departure was the philosophy of Kant—Kant's characterization of the cognitive subject in particular.[4] Rejecting the Cartesian notion that the mind can achieve some unmediated intuition of truth, Peirce followed Kant in holding that general assertions can be proven true of all possible knowledge only in virtue of the dependence of knowledge on logic. But for Peirce, in contrast to Kant, logic develops, and so, too, then must any philosophy based on it. As Peirce went on to make new discoveries in logic, his general philosophy evolved accordingly.

Along the way Peirce signaled his intention to advance a distinctively American contribution to philosophy. In the United States, he mused in 1866, philosophy could show but a few crude homespun products compared to the refined brands imported from Germany, Scotland, England, and France. He hoped his country might some day take the place she ought before the world in philosophy. It was time for "Yankee ingenuity" to realize the potential of "a people as subtile as any under the sun and who promise to eclipse every nation since the Greeks in their genius for abstract studies" (1982, 1:456–58, 358). Some three decades later Peirce declared his ambition "to erect a philosophical edifice that shall outlast the vicissitudes of time," to create nothing less than "a theory so comprehensive that, for a long time to come, the entire work of human reason, in philosophy of every school and kind, in mathematics, in psychology, in physical science, in sociology . . . shall appear as the filling up of its details" ([1898] 1931–58, 1:1).

Although Peirce's philosophic views changed over the years, his different systems deal with similar problems and espouse fundamentally similar conceptions. In two seminal articles—"The Fixation of Belief" and "How to Make Our Ideas Clear"—which first appeared in the *Pop-*

3. This estimation of Peirce is shared by scholars of widely divergent orientations, including C. Wright Mills (1964, 127–28), Josiah Lee Auspitz (1983, 51), and Philip Wiener (1958, ix).

4. When Peirce was sixteen, his father, an eminent professor of mathematics at Harvard, began supervising him for three years of regular readings in German of Kant's *Critique of Pure Reason,* so that he committed whole chunks to memory. Although Peirce read extensively in the history of philosophy, "he seems to have been influenced by Kant far more than by anyone else" (Thompson 1953, xvii).

*ular Science Monthly* in 1877–78 and in France in the *Revue Philoso-phique* the following year, Peirce presented two key tenets of his evolving doctrine. The first construed beliefs as habits used to satisfy wants, and doubt as a disruption of habit—an unpleasant state of not knowing what to do. The second tenet was that the meaning of a concept resides wholly in the practical effects that might follow from holding the concept. This permits concepts to be translated into results observable under test conditions; thus, the meaning of "boiling hot" is that the temperature of water will register around 212 degrees on a Fahrenheit thermometer. With these formulas, Peirce expressed his fundamental principle that *thought is essentially a purposive action.*

In conversations with William James and others at Harvard in the early 1870s, Peirce had begun to refer to this doctrine as pragmatism. He adapted the name from Kant's use of *pragmatic* in the *Critique of Pure Reason* to designate the kind of belief that, while contingent, provides a basis for selecting means to carry out intended actions—in pointed contrast to the concept of *practical.*[5] The term was little noticed until the late 1890s, when James made use of it in a lecture at the University of California, "Philosophical Conceptions and Practical Results." Peirce himself first used in it print in an article for a philosophical dictionary in 1902. With the publication of James's *Pragmatism* in 1907, the term became widely known. By that time Peirce wanted to disavow the name, claiming that its popularization had distorted what he meant by the word. Peirce proposed to substitute pragmaticism as a word "ugly enough to be safe from kidnappers" ([1905] 1931–58, 5:277). But pragmatism came to be the rallying symbol for an army of American social theorists, all of whom shared certain notions he had pioneered.

Peirce's pragmatist doctrine reflects a fivefold modification of Kant's notion that the knower secures knowledge through the applica-

---

5. Some of Peirce's friends, he later recalled, wanted him to call his doctrine 'practicism' or 'practicalism,' terms closer to the Greek *praktikos,* but "for one who had learned philosophy out of Kant . . . and who still thought in Kantian terms most readily, *praktisch* and *pragmatisch* were as far apart as the two poles, the former belonging in a region of thought where no mind of the experimentalist can ever make sure of solid ground under his feet, the latter expressing relation to some definite human purpose. Now quite the most striking feature of [my] new theory was its recognition of an inseparable connection between rational cognition and rational purpose" ([1905] 1931–58, 5:274). The locus classicus in Kant's first *Critique* is A824, B852: "Ich nenne dergleichen zufälligen Glauben, der aber dem wirklichen Gebrauche der Mittel zu gewissen Handlungen zum Grunde liegt, den *pragmatischen Glauben.*"

tion of a priori categories. He redefined cognition as an activity that alternates between fixed modes of acting (habits) and disruptive experiences (doubts). He viewed this activity as a process involving change: cognitive categories are not fixed and innate, but admit novelty in the course of fresh inquiry stimulated by doubts. He identified the medium of this process as a third element outside of sense impressions and mental dispositions—language or, more generally, signs. He situated this activity in the work of an indefinite community of experimental investigators. And he located the collective process of inquiry in a larger context of human evolutionary development. This treatment of the cognitive subject by reference to the concepts of experience, habits, novelty, language, community, inquiry, and evolution was shared by all the authors who came to be associated with the pragmatist movement, however much they differed among themselves.

Although Peirce himself lived, tragically, on the margins of American academic institutions, pragmatist ideas were developed through the work of professors at three universities—Harvard, the University of Michigan, and the University of Chicago. The pragmatist philosophy cultivated at these institutions would orient the preeminent shapers of American sociology in the first decades of the twentieth century. But first it had to undergo transformation from a theory of meaning, as Peirce conceived it, to a theory of ethics and society.

Part of the transformation was carried out by William James, Peirce's longtime friend and colleague at Harvard. James applied Darwin's evolutionary theory more radically and consistently than had Peirce, seeking to understand all aspects of human action—all beliefs and feelings, including religious sentiments—as forms of evolutionary adaptation. James also developed further Peirce's notion of the self as based on internal conversation, distinguishing between an 'I' and a 'Me' and identifying an externally constituted 'Social Me' as part of the latter. Above all, he shifted the core pragmatist interest in the practical consequences of beliefs *from a concern with what a belief might signify for an audience of scientific observers to a concern with the repercussions the belief might have on how humans live.* Through these innovations and his more successful public activities James played a key role in developing and disseminating pragmatist philosophy. However, his impact on American sociology was indirect, since he was known primarily as a psychologist and remained preoccupied with the vagaries of individual consciousness. The pivotal figures for adapting pragmatism to social theory were John Dewey and George Herbert Mead.

## FROM HEGEL TO DEWEY AND MEAD

Young John Dewey took graduate courses with Peirce during the brief period Peirce lectured at Johns Hopkins, but it was only decades later, he confessed, that he came to appreciate what Peirce was doing. Initially, Dewey evolved a pragmatist point of view in reaction against German idealism via a route rather different from that taken by Peirce.

Following an exposure to Scottish moral philosophy standard for American undergraduates of the time, Dewey came under the influence of the neo-Hegelian George Morris at Hopkins and began his adult philosophical journey as a follower of Hegel. Dewey's dissertation depicted Kant as the founder of modern philosophic method insofar as he remained true to the conception of reason or spirit as the center of human experience, but held that insofar as Kant deviated from that conception he fell into contradictions which Hegel then resolved.[6] At Hopkins Dewey also was attracted to G. Stanley Hall, whose work moved him to write an essay, "The New Psychology," that celebrated physiology for introducing experimental techniques into the exploration of psychic processes. The essay further acclaimed the new psychology for its ethical overtones in recognizing human tendencies to realize purposes and pursue religious experience. It thus signaled a latent tension in Dewey's thought between finding morality in the supra-individual unfolding of the absolute idea and locating it in the needs of a striving organism.

In 1884 Dewey followed Morris to the University of Michigan as an instructor and began to work out the problems involved in his dual allegiance to Hegelian philosophy and empirical psychology. From Hegel he had derived a lifelong aversion to formalism in logic and to the British tendency to depict psychic processes and individual actors as self-subsistent entities. The Hegelian doctrine, he later recalled, helped him scrap the common assumption that man has a "ready-made mind over against a physical world as an object" and convinced him "that the only possible psychology . . . is a social psychology" (Jane Dewey 1939, 17–18). But his devotion to psychological naturalism was heightened by reading James's *Psychology* in 1891, which finally moved him to challenge the Hegelian outlook by stressing the nonreflective aspects of human experience—treating humans less as cognitive subjects and more as beings who act, suffer, and enjoy—as well as aspects of cogni-

---

6. The dissertation itself has been lost. This summary is based on a letter Dewey wrote about it at the time, quoted in Coughlan 1975 (41).

tion that could be directly elucidated by experimental inquiry. Eventually, Dewey's critical rejoinder to German idealism would turn to outright opposition. At the outbreak of World War I he published a tract indicting German philosophy for idealizing duty to the state in ways that favored militarism and calling for an "American philosophy" that would promote "a future in which freedom and fullness of companionship is the aim, and intelligent cooperative experimentation the method" ([1915] 1942, 145).

Like Dewey, George Herbert Mead turned to German philosophy for a secular worldview that would replace his even more tortuously abandoned religious beliefs and ended up working on a doctoral critique of Kant (which he never completed). In 1887 Mead began graduate study in pursuit of a secular philosophical ethic, drawn to Harvard by another of Hegel's American devotees, Josiah Royce. Royce had studied at Hopkins before Peirce taught there (and, like Dewey, took his degree under Morris) but subsequently came under the influence of Peircean ideas. Even so, he remained loyal to Germanic idealism in his search for a way to join philosophy to a Christian theological view of reality; at times Royce described his own position as "absolute pragmatism." Royce offered Mead a philosophy of history that interpreted the kingdom of God as the historical realization of a "Beloved Community" of mutually uplifting beings. However much Mead appreciated the freedom of intellectual exploration Royce manifested, he declined to commit himself to Royce's Germanic idealism, for he felt it "was the product of another culture grafted onto American culture, not an authentic interpretation of American life and a guide for action in . . . his American present" (Joas 1980, 17).

Like Dewey, too, Mead became attracted early on by the promises of physiological psychology, writing that "the scientific spirit of modern psychology . . . saves the class of philosophers as a whole from wasting themselves upon meaningless formulae."[7] Mead also enjoyed some informal association with James, tutoring James's son the summer after his first year at Harvard. James probably reinforced Mead's decision to leave philosophy for the study of psychology, which he then pursued at Leipzig (with Wundt) and Berlin (with Dilthey and others). In 1891

7. The statement comes from a letter to his friend Henry Castle in May 1887. Mead's decision to turn to psychology was also prompted by a sense of career opportunities in that new field. He feared trying to pursue a career in philosophy in American universities, which at the time were almost totally controlled by intolerant Protestant churches (Joas 1980, 17, 218 nn. 11, 12).

Mead accepted a call to leave Berlin for the University of Michigan, where he taught courses on Kant and the history of philosophy as well as on physiological psychology and evolutionary theory. At Michigan he began a long cordial association with Dewey, Tufts, and the psychologist James Angell (who had studied with James at Harvard). One reason Mead was attracted to Michigan was the prospect of achieving some clarification of his philosophical belief system through a deepened study of Hegel with the renowned Hegelians there. His arrival coincided with a period of intense creativity during which Dewey was forging the core ideas of his pragmatist philosophy. He found Dewey an inspiring exponent of idealism yet devoted to naturalistic science. The situation made Mead ecstatic: "I have at last reached a position I used to dream of in Harvard where it is possible at least to apply good straight phy[siological] psy[chology] to Hegel and I don't know what more a mortal can want on this earth," he wrote a friend.[8]

In 1892 Tufts left Michigan to join the new University of Chicago. At the urging of Tufts, two years later President Harper appointed Dewey, with Mead and Angell in tow, as head professor in philosophy. The four erstwhile Michigan colleagues oriented the new department of philosophy along pragmatist lines.[9] Energized by the intense sense of common endeavor that marked the new university, Dewey, his colleagues, and their graduate students cooperatively produced a wealth of ideas that stimulated fresh thought and inquiry in economics, education, psychology, sociology, and theology as well as philosophy. They aspired to nothing less than a program to resolve all philosophical questions through analyses of practical action. They pushed pragmatism beyond Peirce and James to create what Darnell Rucker in *The Chicago Pragmatists* (1969) has described as the first authentic school of Ameri-

8. Mead to Henry Castle, 12 January 1894. The letter continues, in lines that anticipate Mead's exposition in *Movements of Thought in the Nineteenth Century:* "I have been reading some Fichte lately and was impressed with the idea that he brought out the principle of the subject category—that Schelling objectified it and that Hegel put content into it—unravelled it" (Mead Papers, University of Chicago Library, box 1, folder 3).

9. James had recommended the appointment of Peirce to Harper, but a snide letter from another Harvard professor impugning Peirce's character was apparently sufficient to dissuade Harper (Rucker 1969, 10). Dewey later quarreled with Harper about arrangements at the laboratory school and resigned. However, the Chicago department continued to be dominated by pragmatist philosophers long after 1905, when Dewey left for Columbia and Angell turned to psychology, since Mead and Tufts were joined by fellow pragmatists Edward Ames and A. W. Moore. Their hegemony lasted through the late 1920s.

can philosophy.[10] Dewey's seminar in logic formed the epicenter of the school. A collection of papers from that seminar appeared in 1903 as *Studies in Logical Theory*, a publication that aroused hyperbolic admiration in William James.[11] Advancing the generic pragmatist program of rooting all beliefs in the exigencies of action, it affirmed intimate connections between actual thought processes as studied in the lab and the normative principles of logic, and between how we ascertain physical facts and how we make value judgments.

The foundational notions for that development got crystallized in Dewey's famous 1896 paper, "The Reflex Arc Concept in Psychology." There he challenged the reflex arc model of psychic phenomena he had favored until but a few years earlier, a model that depicts psychic reactions as passive responses to external stimuli. Now he depicted humans as creative rather than passive, agents who actively select stimuli and impart meaning to them and to their effects. Dewey went on to distinguish habitual activities, in which there is no stimulus response at all because the action simply follows an orderly sequence of events, from actions in problematic situations, in which the organism encounters stimuli of uncertain meaning to which the appropriate response is far from clear. In the latter case, the organism must imaginatively rehearse anticipatory images of various responses it might make and their consequences. With this formulation Dewey succeeded in giving a naturalistic account of human thinking and thereby laid foundations for his later analyses of the phenomena of intelligence, the logic of inquiry, the techniques of education, and the process of valuation.

Mead expanded this conception in ways that Dewey quickly embraced. On the one hand, Mead rooted human thinking more radically in biological processes, showing how it emerged from adaptive response patterns that organisms found selectively advantageous in the course of natural evolution. In its trial-and-error responses to situa-

10. "Only at the new University of Chicago at the turn of the century did there grow up a school of American philosophy. The pragmatism that John Dewey and his colleagues and their students collaborated on there had its roots in James and Peirce, but what emerged from their efforts was distinctively their own and reflected more truly the soil from which it sprang than did either James's or Peirce's thought" (Rucker 1969, vi).

11. On reading the volume James exclaimed: "Chicago University has during the past six months given birth to the fruit of its ten years of gestation under John Dewey. The result is wonderful—a *real school*, and *real Thought*. Important thought, too! Did you ever hear of such a city or such a University? Here [at Harvard] we have thought but no school. At Yale a school but no thought. Chicago has both" (Rucker 1969, 3).

tional problems, Mead later wrote, "the animal is doing the same thing the scientist is doing" (1936, 419). On the other hand, Mead connected thinking more radically to societal phenomena, tying the evolution of mind to the evolution of the self and making the latter in turn an outcome of social interactions. Finally, he provided a more sophisticated way to determine ethical criteria by linking the whole process to the evolution of an increasingly inclusive and universally oriented society.

Between them Dewey and Mead worked out a synthesis of principles evolved by Peirce and James and fused it with the social concerns of their own milieu. They accepted Peirce's broad view of the method of science and generalized it to all cognitive activity. By viewing science as the epitome of human creativity and democratic community, they at once defused Jamesian anxieties about science as a threat to human values and transcended Peirce's restriction of the pragmatic emphasis to matters of theory. They also found a way to connect it with their meliorist impulses, tying inquiry to the redress of social grievances and the reform of education, matters to which they both devoted a good deal of energy—Dewey through his work at the university's laboratory school and the settlement programs of Hull House, Mead supplementing those involvements with service to many civic causes, including juvenile penal code reform, the struggle for women's rights, a school for emotionally disturbed children, strike arbitration work, and the reform of municipal health services.[12] Dewey and Mead grandly unified theory and practice—in theory and in practice.

## PRAGMATISM AND AMERICAN SOCIOLOGY

In their formative years each of the major pragmatist philosophers experienced some form of struggle related to the conflict between science and religion.[13] Coming from backgrounds steeped in Puritan piety, they all were eager to follow the way of secular scientific inquiry. In particular, all were devoted to the truths of Darwinian evolutionary theory and to finding a way to reconcile them with the moral verities of their

12. Tufts likewise participated intensely in civic activities, framing legislation that affected the work of social agencies and chairing a board of arbitration in the clothing industry. Probably never before or since have a number of notable philosophers engaged themselves so extensively in constructive social activism.

13. Indeed, according to the authors of an authoritative history of philosophy in America, "the central role of philosophy in American thought has been that of a mediator between or synthesizer of science and religion" (Flower and Murphey 1977, xvii).

Christian backgrounds.[14] The philosophical form this struggle took was twofold. It expressed itself primarily as a conflict between naturalism and idealism or voluntarism. It also appeared as a struggle between the secular appeal of competitive individualism and ideals of communal solidarity and service to society. The conflicts that appeared on the main axes of European social thought—between British individualism and French collectivism, and between German voluntarism and Anglo-French naturalism—thus were internalized in the experience of the pragmatist founders. Their mission became one of reconciling these oppositions, and they did so largely by collapsing them.

This process was particularly prominent in Dewey's biography. Late in life Dewey referred to traumas he had suffered from the culture of his youth with its "divisions by way of isolating of self from the world, of soul from body, of nature from God." These conflicts produced an "inward laceration" and a "demand for unification that was doubtless an intense emotional craving." In the Hegelian syntheses, with their unification "of subject and object, of matter and spirit, the divine and the human" he found "an immense release" (1930, 2:19)—only to experience a new set of tensions between Hegelian idealism and the naturalism of evolutionary biology and physiological psychology. Dewey finally succeeded in resolving all those oppositions by transforming their components into elements of an interactional field. A year before writing the reminiscence just cited he stated:

> Neither self nor world, neither soul nor nature . . . is the center, any more than either earth or sun is the absolute center of a single universal and necessary frame of reference. There is a moving whole of interacting parts; a center emerges wherever there is effort to change them in a particular direction. (1929, 291)[15]

14. At the age of twenty-five, Dewey was still saying, "The statements of Christ and his immediate followers are explicit. . . . There is an obligation to know God, and to fail to meet this obligation is not to err intellectually, but to sin morally" ([1884] 1967–72, 1:61). A decade later, when his outlook had become more secular, Dewey's publications were addressed overwhelmingly to help those struggling to accommodate scientific and evolutionary teachings to Protestant theological backgrounds—and he found hungry audiences. In the biographies of Peirce, James, and Mead, such conflicts induced episodes of acute distress. For a revealing interpretation of the ways such conflicts affected the formation of adult identities among Dewey's contemporaries who gravitated toward sociology, see Henking 1988.

15. Flower and Murphey aptly subtitle their chapter on Dewey, "Battling against Dualisms" (1977, 811). Dewey's experience nicely illustrates Erik Erikson's point that historic leaders are those who resolve intense personal conflicts, which are at the same time the major conflicts of their era (1958). One may question Dewey's assertion that his

The collapse of those oppositions opened the way to a new and distinctive set of responses to the perennial questions we have addressed in examining the earlier traditions. Rather than take sides on the old question of whether individuals alone are real or whether societal phenomena possess an irreducible reality of their own, the pragmatists espoused the notion that individuals are themselves social phenomena—human realities consist of the acts of *social selves*. Rather than take sides on whether natural phenomena provide the exclusive objects of knowledge and grounds for action or whether humans can transcend the constraints of nature, the pragmatists argued that humans possess distinctive mental capacities that nevertheless emerged from the ordinary mechanisms of biological evolution. Mind and self alike are products of a long-term process of organismic adaptations to environment. The pragmatists biologized subjectivity. With respect to how human phenomena are to be constructed and explained, then, Dewey and Mead may be said to have formulated what we may, somewhat awkwardly, call a **Postulate of Evolving Natural Mental Social Selves.**

To the question of how secular thought can provide a rational grounding of moral judgments, they propose what might be called a **Postulate of Social Situational Normativity:** *Defensible norms emerge in concrete situations on the basis of socially executed analyses of the conditions and consequences of alternative actions.* Guides for action derive not from antecedently determined truths about nature nor from the calculations of abstract reason, but take shape in the course of attempting to diagnose a confused situation. The pragmatists marched behind the banner of Dewey's dictum: "As natural science found its outlet by admitting no idea, no theory, as fixed by itself, demanding of every idea that it become fruitful in experiment, so must ethical science purge itself of all conceptions, of all ideals, save those which are developed within and for the sake of practice" ([1893] 1967–72, 4:53). The improvement of normative judgment comes through expanding the social universe in which that diagnosis gets conducted and upgrading collective resources for the determination of facts. It can never claim absolute certainty but involves experimental exploration and continuing reconstruction of conceptions of the desirable. Philosophy has the task of mediating the clash between inherited institutions and newer social ends.

---

philosophical struggles were wholly unrelated to his personal crisis regarding religious beliefs; he himself hints at the point by volunteering the insight that one's external battles are really about a struggle going on inside oneself (1930, 19, 17).

To the question of the source and character of human moral dispositions, they offer a **Postulate of Socially Responsive Morality**: *Morality consists of habits of mind, engendered through interaction with significant others, to process decisions from the point of view of the groups involved in a particular situation.*[16] This postulate differs from that of the French theorists, to which it is perhaps closest, in replacing a notion of socially instilled norms with a more fluid and future-oriented conception of socially engendered dispositions to consider group perspectives in making decisions. Dewey himself sharply contrasted this view of the moral disposition with Benthamite individualism; he aligned his view with Mill's critique of Bentham, but went on to make the capacity for taking the social point of view an integral part of the socially constituted self. The capacity to pursue the reconstruction of ideas in a social framework is the central outcome of educational programs and the indispensable ingredient of successful democracy.

The challenge posed by the pragmatist synthesis for a science of sociology was threefold. Sociology needed to develop a conception of social phenomena that featured the subjective mental processes of actors yet understood those subjective processes both as effects and causes of societal processes. It needed to develop a conception of social dynamics that depicted states of disorder as natural occurrences providing opportunities for adaptive innovation. Above all it needed to help create publics that could exert some kind of informed moral control over current problems and future directions. These tasks were addressed with extraordinary creativity by Charles Horton Cooley, William I. Thomas, and Robert Ezra Park.

Cooley, Thomas, and Park emerged as the three intellectually dominant figures of American sociology in the early decades of this century.[17] As Figure 13 shows, the three men were exact contemporaries, although Cooley's significant publications began to appear well before

16. As Dewey expressed it, "The genuinely moral person is one [who] . . . forms his plans, regulates his desires, and hence performs his acts with reference to the effect they have upon the social groups of which he is a part" (Dewey and Tufts 1908, 298).

17. Cooley was mentioned most frequently as an influential author by respondents to the Bernard survey of 258 American sociologists in 1927 and figures invariably among the most frequently cited authors in sociological treatises around that time. Thomas and Park provided the intellectual leadership for the dominant department of sociology in the two decades after 1910, and were cited nearly as often or more than Cooley (Levine, Carter, and Gorman 1976, 840–42). Merton once called Thomas "the dean of American sociologists" ([1949] 1968, 475), and Ralph Turner wrote that "probably no other man has so deeply influenced the direction taken by American empirical sociology as Robert Ezra Park" (1967, ix).

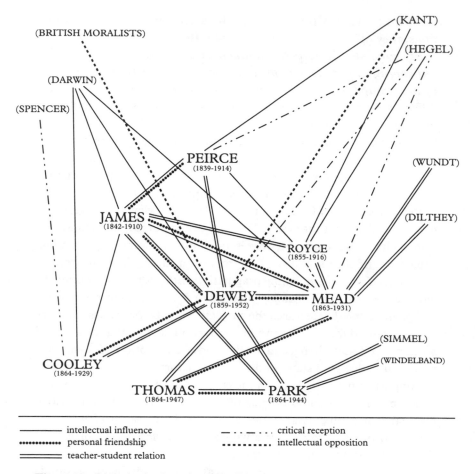

Figure 13. Links in the American Tradition

those of Thomas and Park. All three studied under Dewey, and through that contact and other influences came to inject pragmatist ideas into the American sociological tradition.[18]

All three sociologists elaborated the theme of *social subjectivity*, both theoretically—in formulations regarding the social self—and

18. Cooley and Park attended Dewey's lectures at the University of Michigan, Park as an undergraduate and Cooley as a graduate student. Cooley, like Dewey (and Park in turn), had been strongly influenced by James's *Psychology*. Park later studied with James at Harvard. Thomas began graduate study at Chicago the year after it opened and took courses with Dewey at a more advanced age. Thereafter, Thomas became a particularly intimate colleague of Mead.

methodologically—through special procedures for securing data on subjective phenomena. Cooley was perhaps the most radical in his theoretical formulations, declaring that 'society' and 'individual' denote not separable phenomena but different aspects of the same thing, for "a separate individual is an abstraction unknown to experience, and so likewise is society when regarded as something apart from individuals" (1902, 36). He came to refer to the individual mind as a "mental-social complex" (1930, 295 ff.). Cooley expanded on James's notion of the Me with his concept of the looking-glass self: the self gets constructed by imagining how one appears to another person, imagining the other's judgment of that appearance, and then experiencing some sort of self-feeling, like pride or mortification. Society in Cooley's view consists of the interweaving of these mental selves into one large social mind.

Thomas similarly emphasized the conjoint functioning of social and individual phenomena and what he called the "reciprocal dependence between social organization and individual life organization." In his masterwork *The Polish Peasant in Europe and America* (coauthored with Florian Znaniecki), Thomas presented his central concept for representing this interdependence as the "attitude," defined as a conscious disposition to act in a certain way in the social world. The study of these attitudes belonged to the province of social psychology, defined as the "science of the subjective side of social culture." On the other hand, certain attitudes become manifest in rules of behavior embodied in customs and rituals, in legal and educational norms and the like. These rules are "values" that cluster into organized systems called social institutions, which in turn form the subject matter of sociology. Thomas identified three major types of actors on the basis of their dominant attitude toward social values: the conformist, the rebel, and the creative person. And he resuscitated Dewey's notion of the generic creative actor with his notion that prior to self-determined action people examine and reflect on what is before them in order to produce a "definition of the situation," and his famous theorem that "if [people] define situations as real, they are real in their consequences" (1966, chs. 15, 10, 9; 1928, 572).

Park carried understanding of the social self forward by renaming Thomas's notion of life organization "self-conception" and by linking it with the notion of social roles. He argued that everyone is always and everywhere more or less consciously playing a role, that it is in these roles that we know each other and know ourselves, and that the conceptions that persons form of themselves seem to depend upon the recognition and status that society accords them in these roles. Persons who are subject to conflicting definitions of themselves owing to participation in dual cultures, he observed in his famous analysis of the "marginal man," experience stress and uncertain self-conceptions but also wider horizons and a more "civilized" outlook (1967, xxxvii–xl).

Because of their conviction of the explanatory salience of socially situated subjectivity, all three men pioneered the creation of methodologies designed to capture subjective realities. Cooley identified the process of sympathetic introspection—what psychoanalysts more than half a century later would reinvent as the method of "empathic introspection"—as the indispensable method for obtaining social knowledge. True knowledge of others, he argued, consists of putting oneself in contact with various sorts of persons in various situations and becoming aware of the sentiments one feels when thinking of them in those situations (1909, 7; 1930, 289–309). Thomas devised a set of techniques in order to provide more objective access to subjective realities: the systematic collection of personal life records, including diaries, letters, autobiographies, poems, and the like. Park urged his students to study the attitudes of different social strata by hanging out and getting closely acquainted with them, an empirical approach that came to be known as participant observation.

In probing societal phenomena the three germinal American sociologists elucidated the *alternation of social order and disorder.* Their interpretations reflect two emphases. One is the effort to describe social organization with reference to consensual norms rather than as a mere outcome of impersonal market forces. Cooley disputed the view that even economic institutions could be understood solely as a result of such forces. They necessarily involve human thought and moral judgment; all forms of social organization embody "the slow crystallization in many forms and colors of the life of the human spirit" (1909, 22). Thomas defined social institutions as interconnected systems of rules and regulations, and social organization as the totality of institutions found in any social group. Park depicted a "moral order" supervening over an ecological order generated by unregulated competition.

Their other emphasis is an appreciation of the inexorability and creative possibilities of social disorganization. In this they were at one with the pragmatists' conception of the creative potentialities of periods of doubt alternating with periods of fixed belief and habitual action. Although they did not dismiss the human and social cost of eroded norms, they saw the human and cultural growth such conditions could foster as well. Thomas understood the stability of social institutions to involve a dynamic equilibrium of processes of disorganization and reorganization. He also contrasted the group's desire for normative stability with the individual's wish for new experience and lauded creative persons for reconciling these desires. Creative persons reconcile these opposed desires by redefining situations and creating new norms of a superior social value. In so doing, they become agents of "social reconstruction," the kind of response groups need when disorganization has reached an acute stage (1966, ch. 1). Speaking with an evidently American accent, Cooley observed that the dissolution of traditions has its good side, producing "the sort of virtues, as well as of vices, that we find on the frontier: . . . plain dealing, love of character and force, kindness, hope, hospitality and courage" (1909, 355). The pragmatist sociologists also diverged from the tendency, more common among European social thinkers, to view disorderly crowds with alarm. Thus, where Sighele and Le Bon stressed the disruptive effects of crowds, Cooley and Park saw spontaneous collective gatherings as inherent in the transition to modern urban society and a source of wholesome social stimulation.

These American sociologists thus adapted the pragmatist view of reality as continual flux to the ordinary phenomena of social control and social change. They redefined change as a continuous endogenous process of human group life rather than an episodic result of extraneous facts playing on established structure. In their view, human group life appears always incomplete and undergoing development instead of jumping from one completed state to another. Social disorganization is seen not as a breakdown of existing structure but as an inability to mobilize action effectively in the face of a given problem.

Finally, Cooley, Thomas, and Park espoused a neutral professional role for sociological observers yet defined that role in terms of public service. They found the mission of sociology in enhancing society's capacities for intelligent self-direction, a process they referred to as *social control*. Cooley saw sociology as contributing to the growing efficiency of the intellectual processes that would enlighten the larger public will. Thomas viewed his efforts as contributing to a science of purposive social intervention and held that "ultimate practical applicability" would constitute "the only secure and intrinsic criterion" of sociology as of any science (1966, 53).

Park's whole career, in a sense, can be interpreted as an effort to realize Dewey's vision of the modern democratic public. After collaborating with Dewey on an ill-fated project to found a magazine devoted to enlightening the public with reliable factual reporting on matters of societal interest, he spent several years as a journalist and several more working on public relations for Booker T. Washington. Park's German dissertation portrayed the public as a creative collectivity unbound by conventional norms, one that differed from the crowd by being open to different value orientations yet oriented to a shared body of reliable facts; he offered an annual course on that subject, The Crowd and the Public, during the first decade he taught at Chicago. For Park, the mission of sociology was to help *create* the larger public Dewey and Mead advocated by enabling diverse sectors of the great society to learn about one another and to help *inform* the public by presenting dispassionately observed and analyzed facts about the natural processes of social life. To this end he guided his students into such little-known lifeworlds as those of black urban communities, Chinese laundrymen, Jewish ghettoes, juvenile gangs, hoboes, taxi dance halls, slums, and elite residential districts. By thus raising the public's consciousness about itself and by revealing the "perturbing causes" of social problems, sociology could become part of the grand process of enlightened social control.

# PART THREE

# Visions of the Present

## SOCIAL SCIENCE IN CRISIS OR TRANSFORMATION?

The chronological order of historic epochs is not their philosophical order. In place of saying: the past, the present, and the future, we should say the past, the future, and the present. In truth it is only when we have conceived the future by aid of the past that we can with advantage revert to the present so as to seize its true character.

AUGUSTE COMTE

# CHAPTER THIRTEEN

# Forming and Transforming a Discipline

The landscape of contemporary sociology contains a multitude of formations. A close look at the field reveals three main kinds of differences among them. As in other sciences, sociologists divide according to different topical specialties—whether they study age groups, cities, ethnic groups, families, firms, gender, religious groups, and the like. They also divide on the basis of methodologies: survey research, historiography, ethnography, experimentation, discourse analysis, aggregate data analysis. These correspond to specialties familiar from the natural sciences, similar to the way that chemists, for example, divide into inorganic and organic according to interests in different kinds of molecules, and further into groupings based on methodologies like chromatography, spectroscopy, and thermal chemistry.

What distinguishes sociology and, to a certain degree, all other social sciences is their further division according to presuppositions that reflect philosophical differences. How one classifies these diverse approaches is to some extent arbitrary.[1] Any such schema needs be handled with caution since it necessarily simplifies matters. Here are what I consider to be the main positions that had emerged by the early 1970s, along with one prominent representative of each:

| | |
|---|---|
| comparative historicism | Reinhard Bendix |
| class-state theory | Erik Olin Wright |
| critical theory | Jürgen Habermas |
| cultural structuralism | Claude Lévi-Strauss |
| eco-evolutionism | Gerhard Lenski |
| elite theory | Suzanne Keller |
| ethnomethodology | Harold Garfinkel |
| functionalism | Talcott Parsons |
| geometric formalism | Ronald Breiger |
| integralist sociology | Pitirim Sorokin |
| interactional formalism | Peter Blau |
| phenomenological formalism | Erving Goffman |

1. Different taxonomies appear, for example, in Eisenstadt 1976, Martindale 1981, and Alexander 1987.

pragmatist sociology          Morris Janowitz
rational choice theory          James Coleman
sociobiology          Pierre van der Berghe
social structuralism          Robert Merton
symbolic interactionism          Herbert Blumer
world-system/dependency theory          Immanuel Wallerstein

Where did all these orientations come from? What is their significance today? It is time to review and complete the story.

## DEPARTURES FROM ARISTOTLE

The philosophical assumptions that organize present-day sociology represent the outcome of an age-old European quest to establish a rational secular ethic based on the nature of things. The quest is generally understood to begin with Socrates and Plato and to find expression in a schematic organization of the social sciences in Aristotle. In chapter 6 I characterized the Aristotelian achievement as an effort to create a set of practical sciences of action with reference to a clearly formulated view of nature, yet in a way that kept them distinct from the aims and methods of the natural sciences. Aristotle found the good life to be constituted by happiness, the source of happiness in nature to lie in the individual's natural potential for virtue, and the cultivation of virtues to depend on social groupings that exist by nature. Yet the shaping of human virtues varies with the highly variable constitutions of communities, and the best ways to organize polities depend on particularities of circumstance and on judgments arrived at through deliberation, not rigorous proof. The ability to make such judgments draws on the distinctive human capacities for free choice and for communication through language, and the surest way to promote a good society is to have it governed by an aristocracy of well-qualified citizens.

The intellectual revolution associated with Thomas Hobbes discarded nearly all of these postulates. Hobbes viewed nature not as a kind of potential to be realized but as an inherent force that directs a universe of atoms in perpetual motion. The essentially natural feature of humans is not their potentiality for nobility and justice, but the appetites and aversions that motivate their actions. Human social order derives not from naturally formed associations but from an artificial compact geared to reaching social equilibrium through the reciprocal adjustment of interests. Instead of searching for the best way to organize human societies to promote the attainment of virtue, the key moral question becomes one of resolving the dilemma posed by the free interplay of human desires. Instead of looking to well-qualified elites to govern a good society, Hobbes contents himself with the institution of a sovereign entrusted simply to establish civil order. The science that can solve the moral question is no longer based on voluntary discourse, which must remain probabilistic, but on a rigorous discourse that reaches precise and determinate conclusions. Ordinary human language poses a major obstacle to securing such a science.

At this point, it is plausible to interpret the series of explicit and implicit rejoinders to Hobbes traced in Part Two as a complex set of responses which in effect recovered the several components of the Aristotelian position that Hobbes had rejected. There simply was too much human experience to support Aristotle's ideas for some social thinkers not to reaffirm the assumptions of

1) a naturally sociable disposition in humans;

2a) a natural basis for human associations, and

2b) the essential variability of social structures and related moral habits;

3a) the key role of human freedom in making moral decisions, and

3b) the distinctive dignity humans acquire through language;

4) the idea of nature as having a goal-directed potentiality;

5) the need for well-qualified elites to direct a good society; and

6) the futility of requiring rigorously certain proofs for practical judgments.

These assumptions did not return all at one time or in one place, or—except for Hegel and Durkheim—with any consciousness of being engaged in an effort to resurrect Aristotelian ideas. They returned piecemeal and were developed as separate doctrines. Those doctrines reflected intellectual dispositions that expressed the peculiar bents of a number of modernizing nations. What cultural and political structures engendered those characteristic dispositions? The question is fascinating and deserves closer examination. Here I only speculate briefly on the matter.

1. The notion of a *naturally sociable disposition* in humans found its champions in the British opponents of Hobbes. Shaftesbury, Hutcheson, Hume, Smith, Mill, and Spencer figured among those who affirmed the natural sources of social sentiments. They found ways to do so while still affirming the Hobbesian postulates of atomic naturalism, which is why I have called them the loyal opposition to Hobbes. The British preoccupation with the properties, rights, and utilities of

individual actors fits well with the long British struggle for personal liberties and with Calvinist strains, in Scotland and England, that focused attention on the individual's personal conduct, while the ability to take the nation-state for granted relieved British thinkers from attending to issues of collective identity and organization that preoccupied their counterparts in France, Germany, and Italy.

2. The doctrine that societies represent *suprapersonal formations whose variable structures determine variable moral habits* found its champion in the French tradition. The conviction of the French originators of modern social science—from Montesquieu, Rousseau, and Maistre through Saint-Simon and Comte to Durkheim—echoed by ideologues of the left, right, and center, was that society formed a suprapersonal entity with properties and needs of its own, above all needs for normative regulation and solidaristic integration. Comte and Durkheim crystallized the view that those properties and needs are natural phenomena, to be considered just like any other order of natural objects. The persisting French political need to integrate its disparate provinces into a national whole and the communal orientations of organized Catholicism (and, in Durkheim's case, Judaism) can be seen as underlying characteristics that disposed French thinkers toward such emphases.

3. Certain features of German culture made their thinkers especially averse to the project of grounding an ethic on foundations supplied by the lawful properties of natural phenomena. These included the inward-looking cast of Lutheranism, with its doctrines of salvation through faith and its celebration of subjective freedom. In addition, the highly repressive character of German political life has often been associated with a German tendency to find freedom in an ideal realm since it was unavailable in political reality. Thus, starting with Kant, German opponents of naturalistic ethics raised to a high pitch Aristotle's paean for *human freedom as an essential element of moral decision making.* Similarly, with Herder and Schleiermacher, they went beyond Aristotle in affirming the *creative power of language* as a distinctive feature of human action and morality.

4. Marx's attitude toward nature was ambivalent. Although he retained the idealist wish to overcome nature through voluntarism, he also restored the project of looking to nature as a source of human fulfillment. Marx was inclined to do so in part by a thoroughgoing revulsion against German religiosity. Yet his no less deeply felt antagonism to the German secular order precluded a view of nature that affirmed

any existing national society. Marx came to embrace a view of *nature as directed toward the transformative actualization of a potentiality,* a conception for which Hegel's restoration of the Aristotelian notion of telos prepared the way. Marx turned the notion of history as the realization of a telic potential into one that forecast the convulsive transformation of all existing nations—into egalitarian societies that functioned without religion or state organizations. His message thus became a beacon for intellectuals alienated from their national societies.

5. The Marxian doctrine of inexorable natural evolution into a classless society ran exactly counter to what Italian thinkers understood as an ethic grounded on the laws of nature. Like the French, Italians sought laws about societies as natural systems. In Italy the preeminent features of those systems proved to be the functioning of ruling classes. Italian thinkers thus restored the Aristotelian assumption that *good societies require good elites.* They were disposed to do so by long traditions that featured the benign effects of proper governance and by a late-blooming nation-state that looked anxiously for a stratum of competent rulers.[2]

6. Conditions in the United States were markedly different. These included the formative influences of frontier improvisationalism, the relatively modest role played by hereditary social status, and the expanded role of voluntary associations. Accordingly, American culture favored both skepticism of rigid categories and established authorities, and a tendency toward social activism disposed to solve problems on an experimental, commonsense basis. These features were embodied in the pragmatists' model of science as a community of democratically organized enquirers, a model they linked to a democratic public and extended to the whole universe of ethical and social problems. For the first time since Hobbes turned the quest for a rational ethic into a quest for doctrines supported with mathematical certainty, American philosophers retrieved the Aristotelian notion that *practical inquiry should be envisioned as open-ended and ongoing, and that the quest for certainty in moral matters was grievously misguided.*[3]

Although most of the assumptions that informed the Aristotelian philosophy were recovered one by one in post-Hobbesian social

2. For an analysis of modern Italian social theory that relates it to its historical context, see Bellamy 1987.

3. Far from viewing Aristotle as inspiration for this view, Dewey *misrepresented* him as one of the Hellenic philosophers who advocated the quest for certainty in all philosophical questions.

thought, by the time sociology was ready to be institutionalized no one had attempted to recover his system as a whole.[4] Instead, specialized cultivation of Aristotelian themes in different national settings produced philosophical traditions that led to an array of distinctive sociological orientations. Those traditions constituted themselves through two continuous forms of dialogue: continuous dialogues within the traditions, producing more differentiated versions of their original statements; and intermittent dialogues among the traditions, through which they defined and sophisticated themselves. Conjoined to intercourse with diverse empirical traditions, those dialogues helped form the discipline of modern sociology.

## FROM NATIONAL TRADITIONS TO A UNIVERSAL DISCIPLINE

Sociology came into being through a confluence of traditions, traditions that were empirical and practical as well as philosophic and theoretical. The empirical traditions also bore the mark of national dispositions, if not in such pronounced form as the philosophical ones. England led the way with social surveys, systematic investigations of living and working conditions, mainly of members of the working classes. France and Italy pursued the collection of national social statistics, work that enabled Durkheim to lead off so impressively with his analyses of divorce rates, educational levels, mental illness data, religious affiliation and the like in *Suicide*. Germany pioneered the experimental manipulation of subjects and also the systematic collection of ethnographic data in broadly defined culture areas. The United States pioneered in producing census data and later in the systematic gathering of information through personal documents and direct observation as well as interviews.

These diverse methods of generating data expressed a common impulse, the wish to apply scientific methods to human affairs. That impulse in turn sprang from two general sources. It represented a secular impulse to reform society through the application of scientific reason—the legacy of the European Enlightenment. In addition, it reflected a need to replace religious beliefs with a secular kind of orientation. Although both the reforming impulse and the recourse to sociology as a

---

4. Durkheim came closest, and in fact was the only originary sociologist who appears to have identified himself with Aristotle. In the present generation, MacIntyre (1981) has called for an explicitly neo-Aristotelian social science.

substitute for religion were particularly pronounced in the United States, the institutionalization of sociology was a truly international process.

The era when professional sociology took shape was a time of international and multilingual scholarship. Participants in scholarly conferences were generally assumed to be conversant at least in English, French, German, and Italian. Moreover, there were so few sociologists anywhere in the 1890s that they looked eagerly to colleagues in other countries for stimulation and moral support. At the Paris World Exposition of 1900, many of them convened to talk about teaching social science, plan exchange programs, and dream about an international university. Sociologists created international associations before they had formed any national sociological associations.[5] Members of the Institut international de sociologie came from more than half a dozen countries and included Gumplowicz from Austria, de Greef from Belgium, Marshall from England, Tarde from France, Schmoller from Germany, Loria from Italy, Kovalevsky from Russia, Stein from Switzerland, and Ross from the United States. When a group of British intellectuals tried to establish sociology in England, they turned to Durkheim in France and Tönnies in Germany for advice. When Simmel was confronted with hostility to sociology in the German academy, he turned first mainly to colleagues in France and then to the United States to secure a responsive audience.[6]

An active part of this international movement, academics in the United States offered dispositions exceptionally favorable to the new discipline. The upsurge of social problems in American cities of the 1890s aroused public sentiment to pursue reforms and to use the best available social knowledge for that purpose. This occurred at a time when many college-educated Protestants were searching for vehicles to bear their secularizing cultural identity. The disproportionate number

5. The Institut international de sociologie was founded at Paris by René Worms in 1893, the École libre et internationale d'enseignement supérieur at Brussels in 1894. The first national sociological societies were founded in England 1903, in the United States in 1905, and in Germany in 1910. In France and most other countries, the organization of academic work through patron-client networks inhibited the formation of national associations of sociologists until well into the twentieth century. On the role of international scientific cooperation in the early establishment of sociology, see Gülich 1992b.

6. Simmel's programmatic essay, "The Problem of Sociology," got published in five languages in five countries between 1894 and 1899. On Simmel's dependence on French audiences for his sociological identity, see Gülich 1993/2a. On his reception in the United States, see Levine, Carter, and Gorman 1976.

of early American sociologists from families of Protestant ministers has often been noted. Some used sociology as an outlet for directly expressing their religious impulses; perhaps more used it to replace their religious yearnings.[7]

The other main condition favoring sociology in the United States was the receptivity of its newer academic institutions. Uninhibited by the conservative resistances to sociology found at most European universities and at older American ones like Harvard and Princeton (but not Columbia), new private universities like Chicago and Stanford and land-grant state universities like Kansas, Minnesota, and Wisconsin encouraged new disciplines and innovative methods. This openness was exploited by a group of upwardly mobile men who could not otherwise have gained academic entree through the established disciplines (Oberschall 1972, 189).

American sociologists' experimental frame of mind enabled them to play with new empirical techniques and kept them open to diverse theories. Dependent on European—mainly German—academics for intellectual inspiration, early American sociologists nonetheless avoided strict adherence to any particular tradition.[8] The dominant American works that sought to define and systematize the field—Park and Burgess (1921), Sorokin, (1928), and Parsons (1937)—were, for all their differences, united in projecting a discipline whose germinal ideas they derived from many nations. The Park and Burgess textbook that oriented so many American sociologists in the 1920s and 1930s evinced an unmistakably cosmopolitan as well as eclectic spirit, including as it did selections by authors from no fewer than seven countries.

Although sociological work went on in several European countries during the interwar years,[9] by World War II the United States had emerged as the leader in world sociology. By the 1960s, American academics led the world in the social sciences generally, and brought soci-

7. The words of Albion Small are an exceptionally flamboyant expression of the sentiments that animated the new professors: "Sociology is really assuming the same prophetic role in social science which tradition credits to Moses in the training of his nation. . . . In all seriousness, then, and with careful weighing of my words, I register my belief that social science is the holiest sacrament open to men" (1910, 398, 277).

For insightful descriptions and interpretations of the issue of cultural identity and Protestantism among early American sociologists, see Henking 1988 and 1992.

8. This can be seen in the ways in which Park casually adapted the ideas of his erstwhile mentor Georg Simmel (Levine 1985a, 112–18).

9. Significant sociological work appeared in Austria, Belgium, Denmark, Finland, France, Germany, Netherlands, Norway, Poland, and Sweden, not to mention parts of Asia and Latin America.

ology to unprecedented heights of accomplishment and acclaim. The past two decades have witnessed a resurgence of sociology in Europe and a thorough internationalization of the discipline, with significant new centers of sociological activity in Canada and Mexico, Bulgaria and Poland, Russia and India, China and Taiwan, Korea and Japan. A wide inventory of concepts, methods, and problems that originated in separate countries now constitute a single universal discipline.

## THE FRAGMENTATION OF CURRENT SOCIOLOGY

For most of its first century as an institutionalized discipline, the proponents of sociology envisioned it as a unified field. The vision was elusive and consensus hard to come by.[10] Yet for all their profound differences about what sociology should be and do, its principal spokesmen —figures like Durkheim, Simmel, Weber, Park, and Parsons—agreed that sociology should be framed as a coherent enterprise demarcated by clear and defensible boundaries. The narratives constructed by Park and Burgess, Sorokin, Parsons, and others were part of the more general effort to justify such a unified vision.

The struggle of sociology to present itself as a unified discipline persisted into the middle decades of this century, until the eruptions of the late 1960s shattered the vision once and for all. Traditions had persisted along fault lines set by the oppositions we have traced within earlier Western social thought. These oppositions, I have argued, emerged after Aristotelian social philosophy was overthrown by Hobbes. They took the form of a transgenerational series of reactions to the Hobbesian program, which involved progressively developed but contrasting solutions to common problems. Formed initially within channels that followed the distinctive contours of national cultures, the several traditions came together in the mainstream of world sociology as an outpouring of diverse theoretical approaches that populated American and thence world sociology in the 1970s. The outcome in present-day sociology is the complex of approaches listed at the start of this chapter and traced genealogically in Figure 14.

The British tradition gave rise to three contemporary orientations: economistic sociology, sociobiology, and what may be termed eco-evolutionary sociology. The first manifests itself in current work called

---

10. The three volumes of papers issued by the Sociological Society of London from 1905 on contain sixty-one definitions of the nature and aims of sociology (Abrams 1968, 3).

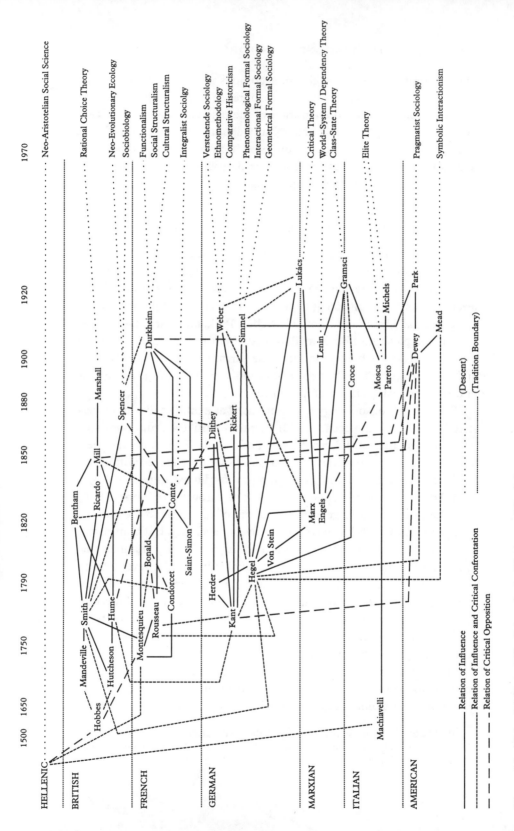

Figure 14. Major Dialogical Traditions in the Heritage of Sociology

rational choice theory, which analyzes social phenomena as deriving from the decisions of individual actors pursuing utilities in an instrumentally rational manner—the main thrust of the utilitarian tradition from Hobbes through Bentham. An eco-evolutionary approach, inspired by Spencer, focuses on changes in social structures brought about by the rational adaptations to environmental conditions made by successive generations of populations. Sociobiology revives the strain of British thinking, from Shaftesbury through Smith, that emphasizes biological endowments as the ultimate cause of human behavior.

The principal legacy of the French tradition was the functionalist approach. Functionalism entered via two routes. One was through British social anthropology, whose germinal moment can be traced to A. R. Radcliffe-Brown's conversion to a functionalist perspective after he encountered Durkheim in 1910 (Stocking 1984). The other was through the direct appropriation of Durkheim by Parsons and Merton in the 1930s. Merton converted this interest into a program to analyze the functions and dysfunctions of various types of social structures in a manner he came to call structural analysis. Parsons pursued grander theoretical ambitions: he sought to combine Durkheimian functionalism with aspects of British individualism and German idealism into a synthesis he referred to as a general theory of action, but which became labeled as functionalism due to Parson's concern for specifying the functional requisites of all systems of action. Reviving the Durkheimian interest in structural properties of collective representations in conjunction with ideas derived from the linguist Ferdinand de Saussure, the French anthropologist Claude Lévi-Strauss opened another avenue of theoretical work, one that looked to the "deep structures" of cultural systems to find the fundamental source of human organization.

A minor stream from the French tradition appeared in the work of those whose inspiration came directly from Comte rather than from Durkheim. The emphasis here was on the emergence of world community and of commensurately altruistic sentiments and beliefs. Although this strain disappeared during the early twentieth century, it was resurrected and championed by Sorokin in his final phase of work, which focused on promoting the process of "altruization" and the creation of an integral humanity.

The Italian legacy appeared as a substantive specialty, elite theory, which gained headway in political science and sociology in the 1950s, through the work of scholars like Harold Lasswell and Karl Deutsch.

The German tradition was internally most complex, as we have seen, and also most prolific in spawning distinctive orientations within sociology. I identify five distinct approaches in contemporary sociology that are of German inspiration, two deriving from Dilthey and Weber and three from Simmel. The hermeneutic tradition appears in two forms, one focusing on the distinctive outlooks of cultural configurations or historical periods and one on the subjective meanings of individual actors. The former, which emphasizes the uniqueness of cultural/historical formations, was preeminently developed by a major interpreter of Weber, Reinhard Bendix. The latter was developed by Alfred Schutz and his American followers, Garfinkel and Cicourel, in the approach labeled ethnomethodology. A closely related approach is the one I am calling phenomenological formal sociology. Its inspiration is the subjectivist interpretation of social forms, as in Simmel; its exemplary representative is Erving Goffman. Two other approaches derive from other features of Simmel's sociology. From Simmel's attention to the interactive process as a structured exchange of sacrifices and rewards stems the exchange theory propounded by Peter Blau. From his suggestion to represent those forms of interaction in geometric terms comes the earlier work in sociometry pioneered by Moreno, a good deal of small group work in the 1950s, and more recently the kinds of network theory cultivated by Laumann and Breiger.

At least three distinguishable orientations have come from the Marxian tradition. One follows the essential guidelines of historical materialism in delineating the socioeconomic foundations of power structures, as in the class-state theory of Erik Olin Wright. Another follows the Leninist development of analyzing structures of imperial power and world domination, as in the world systems and dependency theories of Immanuel Wallerstein. A third hearkens to the Hegelian side of Marxism with its critical humanistic perspective, represented by the "critical theory" of the Frankfurt School.

In the United States, finally, two other perspectives crystallized in the decades after World War II. Symbolic interactionism was codified by Herbert Blumer following the social psychology of Dewey and Mead. What may be called pragmatist sociology was later formulated by Morris Janowitz, who called for a return to the pragmatists' emphasis on informed public opinion and enlightened social control.[11]

11. In developing what he called symbolic interactionism, Blumer has been faulted for claiming to represent Mead but in fact following the more individualized psychology of James. On the complex question of the relation between pragmatist philosophy and symbolic interactionism, see, for example, Joas 1980, Lewis and Smith 1980, and Shalin

In the two decades since this array of approaches gained prominence, new European variants on these positions have flourished. To name but a few: Anthony Giddens developed a theory of "structuration" that claimed to link the dynamics of human agency more effectively with the realities and reproduction of institutionalized structures. Niklas Luhman outlined a theory of "autopoietic systems," geared to analyzing the dynamics of functionally specialized systems that operate under their own laws, in a manner reminiscent of Weber's concept of autonomization (*Eigengesetzlichkeit*) and Buckley's concept of morphogenesis. Habermas recast key pragmatist notions regarding social disorganization and the public sphere, the former through fresh interpretations of social and cultural crises, the latter through searching analyses of the structuring of public opinion.

Norbert Elias and his followers promoted "figurational sociology" as an effort to represent societies as webs of interdependent individuals whose affects, actions, and relationships change in response to "civilizing" and "decivilizing" developments, processes they explore through the (largely Weberian) themes of monopolization of violence, control of taxation, and the search for distinction. In the course of fruitful analyses of many empirical domains, Pierre Bourdieu developed further some of Elias's key concepts, including the notion of multiple forms of capital and the concept of habitus, defined as enduring tendencies incarnated in human bodily dispositions. The idea of attending explicitly to the body again became the focus of a number of theoretical departures, including work by Bryan Turner and others on the bodily dimension of action and social order as well as work by American and European feminists that raised gender, the relationship between the sexes, and the question of historically male-dominated science to questions of general theoretical significance. Other recent theoretical initiatives regarding modernization will be mentioned in the section on modernity in chapter 15.

The proliferation of orienting frameworks reviewed in this chapter grievously weakened whatever center the discipline of sociology had managed to create. This has made the effort to conceive sociology as a unific discipline deeply problematic. Such a condition may be experienced as a loss for those with strong professional attachments to the field. Yet facing up to that loss may be a precondition of new gains.

---

1986. For an exposition of Janowitz's work as an embodiment of the pragmatist tradition, see Burk 1991.

# CHAPTER FOURTEEN

# Diagnoses of Our Time

On the surface, sociology of the 1990s has seemed healthy. Research programs multiply; conferences abound; professional groupings form; journals flourish. Nearly every year occasions a centenary celebration: the first department of sociology (University of Chicago, 1892); the first international professional association (Institut international de sociologie, 1893); the first professional journals (*American Journal of Sociology*, 1895; *Annales de Sociologie*, 1896); some landmark publications (Simmels' "Das Problem der Soziologie," 1894; Durkheim's *Le Suicide*, 1897). Yet beneath the surface there lingers muted disquiet. The decade followed a period when sociology, along with the other social sciences, was wracked by debilitating changes.

## A SENSE OF UNEASE

The proliferation of outlooks described in the previous chapter prompted a number of sociologists to diagnose a deep malaise in the field. Eisenstadt and Curelaru described a widespread perception of crisis in sociology:

> As a result of these tendencies [toward proliferation in the 1970s], sociology could be presented as consisting of completely closed, "totalistic" paradigms which differed not only in their analytic premises but also in their philosophic, ideological, and political assumptions, minimizing the possibility of scholarly discourse on problems of common interest. . . . It was the continuing spread of these developments that produced a widespread malaise in sociology; an acceptance of its being in a time of crisis. This feeling was intensified by the fact that . . . these developments were worldwide and communication among different sociological communities intensive. (1976, 311–12)[1]

1. The passage continues: "Thus, indeed, sociology has arrived at a critical juncture, a point of both great promise and of possible disintegration." Questioned about the matter in 1990, Eisenstadt said he believed that the tendencies toward disintegration had gained the upper hand.

In 1980 the outgoing president of the American Sociological Association, Peter Rossi, observed that the organization's very openness in reflecting so many of the divergent viewpoints in current sociology had produced a condition of intellectual paralysis, while a noted historian of the field took it as given that sociology had been suffering an "identity crisis" (Kuklick 1980, 210). A decade later, Randall Collins sharpened the diagnosis: "We have lost all coherence as a discipline; we are breaking up into a conglomerate of specialties, each going its own way and with none too high regard for each other" (1990, 311). By 1994, the only point a group of scholars trying to define a distinctive European sociology could agree on was that "contemporary European sociology is highly fragmented" (Nedelmann and Sztompka 1993, 6).

Expressions of this sort had been emanating from other social science disciplines as well. On the eve of the 1980 meeting of the American Anthropological Association, Eric Wolf wrote that "the annual meeting operates as a giant fair, in which . . . diverse activities and their results are exhibited, discussed and savored." Commenting on the display, Wolf noted:

> Yet this multifarious activity is accompanied by a sense of unease, which feeds on that very proliferation of purposes and tasks. What was once a secular church of believers in the primacy of Culture has now become a holding company of diverse interests, defined by what the members do rather than by what they do it for. There are unvoiced concerns within the profession about what anthropology has become and where it is headed. (1980, E9)

Voicing such concerns, Adam Kuper observed that anthropologists had become "accustomed even to accuse each other of ignoring 'reality.' . . . And the very possibility of comparison, traditionally the corner-stone of anthropological method, remains contentious" (1980, 14).

Shortly before, a high-ranking psychologist had observed that "the field of psychology, after one century as an experimental discipline, seems to be in a state of crisis. At least that is what a lot of people tell me; and everywhere I turn I see psychologists searching for that holy grail called a 'paradigm' and arguing about the true nature, proper subject matter, and relevant methods of psychology" (Leary 1979, 231). Reviewing two decades of work in social psychology, Sheldon Stryker noted that "a sense of crisis . . . has been said to pervade the field"

(1981, 388), a judgment echoed by a commentator who found it amazing that eleven of the best minds in the field failed to agree on almost anything about what constituted significant work in psychology (Wade 1982).

Comparable statements from economics and political science had been circulating for years. The 1970s began with Wassily Leontief's presidential address to the American Economics Association regarding his "uneasy feeling" about the state of economics due to the "palpable inadequacy" of the scientific means with which economists try to solve their problems (1971), followed shortly by Oskar Morgenstern's (1972) diagnosis of a critical condition in economics because it lacks the concepts and methods needed to deal with social realities. The decade ended with a special issue of *The Public Interest* devoted to the imputed crisis of that field, in which Irving Kristol wrote that "it is widely conceded that something like a 'crisis' in economic theory exists, but there is vehement disagreement about the extent and nature of this crisis" (1980, 201). Kristol proceeded to identify more than half a dozen divergent views about what was wrong with economics and where it should be heading.

In political science, expressions of unease took many forms. Already in 1960 Sheldon Wolin was lamenting that "the sense of the political has been lost" (1960, 288). A decade later, David Easton offered the diagnosis that the discipline was suffering an identity crisis. Gabriel Almond subsequently described a condition of demoralization in major areas of political science such that these subjects were no longer being transmitted effectively to younger generations (Almond and Genco [1977] 1988). He went on to say that political science "is not a happy profession" for being divided into schools and sects that sit at "separate tables . . . each protecting some secret island of vulnerability" (1988, 14).

In the discipline of history, finally, the 1981 meeting of the Organization of American Historians featured a keynote session on the topic "History in Crisis," a session introduced in the program with these words: "Many historians complain of a malaise, a loss of confidence in the role of their discipline, a lack of certainty about its nature and function, its place among the other disciplines, its appeal to a wider public. Why should we study history?"

It takes little inductive skill to conclude from these statements that many social scientists shared the perception that their disciplines were experiencing a condition of crisis. Even if it is true that statements like the above are scarcely unprecedented—after all, recent sighs over the death of history were prefigured in the United States by a comparable loss of historiographic nerve following World War I, and sociology has been described as experiencing a condition of crisis throughout its history (Pizzorno 1972; Merton 1975, 21)—it is hard to deny that those statements bespeak a state of mind and morale that varied sharply from the outlook in the social sciences during the two decades that followed World War II. Consider, for example, the bold projections about these disciplines conveyed by *The Human Meaning of the Social Sciences,* a collection of essays published in 1959. In that volume Clyde Kluckhohn reviews the achievements of anthropology proudly—a "lusty . . . hybrid monster" he fondly calls it—and proclaims that "the fate of our Western civilization and perhaps of civilization in general may hang upon humanity's gaining some orderly and systematic insight into the nonrational and irrational factors in human behavior" (Lerner 1959, 248, 281). Speaking for psychology, Lawrence Frank concludes that "psychological concepts are giving man a new conception of human nature—a confident new image of himself as an essential participant in his society" (241). Paul Samuelson celebrates the great advances in economics and the therapeutic techniques it has produced to "wipe out persistent slump or unsought inflation" (211). The volume editor, Daniel Lerner, hails the "unique function of social science—as a method of inquiry into the social process whereby its operations are continuously recorded and regulated," and concludes that "the great current issue for Social Science is how to increase democracy's chances for survival in our time. One part of this task is to improve continuously the intellectual quality and social utility of its own products. . . . Social scientists, both West and East, have made a start in this direction" (37, 38). Echoes of these sentiments reverberated throughout the field in the early 1960s. Lipset and Smelser, for example, introduced a set of papers on the progress of sociology in the 1950s by saying that those articles reflected "the complete triumph since World War I of the new 'scientific sociology'" (1961, 1); Boulding found the social sciences to be occupying a position of central power and responsibility in contemporary society, and he forecast "the greatest changes in the future to come from social telescopes and microscopes" (1966, 23).

Two decades later one would have been hard pressed to locate a set of comparably confident and hopeful statements. Although the later expressions of malaise reveal different emphases in the various disciplines, one feature seems common to them all. They all portray a high degree of dissensus.

That dissensus had come to permeate the social science community cannot be denied, even if it was not so severe as alleged by a political scientist who quipped that "the only thing two social scientists can agree on is that the work of a third is no good." Even so, dissensus among social scientists is neither a new phenomenon nor inherently demoralizing. Scientific fields generally exhibit a good deal of dissensus. Imre Lakatos was surely right to say that "*the history of science has been and should be a history of competing research programmes (or, if you wish, 'paradigms') . . . the sooner competition starts, the better for progress. . . . Continuity* in science . . . can only be explained if we construe science as a battleground of research programmes" (1978, 69, 87). The history of each of the social sciences is constituted by prolonged and acrimonious controversies—among diffusionists, evolutionists, and functionalists in anthropology; institutionalists, monetarists, and Keynesians in economics; Rankeans, Burckhardtians, and Marxians in history; theorists and empiricists in political science; introspectivists, behaviorists, and Gestaltists in psychology; field workers and quantifiers in sociology— to name but a few of the dozes of axes of divisiveness in these fields. And many of these controversies raged during times of high morale in those disciplines.

Perhaps one could argue that the dissensus of the 1970s was of an order of magnitude greater than that which obtained in the past. This may be so, though the claim is not easy to substantiate. In any case, it is possible to identify factors other than an escalation of dissensus that contributed to those expressions of unease. Since the early 1970s, three sorts of changes in the external environment of the social sciences posed a threat to their continued vitality. For one thing, resources available to academic social science were reduced. Although social scientific enterprises in the private sector continued to prosper—indeed, multimillion-dollar industries based on techniques and findings of the social sciences emerged in the United States—the flow of resources to the academic terrain where these disciplines get grounded steadily diminished. Reduced funds for training graduate students and shortages of academic openings hampered the recruitment of talented and dedicated social scientists. Constraints and threats of constraint on research emanated from new federal regulations and from reduced access to research sites in many other countries. Funds for basic social research declined in all the European centers of social science as well as in North America. Throughout the 1970s there was an overall decline of about 21 percent in constant dollar support for the social sciences from the National Science Foundation. More recently, budgetary alarms have motivated efforts to shut down departments of sociology in some universities.

A second change was the reduction in public deference shown to the social science enterprise, following a period in the 1950s and early 1960s when virtually all branches of the U.S. federal government— from the Supreme Court to Congress to many executive departments —made unprecedented use of social scientists in such areas as the fight against segregation, analysis of foreign elites, international economic development, and domestic antipoverty programs. In part this drop in status reflected a secular trend toward the withdrawal of deference from professionals and experts generally. Just as medicine and law were being criticized for the allegedly inefficient, exploitative, injurious, or otherwise unethical practices of some of their members, so scientific "experts" became targets of consumerist critiques that demoted them from whatever pedestals they might have occupied.[2] In the case of the social sciences, the backlash was not so much aimed against real or alleged abuses by professionals—who after all never enjoyed that much potency—but rather seemed to spring from the fact that the demand for solutions to social problems far exceeded the capacity of the social sciences to deliver them. There grew a sense that the social sciences have not been and do not seem likely to produce the kinds of results their earlier proponents anticipated.[3]

A third source of weakened support came from changes in the philosophical environment of social science. The net effect of two decades of tumultuous activity in the philosophy of science had been to undermine the belief of social scientists in the viability of objective standards and arguments. Ideas variously advanced by Popper, Kuhn, Lakatos, Feyerabend, Toulmin, and others were taken to indicate that subjectivity reigns supreme in the natural sciences, "and so, it is inferred, [subjectivity] must surely reign in the social and behavioral sciences. [Social scientists] drawing this gratuitous inference take it

2. Some social scientists abetted this tendency to debunk professionals through scholarly analyses that stressed socially dysfunctional features of professional behavior and the self-serving aspects of professional rhetoric (Kuklick 1980, 202).

3. For a compendium of searching analyses of issues regarding the reception of sociology in the 1980s, see Halliday and Janowitz 1992.

as license legitimizing a total subjectivity in which anything goes" (Merton 1975, 26). The new penchant for subjectivism in social science exacerbated tendencies toward the privatization of scholarly work and the politicization of scholarly interchange.

Given this convergence of external changes that weakened the social sciences, it is understandable why internal dissensus seemed so threatening. Human groups can respond to external threats with focused energy only when united behind some minimal set of shared understandings. Yet many social scientists, far from providing the core of beliefs to unify and direct modern societies that Saint-Simon and Comte expected social science to produce, lost plausible conceptions even of themselves as members of viable intellectual communities.

To regain such conceptions would seem to require an effort to resuscitate the traditional disciplines of the social sciences as sharply defined, strongly energized, and well-defended corporate entities. There are reasons, however, for thinking that such an effort is no long viable. The primary reason is that the old disciplinary boundaries have become less salient, if not obsolete. The other reason is that these disciplines no longer possess narratives about their historic development with sufficient credibility to anchor a charter for their future. These considerations imply that the social sciences face a genuine crisis. I call it an *evolutionary crisis* to signal the fact that *their established forms no long fulfill the function of providing orienting frameworks for intellectual communities.*

Those considerations open the door to what may be a more productive way to analyze the situation of the late 1990s. Although one no longer hears strident cries of crisis, that does not mean that the underlying difficulties which gave rise to them have disappeared. It is more likely that scholars have made private, temporizing adaptations to them. After all, as Erich Fromm once remarked, "probably never have the majority of people in a radically critical situation been aware of the crisis" (1960, 2). Let us examine the notion that the social sciences face an evolutionary crisis, both because their disciplinary frameworks have become obsolete and because they no longer possess persuasive narratives about their historic development to chart a course for their future.

## THE ASSAULT ON DISCIPLINARY BOUNDARIES

Since the late 1960s a number of secular developments weakened the boundaries of the several social sciences that had grown so robust in the two postwar decades. For one thing, each of those disciplines established beachheads or won converts among the practitioners of other disciplines. At present few major concepts, methods, or problems belong exclusively to a single social science discipline. Anthropologists interpret dreams to find motives; psychoanalysts scrutinize documents to find the causes of war; sociologists and political scientists use "economistic" modes of analysis to study decision making; economists do field work to study behavioral patterns in primitive societies; psychologists and anthropologists use survey research methods to examine processes of modernization. Terms like motivation, reinforcement, status, legitimacy, authority, exchange, unconscious, symbolism, norms, and cost-benefit analysis have come to be used with decreasing self-consciousness by people in disciplines other than those in which these terms were formed. Even psychoanalysis, traditionally one of the most self-contained and sharply bounded of the human disciplines, has long since reached the point where, as George Klein put it, "the eclectic spirit has been so insistent that it is hard to trace the common thread among the diverse groups who pre-empt the label 'psychoanalysis'" (1976, 17).

Even more significant than this movement among disciplines has been the emergence of research programs that defy any disciplinary labeling altogether. Brian Barry aptly described this sort of change:

> Already it is possible in certain contexts (for example at certain sessions of the Public Choice Society) to listen to a discussion without being able to tell from what is said that one speaker is from economics, another from law, another from philosophy, and another from political science. What we are seeing, in other words, is a new kind of interdisciplinary development: not a wary rapprochement across disciplinary boundaries but the creation of autonomous spheres of discourse that draw on existing disciplines but represent a genuine synthesis. (1979, 3)

Such "autonomous spheres of discourse" developed profusely over the past generation. They came to be firmly planted on the academic landscape with the flowering of area studies specialties in the 1960s—spheres of discourse concerned with a country like India, a religion like Islam, a region like sub-Saharan Africa. They emerged as new supradisciplinary analytic approaches like social choice theory, including that amalgam of notions from anthropology, linguistics, mathematics, and psychology known as "structuralism"; that blend of analytic techniques from econometrics, psychometrics, and genetics known as "causal modeling"; those syntheses of ideas from philosophy, cognitive anthropology, cognitive psychology, linguistics, and sociology called "ethnomethodology" and "cognitive science"; and those generic examinations of genres, myths, texts, and tropes known as "cultural studies." They flourished in numerous fields devoted to the investigation of particular subject matters, from studies of ethnicity, gender, health care, and sports to the analyses of human evolution, civilizational configurations, and advanced capitalist systems. The burgeoning of "evaluation research" in the late 1970s added fresh momentum to this new mode of supradisciplinary collaboration.

The old disciplinary boundaries became weakened further, finally, by the proliferation of diverse orientations within each discipline. As a result, most of the disciplines have become so fragmented internally that no formula can designate an intellectual universe with which their practitioners can all identify and to which they can feel allegiance. Even if such agreement could be achieved in individual cases, it would not be respected by those outside the discipline. Who, now, is prepared to grant anthropology sole jurisdiction over the study of culture, economics over rational exchange, political science over power, or psychology over motivation?

These changes lead us to suspect that efforts to resuscitate the conventional disciplines of the social sciences would be retrogressive. Quite the most interesting work now takes place within other kinds of boundaries: in *subdisciplinary specialties, transdisciplinary forays,* and *supradisciplinary syntheses.* The blurring of disciplinary genres, as Clifford Geertz once described the matter, has proceeded at such a pace and in so many areas that we seem to live amidst a vast cultural ferment: "a phenomenon general enough and distinctive enough to suggest that what we are seeing is not just another drawing of the cultural map—the moving of a few disputed borders, the marking of some more picturesque mountain lakes—but an alteration of the principles of mapping" (1983, 20).

These changes further suggest that even if the social sciences faced no threat to the supply of material and human resources needed to sustain them, they would nonetheless confront an orientational crisis—call it opportunity, challenge, or transitional period if you prefer—of no mean proportions. *Older mappings of the social sciences persist in the face of circumstances that call for radical alterations of that mapping.* In this view the malaise in social science is to a great extent internally induced. It reflects the inadequacy of the forms by which social scientists organize their understanding of what they are about; it reflects the lack of a set of accurate and mutually acceptable self-images. This deficiency arguably has produced the symptoms described above, including the diminished sense of commitment ("what they do it for") and a weakened capacity for collaboration ("minimizing the possibility for scholarly discourse on problems of common interest"). Without a credible sense of professional identity it is indeed difficult to devise morally intact programs of education and research. Perhaps this deficiency is related to what some have identified as a new order of cynicism in our teaching, technical fetishism in our research, and sterile polemics in our scholarly exchanges.

To rescue our scholarly integrity, an effort to articulate new principles for mapping our intellectual universe is mandated. That the older mappings will be defended in many quarters there can be no doubt, nor is there reason to think that our professional associations will close down in the imaginable future. What may be plausible—the most we actually need aspire to—is to gain acceptance for redrawing the map of the social sciences in ways that give those professional boundaries less salience and that insert other kinds of lines for purposes of demarcating genuine intellectual communities.

Carrying the cartographic metaphor further, I find it useful to liken the established disciplines to nation-states. As the latter emerged worldwide in the last few centuries to provide security, identity, prestige, welfare, and civic rights for populations somehow historically connected, so the disciplines emerged to provide professional status, intellectual identity, academic benefits, and collegial support for those who came to profess them. As certain periods of history produced strong expressions of national sentiment and allegiance, so the disciplines, in their years of consolidation and expansion, evoked strong expressions of loyalty and solidarity. And just as now, in our generation, commitments to national political entities compete increasingly with allegiances that are subnational (ethnic, regional), transnational (professional groups), and supranational (multinational corporations, multinational religious communities), so now the allegiance to disciplinary fields competes with intellectual alliances that I have glossed above as subdisciplinary, transdisciplinary, and supradisciplinary.[4]

4. Recent scholarship confirms and extends these interpretations on the challenges to national identities. Thus Yasemin Soysal (1995) analyzes the impact of international migration on criteria of nationhood and citizenship, and Getinet Belay (1995) traces the ramifications of new forms of collective identity that are subnational and transnational in

Like nation-states, the disciplines are here to stay, but in forms more circumscribed than in the past. They will remain valuable for supplying elements of professional identity, conveying some aspects of shared traditions, and providing vocational certification. They will continue to provide channels through which scholars may gain access to resources, collegial support, and related benefits. But, to the extent that they were before, they can and should no longer be looked to for providing charters for the supreme point of scholarly work—the generation of research programs and of educational curricula. They will probably remain sources of malaise unless we manage to formulate more appropriate bases for those charters, including a reconstructed narrative that affirms the identity of those who follow them.

## THE COLLAPSE OF OLD NARRATIVES

Returning to the case of sociology, I propose now to resume the argument that none of the earlier types of narrative reviewed in Part One remains credible as a basis for orienting the sociological community today. Viable when they were originally conceived, the shortcomings of these narratives have become apparent over time and their strengths no longer minister to the kinds of need for meaning the present generation of social scientists displays.

The positivist narrative—viewing the story of sociology as a succession of cognitive improvements due to the refinement and application of empirical techniques—appears vulnerable on two counts at least. For one thing, it ignores the numerous instances when sociological propositions have been consensually repudiated, not on the basis of empirical disconfirmation, but in a manner comparable to changes in fashion: due to shifts in the popularity of their author, changes in interest in their subject matter, or the intrusion of ideological elements. In addition, it ignores the extent to which observations are embedded in conceptual frameworks, in such a manner that they cannot be absorbed

---

scope. However, while arguing that the nation-state has been significantly eroded as the predominant organizing principle of identity due to these multidirectional shifts of identification, Belay notes that it is still salient, for "the nation-state remains the only legally and politically constituted territorial unit of collective identification, within . . . which the basic rights and duties of the human individual are defined, and [where] political struggle over democracy and social justice takes place. . . . There is nothing archaic about citizenship" (332).

in the cumulative advance of knowledge when inquiry is pursued in accord with other frames of reference.

The pluralist type of narrative is able to accommodate those pieces of the story having to do with perspectival embeddedness, which positivist narratives neglect. However, by treating different schools or approaches as discrete entities it ignores the demonstrable interactions among them. No less important, pluralist narratives fail to consider plausible syntheses that have actually occurred. Such syntheses form the dramatic core of the narratives I have referred to as synthetic. The shortcoming of the synthetic type of narrative is the obverse: its inability to deal with persisting incommensurable philosophic or theoretic perspectives in the discipline.

All three of these narratives are vulnerable to another kind of criticism, one raised by the perspective of the humanistic narratives. They all view the classics purely instrumentally—as stepping stones toward current achievements of positive knowledge. They fail to consider what are arguably the perduring aesthetic, moral, and philosophical values of the classics. More particularly, they exclude achievements of the classics that do not fit the criteria of progressive science, achievements that rely upon irreducibly philosophical, nonempirical formulations. As formulated by Simmel, these achievements occupy domains that lie at the "lower" and "upper" boundaries of any positive science. Beneath every scientific discipline sits a set of assumptions about the principles and methods that organize its practice. These assumptions cannot themselves be proved through empirical research, for the latter can proceed only by taking those assumptions for granted. Above and beyond the findings of every empirical discipline, moreover, exist interpretations that relate such empirical material to the totality of life. These interpretations constitute a response to questions "that we have so far been unable either to answer or to dismiss." Such work either incorporates the discrete threads of specialized research into the tapestry of a worldview or else weaves them into a selectively colored interpretation that imbues them with special meaning or evaluative significance (Simmel [1907] 1978, 53).

For all its value in calling attention to the philosophical achievements of the sociological tradition, the humanist approach, like the other three narrative types, tells a story that is essentially internalist. All four internalist narratives are vulnerable to criticisms about their failure to consider the ways in which extrascientific and indeed extracognitive needs—political ambition, economic interest, religious aspiration, aesthetic inclination—inform the strivings of those who created the sociological tradition. These are the matters that make up the texture of the contextual narratives that have become so prominent in the past two decades.

Nevertheless, contemporary sociology is by no means merely an expression of extrascientific cultural themes nor a simple falling away from peerless classic analyses. Contextual narratives along with humanistic ones stand vulnerable to criticisms based on evidence that sociology has made substantial progress in many respects, both empirical and theoretical. Sociology has presented and conducted itself, to some extent at least, as a science. And no one denies that cumulative character of science—that it develops thanks to the progressive resolution of problems.

None of the shortcomings just noted would be so critical if it could satisfy the present cultural need. I have suggested that the kind of meaning sought by the sociological profession today (along with that of the other social sciences) is one that ministers to a frustrating sense of factionalism and fragmentation. In other words, the kind of story that sociologists seem to need is one that finds a place for the various specialized outlooks in a more encompassing enterprise. Each of the earlier types of narratives has the effect of excluding some constituency or other. The positivist narrative excludes those who affirm an inexpungeable need for philosophic accompaniments to sociology. The pluralist excludes those who crave synthesis and believe synthesis has been accomplished. The synthetic narrative excludes adherents to approaches that resist the effort to subsume their doctrines into such syntheses. The humanist excludes those who believe genuine, nontrivial scientific progress has been made. The contextualist excludes those committed to sociology as an enterprise that pursues the truth and makes advances in that pursuit. None of the old narratives seems suited to carry the moral of inclusiveness.

## BEYOND POSTMODERNISM

To debunk other people's narratives is no new thing. The act of undermining the stories that people live by has reached a high art in the form of intellectual activity that has become known as deconstructionism. This activity is said to express one of the key impulses in the more general cultural condition described as postmodernism. In *The Postmodern*

*Condition,* Jean-François Lyotard makes an argument that to some extent parallels what I have presented here. Lyotard argues that the old grand narratives that legitimated the scientific enterprise in the West—which he identifies as the Enlightenment narrative that science will emancipate humanity and the largely Hegelian narrative that the growth of knowledge constitutes the unfolding of the world spirit—have lost their credibility. Consequently, they can no longer serve to valorize contemporary science. Lyotard dismisses calls for a new set of beliefs to replace them on grounds that "consensus has become an outmoded and suspect value." He depicts a scientific universe constituted by nothing but episodes of combat—"to speak is to fight"—and no consensus beyond that of local networks of partners unified on the basis of short-term contracts ([1979] 1984, 66, 10).

No sooner has Lyotard done this, however, than he proceeds to state principles he assumes will be consensually affirmed. He observes that justice as a value is neither outmoded nor suspect. He notes that the pursuit of knowledge entails the renunciation of terror (defined as eliminating or threatening to eliminate any players from a language game one shares with them). It seems Lyotard acknowledges the need for some consensual constitutive beliefs after all. If that is so, it is hard to understand why he would not want to wrap them in a narrative that gives them historic depth and inspires future commitments.

I believe it possible to construct a narrative that avoids the intellectual pitfalls of the earlier approaches and that ministers to our present-day need for meaning. The current context, shaped by the perception of crisis and dissensus within the social sciences, is one of fragmentation and anomie within an intellectual community. The healing response needs to be one that connects different parts of the community while fully respecting what appear to be irreducible differences. The prescription must be for dialogue, the narrative one that embodies a dialogic view of the tradition.

# CHAPTER FIFTEEN

# On the Heritage of Sociology

A single assumption has guided the interpretation of narratives, traditions, and crises presented in this book. I have assumed that humans create social and cultural forms in order to organize the pursuit of goals and the expression of sentiments and that, as our needs, goals, and sentiments shift in response to environmental change and internal evolution, we experience a wish to modify old forms and create new ones. This wish conflicts with the attachment to old forms that persists due to habituation, sentiment, and vested interests.

In this perspective we can interpret the creation of narratives of the sociological tradition, like those of any tradition, as a response to the need for meaning about the enterprise. Such meaning imparts identity to those who embrace it and moral support to those who carry out its mission. Thus I have portrayed the story of sociology in Part One as a series of narrative reconstructions serving to adapt sociologists to the changing situation of their discipline. As new needs emerged, new narratives were constructed.

This is also the spirit in which I presented a dialogical narrative of the sociological tradition in Part Two. I interpreted the rise of sociology as an effort to provide forms for understanding social phenomena, an effort deriving from a sense that traditional worldviews no longer provide a sufficiently credible basis to guide human action. The quest for such forms began as moral and political philosophy. This quest was pursued in a number of Western nations in ways that reflected distinctive cultural preoccupations and emphases. It was constituted by a complex series of transgenerational conversations, conversations that exhibited remarkable continuities within national communities as well as creative interactions with other national traditions. By differentiating itself from philosophy, reformism, policy questions, and social work, sociology emerged as a purely investigative discipline no longer directly connected to moral concerns. Nevertheless, its guiding conceptions remained linked to their origins in the earlier forms.

The visions of society that came to constitute the sociological tradition succeeded overarching visions of the human world previously found first in religion and then philosophy. The business of defining sociology thus became a matter of no small import. For this reason one can understand why figures like Comte and Spencer, Durkheim and Weber, Parsons and Mills, Berger and Nisbet, invested so much passion in the definition of sociology.

## AN EVOLUTIONARY CHALLENGE

*The form of sociology no longer appears to satisfy the sociologist's quest for meaning.* This is how I have interpreted the symbolic side of the evolutionary crisis I depicted in the previous chapter. The aspiration to create a coherent discipline of sociology represents a way station between the global philosophic forms of the eighteenth and early nineteenth centuries and the variously contoured intellectual forms of the late twentieth century—just as I suggested, nation-states became objects of transcendent loyalty midway between the grand empires of the preindustrial civilizations and the contemporary universe of subnational, multinational, and supranational forms. It may be time, then, to relinquish the form of sociology as an exclusive object of intellectual loyalty. This is needed to legitimate solid commitments to other forms, which I have glossed as subdisciplinary, multidisciplinary, and supradisciplinary in character.

Giving up such an attachment is not without cost, but the evolution of knowledge is strewn with abandoned cultural forms.[1] In this case the cost need not be substantial. Perhaps the main adjustment that is needed is to develop more internally differentiated constructions of our disciplinary identities. Meeting in this way the adaptive challenge posed by the obsolescence of older disciplinary forms and narratives promises substantial benefits. For one thing, it may enable us, as social scientists, to overcome our subliminal malaise and reenergize our intellectual projects. It may lead as well to a way of imagining sociology that gives it a vibrant new role: as preeminent host, by virtue of its classic tradition, of the social science dialogue.

---

1. Interpretations like those of Susan Henking and Peter Homans afford insight into this process. Henking (1988) interprets the emergence of commitments to sociology among early American academics as an outgrowth of struggles with traditional religious commitments or yearnings—struggles of the sort encountered in many earlier figures, including Hobbes, Spencer, Saint-Simon, Comte, Hegel, Weber, Mead, and Dewey. Homans (1989) interprets the emergence of the psychoanalytic psychologies as a response to the loss of traditional cultural attachments. He also illuminates the process by which mourning those lost objects leads to new psychic structures that constitute and enhance greater individuation.

We thus arrive at the paradoxical conclusion that the optimal solution to the identity crisis of sociology—and perhaps of other social sciences as well—is to relax attachments to conventional ways of conceiving the discipline. After all, the currently circumscribed disciplines were not the first forms of privileged knowledge nor need they be the last. They are historically evolved forms that once corresponded to presenting intellectual needs and no longer serve them optimally. The final segment of our dialogical narrative returns sociology and the other social sciences to a state in which their story is no longer encapsulated within the boundaries of each discipline. It returns us to the broad quest for social understanding and for a secular ethic.

Such a quest involves sketching some of the most general features of the social science enterprise. This includes an inventory of some of its fundamental postulates: about the nature of social reality, about the nature of the modern world, and about the proper relation between theory and praxis. These tasks form the agenda for this and the next chapter. In concluding I return to the issue of how a dialogical narrative can serve to integrate a fragmented community.

## THE LEGACY OF THE QUEST

The quest of European and American thinkers to produce a rationally grounded ethic has left us a wealth of intellectual resources to help describe and explain social phenomena and to guide our social actions. I have characterized the philosophical foundations of modern social science as a complex of response to Hobbes's reaction to Aristotle. These responses took four fundamental forms. They can be represented by the postulates outlined in Part Two.

The Postulate of Methodological Individualism holds that social phenomena are best explained by analyzing the natural propensities of the individual actors that constitute them. This has led to a number of theories that account for social phenomena in terms of universal human passions, constitutive interests, and/or rational dispositions—the stock in trade of the British tradition from Hobbes and Locke through Hutcheson, Hume, and Smith to Bentham, Mill, Spencer, and Marshall.

The Postulate of Societal Realism holds that society is a supraindividual phenomenon with determinate properties not reducible to individual propensities. It has taken two forms, both inspired by Saint-Simon. One, represented by Comte and Durkheim along with others in the French tradition, emphasizes the integrative mechanisms of society, such as collective rituals and legal codes; the other, represented by Mosca and Pareto, emphasizes the structural and functional necessity for ruling elites.

The two other forms derive from the Postulate of Subjective Meaning, which holds that human phenomena cannot be reduced to natural propensities and mechanisms, individual or collective, but that they manifest themselves distinctively through the meanings with which actors imbue their actions. This has been the guiding postulate of the complex German tradition. Its two major forms reproduce the individual-collective opposition so prominent within the naturalistic traditions. One form emphasizes the meaningful orientations of individual subjects (Kant, early Dilthey, Weber); the other emphasizes the meaningful orientations of collective subjects (Herder, Hegel, late Dilthey, Weber).

Virtually all accounts of the sociological tradition take these two dichotomies into account, however much they vary in describing them and in the significance they accord them. The opposition between individualistic and collectivistic principles formed a central dichotomy, for example, in the accounts of the sociological tradition by Sorokin, Parsons, and Stark, and pervades more recent schematizations of social theory. The opposition between those naturalistic postulates and contrasting positions that insist on the radically distinct properties of human subjects appears in various forms, including Parson's distinction between "positivism" and "idealism" and Wallace's typification of theories according to whether they conceive behavioral relations as "objective" or "subjective." Combining these two dichotomies in the 1981 edition of *The Nature and Types of Sociological Theory*, Martindale classified all sociological theories into four types: Scientific Elementarism, Scientific Holism, Humanistic Elementarism, and Humanistic Holism. This typology exactly parallels what emerges from juxtaposing the perspectives of the British, French, Italian, and German traditions described in Part Two. There I termed the four types atomic naturalism, societal naturalism, individual voluntarism, and collective voluntarism.[2]

Although Martindale and I evolved this typology in order to classify

---

2. Although the typology I developed corresponds exactly to that of Martindale (1981), I find problems with his terminology. 'Holism' is problematic because the term can be taken to refer to the assumption of emergent organizational properties at any level; one speaks, for example, of Gestalt psychology as representing a holistic view of personality. 'Humanistic' is problematic because it implies that theories which stress the natural properties of human beings are somehow non- or antihumane.

theories within sociology, it can in fact represent the entire spectrum of the social sciences. The approach of atomic naturalism organizes a great deal of the work in behavioral psychology, neoclassical economics, and behavioral political science, as well as the work within sociology associated with the approaches known as rational choice theory and exchange theory. The approach of societal naturalism has manifested itself in such fields as British social anthropology and structural-functional political science as well as such work in sociology as Blau's compositional structuralism, Merton's structural analysis, Parson's functionalism, class-state theory, elite theory, and geometric formal sociology. The approach of voluntaristic individualism appears in psychoanalytic self-psychology as well as in ethnomethodology, symbolic interactionism, and what I have called phenomenological formal sociology. The approach of voluntaristic collectivism appears in cultural anthropology and civilizational studies as well as in critical theory and pragmatic sociology.

In addition to these four discrete and contending positions, however, we have seen that other traditions have sought to overcome these oppositions. All together, one can identify four strategic routes to synthesizing them. I refer to these as the strategies of progressive substitution, collapsing distinctions, architectonic combination, and reciprocal priority. Figure 15 represents them in graphic form.

The strategy of *progressive substitution* proceeds by rejecting one feature of a tradition and replacing it with something from another. Wiley (1995) describes this sort of strategy more concretely as a method of effacement and replacement. This is the approach I identified in the synthesis attempted by Karl Marx.

The strategy of *collapsing distinctions* proceeds by overcoming the oppositions in question by declaring that they are really false oppositions. The opposition between individual and collectivity is collapsed by declaring the essential agentic reality to be one of social selves. The opposition between nature and subject is collapsed by showing the subject to be a higher order of natural process. Thus, there is one human reality that combines all four principles, the reality of naturally emergent social selves. This is the approach I associated with Dewey and Mead.

The modes of progressive substitution and of collapsing distinctions both require the sacrifice of some features of the originative contending positions. The two other approaches to synthesis do not entail such a sacrifice. These are represented in the thought of Parsons and Simmel, respectively.

## A. Marx: Synthesis through progressive substitution

| | | PRINCIPLE OF RATIONAL ETHIC | |
|---|---|---|---|
| | | NATURE | FREEDOM |
| LOCUS OF REALITY AND VALUE | INDIVIDUALS | Atomic Naturalism | Individual Voluntarism |
| | SOCIETIES | Societal Naturalism | Collective Voluntarism |

*(with circled markers ③ ① ② positioned between the NATURE and FREEDOM cells)*

1. Replaces nature-transcending individual consciousness with collective consciousness
2. Replaces nature-transcending collective consciousness with socially organized classes
3. Replaces naturally-given historical social classes with aggregates of individuals driven by natural interests

## B. Dewey-Mead: Synthesis through collapsing distinctions

| | | PRINCIPLE OF RATIONAL ETHIC | |
|---|---|---|---|
| | | ~~NATURE~~ | ~~FREEDOM~~ |
| | | *Mind as part of nature* | |
| LOCUS OF REALITY AND VALUE | ~~INDIVIDUALS~~ *Society consisting of selves,* ......... *which are social products* ~~SOCIETIES~~ | Evolving natural mental social selves | |

## C. Parsons: Synthesis through architectonic organization of a multileveled reality

| | ULTIMATE SYMBOLIC REALITY | CONSCIOUSNESS (CONTROLS OVER ACTION) |
|---|---|---|
| COLLECTIVE LEVELS | CULTURE | |
| | SOCIETY | |
| INDIVIDUAL LEVELS | PERSONALITY | |
| | BEHAVIORAL SYSTEM | |
| | PHYSICAL-ORGANIC ENVIRONMENT | NATURE (CONDITIONS OF ACTION) |

Figure 15.  Modes of Pursuing Synthesis of Theoretical Oppositions

D.  Simmel: Synthesis through reciprocal priority among a plurality of worlds

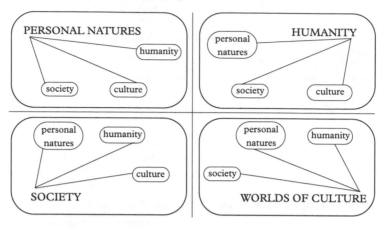

Figure 15.  (*continued*)

In his later thought, Parsons represented human action in a schema that embodied the two dimensions. The individual-collective dimension was represented in terms of different levels. With his formula that the phenomena at each level vary independently, even though they interpenetrate with those at other levels, Parsons resisted both the atomic or elementarist impulse toward downward reduction and the collectivist or holist impulse toward upward reduction without collapsing the distinction between them.

In addition, Parsons represented the natural-subjective dimension with what he called a cybernetic hierarchy. That is, the components at the bottom are high in energy and low in information; those at the top are low in energy and high in information; influence proceeds in both directions. The energies that proceed upward through the system are those commonly represented in terms of natural forces, such as the biologically based propensities featured by writers like Hutcheson, Smith, and Durkheim. The symbolic coding that proceeds downward through the system has commonly been represented in terms of conscious direction, such as the ideas and ideals that figure prominently in the interpretations of writers like Dilthey, Weber, and Mead. With this model (quite similar in conception to that of Max Scheler), too, Parsons resisted the temptation to reduce everything to nature or to subjectivity as well as the temptation to collapse the distinction between them. All together, he connects the four positions in a manner of *architectonic com-*

*bination,* fitting them into a single overarching theoretical framework.[3]

The other way to attempt a synthesis that preserves the distinctive features of each position would be to pursue what, following Walter Watson, may be called the strategy of *reciprocal priority.*[4] This strategy maintains that the four fundamental philosophic approaches—atomic naturalism, societal naturalism, individual voluntarism, collective voluntarism—are truly incompatible only if one tries to follow them all simultaneously. That is to say, each of the positions is capable of interpreting the totality of human phenomena. In this manner each amounts to what Simmel called a world. Simmel's radically pluralistic synthesis would maintain that the entire universe of human phenomena can be understood as part of the world of society, yet those same contents can be understood as part of the world of personality, or of culture, or of humanity (1971, ch. 3). Although at any moment one must operate from the perspective of a particular world, one need not be forever tied to that perspective. At the very least, one can listen to and learn from the interpretations of those who speak from the standpoint of other worlds.

The above remarks just begin to stake out the harvest of intellectual resources available to the social sciences today. Many more taxonomies could be developed to take stock of our manifold forms of social knowledge. Inventories of this sort offer substantial benefits. They help us analyze more efficiently the structure of a given approach by constraining us to identify and locate its central defining features. They provide a common vocabulary that social scientists of all persuasions can use to engage in constructive conversations about their differences. They provide a more comprehensive and balanced way for critics to assess the value of different kinds of social knowledge.[5]

The resources just considered concern only the most general assumptions about basic modes of representing social phenomena. The chief accomplishments of the sociological tradition, however, reside in

3. Wiley (1995) has recently proposed a more differentiated version of this architectonic. To a certain extent, the frameworks formulated by Elias, Bourdieu, Giddens, Habermas, and Luhmann represent efforts to articulate comparable architectonic syntheses.

4. Watson develops this approach in *The Architectonics of Meaning* ([1985] 1993), following the work of Richard McKeon. In an earlier essay (1989), I argued that the McKeon-Watson approach was adumbrated by Simmel.

5. In an earlier paper, "The Forms and Functions of Social Knowledge" (1986a), I offered a much more differentiated paradigm for taking an inventory of the universe of cognitive forms that social scientists have developed.

the wealth of its analyses regarding the contents, forms, causes, and consequences of diverse social phenomena. Even to begin to identify these lies well beyond the scope of this book. Yet there is one major problem they all address and to which the diverse dialogical traditions supply partial answers. As many have observed, the very project of modern sociology was triggered by the societal transformations that took place in Western Europe and North America from the seventeenth to the nineteenth centuries. From the time of Hobbes on, the quest for a rational ethic is also a quest to understand these transformations and to define appropriate ways of responding to them. Above all else, sociology's mission has been to identify and diagnose the most salient features of the modern order.

## THE PROBLEM OF MODERNITY

Serge Moscovici has expressed the point pithily, defining sociology as the "science du problème de la modernité" (1988, 414). Sociology has indeed wrestled continuously with the problem of modernity, largely as a metascientific enterprise of the sort Simmel described: one that pursues questions that science may not answer but which we feel compelled to pursue nonetheless. The traditions of sociology and protosociology remain fruitful as points of departure for orienting humanity to the condition of the modern world. I shall discuss nine major features of the modern order that these traditions have analyzed: 1) commercial prosperity and its attendant amenities; 2) personal rights and liberties; 3) declining warfare; 4) expanded social integration; 5) tension between egalitarianism and elitism; 6) subjective freedom; 7) rationalism; 8) differentiation and sectoral autonomy; and 9) lineal human progress. Many of these features have been discussed in most of the constitutive traditions, but they tend to have a particularly prominent association with one tradition or another.

### THE BRITISH CONTRIBUTION

The sociological theory of modernity may be said to begin with Adam Ferguson, whose *Essay on the History of Civil Society* (1767) offered a theory of the development of society from a "rude" to a "polished" state. The characteristics of polished society include the cultivation of arts and sciences, the attainment of efficient administration, and the refinement of commercial practices. Ferguson's contemporary Adam Smith advanced a similar yet more differentiated model, which identi-

fied the progress of society through four stages—hunting, herding, ag-
ricultural, and commercial. While Ferguson was willing to identify
ancient societies like Rome and Sparta as civilized, for Smith the full
progress of society, culminating in the commercial stage, had taken
place only in Western Europe. With Smith's delineation of key features
of commercial society, modernization theory received its first sharp
formulation.

For Smith, the central features of modern society included a remarkable improvement in the dexterity of productive labor and a disposition to invest wealth in productive enterprise; and, in consequence
of these factors, an unprecedented rise in the standard of living of the
population at large. Smith's analysis was carried forward by John
Millar, who explored the impact of progress in the arts and manufactures upon the relations of the sexes and the structures of government.

Another key feature of the modern order that the Scottish writers
highlighted was its promotion of personal liberty through the progress
of the rule of law and the declining intervention of government in civil
society. This ties into the many-sided individualism that we have found
in the British tradition. Smith hailed the emerging "system of natural
liberty" associated with the progress of society, which, in his book,
leaves everyone "perfectly free to pursue his own interest his own way"
([1759] 1976, 208). J. S. Mill referred to the age-old struggle between
liberty and authority as having traversed a series of stages, from the attainment of political rights vis-à-vis rulers and the establishment of
constitutional checks on governing powers to the institution of elective
and temporary rulers and, finally, to the protection of individual choice
and expression against penal coercion or the moral coercion of public
opinion.

Spencer theorized this development as the progression from a militant to an industrial type of society. Militaristic societies require centralized power. In peacetime, this type of society is perforce organized
as a quiescent army, the claims of individuals are strictly subordinated
to the state, and cooperation is secured through compulsion. With the
transition to societies oriented primarily to industrial pursuits, coercive
rule declines, personal liberties and rights become assured, and cooperation becomes voluntary. The fully modern society of the future may
evolve even further, as the shift from a martial ethic to a work ethic is
followed by the subordination of the work imperative to an ethic of personal fulfillment.

The Scots' account of the advances of civilization set the tone for a number of other accounts that hailed the progress of arts, amenities, and manners in the modern era. Comte defined the advancement of civilization as an evolutionary process that diminished the urgency of physical wants and stimulated humans' intellectual powers. The boons of the new civilized order were thought to include a diminution of the scourge of war. Like Spencer later, Comte advanced a sociology of modernity that emphasized the replacement of warfare as the preeminent societal goal by pacific pursuits centered on commerce and industry. Among the civilizing aspects of modern society Durkheim took special note of the reduction in the severity of penal sanctions.

Although writers of the British tradition identified commercial arts and prosperity, peaceful pursuits, and individual liberties and well-being as the hallmarks of modernity, they nevertheless drew attention to developments that evinced precisely the opposite properties. At the same that Ferguson, Smith, and Millar extolled the advances of civilized living in the modern order, they decried the attendant degradations manifested in declining public spirit, impoverished mental abilities, and corruption by luxury. As Forbes sums up the analyses of these Scottish writers, they "took a long, cool look at both sides of the medal of modern civilization, and what they saw was the paradox of the progress of commerce and manufactures . . . inevitably producing a second-rate sort of society full of second-rate citizens pursuing comparatively worthless objects" (Ferguson [1767] 1966, xiii). If the division of labor in industry was good for productivity, Smith argued, it was terrible for the welfare of industrial workers, for it rendered them "as stupid and ignorant as it is possible for a human to become" ([1776] 1976, 2:303). Even the improvement in standard of living touted by Smith became problematic in the analyses of Ricardo, who showed how the workings of the modern market economy produced an increasingly impoverished working class. Marx combined both these indictments in his diagnosis of the inexorable immiseration of the working class under modern capitalism. Finally, Malthus prognosticated immiseration due to the increased pressure of population on resources. Lowered death rates and unchecked birth rates promised to boost population growth well above what the earth's resources could provide, anticipating recent accounts of the depletion of earth's finite resources due to the explosion of world population.

Moreover, the same Spencer who hailed the transition from militant to industrial society took note, especially in his later years, of developments in a contrary direction. He saw the societies of Europe returning to a state of militarism, in which "the white savages of Europe are over-running the dark savages everywhere." With the return to militaristic society would come a return to despotic orders and the undoing of personal freedoms. Spencer's only hope was that this "re-barbarization which is continually undoing civilization" would eventually be curtailed by a federation of the most highly developed nations and the inculcation of habits proper for human living in a social state (1972, 258–63).

## THE FRENCH CONTRIBUTION

As might be expected, the features of modernity emphasized within the French tradition concern the enhancement of *society*. Their analyses highlight the expanded compass of societal organization and the strengthening of social integration or solidarity. Comte saw modern society as the outgrowth of a millennial process by which social groupings expanded in size, from the small-scale units of clan and tribe through city-states and empires to the final stage of the Great Being, the whole of humanity. Durkheim followed Spencer in using biological language to delineate this evolutionary process, which went from homogeneous hordes and clans and aggregations of clans, through simply and doubly polysegmentary societies, to the internally differentiated organic societies of modernity.

What is more, Durkheim saw modern organic societies not only as vaster in scope than earlier societies but also as fundamentally more cohesive. Their greater cohesiveness rests on two factors. One is the functional interdependence that comes from the fact that highly specialized organs necessarily rely much more upon one another than do members of homogeneous societies. The other consists of the vast networks of legal codes and moral norms that arise to regulate the interactions among specialized structures. These connective links are so effective, Durkheim proposed, that modern societies can achieve an unprecedented degree of solidarity without requiring a substantial body of shared beliefs and values.

Although these French theorists were pleased to identify an extensive growth of society in the modern era, they also took note of opposed tendencies. Comte criticized modern civilization not only for creating "minds that are very able in some one respect and monstrously incapable in all others" but for undermining the essential consensus needed for societies to function in the first place. The very division of labor that makes possible an expanded social order produces mutually alienated strata and exorbitantly privatized individuals, with the result that "the principle by which alone general society could be developed and extended threatens, in another view, to decompose it into a multitude of unconnected corporations, which almost seem not to belong to the same species" ([1855] 1974, 511). Durkheim also associated a notable increase of egoism with the modern social order. He referred not only to the socially sanctioned cult of the individual—a phenomenon that Parsons later represented by the felicitous phrase "institutionalized individualism"—but also to the completely unregulated separation of individuals from their social moorings that in extreme cases led to egoistic suicide.

Another feature of the modern social order that Comte analyzed was the emergence of new kinds of elites. Following Saint-Simon, Comte held that the new industrial order required new types of leaders to provide direction, captains of industry and engineers for the productive sector, secular intellectuals for the scientific and moral sectors. Their theories would later inspire Italian sociologists, Mosca in particular, who connected society's need for oligarchic rulership with the changing functional needs of society. So convinced was Comte of the need for authority from qualified experts that he dismissed appeals for freedom of speech and press as a bid to elevate ignorant rabble.

Alexis de Tocqueville contributed a countervailing argument to this part of the French component of modernization theory. Although his analysis of the ancien régime and the French Revolution focused on the growing strength of the national center in modernizing societies, his analysis of democracy in America proceeded from the assumption that egalitarian values and arrangements were becoming the defining mark of modern societies—a point echoed by Spencer's forecast of the increasingly equal status of women and children in families. Nevertheless, anticipating Durkheim's argument about the need for a stronger state in modern societies, Tocqueville saw a connection between guarantees of equal rights under the law and strengthened institutions of central authority in modern societies.

THE GERMAN CONTRIBUTION

While British theories of modernity focused on the themes of commercial civilization and individual rights, and French theories on the expansion of society and contradictory trends regarding social stratification, for writers of the German tradition, developments relating to subjective freedom and the growth of rationality became the center of attention. Kant celebrated the era of the European Enlightenment as a time when humans passed from a state of tutelage to a position where they make decisions for themselves, and Hegel identified the refusal to recognize anything that has not been justified by reason as the "characteristic property of the modern age" ([1821] 1991, 22).

Both for Kant and for Hegel, the growth in the capacity of human subjects for free choice was part and parcel of a growth in their capacity for rationality. Hegel associated this development with the creation of the rational structures of modern life: civil society and the state. Tönnies carried this line of analysis further by depicting the whole historical development since the Middle Ages as a process of the increasing domination of rationalism, a process he associated with the ascendance of a new type of human volition, *Kürwille*, or "elective will." In *Kürwille*, rational activity attains a kind of independence: it can conceive novel ends, project alternative futures, and calculate a variety of means. By using this rational elective will, persons come to associate on the basis of instrumental considerations and contractual arrangements, thereby producing such characteristically modern social formations as constitutions, corporations, political parties, and bureaucratic staffs.

The themes of freedom and rationality figure prominently in the famous analyses of modernity produced by Simmel and Weber, with Simmel featuring the former and Weber the latter. Simmel highlighted two structural aspects of modern life, an advanced money economy and metropolitan residence, both of which favored an enormous expansion of the domain of subjective freedom. Urban life does so by liberating persons from the conventional constraints of local communities; money does so by enlarging the universe of options and by permitting individuals to develop their subjective centers independent of extraneous factors. Weber treated rationality as the defining characteristic of modernity in analyses that delineate the organization of modern capitalist enterprise, bureaucratic authority, the codification of law, the proliferation of rational technology, and the institution of modern science.

As Weber characterized the growth of rationality, however, it moved in directions that brought about a marked curtailment of subjective freedom. The formal and instrumental rationalities of the productive process in modern capitalism forced the experience of humans away from their natural rhythms and personal desires, and the codified routines of the bureaucratic machines that were engulfing the modern world threatened to fabricate a cage every bit as enslaving as the condition of ancient Egyptian fellahs. In Simmel's perspective, workers were not only becoming enslaved to an impersonal production process and, as consumers, in thrall to dispensable products, but the objectified forms of rational culture were beginning to oppress the individual subject in ways that constituted a characteristic tragedy of modern life.

## OTHER CLASSIC CONTRIBUTIONS

The heightened rationality of the modern era was also highlighted by American pragmatists. In analyses that featured the crucial role of the media that shape public opinion, Dewey, Mead, and Park viewed modernity as a scene of unprecedented opportunities for rational discourse and public deliberation modeled on the workings of the scientific community.

Even so, other lines of analysis pointed to tendencies toward increased *irrationality* thrown up in the course of modern developments. Writers in the Italian tradition might be expected to make much of this theme, but it can be found in a number of other writers as well. Pareto identified the enduring irrationalities of human sentiment in the various ideologies of modernity, and Sighele discussed the irrationalities of collective behavior that surfaced in the modern crowd. Durkheim spoke of the maladies of unchecked impulsiveness unleashed by the erosion of binding moralities. Although Simmel argued that the impersonal calculations required for living in a money economy and the modern metropolis promote intellectuality at the expense of sentiment, he delineated some contrary dynamics as well: one effect of money economies and their attendant division of labor is to transfer the intellectual potential of modern life from the individual subject to objectified forms, thereby weakening the intellectual capacities of subjects; and the modern metropolis spawns such irrational reactions as compulsive aversion to strangers and forms of rebellious individuality. Max Scheler diagnosed an enormous increase in waves of ressentiment in the modern world, and Karl Mannheim went on to diagnose an upsurge of "substantive irrationality" that accompanies the diffusion of functional rationalization.

Writers from nearly all traditions discussed the theme of functional differentiation as a major feature of the modern order. Smith noted the ways in which occupational specialization enhances productivity. Spencer made the principle of differentiation the foundation of a whole cosmology. He located the progressive aspect of modern societies in their ability to embody functionally differentiated structures, even though he acknowledged the problems posed by functionaries who acquire vested interests in their specialized roles. Durkheim found that the enhanced solidarity made possible by functional specialization fostered a higher level of morality. Simmel and Weber brought the discourse on specialization to a new level by discussing the autonomization of diverse spheres of human activity, Simmel with his discussion of ways in which initially instrumental activities like singing or stargazing become transformed into domains cultivated for their own sake, Weber with his analysis of the ways in which specialized spheres come to be *eigengesetzlich*—governed by their own internally generated norms.

The Marxian tradition offered a contrasting view of the phenomena of differentiation. On the one hand, Marx and Engels attributed pernicious effects to the division of labor, both in society at large and within the modern factory. On the other hand, they denied the principle of the autonomy of specialized spheres by seeing the whole process driven by the economic imperatives of the capitalist system and the integrity of putatively autonomous domains undermined by the all-pervasive dynamics of the market.

A final aspect of the modern order theorized by the classic tradition concerns the general form of modern history. Perhaps the most common assumption has been that this history takes the shape of a lineal evolution. The classic articulations of this model include Condorcet's outline of ten epochs in the evolution of the human mind, Schelling's interpretation of the process of history as a progressive realization of law culminating in a sovereign world federation, Maine's depiction of the transformation of social arrangements from determination through social status to determination through voluntary contract, Hobhouse's account of the ever-expanding efficiency and scale of human organization. Indeed, many of the hallmarks of modernity mentioned above were represented in ways that assumed a kind of lineal evolution—for example, Mill's sketch of the several stages in the evolution of human liberty, Hegel's account of the evolution of human consciousness in history, or Spencer's theory of the evolutionary trend from homogeneity to differentiation.

Although the notion that modernity unfolds in lineal form was widespread, it was challenged by a number of views that upheld alternative models. Thinkers of the Italian tradition rejected the notion of progressive evolution in favor of a cyclical view of history, which followed Polybius and Machiavelli. In a similar vein, Central European scholars like Gumplowicz and Spengler viewed the historical process as a record of the rise and fall of states and civilizations, one that follows an inevitable cyclical course of growth and decline. Such views can be seen as a latter-day extension of the views of Vico and Herder, for whom the grand tableau of historical experience presents not a single story of human or societal evolution but a harvest of diverse, colorful, and irreducibly distinct cultures. In this kind of perspective, modernity appears not as the convergent endpoint of all previous history but as a particular culture that will in turn decline and give way to other cultural formations.

Yet another model appears in the conceptions of those who view the trajectory of modernization as proceeding not in a straight line but more like a spiral with alternating crests and troughs. To some extent, Marxian analyses fit this model, with their charting of historical development in terms of sequence of theses and antitheses, and the vicissitudes of capitalism in terms of cycles of inflation and depression. Spencer, often thought of as a lineal evolutionist, took pains to voice his objection to such a notion. In Spencer's words:

> The cosmic process brings about retrogression as well as progression. . . . Evolution does not imply a latent tendency to improve, everywhere in operation. There is no uniform ascent from lower to higher, but only an occasional production of a form which, in virtue of greater fitness for more complex conditions, becomes capable of a longer life of a more varied kind. (1972, 261)

Such words gave Spencer a consoling perspective at a time when the nations of Europe seemed to be descending to a new barbarism, leading him to predict that civilized mankind would have to be uncivilized again before civilization could once more advance (260).

Perhaps the most striking conclusion one reaches from bringing together the numerous analyses of modernity in the sociological tradition is that time and again they identify diametrically opposed developmental tendencies. Often enough, one sees this only by bringing together the analyses of different authors or traditions, as in Tocqueville's egalitarianism versus Saint-Simon's neoelitism, or Tönnies's rationalization versus Sighele's new irrationality. In other cases, the authors are themselves conscious of opposed tendencies in the modern order, as in Smith's and Marx's account of commercial society as providing both increased amenities and impoverished lives, or in Weber's account of the simultaneous increase and decrease of freedom in modern society (Levine 1985a, ch. 7). Indeed, Durkheim began his career by wondering how it could be that the modern order produced an expansion of society at the same time that it promoted an unprecedented individualism.

It was this very condition of amplified dualisms that Simmel made the cornerstone of his general theory of modernity. Simmel's magisterial essay on the metropolis and mental life describes the modern city as "one of those great historical structures in which conflicting life-embracing currents find themselves with equal legitimacy" ([1903] 1971, 339). His multipronged attack on the problem of money yielded the proposition that money "cultivates all the opposites of historical-psychological possibilities" ([1907] 1978, 409). He tendered the propositions that individualization and societal expansion go hand in hand, that accelerated change in fashions intensifies the oscillation between desires for conformity and distinction, that in modernity the public realm becomes ever more public and the private ever more private. For Simmel, the most basic feature of the modern order is its capacity to *differentiate and promote opposed characteristics.*

## CONTEMPORARY CONTRIBUTIONS

Contemporary discourse about modernity revives and extends the contrasting analyses of its central features formulated in the classic tradition. The *civilizing process* has been celebrated in renewed attention to the seminal work of Norbert Elias, while S. N. Eisenstadt has reconsidered the relation between *barbarism* and modernity, and Hans Joas has raised fresh questions about the relationship between modernity and *military violence.* The argument that modern economic systems bring both greater benefits and costs to human welfare has been updated in the seminal work of Ulrich Beck, who finds late moderns living on a "volcano of civilization" in which the social production of *wealth* is systematically accompanied by the social production of *risks.* T. H. Marshall extended Mill's analysis of the progressive institutionalization of *human rights* while Hannah Arendt and Zygmunt Bauman have explored the connections between modernity and *totalitarianism.* Mark Gould offers a fresh account of the trend toward *equity* as the final stage of modernization, yet Daniel Bell's analyses of postindustrial society portray the rise of a *new kind of elite* in ways Saint-Simon would surely have appreciated. Roland Robertson explores the essential movement of modern societies toward *globalism,* Clifford Geertz offers a trenchant analysis of new sources of *primordial mobilization* in modernizing societies, while Benjamin Barber identifies tribalism and globalism as the two axial principles of our age. Educators revive the discourse about new realms of subjective choice and the modern mode of *values clari-*

*fication* while critical theorists revive talk about new forms of objectification and *repression*. The opposition between enhanced *personal autonomy* and expanded *social control* has been pondered by scholars like Anthony Giddens, Peter Wagner, and Alan Touraine.

Over the course of many publications Parsons continued Tönnies's project of depicting modernization as a depth-historical process of *rationalization* and Spencer's project of depicting *functional differentiation*, which Luhmann extended with his notion of *autopoietic systems*. Nevertheless, a follower of Parsons, Leon Mayhew, argues that *ascriptive solidarities* become more salient in modernity and another follower of Parsons, Richard Münch, uses Parson's own notion of *interpenetration* to criticize Luhmann's notion of sectoral autonomy; meanwhile, Tom Scheff and Tom Smith explore new waves of *irrationality* endemic to the modern order. At the most general level, *convergence* theorists revive notions of a world-historical progression toward a single type of sociocultural system, and David Livingston actually proclaims a single Central Civilization which all world civilizations have entered over millennia. Meanwhile, other theorists stress persisting divergences among nations and regions, and Robertson argues that the demonstrable trend toward globalization nevertheless involves radically diverse conceptions of what globality means.

It has become fashionable in recent decades to eschew the entire project of coming to grips with the character of the modern order. This may have succeeded in keeping courses on modernization out of the curriculum; it can scarcely halt the inexorable processes of modernization, which the originative thinkers of the sociological tradition identified and analyzed so suggestively. When social scientists do focus on modernization, they customarily align themselves with one particular mode of interpreting modernity. I leave it to the reader to decide whether that custom is most productive, or whether one does not secure a more realistic, interesting, and helpful picture by bringing the diverse takes on modernity into dialogue with one another.

# CHAPTER SIXTEEN

# In Quest of a Secular Ethic

On the face of it, the ethical concerns that propelled philosophers into creating the social sciences seem to have dropped out of sight. A metaphor I like to use for this process is launching a spacecraft. The quest for a rational ethic was the booster that launched the social scientific disciplines into orbit. Once the disciplines were launched, the booster dropped away and disappeared. Yet the trajectory of those disciplines continues to be determined by the direction of the programming that first set them into motion.

What is more, no matter how hard social scientists struggle to divest themselves of considerations of practice, practical concerns rarely lurk far from the surface. Many if not most enter the social sciences because of a desire to improve the human world in some way. Insofar as they study earlier authors for whom moral concerns remained silent, they become dimly aware of a great stretch of unfinished business on the agenda of the social sciences. Although the ethical boosters have accomplished their originary task and sunk into oblivion, there remains some nagging sense of a need to address still-unresolved issues from the debate about the proper relation of normative principles to the laws of nature. Even when that need is not felt, the ethical concerns often permeate work subliminally. Using a different metaphor, one astute observer of contemporary sociology suggests that ethics is "the ghost in the social-science machine" (Horowitz 1993, 227).[1]

## THEORY AND PRACTICE REVISITED

What has the heritage of sociology and its predecessors left us as the result of their transgenerational, multinational quest for a rational, secular ethic? Taking Aristotle once again as a point of departure, we can identify six general ways of responding to the question. These can be

1. Describing how the ghost works, he writes: "At the start and conclusion of every major piece of empirical research, or theoretical paradigm developed by social scientists, has been some driving moral imperative about personal rights, racial balance, or sexual equality. But this moral dimension has been obscured by those for whom facts speak for themselves" (227).

associated, respectively, with Aristotle himself, Hobbes and his followers, the French and Italian traditions, Kant and his followers, Marx,
and the American pragmatists. The solutions, I suggested earlier, hinge
largely on how one defines nature and how one assesses the pertinence
of reliable knowledge about nature to directives for human action.

The quest began by defining nature as a partial guide to action that
needs to be supplemented by a separate and distinct practical discourse. It then entered a phase in which knowledge of nature was
viewed in different ways as a truly reliable guide to action. This led to a
critique in which knowledge of nature is rejected altogether as a reliable
basis for a rational ethic. Finally, the very distinction between knowledge of nature and practical knowledge was questioned in different
ways.

As Aristotle framed the matter, sciences of natural phenomena identify the properties of substances that exist apart from human intervention. The natural science of botany studies the properties of plants,
whereas arts like medicine or painting study ways to modify plants
for human purposes. Because humans intervene regularly to modify
human material, a great deal of human experience lies outside the
purview of theoretic natural science. Nevertheless, some human formations exist by nature, and these lend themselves to theoretic examination. One set consists of the formations of the human psyche. These
comprise the subject matter of the natural science of psychology, which
examines such natural faculties as vision, hearing, moving, desiring,
and calculating. Psychology discloses the natural potentials of individual human life. It cannot encompass the domain of personal action,
however, because natural sciences formulate universals and action
consists of particulars; because natural sciences formulate necessary
propositions and action depends on voluntary decisions; and because
psychology deals merely with what happens as a matter of course, while
humans are concerned with action in order to know what is the best
way to act. Accordingly, a distinctive science concerned with action, a
practical science, must be cultivated to deal with the concrete, indeterminate, and goal-oriented subject matter of individual human action.
That discipline is ethics, which employs a method of deliberation different from the induction of universals on which psychology is founded.

Other practical disciplines are required to examine questions regarding the good life in human associations. Although Aristotle considered only two of these—the household and the polis—in principle the

kind of practical disciplines he envisioned could be organized to deal with action in any form of human association. Aristotle did not posit a natural science of human associations comparable to the natural science of psychology. He did, however, stipulate that human associations get formed by nature: they occur as a matter of course, and they constitute a complex of potentialities shaped in varying ways by different constitutions. In principle there could therefore be an Aristotelian natural science of society parallel to psychology, a point that Aquinas made in commenting on Aristotle's organization of the social sciences. Again, however, a naturalistic sociology could only indicate the universal regularities and raw potentialities of forms of social intercourse, not the ways in which associations should be shaped and directed under particular circumstances. Guides for action require disciplines like economics and politics that can proceed only by deliberation and never with the kind of exactitude one would expect in sciences of natural substances.

The reorientation of social thought in the seventeenth and eighteenth centuries included changes in conceptions both of nature and of how to employ knowledge of nature in pursuit of a rational ethic. Hobbes initiated a long line of efforts to conceptualize society, not as a natural association possessing potentials that can be actualized to promote human excellence, but as the outcome of individual psychic processes that occur in accord with laws as determinate and universal as the law of gravity. In this perspective, no separate discourse is needed to determine the best ways to act. Practical knowledge follows logically from the foundations set by a natural psychology. For Hobbes, the need for sovereign political authority presents itself as a "law of nature," recognition of which will bring humanity the blessings of civil peace; for Smith, the "obvious and simple system of natural liberty" establishes itself as a beneficial order once its theoretical understanding enables regimes to remove all artificial preferences and restraints from human commerce; for Bentham, a natural science of utility establishes the dominance of pain and pleasure, and determines standards of right and wrong in the same breath that it determines chains of causes and effects.

French thinkers of that period were no less enthused than the British about the achievements of the new physics and its potential for establishing a rational ethic on a comparably secure footing. Comte called this the positive method and created a philosophy of positivism to realize its promise. For Comte and the principal social thinkers of the

French tradition, however, the way to achieve this was not by making all phenomena explicable through the properties of their atomic elements. Nature did not consist of a uniform universe of atomic motions but of phenomena organized on different levels of complexity. Just as organisms have properties that cannot be reduced to those of their constitutive elements, so societies have properties not reducible to those of their individual members. Once this is understood, natural sciences can provide standards for action by determining what is normal for the phenomena at a given level. This means that those who promulgate social laws should wait on the conclusions of the newly emerging theoretical science of society. Durkheim reinforced this position, arguing for a theoretically grounded calculus of societal normality and pathology, that is, for a theoretical sociology that had to be pursued with the full rigor of natural science but whose ultimate rationale was to establish standards of societal health.

It was to counter this entire approach—one presupposing that practical wisdom could and should be derived from foundations supplied by a naturalistic theoretic science of human behavior or societal functioning—that Kant revolutionized the quest for a rational ethic by divorcing it from knowledge of nature altogether. What seemed to clinch the matter for Kant was the logical impossibility of obtaining on naturalistic grounds a rational ethic that possessed the universally compelling character he thought that moral laws ought to have, and that naturalists from Hobbes on promised it would have. At the same time that Kant secured a universally compelling moral imperative through the operations of the human mind alone, he also preserved the dignity of human subjects by protecting their autonomy. Respect for the free will of actors was built into the process of determining the ethic as well as into the content of the moral imperative. Long after the rationally compelling universality of ethical norms had been dropped from the agenda of those who developed the social sciences in Germany, figures like Dilthey, Simmel, and Weber continued to proclaim the impossibility of deriving ethical imperatives from natural science. This led to two distinct formulations regarding the relations between theoretical science and practice. On the one hand, in continuing to make the free creations of the human subject the touchstone of their normative positions, Simmel and Weber moved toward an existentialist ethics in which the authentic personal decisions of each actor become the principle for directing action. On the other hand, they laid a philosophical foundation for the position that has come to inform the orientations of most professional sociologists today: that although scientific theory cannot serve to ground the ends of action, it can and should provide information that will help actors select the most appropriate means for attaining their ends. In Kantian terms, theories about human conduct viewed as a natural phenomenon can provide no categorical imperatives, but they can provide hypothetical imperatives, propositions that indicate one what should do if one wants to attain a certain end.

The effort to divorce autonomous human ideals from the processes of nature was sharply challenged by Marx and his followers. Reversing his earlier veneration of Kant, Fichte, and Hegel, Marx ridiculed the German tendency to concoct abstract ideals instead of attending to the actual miseries of those engaged in laboring to satisfy everyday wants. Where Kant had found nature unsatisfactory as a source of morality because of its constitution by sensuous needs that corrupt or at least tempt moral judgment and fail to provide a logic of obligation, Marx found ideals based on a supersensuous domain to be alienated from man's only reality—sensuous experience. Although Marx acknowledged the historical existence of a distinct domain of theoretical knowledge separate from practical concerns, he considered that domain detrimental to human well-being. Theoretical knowledge reflects the historic separation of mental work from physical labor and the ministrations of an intellectual elite that lives off the surplus value created by manual workers. Support for such knowledge buttresses the position of an exploitative ruling class and distracts energies from the effort to abolish human misery.

For Marx, then, true consciousness can only be consciousness of existing practice. Theoretical knowledge separate from practice is alienated, whether that separation stems from a theoretic science antecedent and foundational to practice, as with Hobbes and Comte, or from a pure practical reason independent of natural processes, as with Kant. Rational practice begins with an acknowledgment of true human needs—for eating and drinking, clothing, housing, but also for expressing oneself creatively in work—and any intellectual activity that does not minister to the satisfaction of these needs represents false consciousness. "Social life is essentially practical, [and] all mysteries which mislead theory into mysticism find their rational solution in human practice and in the comprehension of this practice," said Marx (Tucker 1978, 145). Suitable directives for action can only stem from the reality of man's sensuous experience, and the only legitimate way to organize science is as a single science of nature and humanity whose sole con-

cern would be the fulfillment of human wants through dominating nature, emancipating labor, and socializing all human activity.

Another type of reaction, finally, occurred in the United States,
where pragmatist philosophers also rebelled against the tendency of
German idealism to divorce ideals from nature. Instead of repudiating
the ideals because of their imputed alienation from natural wants, however, philosophers like Dewey and Mead reconceived the whole process of forming ideals as a phenomenon that emerges in nature. Rather
than pursue a separate theoretic science of nature to determine human
ideals, pragmatism sought to legitimate natural social processes as a
source of ideals. Ideals emerge through efforts to solve problems and
through recollection of previous solutions that have proven satisfactory.

Like Marx, Dewey interpreted the idea of a separate domain of pure
theory as a residue of an elitist social structure. He, too, believed that
the mysteries of pure theory find their resolution in human practice.
But Dewey regarded the effort to establish a list of absolute human
needs as itself a kind of alienation, just another by-product of the age-
old, all-too-human wish for certainty.

For Dewey and Mead, theory is simply a name for a special kind of
practice, so the quest for a theoretical knowledge either prior to or seg-
regated from practice must be rejected as a reflection of human anxieties. Just as the pragmatists collapsed the distinctions between
individual and society and between nature and mind, so they collapsed
the distinction between theory and practice. They resurrected Aristotle's method of deliberation to deal with practical problems but made
that method appropriate to theory as well: in science as in daily life,
action gets initiated in situations marked by indeterminacy or conflict,
in which felt difficulties prompt efforts to formulate problems, suggest
hypotheses, and carry out activities designed to test those hypotheses.

The quest for a rational ethic that inspired the sociological tradition
thus has produced an interesting range of positions on the question of
how to relate theory and the sciences of nature to questions of ethics
and practice. Social scientists today have little awareness of this range
of positions. They have lost the insights associated with them and have
not cultivated the ability to bring them into a joint inquiry or investigation. They tend either to proceed in stubborn attachment to the notion
that nothing they do as social scientists is colored by their practical concerns, or else that the way they conceive of the relationship between
social science and practice is the only legitimate way to do so. Part of

the benefit of reconstructing the tradition in the form of a dialogical narrative may be to recover the rich legacy of arguments on this question and to bring them to bear on the quest in a novel way.

## A DIALOGICAL APPROACH TO THE QUEST

All of this begs the question of how to select one of these positions in the first place. For the most part, such selections reflect accidental combinations of educational background, personal identifications, and situational incentives. Yet the process of selecting resources from the tradition can be subjected to more intelligent direction by invoking the principle I stated at the beginning of this chapter. This is the same principle that informed our interpretations of the sequence of narratives, the constitutive subtraditions, and the contemporary crises of the sociological tradition. It is the principle of *evaluating forms with respect to their adequacy to the functional requirements of a particular situation of action*. This principle holds good whether the forms in question are categorical frameworks, empirical procedures, descriptive modalities, explanatory logics, epistemic methods, interpretations, or epistemic products (Levine 1986a).

If this principle is to be followed, it is useful to have recourse to a schema of systemic functions. One functional schema that has passed the test of time is the so-called AGIL scheme propounded by Parsons. Developed initially at the level of social systems, it parallels the functional schema of personality created by Freud and his followers. I shall apply that schema of systemic functions to the question of how to select a particular conception of the relationship between theory and praxis.

The functions are divided according to whether they concern the system's relation to its external environment or to its internal processes, and whether they concern the acquisition of means to obtain goals (instrumental) or the attainment of the goals (consummatory). The external functions comprise those that have to do with marshaling adaptive resources (A), and those involved in coordinating energies to attain goals (G). The internal functions have to do with integrating the elements of the system (I) and providing support for maintaining its latent patterns (L). At the level of the personality, the A, or adaptive, functions are served by what Freud called the ego; the G, or goal-attainment, functions by the id; the I, or normative integrative, function by the superego; and the L, or pattern maintenance, function by the ego ideal.

With this schema in mind, different constructions of the theory-practice relationship identified as we moved from Aristotle to Dewey can be interpreted as responses to different kinds of systemic problems.[2]

1. The setting of ends through deliberation as in Aristotle and the diagnoses of natural health or normality as in the British and French theorists concern the internal function of pattern maintenance. This is akin to the ego ideal in the personality.

2. The specification of norms that formed the heart of Kant's practical philosophy concerns the internal function of integration, akin to the superego function of the personality.

3. Marx's identification of practice with the satisfaction of sensuous needs corresponds to the function of goal attainment. This corresponds to what has been called the id function.

4. Dewey's identification of practice with problem solving corresponds to the ego function of the personality, and to the more general system function of adaptation, as does the position of standard professional sociology. This position finds a separable theoretical knowledge important for identifying optimum means, although it is not usable for specifying ends of action.

Others may prefer different functional schemata. What is important here are not the details of any particular schema, but the way in which such analyses of functions both facilitate selection and enhance assessment. Thus, one could argue that in times when pattern-maintenance problems predominate, the versions of the theory-praxis relationship that feature the setting of ends should prevail; at times when goal-attainment problems predominate, a view of theory as fused with and governed by practice should prevail.

## THE USES AND ETHICS OF DIALOGUE

Comprehensive schemas of themes and ideas facilitate the uses of dialogue, and these uses are extraordinary.

By opening ourselves to a wider range of options, we learn of other resources for our projects. We also learn of resources pertinent to problems we are not now addressing but may address in the future.

By opening ourselves to the positions of others, we learn more about the character and value of the positions we ourselves espouse. If we are

2. A more extended discussion of this paradigm appears in Levine 1992.

lively, we may be stimulated to defend our positions in creative and fruitful ways. Part Two has revealed the exceptionally deep and complex range of insights produced by the transgenerational and transnational dialogues among participants in the constitutive intellectual traditions of Western social theory. Referring to more recent developments, Portes (1994) emphasizes the value of intellectual trespassing across boundaries as a goad to creative developments in the social sciences—in this case, not national but disciplinary boundaries.

By participating in dialogue one learns to respect the position of the other while presenting the position that comes from one's own center. It means to pursue a project in continuing communication with those who inhabit the same universe, whether or not they support different projects and positions. When practitioners do this, disciplines replace wasteful polemics with creative inquiry.

They may also overcome the fragmentation that so many diagnoses of our crisis have identified. A dialogical approach offers the basis for a narrative that is maximally informative and inclusive. It offers a way to pursue our quest that enables us to take advantage of the contributions of others rather than isolate ourselves from one another. It allows us to stop sitting at "separate tables," as Almond put it.

And what of the quest for a rational, secular ethic? Beyond indicating a range of defensible positions regarding the relation between rational knowledge of nature and the domain of practice, can the dialogical narrative constructed in Part Two and reviewed above make any substantive contribution to the question of how rational inquiry can contribute to the provision of ethical directives? One could claim, ironically, that one significant outcome of the quest has been the finding that nonrational elements remain essential for moral conduct. Among many other notions, Aristotle's character states, Shaftesbury's affections, Smith's sentiments, Durkheim's rituals, Pareto's nonlogical elements, Freud's affects, and Dewey's habits attest in diverse ways to the indispensable role of nonrational factors in the constitution of a viable morality. Weber alludes to some of this thinking with his assertion that most human conduct is governed by impulse or habit, pursued in a state of "inarticulate half-consciousness or actual unconsciousness of its subjective meaning," and that social scientists need to remain mindful of the danger of inappropriately using rationalistic interpretations of human conduct (1968, 21, 7).

Yet Weber preached and practiced communication as an aid to clarifying value positions as well as for scientific purposes. Paradoxically, the final outcome of the quest for a rational ethic may be to locate such an ethic in the structure of the quest itself. Dialogue is not just a way to overcome fragmentation and promote coherence in academic disciplines, nor is it only a way to replace wasteful polemics with creative inquiry. The very form of dialogue offers a kind of model for the ethical life, as Martin Buber imagined and as a number of more recent theorists have been arguing.[3] Buber located the ethical dimension of dialogue in the manner in which it promotes authentic humanity. Others have attended to the ways in which participation in dialogue imposes certain moral preconditions for human interaction—such as the obligation to speak the truth, not to distort the meanings of one's interlocutors, and not to eliminate by force or other means any eligible participants.

As Durkheim might have put it, there are nondialogical foundations of dialogue that contain moral directives in themselves.

3. In addition to Buber, this theme has been explored in diverse directions by philosophers like Mikhail Bakhtin, Hans-Georg Gadamer, Jürgen Habermas, Emanuel Levinas, Richard McKeon, and Richard Rorty. For an effort to synthesize Habermas and Levinas, see Trey 1992. For an effort to link Bakhtin with Gadamer and Habermas, see Gardiner 1992.

# Dialogue as an Antidote to Fragmentation?

At a time when the social science community, like the global human community, is riven by contentions among members holding different narratives from the past, perhaps the prime task of a dialogical approach may be to make respectful contact with each of the other narratives and to bring them into fruitful conversation with one another.[1]

Like personal stories, collective narratives define present identities in order to direct future action. What kind of past Me the self depicts affects the kind of You it speaks to when giving itself directions toward the future. Each type of sociological narrative implies a certain view of knowledge and legitimates a certain orientation to scholarly work.

The positivist narrative directs the sociologist to move forward by improving and applying observational technologies. It supports the rigorous work of formalization and codification that organizes continuities within and among research programs. In this sort of narrative, theory emerges relatively unproblematically through careful attention to relationships observed among precisely defined variables.

The pluralist narrative adds to the theme of empirical work the value of considering a theoretical perspective. Its moral is that empiricism is not enough, and that one should become aware of the universe of theoretical possibilities even while orienting one's work by some partial perspective. Even the most resolutely empirical research involves a certain amount of prestructuring provided by a theoretical tradition.

The synthetic narrative adds to the pluralist's awareness of theoretical issues the conviction that prior theoretical divergences have been overcome within a common synthetic framework. It enjoins the sociologist to work with full awareness of that synthesis and to carry out all investigations with that in mind, and to employ that framework as a tool to lend particular investigations greater resonance and generality.

---

1. Pursuing the therapeutic metaphor further, one reader has likened the current fragmentative character of the social sciences to a multiple personality disorder. As the therapist's task in such a case is to help the dissociated identities within the same person begin to make respectful contact with on another, so the task of a dialogical narrative must be to help those who hold divergent narratives that define different disciplinary identities begin to communicate respectfully with one another.

The humanist is wary of restricting all sociological work to the accumulation of narrowly circumscribed empirical studies. Great classic works provide the touchstone of sociological excellence. These exemplars conjoin aesthetic creativity, moral sensibility, philosophical depth, and historical awareness to whatever particular investigations are being prosecuted. One should imitate some features of them in current work or at least show how what one is doing relates to them.

Contextualist narratives legitimate work that expresses ideological themes of historians or their subjects. Marxian versions favor work that speaks for oppressed strata or on behalf of what is called an "emancipatory" interest. Other perspectives express some partisan interest based on gender, nation, race, or religion, or they seek simply to define the accomplishments of social science as expressions of a concrete set of cultural themes and dispositions.

The dialogical approach to narrative can take something of value from each of these other narratives without insisting, in turn, that it is the only valid mode of telling the story. With the positivist narrative it shares an affirmation that careful, sustained communication is able to yield cumulative and improved understanding. With the pluralist narrative, it acknowledges the legitimacy of an irreducible plurality of philosophical positions. With the synthetic approach, it seeks to bring diverse positions into communication with one another, even though no single formulation of an encompassing synthesis can be acceptable to all parties or do justice to the complexity of human concerns and realities. With the humanist position, it affirms the classics as indispensable resources for the constitution of the conversation. With the contextualist, it seeks to understand the historical contexts in which narratives arise, and to anchor its own espousal of dialogue in the contemporary crisis of social science and the human community.

Even so, the dialogical approach is not wantonly eclectic, for it propounds a distinctive way of constructing narratives. It is certainly not casually permissive, for it can insist on criteria of validity, criteria of significance, and criteria of quality of performance.

The mission of a dialogical narrative is to display connections. It may thereby encourage members of a community who share that narrative to forge and enjoy connections among themselves. Yet dialogue connects without enforcing uniformity. It promotes, as Buber held true for "genuine conversation"—and therefore for every actual fulfillment of interhuman relationship—the "acceptance of otherness" (1992, 65).

Not all conversations represented in this book follow the norm of respect for the other, let alone that effort to experience the intersubjective encounter with the other advocated by Buber. Yet many of them do, and the record of those dialogues may remind us of the ideal that Durkheim and others have articulated—to develop social ties strong enough to provide emotional support and normative integration yet not so strong as to inhibit diversity of roles and personal autonomy. If this spirit of dialogue gets cultivated, it may serve not only to overcome the epistemological fragmentation of our discipline but its growing division along particularistic lines. Perhaps it is time for sociology to recover the robustly ecumenical outlook it evinced when the discipline was being established a century ago and to model, for the world community, a way of resolving the cultural crisis of our time.

# Appendixes

## BRITAIN

1642: Hobbes, *De Cive*
1651: Hobbes, *Leviathan*
1690: Locke, *Two Treatises of Government*
1711: Shaftesbury, *Characteristicks . . .*
1714: Mandeville, *The Fable of the Bees*
1728: Hutcheson, *The Essay on . . . Passions and Affections*
1739: Hume, *A Treatise of Human Nature*

1751: Hume, *Enquiry Conc. the Principles of Morals*

1755: Hutcheson, *System of Moral Philosophy*
1759: Smith, *The Theory of Moral Sentiments*
1767: Ferguson, *Essay on the History of Civil Society*
1776: Smith, *The Wealth of Nations*
1776: Bentham, *Fragment on Government*
1779: Millar, *The Origin of the Distinction of Ranks*

1789: Bentham, *Introduction to the Principles of Morals and Legislation*
1792: Ferguson, *Principles of Moral and Political Science*

1798: Malthus, *Essay on the Principle of Population*

1817: Ricardo, *Principles of Political Economy . . .*
1820: Malthus, *Principles of Political Economy*
1821: James Mill, *Elements of Political Economy*

1823–33: Utilitarian Society flourishes

1843: J. S. Mill, *System of Logic*

1848: J. S. Mill, *Principles of Political Economy*
1850: Spencer, *Social Statics*
1859: J. S. Mill, *On Liberty*
1861: Maine, *Ancient Law*
1864: Spencer, "Reasons for Dissenting from the Philosophy of M. Comte"
1865: J. S. Mill, *Auguste Comte and Positivism*
1872: Darwin, *The Expressions of the Emotions in Man and Animals*
1873: Spencer, *The Study of Sociology*
1876–96: Spencer, *Principles of Sociology* (vol. I, 1876; vol. II, 1882; vol. III, 1896)

1890: Marshall, *Principles of Economics*

1906: Hobhouse, *Morals in Evolution*

1922: Radcliffe-Brown, *The Andaman Islanders*

## FRANCE

1748: Montesquieu, *On the Spirit of Laws*
1750: Turgot, *Sorboniques*
1750: Rousseau, *First Discourse*

1762: Rousseau, *Emile, The Social Contract*

1789: Sieyès. *What Is the Third Estate?*

1793 Condorcet, *Sketch for a Historical Picture of the Progress of the Human Mind*
1796: Bonald, *Theory of Political and Religious Authority in Civil Society*
1797: Maistre, *Considérations sur la France*

1813: Saint-Simon, "Essay on Science of Man"
1814: Maistre, *Essay on the Generative Principle of Political Constitutions*
1814: Saint-Simon, "The Reorganization of European Society"

1822: Comte, *Plan of the Scientific Operations Necessary for Reorganizing Society*
1825: Saint-Simon, *New Christianity*
1825–35: Saint-Simonians flourish
1830–42: Comte, *Course of Positive Philosophy*

1835–40: Tocqueville, *Democracy in America*

1840: Proudhon, *What Is Property?*

1845–55: Positivist Society flourishes

1851–54: Comte, *System of Positive Polity*
1855: Le Play, *Les Ouvriers européens*

1864: Fustel de Coulanges, *The Ancient City*

1869: Renouvier, *Science of Ethics*
1871: Le Play: *The Organization of the Family*

1890: Tarde, *The Laws of Imitation*

1893: Durkheim, *On the Division of Social Labor*
1895: Durkheim, *Rules of Sociological Method*
1895: Le Bon, *The Crowd*
1897: Durkheim, *Suicide*
(1898–1900): Durkheim, *Professional Ethics and Civic Morals*
1900: Durkheim, "Two Laws of Penal Evolution"
(1902–03): Durkheim, *Moral Education*

1912: Durkheim, *The Elementary Forms of the Religious Life*

## GERMANY

1781: Kant, *Critique of Pure Reason*
1784: Kant, "Idea for a Universal History . . ."
1785: Kant, *Grundlegung*
1788: Kant, *Critique of Practical Reason*

1784–91: Herder, *Reflections on the Philosophy of the History of Mankind*

1797: Schelling, Philosophy of Nature

1806: Fichte, *Characteristics of the Present Age*
1807: Hegel, *Phenomenology of Mind*
1805–33: Schleiermacher, *Hermeneutics*

1818: Schopenhauer, *The Worlds as Will and Idea*
1818–31: Hegel teaches at Berlin
1821: Hegel, *Philosophy of Right*

1835: Strauss, *The Life of Jesus Critically Examined*
1833–43: Young Hegelians flourish

1841: Feuerbach, *The Essence of Christianity*
1842: Von Stein, *Socialism and Communism in France*

1850: Von Stein, *The History of the Social Movement in France, 1789–1850*

1881: Dilthey, *Introduction to the Geisteswissenschaften*
1887: Tönnies, *Gemeinschaft und Gesellschaft*
1889: Boas, "The Aims of Ethnology"
1891: Simmel, *On Social Differentiation*
1892[1905/07]: Simmel, *Problems of the Philosophy of History*

1900: Freud, *The Interpretation of Dreams*

1900[1907]: Simmel, *Philosophy of Money*
1902: Rickert, *Die Grenzen der naturwissenschaftlichen Begriffsbildung*
1904: Weber, "Objectivity in Social Science & Social Policy"
1905: Weber, "The Protestant Ethic & the Spirit of Capitalism"
1908: Simmel, *Soziologie*

1912: Scheler, *Ressentiment*
1920–21: Weber, *Collected Essays in the Sociology of Religion*

1921: Weber, *Economy & Society*
1921: Buber, *I and Thou*
1923: Mannheim, "On the interpretation of Weltanschauung"
1924: Scheler, *Essays toward a Sociology of Knowledge*
1925: Mannheim, "The Problem of a Sociology of Knowledge"

# the History of Western Social Thought

## MARXISM

1844: Marx, "Introd. to . . . Critique of Hegel. . ."
(1845–46): Marx & Engels, *The German Ideology*
1848: Marx & Engels, *The Communist Manifesto*

(1858): Marx, *Grundrisse*
1859: Marx, *Contribution to the Critique of Political Economy*
1867: Marx, *Capital*, vol. 1

1878: Engels, *Anti-Dühring* (inc. "Socialism: Utopian and Scientific")
1885: Marx, *Capital*, vol. II

1894: Marx, *Capital*, voll. III

1902: Lenin, *What is to Be Done?*

1916: Lenin, *Imperialism*

1923: Lukacs, *History and Class Consciousness*

## ITALY

1884: Mosca, *Sulla teorica dei governi* . . .

1891: Sighele, *The Delinquent Crowd*
1896: Mosca, *Elementi* . . . *(=The Ruling Class)*

1896–97: Pareto, *Cours d'économie politique*

1902: Pareto, *Les systèmes socialistes*

1909: Croce, *Philosophy of the Practical*

1914: Michels, *Political Parties*
1916: Pareto, *Trattato* . . . *(=The Mind and Society)*

## UNITED STATES

1890: James, *Principles of Psychology*

1896: Dewey, "The Reflex Arc Concept in Psychology"

1898: Dewey, "Evolution and Ethics"

1902: Cooley, *Human Nature and the Social Order*

1904: Park, *The Crowd and the Public*

1906: Sumner, *Folkways*
1907: James, *Pragmatism*
1908: Cooley, *Social Organization*
1913: Mead, "The Social Self"

1915: Park, "The City: Suggestions . . ."
1918–20: Thomas and Znaniecki, *The Polish Peasant* . . .
1922: Dewey, *Human Nature and Conduct*

1923: Thomas, *The Unadjusted Girl*
1923: Mead, "Scientific Method and the Moral Sciences"
1924: Mead, "The Genesis of the Self & Social Control"
1927: Dewey, *The Public and its Problems*

# Graphic Depictions of the Six Types of Narrative

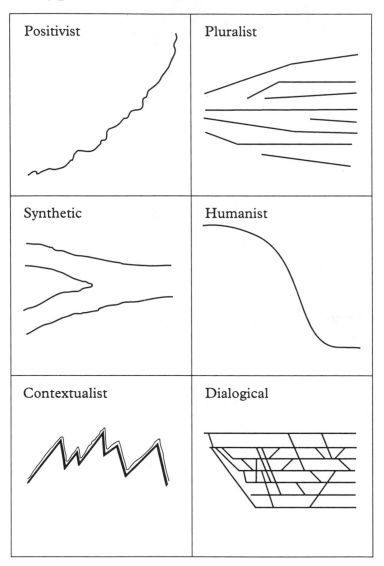

# APPENDIX C
# Basic Postulates of the Seven Traditions

| | CONCEPTION OF NATURE | PRINCIPLE OF GOOD SOCIETY | SOURCE OF MORAL DISPOSITIONS | PHENOMENAL CONSTRUCTS |
|---|---|---|---|---|
| ARISTOTLE | Goal-directed Potentialities | Organized to Promote Virtue and Justice | Socialized Habits and Reflective Capacity | Mutually Determinative Parts and Wholes |
| BRITISH | Atoms in Motion → ATOMIC NATURALISM | Normative Individualism | Natural Individual Morality | Methodological Individualism |
| FRENCH | Different Levels of Phenomenal Reality → SOCIETAL ESSENTIALISM | Societal Normativity | Societal Morality | Societal Realism |
| GERMAN | Lawful Determinism, Opposed to SUBJECTIVE VOLUNTARISM | Normative Self-determination | Subjective Voluntarism (free will) | Subjective Meaning |
| MARXIAN | External Determinism → HISTORICAL MATERIALISM | Communal Production in Classless Society | Class-determined Morality | Dialectical Materialism |
| ITALIAN | Systems in Equilibrium → HIERARCHISTIC NATURALISM | Societal Normativity | Societal Morality | Societal Hierarchism |
| AMERICAN | Complex Flux → PRAGMATISM | Social Situational Normativity | Socially Responsive Morality | Evolving Natural Mental Social Selves |

# References

Abrams, M. H. 1972. "What's the Use of Theorizing about the Arts?" In *In Search of Literary Theory,* ed. M. W. Bloomfield, 1–54. Ithaca, N.Y.: Cornell University Press.

Abrams, Philip. 1968. *The Origins of British Sociology: 1834–1914.* Chicago: University of Chicago Press.

Almond, Gabriel. 1988. "Separate Tables: Schools and Sects in Political Science." In *A Discipline Divided,* 13–31. Newbury Park, Calif.: Sage.

Almond, Gabriel, and Stephen Genco. [1977] 1988. "Clouds, Clocks, and the Study of Politics." In Almond, *A Discipline Divided.*

Alexander, Jeffrey C. 1982–83. *Theoretical Logic in Sociology.* 4 vols. Berkeley and Los Angeles: University of California Press.

———. 1985. "Habermas's New Critical Theory: Its Promise and Problems." *American Journal of Sociology* 97:400–424.

———. 1987. *Twenty Lectures: Sociological Theory since World War II.* New York: Columbia University Press.

———. 1989. "Against Historicism/for Theory: A Reply to Levine." *Sociological Theory* 7:118–21.

Anderson, Kevin. 1995. *Lenin, Hegel, and Western Marxism: A Critical Study.* Urbana-Champaign and Chicago: University of Illinois Press.

Aron, Raymond. 1957. *The Opium of the Intellectuals.* New York: Doubleday.

———. 1962. *The Opium of the Intellectuals.* New York: Norton.

———. 1965–67. *Main Currents in Sociological Thought.* Trans. Richard Howard and Helen Weaver. 2 vols. New York: Basic Books. [Published in France in 1967 as *Les Étapes de la pensée sociologique,* by Editions Gallimard.]

Assmann, Georg, and Rudhard Stollberg, eds. [1977] 1979. *Grundlagen der marxistisch-leninistischen Soziologie.* 2d ed. Berlin: Dietz Verlag.

Aubrey, John. 1949. *Brief Lives and Other Selected Writings.* Ed. Anthony Powell. London: The Cresset Press.

Auspitz, Josiah Lee. 1983. "The Greatest Living American Philosopher." *Commentary* 76:51–64.

Baker, Keith M. 1964. "The Early History of the Term 'Social Science.'" *Annals of Science* 20:211–26.

———. 1975. *Condorcet: From National Philosophy to Social Mathematics.* Chicago: University of Chicago Press.

Barnard, F. M. 1979. *Herder on Social and Political Culture.* Cambridge: Cambridge University Press.

Barry, Brian. 1979. "On Editing Ethics." *Ethics* 90:312–18.

Bauman, Zygmunt. 1992. *Intimations of Postmodernity.* London: Routledge.

Belay, Getinet. 1995. "The Reconstruction and Negotiation of Cultural Identities in the Age of Globalization." In *Interaction and Identity: Information and*

*Behavior* five, ed. Hartmut B. Mokros. New Brunswick, N.J.: Rutgers University, Transaction Publishers.

Belke, Ingrid, ed. 1971. *Moritz Lazarus und Heymann Steinthal: Die Begründer der Völkerpsychologie in ihren Briefen.* Tübingen: J. C. B. Mohr.

Bellah, Robert N. 1959. "Durkheim and History." *American Sociological Review* 24:447–61.

Bellamy, Richard. 1987. *Modern Italian Social Theory.* Stanford, Calif.: Stanford University Press.

Bendix, Reinhard. 1971. "Two Sociological Traditions." In *Scholarship and Partisanship,* by Reinhard Bendix and Guenther Roth, 282–98. Berkeley: University of California Press.

———. 1977. *Max Weber: An Intellectual Portrait.* Berkeley: University of California Press.

Bentham, Jeremy. [1789] 1948. *An Introduction to the Principles of Morals and Legislation.* New York: Hafner Press.

———. 1843. *The Works of Jeremy Bentham.* Ed. John Bowring. 11 vols. Edinburgh: W. Tait; London: Simpkin, Marshall.

Berlin, Isaiah. 1976. *Two Studies in the History of Ideas.* New York: Vintage.

———. 1978. *Karl Marx: His Life and Environment.* 4th ed. Oxford: Oxford University Press.

———. 1990. "Joseph de Maistre and the Origins of Fascism: III." *The New York Review of Books,* October 25.

Borgese, Guiseppe Antonio. 1938. *Goliath: The March of Fascism.* London: Victor Gollancz.

Bottomore, Tom. 1969. "Out of This World." *The New York Review of Books,* November 6, 34–39.

Boulding, Kenneth. 1966. *The Impact of the Social Sciences.* New Brunswick, N.J.: Rutgers University Press.

Brown, Kevin L. 1994. "Fleshing out Economic Man: The 'Utilitarian Dilemma' in Historical Perspective." Ph.D. diss., University of Chicago.

Buber, Martin. 1992. *On Intersubjectivity and Cultural Creativity.* Ed. S. N. Eisenstadt. Chicago: University of Chicago Press.

Buckley, Walter. 1967. *Sociology and Modern Systems Theory.* Englewood Cliffs, N.J.: Prentice-Hall.

Burgalassi, Marco M. 1990. *Il Destino della sociologia: Un Modello interpretativo della prima sociologia italiana.* Pisa: Giardini.

Burk, James. 1991. Introduction to Janowitz 1991.

Camic, Charles. 1979. "The Utilitarians Revisited." *American Journal of Sociology* 85:516–50.

———. 1989. "*Structure* after 50 Years: The Anatomy of a Charter." *American Journal of Sociology* 95:38–107.

———. 1991. Introduction to *Talcott Parsons: The Early Essays,* ed. Camic, ix–lxix. Chicago: University of Chicago Press.

———. 1992. "Reputation and Predecessor Selection: Parsons and the Institutionalists." *American Sociological Review* 57:421–45.

Cammett, John M. 1967. *Antonio Gramsci and the Origins of Italian Communism.* Stanford, Calif.: Stanford University Press.

Catton, William R. 1966. *From Animistic to Naturalistic Sociology.* New York: McGraw-Hill.

Clark, Terry N. 1968. "Gabriel Tarde." In vol. 15 of *International Encyclopedia of the Social Sciences,* ed. David L. Sills, 509–14. New York: Macmillan and The Free Press.

———. 1969. Introduction to *Gabriel Tarde: On Communication and Social Influence,* ed. Clark, 1–69. Chicago: University of Chicago Press.

———. 1973. *Prophets and Patrons: The French University and the Emergence of the Social Sciences.* Cambridge, Mass.: Harvard University Press.

Cochrane, Eric W. 1973. *Florence in the Forgotten Centuries, 1527–1800.* Chicago: University of Chicago Press.

Cohler, Bertram J. 1982. "Personal Narrative and Life-Course." In vol. 4 of *Life-Span Development and Behavior,* ed. Paul Bates and Orville Brim, 205–41. New York: Academic Press.

Collins, Randall. 1987. "A Micro-Macro Theory of Intellectual Creativity: The Case of German Idealist Philosophy." *Sociological Theory* 5:47–69.

———. 1990. "The Organizational Politics of the ASA." *American Sociologist* 21:311.

Comte, Auguste. [1822] 1974. "Plan of the Scientific Operations Necessary for Reorganizing Society." In Comte 1974, 111–81.

———. [1825] 1974. "Philosophical Considerations on the Sciences and Savants." In Comte 1974, 182–213.

———. [1830–42] 1877. *Cours de philosophie positive.* 4th ed. 4 vols. Paris: J.-B. Baillière.

———. [1848–51] 1875. *System of Positive Polity.* 4 vols. London: Longmans, Green, and Co.

———. [1855] 1974. *The Positive Philosophy.* Trans. and ed. Harriet Martineau. New York: AMS Press.

———. 1974. *The Crisis of Industrial Civilization: The Early Essays of Auguste Comte.* Ed. Ronald Fletcher. London: Heinemann.

Cooley, Charles Horton. [1902] 1964. *Human Nature and the Social Order.* New York: Schocken Books.

———. 1909. *Social Organization.* New York: Scribner's.

———. 1930. *Sociological Theory and Social Research.* New York: Holt.

Corry, Bernard. 1968. "Alfred Marshall." In vol. 10 of *International Encyclopedia of the Social Sciences,* ed. David L. Sills, 25–33. New York: Macmillan and The Free Press.

Coser, Lewis A. 1963. *Sociology Through Literature: An Introductory Reader.* Englewood Cliffs, N.J.: Prentice Hall.

———. [1971] 1977. *Masters of Sociological Thought: Ideas in Historical and Social Context.* 2d ed. New York: Harcourt Brace Jovanovich.

———. 1975. "Merton's Uses of the European Sociological Tradition." In *The Idea of Social Structure: Essays in Honor of Robert K. Merton,* ed. Coser, 85–99. New York: Harcourt Brace Jovanovich.

———. 1981. "The Uses of Classical Sociological Theory." In *The Future of the Sociological Classics,* ed. Buford Rhea, 170–82. London: Allen & Unwin.

Coughlan, Neil. 1975. *Young John Dewey: An Essay in American Intellectual History.* Chicago: University of Chicago Press.

Dahme, Heinz-Jürgen. 1981. *Soziologie als exakte Wissenschaft: Georg Simmels Ansatz und seine Bedeutung in der gegenwärtigen Soziologie.* 2 vols. Stuttgart: Ferdinand Enke Verlag.

Davis, Murray S. 1984. "'That's Classic!' The Phenomenology and Rhetoric of Successful Social Theories." Typescript. [Revised version published in *Philosophy of the Social Sciences* 16(1986):285–301.]

Deploige, Simon. [1911] 1938. *The Conflict between Ethics and Sociology.* Trans. C. C. Miltner. London and St. Louis: Herder.

Dewey, Jane. 1939. "Biography of John Dewey." In *The Philosophy of John Dewey,* ed. Paul A. Schilpp, 3–45. Evanston and Chicago: Northwestern University Press.

Dewey, John. [1915] 1942. *German Philosophy and Politics.* New York: Van Rees Press.

———. 1929. *The Quest for Certainty: A Study of the Relation of Knowledge and Action.* New York: Minton, Balch, & Co.

———. 1930. "From Absolutism to Experimentalism." In *Contemporary American Philosophy,* ed. George P. Adams and William P. Montague, 2 vols., 2:13–27. New York: Macmillan.

———. 1967–72. *The Early Works 1882–1898.* 5 vols. Carbondale and Edwardsville: Southern Illinois University Press.

Dewey, John, and James Tufts. 1908. *Ethics.* New York: Holt.

Dilthey, Wilhelm. [1883] 1976. Preface to *An Introduction to the Human Sciences.* In *W. Dilthey: Selected Writings,* ed. H. P. Rickman, 159–67. Cambridge: Cambridge University Press.

———. 1921. *Gesammelte Schriften.* Vol. 4. Leipzig: B. G. Teubner.

Durkheim, Émile. [1892] 1960. *Montesquieu and Rousseau.* Trans. Ralph Manheim. Ann Arbor: University of Michigan Press.

———. [1893] 1984. *The Division of Labor in Society.* New York: The Free Press.

———. [1895] 1982. *The Rules of Sociological Method and Selected Texts on Sociology and Its Method.* New York: The Free Press.

———. [1912] 1965. *The Elementary Forms of Religious Life.* New York: The Free Press.

———. 1915. *"L'Allemagne au-dessus de tout": La mentalité allemande et la guerre.* Paris: Colin.

———. 1973. "Sociology in France in the Nineteenth Century." In *On Morality and Society,* ed. Robert Bellah, 3–22. Chicago: University of Chicago Press.

———. 1975. *Textes* (1). Ed. Victor Karady. Paris: Minuit.

Eisenstadt, S. N., with M. Curelaru. 1976. *The Form of Sociology—Paradigms and Crises.* New York: John Wiley & Sons.

Eley, Geoff. 1984. "Reading Gramsci in English: Observations on the Reception of Antonio Gramsci in the English-Speaking World 1957–82." *European History Quarterly* 14:441–78.

Erikson, Erik. 1958. *Young Luther: A Study in Psychoanalysis and History.* New York: Norton.

Ermarth, Michael. 1978. *Wilhelm Dilthey: The Critique of Historical Reason.* Chicago: University of Chicago Press.

Evans-Pritchard, E. E. 1970. *The Sociology of Comte.* Manchester: Manchester University Press.

Ferguson, Adam. [1767] 1966. *An Essay on the History of Civil Society.* Ed. Duncan Forbes. Edinburgh: Edinburgh University Press.

———. [1792] 1973. *Principles of Moral and Political Science.* New York: AMS Press.

Feuer, Lewis S. 1969. *Marx and the Intellectuals: A Set of Post-Ideological Essays.* Garden City, N.Y.: Anchor.

Flower, Elizabeth, and Murray G. Murphey. 1977. *A History of Philosophy in America.* Vol. 1. New York: Capricorn.

Foucault, Michel. 1980. *Power/Knowledge: Selected Interviews and Other Writings 1972–1977.* Ed. Colin Gordon. New York: Pantheon.

Frank, Art. 1992. "Only by Daylight: Habermas's Postmodern Modernism." *Theory, Culture and Society* 9:149–65.

Friedrichs, Robert W. 1970. *A Sociology of Sociology.* New York: The Free Press.

Freese, Lee, ed. 1980. *Theoretical Methods in Sociology: Seven Essays.* Pittsburgh: University of Pittsburgh Press.

Freyer, Hans. 1923. *Theorie des objektiven Geistes: Eine Einleitung in die Kulturphilosophie..* Leipzig: Teubner.

Fromm, Erich, ed. 1960. *Zen Buddhism and Psychoanalysis.* New York: Harper & Row.

Galston, William A. 1975. *Kant and the Problem of History.* Chicago: University of Chicago Press.

Gane, Mike. 1988. *On Durkheim's Rules of Sociological Method.* New York: Routledge.

Gardiner, Michael. 1992. *The Dialogics of Critique: M. M. Bakhtin and the Theory of Ideology.* London: Routledge.

Garin, Eugenio. 1958. "Gramsci nell cultura italiana." In *Studi Gramsciani,* ed. Istituto Gramsci, 395–418. Rome: Editori Riuniti.

Geertz, Clifford. 1973. *The Interpretation of Cultures.* New York: Basic Books.

———. 1983. "Blurred Genres: The Refiguration of Social Thought." In *Local Knowledge: Further Essays in Interpretive Anthropology,* 19–35. New York: Basic Books.

Giddens, Anthony, ed. *Émile Durkheim: Selected Writings.* New York: Cambridge University Press.

Gilligan, S. G. 1987. *Therapeutic Trances.* New York: Brunner/Mazel.

Gordon, Andrew, ed. 1993. *Postwar Japan as History.* Berkeley: University of California Press.

Gouldner, Alvin W. 1965. *Enter Plato.* New York: Basic Books.

———. 1970. *The Coming Crisis of Western Sociology.* New York: Basic Books.

———. 1980. *The Two Marxisms.* New York: Seabury Press.

———. 1985. *Against Fragmentation: The Origins of Marxism and the Sociology of Intellectuals.* New York: Oxford University Press.

Graham, Loren, Wolf Lepenies, and Peter Weingart, eds. 1983. *Functions and Uses of Disciplinary Histories.* Boston: D. Reidel.

Gramsci, Antonio. 1971. *Selections from the Prison Notebooks of Antonio Gramsci.*

Trans. and ed. Quintin Hoare and Geoffrey Nowell Smith. New York: International Publishers.

———. 1988. *An Antonio Gramsci Reader: Selected Writings 1916–1935.* Ed. David Forgacs. New York: Schocken Books.

Green, Bryan S. R. 1977. "On the Evaluation of Sociological Theory." *Philosophy of Social Sciences* 7:33–50.

Gülich, Christian. 1992a. "Georg Simmel und seine französische Korrespondenz. Historische Rekonstruktion eines wissenschaftlichen Netzwerkes um die Jahrhundertwende." *Critique and Humanism International,* Special Issue 1992:7–29.

———. 1992b. "Le rôle de la coopération scientifique internationale dans la constitution de la sociologie en Europe (1890–1914)." *Communications* 54:105–17.

Habermas, Jürgen. [1981] 1984/1987a. *The Theory of Communicative Action.* Trans. Thomas McCarthy. 2 vols. Boston: Beacon Press.

———. 1987b. *The Philosophical Discourse of Modernity.* Cambridge, Mass.: MIT Press.

Halbwachs, Maurice. 1992. *On Collective Memory.* Trans. and ed. Lewis A. Coser. Chicago: University of Chicago Press.

Harms, Kathy, et al., eds. 1990. *Coping with the Past: Germany and Austria after 1945.* Madison: University of Wisconsin Press.

Halévy, Elie. [1901–4] 1966. *The Growth of Philosophic Radicalism.* Trans. Mary Morris. Boston: Beacon Press.

Halliday, Terence C. 1992. "Introduction: Sociology's Fragile Professionalism." In *Sociology and Its Publics: The Forms and Fates of Disciplinary Organization,* ed. Halliday and Morris Janowitz, 3–42. Chicago: University of Chicago Press.

Halliday, Terence C., and Morris Janowitz, eds. 1992. *Sociology and Its Publics: The Forms and Fates of Disciplinary Organization.* Chicago: University of Chicago Press.

Hayek, F. A. 1952. *The Counter Revolution of Science: Studies on the Abuse of Reason.* Glencoe, Ill.: The Free Press.

Hegel, G. W. F. [1821] 1991. *Elements of the Philosophy of Right.* Trans. H. B. Nisbett. Cambridge: Cambridge University Press.

———. 1988. *Introduction to "The Philosophy of History."* Trans. Leo Rauch. Indianapolis: Hackett.

Heilbroner, Robert L. 1961. *The Worldly Philosophers.* Rev. ed. New York: Simon and Schuster.

Henking, Susan. 1988. "Protestant Religious Experience and the Rise of American Sociology: A Contextual Study of Varieties of Secularization." Ph.D. diss., University of Chicago.

———. 1992. "Protestant Religious Experience and the Rise of American Sociology: Evidence from the Bernard Papers." *Journal of the History of the Behavioral Sciences* 28:325–39.

Herder, Johannes G. [1784–91] 1887. *Sämmtliche Werke.* Vol. 13. Berlin: Weidmannsche.

———. [1784–91] 1968. *Reflections on the Philosophy of the History of Mankind.* Chicago: University of Chicago Press.

_____. 1969. *J. G. Herder on Social and Political Culture*. Trans. and ed. F. M. Barnard. Cambridge: Cambridge University Press.

Hinkle, Roscoe C. 1980. *Founding Theory of American Sociology*. Boston: Routledge and Kegan Paul.

Hobbes, Thomas. [1642] 1972. *De Cive*. In Hobbes 1972.

_____. [1658] 1972. *De Homine*. In Hobbes 1972.

_____. [1843] 1966. *The English Works of Thomas Hobbes of Melmesbury*. Ed. Sir William Molesworth. 11 vols. Darmstadt: Scientia Verlag Aalen.

_____. 1972. *Man and Citizen*. Ed. Bernard Gert. Garden City, N.Y.: Doubleday.

Homans, Peter. 1989. *The Ability to Mourn: Disillusionment and the Social Origins of Psychoanalysis*. Chicago: University of Chicago Press.

Horne, Thomas A. 1978. *The Social Thought of Bernard Mandeville: Virtue and Commerce in Early Eighteenth-Century England*. New York: Columbia University Press.

Horowitz, Irving Louis. 1993. *The Decomposition of Sociology*. New York: Oxford University Press.

Hume, David. [1751] 1975. *An Inquiry Concerning the Principles of Morals*. Reprinted in *Hume: Moral and Political Philosophy*, ed. Henry D. Aiken, 173–249. New York: Hafner Press.

Hutcheson, Francis. [1725] 1971. *An Inquiry into the Original of our Ideas of Beauty and Virtue*. Reprint of 1726 edition. New York: Garland Publishing.

_____. [1728] 1971. *Illustrations on the Moral Sense*. Ed. Bernard Peach. Cambridge, Mass.: Harvard University Press.

_____. [1742] 1772. *A Short Introduction to Moral Philosophy*. Glasgow: Robert & Andrew Foulis.

_____. 1755. *A System of Moral Philosophy*. Vol. 1. London: A. Millar; Glascow: Robert & Andrew Foulis.

Jameson, Fredric. 1984. "Postmodernism, or The Cultural Logic of Late Capitalism." *New Left Review* 146:53–92.

Janowitz, Morris. 1991. *On Social Organization and Social Control*. Chicago: University of Chicago Press.

Joas, Hans. 1980. *G. H. Mead: A Contemporary Re-examination of His Thought*. Trans. Raymond Meyer. Cambridge: Polity Press.

Jones, Robert Alun. 1980. "Myth and Symbol among the Nacirema Tsigoloiocos: A Fragment." *American Sociologist* 15:207–12.

Kalberg, Stephen. 1994. *Max Weber's Comparative Historical Sociology*. Chicago: University of Chicago Press.

Kant, Immanuel. 1785. *Grundelgung zur Metaphysik der Sitten*. Translations include *Groundwork of the Metaphysics of Morals*, trans. H. J. Paton. New York: Harper & Row, 1964.

_____. 1963. *On History*. Ed. Lewis White Beck. Indianapolis: Bobbs-Merrill.

Käsler, Dirk, ed. 1976. *Klassiker des soziologischen Denkens*. 2 vols. Munich: C. H. Beck.

_____. 1988. *Max Weber: An Introduction to His Life and Work*. Chicago: University of Chicago Press.

Kermode, Frank. 1983. *The Classic: Literary Images of Permanence and Change*. Cambridge, Mass.: Harvard University Press.

Klein, George Stuart. 1976. *Psychoanalytic Theory: An Exploration of Essentials.* New York: International Universities Press.

Köhnke, Klaus Christian. 1986. *Entstehung und Aufstieg des Neukantianismus.* Frankfurt am Main: Suhrkamp.

Kristol, Irving. 1980. "Epilogue: Rationalism in Economics." *The Public Interest,* special ed., 201–18.

Kuklick, Henrika. 1980. "Boundary Maintenance in American Sociology: Limitations to Academic 'Professionalization.'" *Journal of the History of the Behavioral Sciences* 16:201–19.

Kuper, Adam. 1980. "The Man in the Study and the Man in the Field." *European Journal of Sociology* 11:14–39.

Lakatos, Imre. 1978. *The Methodology of Scientific Research Programmes.* Cambridge: Cambridge University Press.

Laslett, Peter. 1960. Introduction to *Two Treatises of Government,* by John Locke. New York: New American Library.

Leary, David. 1979. "Wundt and After: Psychology's Shifting Relations with the Natural Sciences, Social Sciences, and Philosophy." *Journal of the History of the Behavioral Sciences* 15:231.

Lee, James L., et al. 1993. *Dynamic Counseling.* 2d ed. Madison, Wis.: Instructional Enterprises.

Leontief, Wassily. 1971. "Theoretical Assumptions and Unobserved Facts." *American Economic Review* 61:1–7.

Lepenies, Wolf. 1988. *Between Literature and Science: The Rise of Sociology.* Cambridge: Cambridge University Press.

Lerner, Daniel, ed. 1959. *The Human Meaning of the Social Sciences.* New York: Meridian Books.

Levin, Michael. 1973. "What Makes a Classic in Political Theory?" *Political Science Quarterly* 88:462–76.

Levine, Donald N. 1970. "Sociology Confronts Student Protest." *School Review* 78:529–41.

———. 1980. *Simmel and Parsons: Two Approaches to the Study of Society.* New York: Arno Press.

———. 1981a. Review of *Economy and Society: An Outline of Interpretive Sociology,* ed. Guenther Roth and Claus Wittich. *Contemporary Sociology* 10:333–35.

———. 1981b. "Sociology's Quest for the Classics: The Case of Simmel." In *The Future of the Sociological Classics,* ed. Buford Rhea, 60–80. London: Allen & Unwin.

———. 1985a. *The Flight from Ambiguity: Essays in Social and Cultural Theory.* Chicago: University of Chicago Press.

———. 1985b. "On the Heritage of Sociology." In *The Challenge of Social Control: Citizenship and Institution Building in Modern Society,* ed. Gerald Suttles and Mayer Zald, 13–19. Norwood, N.J.: Ablex Publishing.

———. 1986a. "The Forms and Functions of Social Knowledge." In *Metatheory in Social Science: Pluralisms and Subjectivities,* ed. D. W. Fiske and R. A. Shweder, 271–83. Chicago: University of Chicago Press.

———. 1986b. Review of *The Classical Attempt at Theoretical Synthesis: Max*

*Weber,* vol. 3 of *Theoretical Logic in Sociology,* by Jeffrey C. Alexander. *American Journal of Sociology* 91:1237–39.

———. 1989. "Simmel as a Resource for Sociological Metatheory." *Sociological Theory* 7:161–74.

———. 1991a. "Simmel as Educator: On Individuality and Modern Culture." *Theory, Culture and Society* 8:99–117.

———. 1991b. "Simmel and Parsons Reconsidered." *American Journal of Sociology* 96:1097–1116.

———. 1992. "Thought, Action, and the Theory of Action: Departures from the Philosophies of Richard McKeon and Talcott Parsons." Paper presented at the Conference on Pluralism and Objectivity in Contemporary Culture: Departures from the Philosophy of Richard McKeon, University of Chicago, March 13–14.

Levine, Donald N., Ellwood B. Carter, and Eleanor Miller Gorman. 1976. "Simmel's Influence on American Sociology." *American Journal of Sociology* 81:813–45, 1112–32.

Lewis, David, and Richard Smith. 1980. *American Sociology and Pragmatism.* Chicago: University of Chicago Press.

Liebmann, Otto. [1865] 1912. *Kant und die Epigonen.* Berlin: Reuther and Reichard.

Linz, Juan J. 1968. "Robert Michels." In vol. 10 of *International Encyclopedia of the Social Sciences,* ed. David L. Sills, 265–72. New York: Macmillan and The Free Press.

Lipset, Seymour Martin, and Neil J. Smelser, eds. 1961. *Sociology, the Progress of a Decade.* Englewood Cliffs, N.J.: Prentice-Hall.

Lively, Jack. 1971. Introduction to Maistre 1971.

Lobkowicz, Nicholas. 1967. *Theory and Practice: History of a Concept from Aristotle to Marx.* Notre Dame, Ind.: University of Notre Dame Press.

Lukács, György. [1954] 1981. *The Destruction of Reason.* Trans. Peter Palmer. Atlantic Highlands, N.J.: Humanities Press.

Lukes, Steven. 1972. *Émile Durkheim: His Life and Work.* New York: Harper & Row.

———. 1985. *Marxism and Morality.* New York: Oxford University Press.

Luther, Martin. 1957. *Christian Liberty.* Trans. W. A. Lambert. Philadelphia: Fortress Press.

Lyotard, Jean-François. [1979] 1984. *The Postmodern Condition: A Report on Knowledge.* Trans. Geoff Bennington and Brian Massumi. Minneapolis: University of Minnesota Press.

Machiavelli, Niccolò. 1950. *The Prince and the Discourses.* Trans. Luigi Ricci and Christian E. Detmold. New York: Random House.

MacIntyre, Alasdair. 1981. *After Virtue: A Study in Moral Theory.* Notre Dame, Ind.: University of Notre Dame Press.

Madge, John. 1962. *The Origins of Scientific Sociology.* New York: The Free Press.

Mah, Harold. 1987. *The End of Philosophy, The Origin of "Ideology."* Berkeley: University of California Press.

Maier, Charles S. 1993. "A Surfeit of Memory? Reflections on History, Melancholy and Denial." *History and Memory* 5:136–52.

Maistre, Joseph de. 1971. *The Works of Joseph de Maistre*. Trans. Jack Lively. New York: Schocken.

Mandeville, Bernard. [1714, 1729] 1924. *The Fable of the Bees: or, Private Vices, Publick Benefits*. Ed. F. B. Kaye. 2 vols. Oxford: Oxford University Press.

Manuel, Frank E. 1962. *The Prophets of Paris*. New York: Harper & Row.

Marcus, Harold G. 1992. "Does the Past Have Any Authority in Ethiopia?" *Ethiopian Review*, April, 18–21.

Martindale, Don. 1960. *The Nature and Types of Sociological Theory*. Boston: Houghton Mifflin.

———. 1981. *The Nature and Types of Sociological Theory*. 2d ed. Prospect Heights, Ill.: Waveland Press.

Marshall, Alfred. [1890; 8th ed. 1920] 1930. *Principles of Economics: An Introductory Volume*. London: Macmillan.

Marx, Karl. [1844] 1975. "Economic and Philosophic Manuscripts of 1844." In vol. 3 of *Karl Marx, Frederick Engels, Collected Works*. New York: International Publishers.

———. [1845] 1965. *The German Ideology*. London: Lawrence & Wishart.

———. [1894] 1964. *Das Kapital: Kritik der politischen Ökonomie*. Vol. 3: *Der Gesamtprozeß der kapitalistischen Produktion*. Ed. Friedrich Engels. *Marx-Engels Werke*, vol. 25. Berlin: Dietz Verlag.

———. 1967. *Writings of the Young Marx on Philosophy and Society*. Trans. and ed. Lloyd D. Easton and Kurt H. Guddat. New York: Doubleday.

———. 1973. *Grundrisse: Foundations of the Critique of Political Economy*. Trans. Martin Nicolaus. Harmondsworth: Penguin.

Mayhew, Leon H. 1982. Introduction to *Talcott Parsons: On Institutions and Social Evolution*, ed. Leon H. Mayhew, 1–62. Chicago: University of Chicago Press.

Mazlish, Bruce. 1984. *The Meaning of Karl Marx*. New York and Oxford: Oxford University Press.

———. 1989. *A New Science: The Breakdown of Connections and the Birth of Sociology*. New York and Oxford: Oxford University Press.

———. 1991. Review of Wolf Lepenies, *Between Literature and Science: The Rise of Sociology*. *Social Forces* 69:1249–56.

McKeon, Richard. 1978. "Person and Community: Metaphysical and Political." *Ethics* 88:207–17.

Mead, George Herbert. 1936. *Movements of Thought in the Nineteenth Century*. Ed. Merritt H. Moore. Chicago: University of Chicago Press.

Melzer, Arthur M. 1990. *The Natural Goodness of Man*. Chicago: University of Chicago Press.

Merton, Robert K. 1968. *Social Theory and Social Structure*. New York: The Free Press.

———. 1975. "Structural Analysis in Sociology." In *Approaches to the Study of Social Structure*, ed. Peter M. Blau, 21–52. New York: The Free Press.

Michels, Robert. [1915] 1958. *Political Parties*. New York: The Free Press.

Mill, John Stuart. [1833] 1969. "Remarks on Bentham's Philosophy." In Mill 1969.

———. [1843; 8th ed. 1872] 1987. *The Logic of the Moral Sciences*. [Book 6 of *A System of Logic*.] LaSalle, Ill.: Open Court Classics.

———. [1861] 1969. *Utilitarianism*. In Mill 1969.

———. [1865] 1969. *Auguste Comte and Positivism*. In Mill 1969.

———. 1969. *Essays on Ethics, Religion and Society*. Vol. 10 of the *Collected Works of John Stuart Mill*. Ed. J. M. Robson. Toronto: University of Toronto Press; London: Routledge & Kegan Paul.

Mills, C. Wright. 1964. *Sociology and Pragmatism: The Higher Learning in America*. New York: Paine-Whitman.

Morgenstern, Oscar. 1972. "13 Critical Points in Contemporary Economic Theory." *Journal of Economic Literature* 10:1163–89.

Mosca, Gaetano. [1896] 1939. *The Ruling Class*. Trans. Hannah D. Khan. New York: McGraw-Hill.

Moscovici, Serge. 1988. *La Machine à faire des dieux*. Paris: Fayard.

Nairn, Tom. 1982. "Antonu Su Gobbu." In *Approaches to Gramsci*, ed. Anne Showstack Sassoon, 159–79. London: Writers and Readers Publishing Cooperative Society, Ltd.

Nedelmann, Birgitta. 1989. "Aestheticization and Stylization: Two Strategies of Lifestyle Management." In *Moderno e Postmoderno*, ed. Carlo Mongardini and Maria Luisa Maniscalco, 91–110. Milan: Bulzoni Editore.

Nedelmann, Birgitta, and Piotr Sztompka, eds. 1993. *Sociology in Europe*. Berlin: Walter de Gruyter.

Newton, Isaac. [1730] 1979. *Opticks; or a Treatise of the Reflections, Refractions, Inflections & Colors of Light*. New York: Dover Publications.

Nietzsche, Friedrich. [1874] 1990. "Schopenhauer as Educator." In *Unmodern Observations*, ed. William Arrowsmith. New Haven, Conn.: Yale University Press.

Nisbet, Robert. 1966. *The Sociological Tradition*. New York: Basic Books.

———. 1974. *The Sociology of Émile Durkheim*. New York: Oxford University Press.

———. 1976. *Sociology as an Art Form*. London: Oxford University Press.

Novick, Peter. 1988. *That Noble Dream: The "Objectivity Question" and the American Historical Profession*. Cambridge: Cambridge University Press.

Oberschall, Anthony, ed. 1972. *The Establishment of Empirical Sociology: Studies in Continuity, Discontinuity, and Institutionalization*. New York: Harper & Row.

O'Brien, George Dennis. 1975. *Hegel on Reason and History*. Chicago: University of Chicago Press.

Ogburn, William Fielding. 1952. "Some Criteria for Appointment to the Department of Sociology." August 12 Memorandum to Dean R. W. Tyler, University of Chicago, Philip M. Hauser Papers & Addenda, Box 14, Folder 11, Department of Special Collections, Joseph Regenstein Library, University of Chicago.

Olafson, Frederick A. 1990. "Habermas as a Philosopher." *Ethics* 100:641–57.

Pareto, Vilfredo. [1916] 1935. *The Mind and Society*. 4 vols. New York: Harcourt, Brace.

———. 1966. *Sociological Writings*. Ed. S. E. Finer. New York: Frederick A. Praeger.

Park, Robert E. 1967. *On Social Control and Collective Behavior*. Ed. Ralph H. Turner. Chicago: University of Chicago Press.

Park, Robert E., and Ernest W. Burgess. [1921] 1924. *Introduction to the Science of Sociology.* Chicago: University of Chicago Press.

Parsons, Talcott. [1935] 1991. "Some Reflections on 'The Nature and Significance of Economics.'" In *Talcott Parsons: The Early Essays,* ed. Charles Camic, 153–80. Chicago: University of Chicago Press.

———. [1937] 1968. *The Structure of Social Action.* New York: The Free Press.

———. 1961. "Comment" on Llewellyn Gross, "Preface to a Metatheoretical Framework for Sociology." *American Journal of Sociology* 67:136–40.

———. 1981. "Revisiting the Classics throughout a Long Career." In *The Future of the Sociological Classics,* ed. Buford Rhea, 183–94. London: Allen & Unwin.

———. 1993. *Talcott Parsons on National Socialism.* Ed. and intro. Uta Gerhardt. New York: Aldine de Gruyter.

Parsons, Talcott, Edward Shils, et al., eds. *Theories of Society: Foundations of Modern Sociological Theory.* 2 vols. New York: The Free Press.

Peel, J. D. Y. 1972. Introduction to Spencer 1972.

———. 1978. "Two Cheers for Empiricism; Or, What Is the Relevance of the History of Sociology to Its Current Practice?" *Sociology* 12:347–59.

Peirce, Charles S. 1931–58. *Collected Papers.* Ed. Charles Hartshorne and Paul Weiss. 6 vols. Cambridge, Mass.: Harvard University Press.

———. 1958. *Values in a Universe of Chance: Selected Writings of Charles S. Peirce.* Ed. Philip P. Wiener. Garden City, N.Y.: Doubleday.

———. 1982. *Writings of Charles S. Peirce: A Chronological Edition.* Ed. Christian J. W. Kloesel. 4 vols. Bloomington: Indiana University Press.

Peyre, Henri. 1960. Foreword to Durkheim 1960.

Pippin, Robert B. 1991. "Hegel, Habermas and Modernity," *Monist* 74:329–57.

Pizzorno, Alessandro. 1972. "Una crisi che non importa superare." In *Ricerca Sociologica e Ruolo del Sociologo,* ed. Pietro Rossi, 327–57. Bologna: Mulino.

Plamenatz, John. 1963. Introduction to *Leviathan,* by Thomas Hobbes. New York: Meridian Books.

Platt, Gerald M. 1992. "Sociology: Origins, Orientations, Crises." *Annals of Scholarship* 9:427–36.

Plattner, Marc F. 1979. *Rousseau's State of Nature: An Interpretation of the Discourse on Inequality.* Dekalb: Northern Illinois University Press.

Pletsch, Carl. 1991. *Young Nietzsche: Becoming a Genius.* New York: The Free Press.

Pope, Whitney, Jere Cohen, and Lawrence E. Hazelrigg. 1975. "On the Divergence of Weber and Durkheim: A Critique of Parsons' Convergence Thesis." *American Sociological Review* 40:417–27.

Portes, Alejandro. 1994. "Contentious Science: The Forms and Functions of Trespassing." Paper presented at the 1994 Dean's Symposium, Division of the Social Sciences, University of Chicago.

Postone, Moishe. 1990. "History and Critical Social Theory." Review of *The Theory of Communicative Action.* Volume 2: *Lifeworld and System: A Critique of Functionalist Reason,* by Jürgen Habermas. *Contemporary Sociology* 19:170–76.

Prior, A. N. 1949. *Logic and the Basis of Ethics.* Oxford: Clarendon Press.

Proust, Jacques. 1962. *Diderot et L'Encyclopédie.* Paris: Armand Colin.

Quetelet, Adolphe. [1835] 1869. *Physique Sociale: Ou, essai sur le développement des facultés de l'homme.* 2 vols. Brussels: Muquardt.

Rammstedt, Otthein. 1986. *Deutsche Soziologie, 1933–1945.* Frankfurt am Main: Suhrkamp.

Ritzer, George. 1975. *Sociology: A Multiple Paradigm Science.* Boston: Allyn and Bacon.

———. 1993. *The McDonaldization of Society.* Newbury Park, Calif.: Pine Forge Press.

Ross, Dorothy. 1991. *The Origins of American Social Science.* New York: Cambridge University Press.

Rossi, Peter H. 1981. "The ASA: A Portrait of Organizational Success and Intellectual Paralysis." *American Sociologist* 16:113–16.

Rousseau, Jean-Jacques. [1762] 1979. *Émile, or On Education.* Trans. Allan Bloom. New York: Basic Books.

———. [1762] 1987. *On the Social Contract.* Trans. Donald A. Cress. Indianapolis: Hackett.

Rucker, Darnell. 1969. *The Chicago Pragmatists.* Minneapolis: University of Minnesota Press.

Saint-Simon, Henri de. 1859. *Oeuvres Choisies de C.-H. de Saint-Simon.* Vol. 1. Bruxelles: Van Meenen.

———. [1952] 1964. *Social Organization, The Science of Man and Other Writings.* Trans. and ed. Felix Markham. New York: Harper & Row. [Originally published as *Henri Comte de Saint-Simon: Selected Writings.*]

Sarton, George. 1936. *The Study of the History of Science.* Cambridge, Mass.: Harvard University Press.

———. 1952. "Auguste Comte, Historian of Science." *Osiris* 10:328–57.

Schopenhauer, Arthur. [1818] 1958. *The World as Will and Representation.* 2 vols. Indian Hills, Colo.: Falcon's Wing Press.

Schudson, Michael. 1989. "The Present in the Past versus the Past in the Present." *Communication* 11:105–13.

Shackelton, Robert. 1961. *Montesquieu: A Critical Biography.* Oxford: Oxford University Press.

Shaftesbury, Anthony Earl of. [1711] 1900. *Characteristics of Men, Manners, Opinions, Times, Etc.* Ed. John M. Robertson. 2 vols. London: Grant Richards.

Shalin, Dimitri. 1986. "Pragmatism and Social Interactionism." *American Sociological Review* 51:9–29.

Shaw, Martin. 1975. *Marxism and Social Science.* London: Pluto Press.

Sheehan, James. 1989. *German History 1770–1866.* Oxford: Oxford University Press.

Shils, Edward. 1961. "The Calling of Sociology." In *Theories of Sociology,* vol. 2, ed. Talcott Parsons et al., 1405–48. New York: The Free Press.

———. 1980. *The Calling of Sociology and Other Essays on the Pursuit of Learning.* Chicago: University of Chicago Press.

———. 1981. *Tradition.* Chicago: University of Chicago Press.

Sidgwick. Henry. [1886] 1954. *Outlines of the History of Ethics.* London: Macmillan.

Sills, David L., and Robert K. Merton, eds. 1991. *International Encyclopedia of the Social Sciences: Social Science Quotations.* New York: Macmillan.

Simmel, Georg. 1890. "Über sociale Differenzierung." *Staats- und Socialwissenschaftliche Forschungen* 10:1–147.

———. [1903] 1971. "The Metropolis and Mental Life." In *Georg Simmel on Individuality and Social Forms,* ed. Donald N. Levine, 324–39. Chicago: University of Chicago Press.

———. [1907] 1978. *Philosophie des Geldes.* 2d ed. Translated as *The Philosophy of Money* by Tom Bottomore and David Frisby. Boston: Routledge.

———. 1907. *Die Probleme der Geschichtsphilosophie.* 3rd ed. Leipzig: Duncker and Humblot.

———. 1918. *Lebensanschauung.* Munich: Duncker and Humblot.

———. 1971. *Georg Simmel on Individuality and Social Forms.* Ed. Donald N. Levine. Chicago: University of Chicago Press.

———. 1977. *The Problems of the Philosophy of History.* Trans. Guy Oakes. New York: The Free Press.

Simon, W. M. 1963. *European Positivism in the Nineteenth Century.* Ithaca, N.Y.: Cornell University Press.

Skinner, Quentin. 1969. "Meaning and Understanding in the History of Ideas." *History and Theory* 8:3–53.

Small, Albion W. 1910. *The Meaning of Social Science.* Chicago: University of Chicago Press.

Smelser, Neil J. 1968. *Essays in Sociological Explanation.* Englewood Cliffs, N.J.: Prentice-Hall.

Smith, Adam. [1759] 1982. *The Theory of Moral Sentiments.* Indianapolis: Liberty Classics.

———. [1776] 1976. *An Inquiry into the Nature and Causes of the Wealth of Nations.* Ed. Edwin Cannan. 2 vols. in 1. Chicago: University of Chicago Press.

Smith, W. G. Pogson. 1909. Introduction to Hobbes, *Leviathan.* Oxford: Clarendon Press.

Sorokin, Pitirim A. 1928. *Contemporary Sociological Theories.* New York: Harper & Brothers.

———. 1966. *Sociological Theories of Today.* New York: Harper & Row.

Soysal, Yasemin. 1995. *The Limits of Citizenship: Migrants and Post-National Membership in Europe.* Chicago: University of Chicago Press.

Spence, J. C. 1897. *The Dawn of Civilization, or England in the Nineteenth Century.* London: Watts & Co.

Spencer, Herbert. [1850] 1972. "The Social Organism." Excerpted in Spencer 1972.

———. [1860] 1972. *Social Statics.* Excerpted in Spencer 1972.

———. [1864] 1968. "Reasons for Dissenting from the Philosophy of M. Comte." In *Reasons for Dissenting from the Philosophy of M. Comte and Other Essays,* 2–25. Berkeley, Calif.: Glendessary Press.

———. 1879–93. *The Principles of Ethics.* 2 vols. London: Williams and Norgate.

_____. 1884. *The Data of Ethics.* New York: D. Appleton and Company.

_____. 1961. *The Study of Sociology.* Ann Arbor: University of Michigan Press.

_____. 1972. *On Social Evolution.* Ed. J. D. Y. Peel. Chicago: University of Chicago Press.

Spykman, Nicholas J. 1925. *The Social Theory of Georg Simmel.* New York: Atherton Press.

Stark, Werner. 1963. *The Fundamental Forms of Social Thought.* New York: Fordham University Press.

Starobinski, Jean. 1990. "Rousseau in the Revolution." *The New York Review of Books,* April 12, 47–50.

Stinchcombe, Arthur L. 1982. "Should Sociologists Forget Their Mothers and Fathers?" *The American Sociologist* 17:2–11.

Stocking, George. 1984. "Dr. Durkheim and Mr. Brown: Comparative Sociology at Cambridge in 1910." In *Functionalism Historicized: Essays on British Social Anthropology,* ed. George W. Stocking, Jr., 106–30. Madison: University of Wisconsin Press.

Strauss, Leo. 1936. *The Political Philosophy of Hobbes: Its Basis and Its Genesis.* Trans. Elsa M. Sinclair. Oxford: Clarendon Press.

_____. 1953. *Natural Right and History.* Chicago: University of Chicago Press.

Stryker, Sheldon. 1981. "Social Psychology." *American Behavioral Scientist* 24:386–404.

Therborn, Goran. 1976. *Science, Class and Society: On the Formation of Sociology and Historical Materialism.* London: New Left Books.

Thomas, William I. 1928. *The Child in America.* New York: Knopf.

_____. 1966. *On Social Organization and Social Personality.* Ed. Morris Janowitz. Chicago: University of Chicago Press.

Thompson, Manley. 1953. *The Pragmatic Philosophy of C. S. Peirce.* Chicago: University of Chicago Press.

Toews, John Edward. 1980. *Hegelianism: The Path toward Dialectical Humanism.* Cambridge: Cambridge University Press.

Tönnies, Ferdinand. 1971. *On Sociology: Pure, Applied and Empirical.* Ed. Werner J. Cahnman and Rudolf Heberle. Chicago: University of Chicago Press.

Trey, George. 1992. "Communicative Ethics in the Face of Alterity: Habermas, Levinas and the Problem of Post-Conventional Universalism." *Praxis International* 11:412–27.

Tucker, Robert C., ed. 1978. *The Marx-Engels Reader.* New York: Norton.

Turner, Jonathan H. 1974. *The Structure of Sociological Theory.* Homewood, Ill.: Dorsey Press.

Turner, Ralph H. 1967. Introduction to Park 1967.

Turner, Stephen P. 1985a. Review of *Theoretical Logic in Sociology.* Volume 1: *Positivisim, Presuppositions, and Current Controversies,* by Jeffrey C. Alexander. *Philosophy of the Social Sciences* 15:77–82.

_____. 1985b. Review of *Theoretical Logic in Sociology.* Volume 2: *The Antinomies of Classical Thought: Marx and Durkheim,* by Jeffrey C. Alexander. *Philosophy of the Social Sciences* 15:211–16.

_____. 1991. "Salvaging Sociology's Past." *ASA Footnotes* 19, no. 5, 6.

Turner, Stephen Park, and Jonathan H. Turner. 1990. *The Impossible Science. An Institutional Analysis of American Sociology.* Newbury Park, Calif.: Sage Publications.

Vidich, Arthur J., and Stanford M. Lyman. 1985. *American Sociology: Worldly Rejections of Religions and Their Directions.* New Haven, Conn.: Yale University Press.

Von Dohlen, Richard Frederick. 1973. "A Case Study in the Explication of Unclear Theories in the Social Sciences: The Relationship of Values to Freedom in the Social Theory of Talcott Parsons." Ph.D. diss., Boston University.

Wade, Nicholas. 1982. "Smart Apes, or Dumb?" *New York Times,* April 30, A30.

Wallace, Walter L., ed. 1969. *Sociological Theory.* Chicago: Aldine.

———. 1984. "Alexandrian Sociology." Review of *Theoretical Logic in Sociology.* Volume 2: *The Antinomies of Classical Thought: Marx and Durkheim,* by Jeffrey C. Alexander. *American Journal of Sociology* 90:640–53.

Wallerstein, Immanuel. 1991. *Unthinking Social Science. The Limits of Nineteenth-Century Paradigms.* Cambridge: Polity Press.

Warner, R. Stephen. 1978. "Toward a Redefinition of Action Theory: Paying the Cognitive Element Its Due." *American Journal of Sociology* 83:1317–49.

———. 1988. Review of *Theoretical Logic in Sociology.* Volume 4: *The Modern Reconstruction of Classical Thought: Talcott Parsons,* by Jeffrey C. Alexander. *American Journal of Sociology* 94:644–55.

Watson, Walter. [1985] 1993. *The Architectonics of Meaning: Foundations of the New Pluralism.* Chicago: University of Chicago Press.

Weber, Max. [1913] 1922. "Über einige Kategorien der verstehenden Soziologie." In Weber 1922, 403–50.

———. 1922. *Gesammelte Aufsätze zur Wissenschaftslehre.* Tübingen: J. C. B. Mohr.

———. 1949. *The Methodology of the Social Sciences.* Trans. Edward Shils and Henry A. Finch. Glencoe, Ill.: The Free Press.

———. 1968. *Economy and Society.* Ed. Guenther Roth and Claus Wittich. 3 vols. New York: Bedminister Press.

———. 1978. *Weber: Selections in Translation.* Trans. Eric Matthews. Ed. W. G. Runciman. Cambridge: Cambridge University Press.

Wiener, Philip P. 1949. *Evolution and the Founders of Pragmatism.* Cambridge, Mass.: Harvard University Press.

Wiley, Norbert. 1995. *The Semiotic Self.* Chicago: University of Chicago Press.

Willey, Thomas E. 1978. *Back to Kant.* Detroit: Wayne State University Press.

Williams, Gwyn A. 1960. "The Concept of 'Egemonia' in the Thought of Antonio Gramsci." *Journal of the History of Ideas* 21:586–99.

Windelband, Wilhelm. 1884. *Präludien.* Freiburg: J. C. B. Mohr.

Wolf, Eric. 1980. "They Divide and Subdivide, and Call It Anthropology." *New York Times,* November 30, E9.

Wolin, Sheldon. 1960. *Politics and Vision: Continuity and Innovation in Western Political Thought.* Boston: Little, Brown.

Yang, Young-Jin. 1986. "Durkheim and Weber: Two Approaches to the Study of Religion and Society." Ph.D. diss., University of Chicago.

Zeitlin, Irving M. [1968] 1981. *Ideology and the Development of Sociological Theory.* 2d ed. Englewood Cliffs, N.J.: Prentice-Hall.

# INDEX